# Advance Praise for
## *Designing the New American University*

"Over the past twelve years, Michael Crow has transformed ASU into one of America's proudest research universities. Now, he and his colleague, William Dabars, share this model of success and the efforts of the university to bring it to scale—presenting untapped opportunities to boost our economic and global competitiveness and to further invest in our next generation of leaders."

**BILL CLINTON, former President of the United States**

"*Designing the New American University* presents a fascinating look at the challenges and opportunities facing our nation's higher education community. Michael Crow is one of the leading college presidents precisely because he understands how we must innovate if we want to continue to lead in today's global knowledge economy, while at the same time expanding access and affordability to ensure more students have the opportunity to achieve the American Dream. This book is an important and insightful read."

**JEB BUSH, former Governor of Florida**

"Instead of dwelling on the past glories of American higher education alone, this book centers on reinvention and the dynamic nature of American universities. At a time when higher education is in flux—some would say in crisis—the clarity of Crow's vision and proposed solutions make *Designing the New American University* essential reading."

**VARTAN GREGORIAN, Carnegie Corporation of New York and former president, Brown University**

"*Designing the New American University* is a brilliant, innovative, lucid, and path-breaking book—arguably the most significant book on higher learning since Clark Kerr's *The Uses of the University,* published more than a half-century ago. No one should miss the delight of engaging in the discussion that this extraordinary book will surely engender about the future of American universities."

**JONATHAN R. COLE, author of *The Great American University: Its Rise to Preeminence, Its Indispensable National Role, Why It Must Be Protected***

"In *Designing the New American University*, Michael Crow and William Dabars have gone one better than just opening a panoramic window on Crow's energetic reinvention at Arizona State of the very idea of the university. Even more importantly, they combine analytic social science, policy studies focused on innovation and on economic and community development, and a humanistic understanding of how institutions and the ideologies and motives underlying them have changed over time, placing bold experiments like Crow's in historical perspective and illuminating how the nation has shaped its institutions of higher learning and how they in turn have shaped, and must continue to shape, the nation."

> DANIEL MARK FOGEL, co-editor of *Precipice or Crossroads? Where America's Great Public Universities Stand and Where They Are Going Midway through Their Second Century*

"At a time when knowledge is the key resource for a robust and prosperous society, Crow and Dabars argue persuasively that we must design a New American University rededicated to the public good and recast to meet society's present and future challenges and opportunities. This book will inspire us to rethink the way we support discovery, creativity, and education—from artistic engagement and humanistic insight to scientific understanding and technological innovation."

> FREEMAN A. HRABOWSKI III, president, University of Maryland, Baltimore County; author of *Holding Fast to Dreams: Empowering Youth from the Civil Rights Crusade to STEM Achievement*

# DESIGNING THE NEW AMERICAN UNIVERSITY

## MICHAEL M. CROW
### AND
## WILLIAM B. DABARS

JOHNS HOPKINS UNIVERSITY PRESS   *Baltimore*

© 2015 Johns Hopkins University Press
All rights reserved. Published 2015
Printed in the United States of America on acid-free paper
9 8 7 6 5 4 3 2 1

Johns Hopkins University Press
2715 North Charles Street
Baltimore, Maryland 21218-4363
www.press.jhu.edu

Library of Congress Cataloging-in-Publication Data

Crow, Michael M. author.
   Designing the new American university / Michael M. Crow and
William B. Dabars.
        pages cm
   Includes bibliographical references and index.
   ISBN 978-1-4214-1723-3 (hardback) — ISBN 978-1-4214-1724-0
(electronic) — ISBN 1-4214-1723-5 (hardcover)   1. Education,
Higher—United States.   2. Universities and colleges—United
States.   I. Dabars, William B.   II. Title.
   LA226.C87 2015
   378.73—dc23      2014036878

A catalog record for this book is available from the British Library.

All figures designed by Charles Shockley.

*Special discounts are available for bulk purchases of this book. For more
information, please contact Special Sales at 410-516-6936 or specialsales
@press.jhu.edu.*

Johns Hopkins University Press uses environmentally friendly book
materials, including recycled text paper that is composed of at least
30 percent post-consumer waste, whenever possible.

# CONTENTS

Preface, by Michael M. Crow    vii

Acknowledgments    xi

Introduction: Solving for X with U    1

1  American Research Universities at a Fork in the Road    17

2  The Gold Standard in American Higher Education    75

3  The Varieties of Academic Tradition    115

4  Discovery, Creativity, and Innovation    151

5  Designing Knowledge Enterprises    177

6  A Pragmatic Approach to Innovation and Sustainability    215

7  Designing a New American University at the Frontier    240

Conclusion: Toward More New American Universities    304

Bibliography    311

Index    329

## PREFACE
*Michael M. Crow*

When I became president of Arizona State University in July 2002, I came to the office following more than a decade at Columbia University, where I had served as a professor of science and technology policy as well as an administrator and designer of new initiatives, culminating in an appointment as executive vice provost. The contrast between Columbia, which began as one of the elite colonial colleges that would come to constitute the Ivy League, and Arizona State, a burgeoning but then still largely undifferentiated regional public university, epitomized the heterogeneity and diversity in mission and scale of operation of the roughly two hundred institutions in the United States characterized as research universities. Established prior to the American Revolution as King's College, Columbia epitomizes the institutional model of the highly successful gold standard in American higher education. Like its institutional peers, public as well as private, the school may boast not only of its achievements but also the rigors of its selectivity. By contrast, ASU is the nation's youngest major research university and, with an enrollment of undergraduate, graduate, and professional students presently exceeding 76,000, one of the nation's largest public universities governed by a single administration. Yet, whereas Columbia and its institutional peers deviate little from a familiar trajectory charted in some cases centuries in the past, ASU has deliberately undertaken an exhaustive reconceptualization to emerge as one of the nation's leading public metropolitan research universities, an institution that combines accessibility to an academic platform underpinned by discovery and knowledge production, inclusiveness to a broad demographic representative of the socioeconomic diversity of the region and nation, and maximum societal impact—a model I have termed the "New American University."

In this book, my colleague William Dabars and I consider both the scope and complexity of the set of American research universities and the various contexts within which their contributions to society, as well as the dilemmas and challenges these institutions routinely encounter, may be addressed. We concur with Frank Rhodes, president emeritus of Cornell University, in his assessment that "the university is the most significant creation of the second millennium."* More than other institutional types, major research universities leverage the potential of knowledge production, and their significance increases with each passing year as the role of knowledge becomes ever more crucial. Our society depends increasingly on the educated citizens and ideas, products, and processes these institutions produce as their integrated platforms of teaching and research contribute to our economic and global competitiveness as well as standard of living and quality of life. These institutions represent our best hope for the survival of our species. While the reconceptualization of ASU represents the pioneering of a foundational prototype for a New American University, more broadly, the "design process" undertaken during the past decade constitutes a recasting of the American research university as a complex and adaptive comprehensive knowledge enterprise committed to discovery, creativity, and innovation, accessible to the broadest possible demographic, both socioeconomically and intellectually. These commitments together imply scalability at a level previously considered improbable if not undesirable.

An objective assessment of our knowledge enterprises undertaken with sufficient perspective—perhaps from the distance of the Oort Cloud, as once suggested by University of Michigan president emeritus James Duderstadt—discloses any number of fundamental design limitations. We face social and environmental challenges of unimaginable complexity, but rather than restructuring institutional operations to embrace and manage complexity, academic culture perpetuates existing organizational structures and practices and restricts its focus with disciplinary entrenchment and increasing specialization. Our universities sometimes appear hesitant to mount operations to address these challenges in real time and retreat instead to the comfort zone of abstract knowledge. The organizational frameworks we call universities—this thousand-year-old institutional form—have not evolved significantly beyond the configurations assumed in the late nineteenth century, nor have differentiated new de-

---

*Frank H. T. Rhodes, *The Creation of the Future: The Role of the American University* (Ithaca, NY: Cornell University Press, 2001), xi.

signs come to the fore. As the lead architect in the design of a new class of large-scale multidisciplinary and transdisciplinary institutions during the past two decades, both at Columbia and now in Arizona, I recognize that although institutional reconceptualization is not without its pitfalls given inherent sociocultural barriers, new models offer new ways of shaping and examining problems and advancing questions through cooperation among large numbers of teams, programs, and initiatives.

Although the effort to transform a large public university into an adaptive knowledge enterprise in real time and at scale is unusual if not unprecedented, the reconceptualization has allowed the academic community to reassess its priorities. In many instances the design process has offered an opportunity for faculty and researchers to reaffirm their commitment to serve society, spurring efforts to advance innovation commensurate with the scale and complexity of the challenges that confront the global community. And because concern with tackling the grand challenges has become engrained in our institutional culture, the teaching and research enterprise of the university sometimes takes on the characteristics of a moonshot project. "Moonshot thinking starts with picking a big problem: something huge, long existing, or on a global scale," writes Astro Teller, who directs Google X, which he describes as the corporate "moonshot factory." "Next it involves articulating a radical solution—one that would actually solve the problem if it existed . . . . Finally, there needs to be some kind of concrete evidence that the proposed solution is not quite as crazy as it first seems; something that justifies at least a close look at whether such a solution could be brought into being if enough creativity, passion, and persistence were brought to bear on it."* The reconceptualization of Arizona State University could in some sense be likened to a moonshot project, as well as some of the initiatives of its teaching and research enterprise, which we delineate in this book. It is therefore to the entire academic community of the past decade, whose commitment to excellence and accessibility and unfailing willingness to innovate have made the design process possible, that I wish to dedicate our book. Creativity, passion, and persistence are hallmarks

---

* Astro Teller, "Google X Head on Moonshots: 10 X Is Easier than 10 Percent," *Wired* (February 11, 2013).

of the American research university, and to adapt a concept from the thinkers at Google, which through innovation has undertaken a corporate initiative to Solve for X, we might well say that a hallmark of a New American University is the willingness to attempt to solve for X with U.

## ACKNOWLEDGMENTS

This, then, is a book about a new model for the American research university, and as befits so complex and varied a topic, our proverbial debt of gratitude to colleagues, scholars, and experts too numerous to cite individually, both within academe and elsewhere, is considerable. We would be remiss, however, if we did not express our appreciation to a number of individuals whose scholarship and expertise—and, in some cases, consultation regarding the project at hand—have inspired and informed the writing of this book. Readers will discover the extent to which the present volume has been inspired by the work of various academic leaders whose vision and effort has advanced the American research university, including most notably Jonathan R. Cole, James Duderstadt, Vartan Gregorian, and Frank Rhodes. Implicit in our discussion of the design process are the contributions of the academic community of Arizona State University, and especially the efforts of those who shaped the design process from the beginning. We attempt to recognize the contributions of colleagues who have brought perspective and nuance to our discussion in endnotes but the endeavor is inevitably futile because too many acknowledgments would soon become tiresome to the reader. Finally, we wish to express our appreciation to Gregory M. Britton, editorial director of Johns Hopkins University Press, for his astute editorial guidance.

Various chapters in our book contain revised portions of texts that appeared previously in articles and book chapters we have either coauthored or authored singly. We wish to express our appreciation to respective editors and publishers for permission to interpolate revised variants of these excerpts into the present volume. Sections from our coauthored book chapter "University-Based Research and Economic Development: The Morrill Act and the Emergence of the American Research University," which appeared in *Precipice or Crossroads: Where America's Great Public Universities Stand and Where They Are Going Midway through*

*Their Second Century*, edited by Daniel Mark Fogel and Elizabeth Malson-Huddle (Albany: State University of New York Press, 2012), inform primarily chapters 2 and 4. Our discussion of interdisciplinarity, which spans chapter 5, includes revised portions of the dissertation by William Dabars, "Disciplinarity and Interdisciplinarity: Rhetoric and Context in the American Research University" (University of California, Los Angeles, 2008), which in turn informed sections of our coauthored book chapter "Interdisciplinarity as a Design Problem: Toward Mutual Intelligibility among Academic Disciplines in the American Research University," which appeared in *Enhancing Communication and Collaboration in Interdisciplinary Research*, edited by Michael O'Rourke et al. (Los Angeles: Sage, 2013). Chapter 5 is substantially constituted by these sources and, to a lesser extent, by a number of paragraphs from our chapter "Toward Interdisciplinarity by Design in the American Research University," which was published in *University Experiments in Interdisciplinarity: Obstacles and Opportunities*, edited by Peter Weingart and Britta Padberg (Bielefeld: Transcript, 2014). Revised excerpts from our article "Knowledge without Borders: American Research Universities in a Global Context," which appeared in the *Cairo Review of Global Affairs* 5 (Spring 2012), inform chapter 1. Our discussion of sustainability in chapter 6 includes revised portions from the book chapter "Sustainability as a Founding Principle of the United States," by Michael Crow, which is to be found in the collection of essays *Moral Ground: Ethical Action for a Planet in Peril*, edited by Kathleen Dean Moore and Michael P. Nelson (San Antonio, TX: Trinity University Press, 2010), and also his article "Overcoming Stone Age Logic," which appeared in *Issues in Science and Technology* 24, no. 2 (2008). The discussion of human limitation that concludes chapter 6 is substantially derived from his article "None Dare Call It Hubris: The Limits of Knowledge," which may be found in *Issues in Science and Technology* 23, no. 2 (2007). Interspersed throughout the book are revised formulations of phrases and paragraphs from his book chapter "The Research University as Comprehensive Knowledge Enterprise: A Prototype for a New American University," which appeared in *University Research for Innovation*, edited by Luc E. Weber and James D. Duderstadt, in the series associated with the Glion Colloquium (London: Economica, 2010). Every effort has been made to cite less substantive variants of remarks, essays, and op-eds contributed over the years in endnotes. Our case study chapter draws substantially from institutional reports that were often the product of unattributed collaborative authorship. In all such cases, we wish to acknowledge the contributions of the respective participants from the academic community of Arizona State University.

# Solving for X with U

"The Only Colleges That Matter." A recent issue of *Forbes* thus proclaimed the magazine's bid to compete in the perennially popular rankings of colleges and universities in a field dominated by *U.S. News and World Report*. The subtitle posed the question "Is Higher Education Still Worth It?" The opinion expressed in the corresponding article is equivocal, citing "outrageously expensive" costs at elite private institutions like Stanford and the University of Chicago that for four years potentially exceed a quarter of a million dollars. "Is it worth it?" the staff writer rhetorically ponders, and without hesitation concludes, "For many students, the answer is probably not—unless they are accomplished enough to be accepted by one of the schools ranked near the top of our annual list of America's 650 Top Colleges."[1] Apparently readers are expected to accept this conclusion at face value because no further effort at justification is forthcoming. But the contention that unless a student is admitted to one of our nation's most selective institutions, college is "probably not" worth the cost and effort speaks eloquently to an increasingly common attitude that is starkly at odds with reality for most individuals and threatens to undermine the future of our collective quality of life, standard of living, and national economic competiveness.

Headlines proclaiming crisis in American higher education seem to proliferate on a daily basis. Accounts of skyrocketing sticker prices at our nation's colleges and universities vie for attention with dire pronouncements from think tanks reinforcing skepticism toward public investment in what has increasingly been framed as a dubious enterprise. Screeds generated from within the bowels of academe purport sober stocktaking but often assume the strident tones of rancorous vitriol one would expect from sworn enemies of the arts and letters. The genre has become so commonplace that it would be superfluous to cobble together even a representative compilation of jeremiads, so a mere few examples should suffice to capture their sense of impending doom. There is a "crisis on campus," Mark C. Taylor, chair of the Department of Religion at Columbia University confidently informs us, and the "education bubble is about to burst."[2] "Higher education is a $420 billion industry," Andrew Hacker, emeritus professor of political science at Queens College of the City University of New York and journalist Claudia Dreifus proclaim, tendentiously steering the discussion toward the association of academe with the corporatist and venal. "What are individuals—and our society as a whole—gaining from it?"[3] Not nearly enough, in their estimation. According to Peter Thiel, cofounder and former CEO of PayPal, who established the Thiel Fellowships, which provide $100,000 grants to pursue entrepreneurial endeavors on the condition that recipients drop out of college, "If you question the economic value of college, the defenders' default answer is that it's priceless." But no matter, Thiel reassures us, as common sense will inevitably prevail over decadence: "Before long, spending four years in a lecture hall with a hangover will be revealed as an antiquated debt-fueled luxury good."[4]

America's students are "academically adrift," according to sociologists Richard Arum and Josipa Roksa. Although institutional mission statements promise to "challenge students to 'think critically and intuitively,' and to ensure that graduates will become adept at 'critical, analytical, and logical thinking'"—capacities that "align with the idea that educational institutions serve to enhance students' human capital—knowledge, skills, and capacities that will be rewarded in the labor market"—Arum and Roksa warn that students experience only "limited learning" from lack of academic rigor on our campuses. As proof the authors cite "emerging empirical evidence that suggests that college students' academic effort has dramatically declined in recent decades," including data that confirm student preference for professors who grade leniently. And inasmuch as academic culture prioritizes research, a symbiotic "disengagement compact" between faculty and students reinforces underachievement: "I'll leave you alone if you leave me alone," the professoriate allegedly implies. "That is, I won't make you work too hard (read a lot, write a lot) so that I won't have to grade as many papers or explain why you are not performing well."[5] In any event, according to Harvard University president emeritus Derek Bok, most faculty members in research universities believe that "teaching is an art that is either too simple to require formal preparation, too personal to be taught to others, or too innate to be conveyed to anyone lacking the necessary gift."[6] After all, the professoriate is concerned primarily with research that is merely academic, according to Nicholas Kristof. In a column in the *New York Times*, he rehearsed the familiar allegation that "to be a scholar is, often, to be irrelevant." And while professors in their monastic isolation "encode their insights into turgid prose" for the benefit of marginalized fellow specialists, the graduate programs they direct have "fostered a culture that glorifies arcane unintelligibility while disdaining impact and audience."[7]

Although the university purports to be a "potential model for free and rational discussion, a site where the community is founded in the sharing of a commitment to an abstraction," Canadian literary scholar Bill Readings found instead a "community of dissensus." An astute observer of the American university, Readings contends, "Few communities are more petty and vicious than university faculties" and offers the following synopsis of common allegations: "Teaching, we are told, is undervalued in favor of research, while research is less and less in touch with the demands of the real world, or with the comprehension of the 'common reader.' " And with the decline of tenure and growth of contingent nontenure and part-time instructional staff, the "professoriate is being proletarianized." We are left with a "university in ruins," which is the title of his equivocal assessment of the contemporary academy.[8] A quarter-century earlier, the political philosopher Allan Bloom had eviscerated contemporary academic culture with far greater resonance. In *The Closing of the American Mind*, he considered "how higher education has failed democracy and impoverished the souls of today's student." Among other ills, he found academia complicit in promulgating an insidious relativism even unto "nihilism, American style." In retrospect we may at least take solace that Bloom accorded our colleges and universities even this measure of impact and relevance.[9]

The drift is obvious, but these sorts of harangues represent only the tip of the iceberg. From the avowedly libertarian perspective of the John William Pope Center for Higher Education Policy, the intent of which is to eradicate liberal bias from the academy and slash education budgets, funding higher education is nothing more than a "boondoggle that robs taxpayers."[10] A report from the National Association of Scholars singles out Bowdoin College as an institutional standard-bearer for liberal bias to "illustrate the intellectual and moral deficit of the American academy." Apparently Bowdoin students are "encouraged to 'think critically' about anything that threatens the college's dogmas on diversity, multiculturalism, gender, and sustainability, etc., but for the most part, not to think critically about those dogmas themselves."[11] Charles Murray, political scientist and fellow of the American Enterprise Institute, finds the pursuit of a baccalaureate degree socially divisive and insidious: "We should prick the B.A. bubble," he warns in a *New York Times* op-ed. "The bachelor's degree has become a driver of class divisions at the same moment in history when it has become educationally meaningless." He recommends that a public interest law firm challenge the constitutionality of a degree as a requirement for employment.[12] Murray may quibble, but he is not wholly oblivious to the imperative for advanced education: "Almost everybody needs more education after high school," he concedes. "What they don't need is to chase after this fraudulent, destructive, antediluvian piece of paper called a BA. The thesis of my argument really is that the BA is the work of the devil."[13]

As befits so complex an institution, the contemporary research university is subject to critique from any number of perspectives, claims to cost inefficiencies being a perennial favorite. Clayton Christensen, the Harvard Business School professor whose influential theory of disruptive innovation revealed patterns of displacement of dominant business models and markets through the application of new and sometimes unexpected—albeit often inferior but cheaper—technologies, has more recently applied this perspective to higher education. Whether the point of reference is academe or "products ranging from computers to breakfast cereals," he and colleague Henry J. Eyring contend that tweaks to the same old model represent merely sustaining innovations. Thus, "institutions that emulate Harvard and strive to climb the Carnegie ladder are doing just as conventional business logic dictates—trying to give customers what they want."[14] Among the various ills Christensen and colleagues perceive in the traditional model are the "multiple value propositions" of "knowledge creation (research), knowledge proliferation and learning (teaching), and preparation for life and careers." As "conflations of the three generic types of business models—solution shops, value-adding process businesses, and facilitated user networks," colleges and universities are faulted for excessive overhead costs. The average state university is thus likened to a merger of "consulting firm McKinsey with Whirlpool's manufacturing operations and Northwestern Mutual Life Insurance Company"—that is to say, "three fundamentally different and incompatible business models all housed within the same organization."[15]

Cultural commentators and academics alike represent higher education in various stages of crisis, but the determinants at issue are symptomatic of a confluence of broader societal trends that threaten to undermine the egalitarian conception of higher education that has been integral to our national identity from the outset of the American republic. Public investment in higher education during the twentieth century produced a level of educational attainment unmatched anywhere in the world. Accessibility to our nation's college and universities served as a springboard to intergenerational economic mobility and a catalyst to innovation, which in turn brought prosperity to a broad middle class.[16] Yet, state funding has progressively declined, and the momentum of increased accessibility that brought growing prosperity to so many during the course of the past century has faltered. At the same time, our leading institutions have become increasingly exclusive and now define their excellence through admissions practices based on the exclusion of the majority of applicants. As a consequence, the egalitarian tenets intrinsic to the vision of the founders of our republic and once embodied in our nation's public universities appear no longer tenable. We address these issues in the first two chapters and deliberate whether there may be some measure of truth in many of the various barbs we have surveyed. Charles Murray's allegation that attainment of the baccalaureate degree has become a "driver of class distinctions," for example, turns out to be not in the least frivolous.

These critiques come at an inflection point in our contemporary society when the significance of knowledge has never been greater. "We are in a transition period where intellectual capital, brainpower, is replacing financial and physical capital as the key to our strength, prosperity, and well-being," writes James Duderstadt. "In a very real sense, we are entering a new age, an age of knowledge, in which the key strategic resource necessary for prosperity has become knowledge itself—that is, educated people and their ideas.[17] Yet, even in the midst of this new knowledge economy, Duderstadt finds that the very institutions that produce and transmit the currency of the realm are besieged by "economic, geopolitical, and demographic factors stimulating powerful market forces that are likely to drive a massive restructuring of the higher education enterprise":

> Whether a deliberate or involuntary response to the tightening fiscal constraints and changing priorities for public funds, the long-standing recognition that higher education is a public good, benefitting all of society, is eroding . . . . Without the constraints of public policy, earned and empowered by public investments, market forces could so dominate and reshape the higher education enterprise that many of the most important values and traditions of the university could fall by the wayside, including its public purpose.[18]

Even a decade ago, Frank Rhodes could foresee the rocky road ahead and introduced his delineation of the challenges that confront our colleges and universities in the following stark terms: "The 'learning industry' is about to face the same wrenching 'restructuring' that health care, manufacturing, and other industries, as well as welfare and public services, have already undergone," he predicted. "Mergers, acquisitions, and strategic alliances are likely to become unwelcome additions to the academic vocabulary. So are the terms 'downsizing' and 'outsourcing.'" Yet, he articulated even more fundamental concerns: "Today's university has no acknowledged center. It is all periphery, a circle of disciplinary and professional strongholds, jostling for position, and surrounding a vacant center." Absent is a "coherent vision" regarding the purposes of the academic endeavor.[19] Toward this end, Gordon Gee, then president of Ohio State University, called for radical reformation for our colleges and universities: "The choice, it seems to me, is this: reinvention or extinction."[20]

"Two major approaches dominate the criticism of colleges and universities," observes John Lombardi, former president of the Louisiana State University system:

> The first seeks to reform existing universities, making them better by improving their operation. This perspective, often pursued by those who be-

lieve the university is fundamentally sound, invokes tradition and values and
attempts to adjust those to the practical realities of contemporary economic
circumstances. The second approach sees universities and many colleges as
beyond repair in their current form or at least in serious crisis . . . . Depending on the spirit of the observer, these critics seek the replacement of existing university structures with much different learning organizations or
propose radical or reformist proposals that would clean house, change
standards, and impose new ones. [21]

Although Lombardi suggests that these alternative approaches are mutually exclusive, we see them as complementary. Indeed, in the following we contend that America's research universities are the most transformative institutions on the planet—or in the course of civilization—yet
that reform in large measure comes precisely with the reconfiguration of
existing organization and rethinking of practices.

In the chapters that follow, we consider the imperative for a new model
for the American research university that is more appropriate to the needs
of our society in the twenty-first century. The inherent limitations of the
present model attenuate the potential of this set of institutions to educate citizens in sufficient numbers and address the host of challenges that
beset the world. There is no single codified model for the American research university, strictly speaking, of course, and there would appear
to be a number of variants, inasmuch as this set of institutions includes
public and private universities that range considerably in scale, from
small private institutions like Dartmouth and MIT to large public universities like Ohio State. But for our purposes, these institutions bear a
striking family resemblance, the commonalities of which, we contend,
justify our reference to a model, which we term the "gold standard" in
American higher education. The model for a New American University
that we delineate is intended to complement the set of highly successful
major research universities and is only one among many possible models for this institutional type. Our reference to this model with each term
capitalized is merely a convention intended to suggest a broadly applicable concept. The New American University model combines accessibility to an academic platform underpinned by discovery and a pedagogical foundation of knowledge production, inclusiveness to a broad
demographic representative of the socioeconomic diversity of the region

and nation, and, through its breadth of functionality, maximization of societal impact commensurate with the scale of enrollment demand and the needs of our nation.

The first chapter examines the contemporary societal context for the American research university and introduces our discussion of the various interrelated dimensions of this set of roughly one hundred major research universities, both public and private, as well as the hundred additional research-grade institutions with less extensive research portfolios. Here and throughout the book, our objective is to contextualize the dilemma of the contemporary American research university, offer perspective on its inherent limitations, and suggest the characteristics of a new and complementary model. As we hope to explain, the implementation of the model represents a reconceptualization of the American research university as a complex and adaptive comprehensive knowledge enterprise committed to discovery, creativity, and innovation, accessible to the broadest possible demographic, socioeconomically as well as intellectually. Each institution, however, must implement the model according to its unique and differentiated profile, determined by its mission and setting; the characteristics of its academic community; the scope of its constituent colleges, schools, and departments; and the extent of its willingness to undertake commitment to public service and community engagement. Any comprehensive reconceptualization of an organization or institution must thus proceed according to its own intrinsic logic, especially in the case of an institution as complex as a major research university. This concept of an intrinsic logic is critical to the processes of adaptation, innovation, and evolution. The purposes of this book, therefore, do not include the articulation of a set of design prescriptions applicable in all contexts. Rather, our intent is to call attention to the explicit focus and extensive deliberation that must be expended on institutional design.

In this chapter we examine the contemporary relevance of the conviction that government has some measure of obligation to support the education of its citizens. We consider the egalitarian conception of higher education articulated from the outset of the American republic and the meritocratic assumptions that have shaped the narrative arc of our democratic experiment. Within the context of the confluence of economic, political, and social currents that enabled the American Dream and produced the American Century, we assess the public values that informed a social compact that produced world-leading levels of educational attainment and research and discovery that contributed to increasingly widely shared prosperity. We consider the evidence that, until the final quarter of the century, access to a college education served for millions as a springboard to intergenerational economic mobility.[22] We survey the subsequent downturn in public investment in higher education despite the success of the model. Disinvestment coincides with declining outcomes in educational attainment and increasingly stark income disparities, as well as declining prospects for younger generations. The reversal comes at a time when more and more Americans are seeking higher education, overwhelming a set of institutions built to accommodate enrollment demand prior to World War II. We introduce our discussion of the impact of the lack of educational infrastructure and evaluate the pernicious effects of admissions practices based on exclusion, which reinforce the social stratification that has been termed the "reproduction of privilege."[23] It is the inherent and fraught complexity of these and interrelated dimensions to the research university that underpins the arguments of the book, and the chapter concludes with a synopsis of the imperative for a new model to guide the transformation of these institutions.

The historical backdrop for the New American University is assessed in chapter 2, which begins with a brief survey of the antecedent models that contributed to the emergence of the American research university as these various strands coalesced into a distinct new institutional type during the final decades of the nineteenth century. The prototype would be consolidated with the establishment in 1876 of Johns Hopkins University, which conjoined the model represented by Oxford and Cambridge, which may be termed collegiate with reference to its focus on teaching undergraduates in a residential setting, with the German model epitomized by the University of Berlin, which sought to advance scientific research and specialized graduate education. The contemporaneous emergence of the various land-grant institutions enabled and enhanced by the Morrill Act, which was enacted into law by Abraham Lincoln in the midst of the Civil War, would serve as the third antecedent institutional model. The utilitarian tenets of the public universities this legislation empowered—as well as several leading private land-grant institutions—would inform the emerging American research university with an orientation conducive to scientific discovery and technological innovation, as well as collaboration with business and industry.

In this chapter we also consider the significance of the decentralization of American higher education, which promoted the competitive engagement of heterogeneous institutions in what has been termed an "academic marketplace."[24] The integration of teaching with research and development capacities consolidated an institutional type capable of educating successive generations of citizens as well as contributing to economic development. In this context we assess the impact of World War II and the expansion of public support for university-based research initiated by Vannevar Bush, advisor to President Franklin D. Roosevelt and the founding director of the Office of Scientific Research and Development (OSRD). His report *Science—The Endless Frontier* determined wartime science policy but also set the precedent for peacetime federal investment in basic research. The outcome of the arrangement in the postwar era led to what has been termed the Cold War university, which Senator J. William Fulbright referred to as the "military-industrial-academic complex."[25] A brief sketch of Harvard University on the occasion of its 375th anniversary suggests the incommensurability of enrollment at the scale characteristic of gold standard institutions with burgeoning demand and national self-interest. We conclude the chapter with a model of the evolutionary trajectory of universities in the Western world that suggests the imperative for differentiated and entrepreneurial institutions operationalized at a scale commensurate with demand.

With the possible exception of organized religion and the courts, few institutions of modern society so rigidly adhere to tradition as academe.[26] Chapter 3 considers what we term the "dark side" of academic tradition and the correlative pursuit of prestige that leads to institutional isomorphism—the paradoxical tendency for organizations and institutions within given sectors to emulate one another and become increasingly homogeneous. Institutional isomorphism is a "constraining process that forces one unit in a population to resemble other units that face the same set of environmental conditions."[27] This excessive veneration of tradition—or filiopietism—inspires the lockstep thinking that produces the set of undifferentiated institutions we designate the Generic Public University, which in private institutional peers spurs the correlate impulse toward Harvardization. We assess the propensity for institutions to attempt to replicate their exemplar peers as evidence of the quest for legitimacy that typifies positioning for prestige.[28] In this context we consider the routine, standardization, inertia, and conformity to rules inherent in large bureaucracies.[29] We then turn to a brief survey of selected episodes of resistance to reform in American higher education and conclude the chapter with a glance at the constructive aspects of tradition embodied in the liberal arts and sciences.

The transformational impact of the American research university on our quality of life, standard of living, and national economic competitiveness is considered in chapter 4. In this chapter we focus on the knowledge production of major research universities, which complements their role in the education of successive generations in all spheres of human endeavor. We consider the important economic impacts of the integrated academic research, development, and education conducted on our nation's campuses, which since the mid-twentieth century have contributed to a remarkable extent to the growth of the American economy. We elaborate on the role of these institutions in the discovery of new knowledge leading to perpetual innovation in the ideas, products, and processes that spur the global knowledge economy, as well as their mediation of the relationship between fundamental research and industrial application, which spawns new industries and anchors innovation clusters. The scientific discovery and technological innovation that are the products of academic research are widely held to have been requisite to the trajectory of economic development that led the United States in the second half of the twentieth century to become the dominant world superpower. We briefly sketch the impact of research universities as hubs of regional innovation clusters, most famously epitomized in the relationship between Stanford University and Silicon Valley and between Harvard University and MIT and Route 128 in Boston, as well as their significance in our national innovation system.

Institutional design is not merely a perfunctory administrative matter adventitious to the production and dissemination of knowledge. In chapter 5 we look closely at the reflexive relationship between institutional design and knowledge production and dissemination. This chapter introduces the concept of institutional design, the implications of the design limitations of the present model, and the possibilities inherent in a new model for the American research university. Design is a central concept for the New American University, and it is precisely the details of practice of institutional design that we consider in this chapter, especially with regard to the organization of research and the implementation of interdisciplinarity and sustainability.

Pragmatism has been termed our nation's most significant contribution to philosophy, and in chapter 6 we briefly sketch its outlines to suggest its influence on the American research university. Pragmatism is characterized by its concern with the practical application of knowledge articulated through social consensus and thus constitutes an insufficiently appreciated grounding for the pedagogical and discovery enterprise of the New American University. The pragmatist stance interrelating knowledge with action implicitly informs the defining tenets of the new model, especially its concern that knowledge should lead to action with the objective of real-world transformational impact. In this context we consider the role of academia in advancing sustainability and the objective of sustainable development, which refers to balancing wealth generation with continuously enhanced environmental quality and social well-being. We contend that the academic sector must assume leadership in managing our accelerating impact on the earth.

Following its comprehensive reconceptualization, Arizona State University serves as a foundational prototype for the New American University model. Chapter 7 offers a case study of the implementation of this model, delineating the design process undertaken to transform ASU from an emerging regional public research university with an uneven academic reputation into an institution that competes academically with the leading universities in the world even as it offers access to a platform of discovery and knowledge production to a broad demographic representative of the socioeconomic diversity of the region. The reconceptualization, initiated in 2002, represents an institutional experiment conducted at scale and in real time, which *Newsweek* termed "one of the most radical redesigns in higher learning since the modern research university took shape in nineteenth-century Germany."[30] An editorial from the journal *Nature* observes that questions about the structure and relevance of the contemporary research university are being examined "nowhere more searchingly than at Arizona State University."[31] "It has become a very different and very exciting institution," comments Frank Rhodes. "It is going to be a prototype for the rest of the country."[32] In conclusion we submit that our colleges and universities must be prepared to lend direction and purpose to the artistic and humanistic insight, social scientific understanding, scientific discoveries, and technological innovations that are the products of an academic culture that represents our best hope as we negotiate the encroaching complexity emerging in the twenty-first century.

If the founding of the colonial colleges, beginning with Harvard in 1636, is representative of a first wave of what was then termed the "higher learning" to sweep up on our shores from Britain and the Continent, the establishment by the various states of a heterogeneous array of public colleges during the subsequent two centuries would constitute a second wave. All of these regional colleges were dedicated almost exclusively to teaching, but with the third wave we see the first stirrings of applied research in an academic setting, albeit closely tied to agriculture and the needs of local industry, and largely confined to what has been termed "hands-on problem-solving."[33] The land-grant colleges and universities that were established in the decades following the Civil War constitute this third wave, which would prove critical to the emergence of the research enterprises of the fifteen institutions that between 1876 and roughly 1915 consolidated the institutional form of the contemporary research university.[34] The roughly one hundred research-extensive and one hundred further research-intensive institutions that constitute the set of American research universities—the fourth wave in American higher education—are the most complex and heterogeneous knowledge enterprises that have ever evolved. No less remarkably, institutions representative of the preceding three iterations we have delineated—elite liberal arts colleges whose scale and purposes depart little from the colonial era; regional colleges focused on teaching; and large public universities more or less limited to instruction in a standardized set of basic disciplines—comingle and thrive in the academic marketplace. This said, we contend that the momentum of the fourth wave has run its course. Or perhaps it would be more accurate to say that a groundswell visible on the horizon signals an impending fifth wave in American higher education.[35]

## Notes

1. Michael Noer, "America's Top Colleges," *Forbes* (August 20, 2012). Arizona State University weighs in at 226 in this tally, far below its ranking in international assessments with rigorous methodologies, where it appears in the top 100 globally. We consider the shortcomings of these spurious assessments in chapter 7.

2. Mark C. Taylor, *Crisis on Campus: A Bold Plan for Reforming Our Colleges and Universities* (New York: Alfred A. Knopf, 2010), 5.

3. Andrew Hacker and Claudia Dreifus, *Higher Education? How Colleges Are Wasting Our Money and Failing Our Kids—And What We Can Do about It* (New York: Henry Holt and Company, 2010), 2–3.

4. Peter Thiel, "College Doesn't Create Success," *New York Times* (August 25, 2011).

5. Richard Arum and Josipa Roksa, *Academically Adrift: Limited Learning on College Campuses* (Chicago: University of Chicago Press, 2010), 2–6. With reference to the "disengagement compact," Arum and Roksa quote George D. Kuh, "What We Are Learning About Student Engagement," *Change* 35 (2003): 28.

6. Derek Bok, *Our Underachieving Colleges: A Candid Look at How Much Students Learn and Why They Should Be Learning More* (Princeton, NJ: Princeton University Press, 2006), 314, cited by Arum and Roksa, 6.

7. Nicholas Kristof, "Smart Minds, Slim Impact," *New York Times* (February 16, 2014).

8. Bill Readings, *The University in Ruins* (Cambridge, MA: Harvard University Press, 1996), 1, 180–181. The decline over the past several decades in the percentage of tenured and tenure-track faculty in American colleges and universities is indeed striking. Figures cited by the American Association of University Professors (AAUP) show that between 1975 and 2007 the percentage of full-time tenure and tenure-track faculty declined from 56.8 percent to 31.2 percent. Another estimate from the U.S. Department of Education shows that in fall 2009 "contingent academics," defined as full-time nontenure-track and part-time faculty and graduate student employees, comprised more than 75 percent of total instructional staff.

9. Allan Bloom, *The Closing of the American Mind* (New York: Simon and Schuster, 2012).

10. John William Pope, quoted by Jane Meyer, "State for Sale," *New Yorker* (October 10, 2011): 100–102.

11. Peter Wood and Michael Toscano, "What Does Bowdoin Teach? How a Contemporary Liberal Arts College Shapes Students" (New York: National Association of Scholars, 2013): 9; 16. The phrase regarding "moral deficit" comes from the foreword to the report by William Bennett. The quote regarding dogma was cited by Dan Berrett, "Bowdoin College Suffers from Moral Deficit, Report Argues," *Chronicle of Higher Education* (April 3, 2013).

12. Charles Murray, "Narrowing the Class Divide," *New York Times* (March 7, 2012).

13. "Too Many Kids Go to College." *Intelligence Squared (IQ²)* debate series, Chicago, October 12, 2011, http://intelligencesquaredus.org/debates/past-debates/item/550-too -many-kids-go-to-college-our-first-debate-in-chicago.

14. Clayton M. Christensen and Henry J. Eyring, *The Innovative University: Changing the DNA of Higher Education from the Inside Out* (San Francisco: Jossey-Bass, 2011), 12–13. Christensen elucidates the theory of disruptive innovation in *The Innovator's Dilemma* (Cambridge, MA: Harvard Business School Press, 1997).

15. Clayton M. Christensen et al., "Disrupting College: How Disruptive Innovation Can Deliver Quality and Affordability to Postsecondary Education" (Washington, DC: Center for American Progress, February 2011), 3.

16. Claudia Goldin and Lawrence F. Katz, *The Race between Education and Technology* (Cambridge, MA: Belknap Press of Harvard University Press, 2008), 11–43.

17. James J. Duderstadt, *A University for the Twenty-First Century* (Ann Arbor: University of Michigan Press, 2000), 13–14.

18. James J. Duderstadt, "Aligning American Higher Education with a Twenty-First Century Public Agenda," remarks to the Association of Governing Boards of Universities and Colleges, Miller Center for Public Affairs, University of Virginia, Charlottesville, June 8–10, 2008.

19. Rhodes, *Creation of the Future*, 44; 230–231.

20. Gordon Gee, "Colleges Face Reinvention or Extinction," *Chronicle of Higher Education* (February 2009): 9.

21. John V. Lombardi, *How Universities Work* (Baltimore: Johns Hopkins University Press, 2013), 30–31.

22. Goldin and Katz, *The Race between Education and Technology*, 11–43.

23. Anthony P. Carnevale, quoted in Thomas B. Edsall, "The Reproduction of Privilege," *New York Times* (March 12, 2012).

24. Hugh Davis Graham and Nancy Diamond, *The Rise of American Research Universities: Elites and Challengers in the Postwar Era* (Baltimore: Johns Hopkins University Press, 1997).

25. Stuart W. Leslie, *The Cold War and American Science: The Military-Industrial-Academic Complex at MIT and Stanford* (New York: Columbia University Press, 1993), 2.

26. William Clark, *Academic Charisma and the Origins of the Research University* (Chicago: University of Chicago Press, 2006).

27. Paul J. DiMaggio and Walter W. Powell, "The Iron Cage Revisited: Institutional Isomorphism and Collective Rationality in Organizational Fields," *American Sociological Review* 48, no. 2 (1983): 149.

28. J. Douglas Toma, "Institutional Strategy: Positioning for Prestige," in *The Organization of Higher Education: Managing Colleges for a New Era*, ed. Michael N. Bastedo (Baltimore: Johns Hopkins University Press, 2012): 119.

29. A classic account of bureaucracy is to be found in Anthony Downs, *Inside Bureaucracy* (Boston: Little Brown, 1967).

30. Stefan Theil, "The Campus of the Future: To Better Compete, A Few Bold Leaders Are Rethinking Their Schools from the Ground Up," *Newsweek* (August 9, 2008).

31. "The University of the Future," *Nature* 446, no. 7139 (April 26, 2007).

32. Frank Rhodes, quoted in Colin Macilwain, "The Arizona Experiment," *Nature* 446, no. 7139 (April 26, 2007).

33. Nathan Rosenberg and Richard R. Nelson, "American Universities and Technical Advance in Industry," *Research Policy* 23, no. 3 (1994): 323–348.

34. Michael M. Crow and William B. Dabars, "University-Based Research and Economic Development: The Morrill Act and the Emergence of the American Research University," in *Precipice or Crossroads: Where America's Great Public Universities Stand and Where They Are Going Midway through Their Second Century,* ed. Daniel Mark Fogel (Albany: State University of New York Press, 2012), 119–158.

35. More elaborate and precise schemata for the trajectory of American higher education have certainly been proposed. Roger Geiger, for example, identifies ten generations over the course of which the character of American higher education is said to have "perceptibly shifted in each generation, or approximately every thirty years" (37). See Geiger, "The Ten Generations of American Higher Education," in *Higher Education in the Twenty-First Century: Social, Political, and Economic Challenges,* 3rd ed., ed. Philip G. Altbach, Patricia J. Gumport, and Robert O. Berdahl (Baltimore: Johns Hopkins University Press, 2011), 37–68.

ONE

# American Research Universities
# at a Fork in the Road

"The university is the most significant creation of the second millennium," observes Frank Rhodes, president emeritus of Cornell University, in the introduction to his eloquent contribution to the vast literature on the American research university. "From modest beginnings over nine hundred years ago, it has become the quiet but decisive catalyst in modern society, the factor essential to its effective functioning and well-being."[1] Although it is possible to trace the lineage of these institutions in the West to the British and continental European universities established in the eleventh or twelfth centuries, and their antecedent institutional forms to the monastery and cathedral schools of the Middle Ages, or even more remotely to the academies of classical antiquity, the American research university emerged only very recently during the modern era. The institutional type we recognize today coalesced in the late nineteenth century when fifteen institutions, both public and private, grafted programs of specialized graduate study, modeled on the practices of German universities, onto their undergraduate programs, which derived from the residential British model epitomized by Oxford and Cambridge. And although what is considered the prototype for the American research university would appear with the establishment of Johns Hopkins University, in Baltimore, Maryland, in 1876, these fifteen institutions, as delineated by the historian Roger L. Geiger, conclusively consolidated the structure and purposes of this institutional type. From a varied evolutionary pool representative of the diversity of American higher education, Geiger explains, the model for the American research university was established by five colonial colleges chartered before the American Revolution (Harvard, Yale, Pennsylvania, Princeton, and Columbia); five

17

state universities (Michigan, Wisconsin, Minnesota, Illinois, and California); and five private institutions conceived from their inception as research universities (MIT, Cornell, Johns Hopkins, Stanford, and Chicago). According to Geiger, these fifteen universities were unified by their collective identity as a unique and differentiated set of institutions and defined by their interrelationships, both competitive and cooperative; capacity to institutionalize and organize the proliferation of specialized knowledge into academic disciplines; success at leveraging burgeoning financial resources and academic infrastructure derived from growth; and commitment to research as a complement to the traditional function of teaching.[2] These fifteen universities collectively determined the gold standard in American higher education—a model the potential and limitations of which we assess from various perspectives in the following chapters.

While the institution famously characterized more than half a century ago by then University of California president Clark Kerr as a "multiversity"—"a whole series of communities and activities held together by a common name, a common governing board, and related purposes"[3]—has undergone incremental change since the nineteenth century, we contend that design limitations inherent to these otherwise highly successful institutions restrict or subvert their vast potential to contribute to knowledge production as well as societal well-being. We take the assessment of Frank Rhodes regarding their transformational impact as a point of departure in our effort to contextualize the dilemma of the contemporary American research university, offer perspective on its inherent limitations, and suggest a new model that is more appropriate to the needs of our society in the twenty-first century. This model for a New American University was initially conceptualized by Michael M. Crow when he became president of Arizona State University, and it has been successfully operationalized there over the course of the past decade through the efforts of its faculty, staff, and students. The New American University represents a differentiated platform for the American research university intended to complement this set of remarkable institutions with a new model for research-grade universities distinguished by their capacity to provide broad accessibility, commensurate with the scale of demand and diversity of our society, to an academic milieu underpinned by discovery and pedagogical foundations informed by knowledge production. The New American University thus represents a reconceptualization of the American research university as a complex and adaptive comprehensive knowledge enterprise committed to discovery, creativity, and innovation, an institution accessible to the broadest possible demographic spectrum, representative of the socioeconomic and intellectual diversity of our nation.

By any measure or set of indicators, American research universities can claim unrivaled global preeminence. Jonathan Cole, provost emeritus of Columbia University, described his experience as an advisor to Chinese provincial leaders determined to build an institution to rival Ivy League schools "starting from scratch." The assignment, writes Cole, was to "create a blueprint for greatness."[4] China is in the midst of massive investment in its national infrastructure for higher education, and policy makers there understand well the correlation between higher education and competitiveness in the global knowledge economy, as attested by an editorial that appeared in the *China Daily* on October 21, 2009.[5] Although the editorial takes the commendable position that government planning for the development of a consortium of world-class institutions—a Chinese Ivy League—places undue emphasis on exclusivity and international status at the cost of access for the majority of citizens, the inherent idealization of the set of elite American research universities underscores the imperative to reconsider the model these institutions represent in the twenty-first century. The commitment to build research universities from scratch offers China the opportunity to design universities that transcend historical models, which in the case of the American research university, as we contend in the following chapters, is limited by its entrenchment in obsolete institutional design, lack of scalability, and residual elitism.[6]

The intent of policy makers in evolving economies around the world to emulate American higher education attests to their realization that this institutional framework represents a uniquely successful model that not only excels in educating students but also contributes inestimably to economic growth and competitiveness. From the perspectives of ruling elites as well as average citizens, the United States offers what by general consensus is held to be the definitive model for higher education. In reality, however, it makes little sense to speak of a single model as if American higher education were governed by a centralized national authority or even guided by a unified and cohesive vision. Contemporary American

higher education is in many important respects the product of a range
of institutional "birth parents" and a long trajectory of ad hoc negotiations taken in response to historical exigencies or fraught political circumstances. The evolution of this set of heterogeneous institutions and
the dynamics of its current success are not easily replicated by fiat, and
efforts by policy makers in developing economies to emulate its broad
contours will almost certainly not produce the same results or outcomes.
The time and place are different, and the definition of success in the future remains to be written. The "blueprint for greatness" will almost certainly require adaptation, depending on the organizational type and the
national context.

The worldwide focus on American research universities also denotes
growing recognition of the significance of knowledge. Because higher
education has been one of the primary sources of the knowledge and innovation that have driven the global economy, the demand for advanced
teaching and research, and for the new ideas, products, and processes that
it yields, has reached fever pitch and exceeds the currently available supply. Even though the production and dissemination of knowledge will
always remain the primary role of colleges and universities, in recent
decades awareness has emerged in both developed and developing
economies that scientific discovery and technological innovation are major drivers of national economic growth and competitiveness, and in
terms of their contributions to economic development, American research universities have been uniquely successful.[7] The consensus that
new knowledge contributes to economic competitiveness has pushed
higher education to the forefront of policy discussions, corresponding to
a ubiquitous new emphasis on science and technology. In the decades
ahead, policy makers' decisions regarding higher education will be major determinants of a given country's economic competitiveness and ability to enhance the well-being of its citizens.

While there are roughly five thousand institutions of higher education in the United States, the Carnegie Foundation for the Advancement
of Teaching categorizes only 108 of them, both public and private, as major research universities. Approximately one hundred additional universities with less extensive research portfolios comprise a second cohort of
research-grade institutions.[8] The status of the research-extensive insti-

tutions in reputable international assessments of academic output reflects the esteem in which they are held worldwide. American institutions consistently occupy seventeen of the top twenty slots in the authoritative ranking of world-class universities conducted by the Institute of Higher Education, Shanghai Jiao Tong University, and fourteen of the top twenty in the most recent edition of the *Times Higher Education* World University Rankings.[9] The number of international students seeking enrollment at American colleges and universities attests to the perception that these institutions offer opportunities that cannot be found elsewhere. Needless to add, all of the institutions assessed in these evaluations are research-grade universities, and in his magisterial discussion of the institutional type, Jonathan Cole differentiates their purposes from colleges and universities devoted primarily to teaching, and in so doing summarizes the scope and breadth of their contribution:

> Although the transmission of knowledge is a core mission of our universities, it is not what makes them the best institutions of higher learning in the world. We are the greatest because our finest universities are able to produce a very high proportion of the most important fundamental knowledge and practical research discoveries in the world. It is the quality of the research produced, and the system that invests in and trains young people to be leading scientists and scholars, that distinguishes them and makes them the envy of the world.[10]

Apart from their role in the formation of successive generations of our nation's scholars, scientists, and leaders in every sphere of human endeavor, the set of research universities, both public and private, has served as the primary source of the discovery, creativity, and innovation that fosters economic growth and social development at all levels of analysis in the global knowledge economy. A geologist by training, Frank Rhodes contrasts our historical dependence on natural resources with the new paradigm of knowledge proliferation realized during the past several decades:

> A nation's present well-being and future destiny are no longer constrained only by its "givens" (its geography, its population, its natural resources). Knowledge has become the prime mover; science and technology represent

the new driving force. Economic prosperity, energy supplies, manufacturing capacity, personal health, public safety, military security, and environmental quality—all these and more will depend on knowledge.[11]

Unlike coal, knowledge is a renewable resource: "Unlike other assets, whose utilization and investment are constrained by the law of diminishing returns, knowledge is autocatalytic, enlarging in the hands of its users; expanding in the range of its usefulness, even as it is applied; growing in scope, even as it is shared, increasing in refinement, even as it is questioned, challenged, and contested." Knowledge is a public good, as the Nobel laureate economist Joseph Stiglitz has elaborated,[12] and the economic impact of knowledge, especially scientific discovery and technological innovation—what the economic historian Joel Mokyr has termed the "gifts of Athena"—is an important correlate of academic research, a point we delineate in chapter 4.[13]

The science-based technological innovation and industrial application that are the products of academic research are widely held to have been requisite to the trajectory of economic development that led the United States in the second half of the twentieth century to become a predominant superpower. Economists contend that as much as 85 percent of measured growth in per capita income in the United States derives from technological change, according to research cited by the National Academies.[14] The innovation advanced by the research and development (R&D) enterprises of American research universities, conducted in coordination with undergraduate and graduate programs, has contributed incalculably to the standard of living and quality of life those of us in developed economies take for granted.[15] Innovation engenders economic growth through the processes of "creative destruction" described by the Austrian American economist Joseph Schumpeter as early as the 1930s. Through creative destruction, new and improved products and processes supersede the outmoded and obsolete.[16] Our focus on the economic development potential of academic research stems from the contention that prosperity promotes social advancement and the values and ideals of our pluralistic democracy. And although academic research and development in the sciences and engineering contribute the predominant share of the new products, processes, and services that impact our daily lives, scholarly and creative endeavor in the arts, the humanities, and the social and behavioral sciences sometimes escape our notice precisely because their pervasive influence already so fully informs our experience.

Yet, although our leading research universities, both public and private, consistently dominate global rankings, our success in establishing world-class excellence in a relative handful of elite institutions does little to ensure the broad distribution of the correlates of educational attainment, nor does it sufficiently advance the innovation that contributes to our continued national competitiveness. Unable or unwilling to accommodate enrollment demand from academically qualified students, our leading institutions have, in recent decades, come to define their status through admissions practices based on exclusion. And even though the global preeminence of our leading institutions may well lead Americans to infer that on the whole our nation has the best colleges and universities in the world, the results of a multinational assessment of adult literacy and quantitative capabilities conducted by the Organisation for Economic Co-operation and Development (OECD) calls this assumption into question. Kevin Carey, an education policy expert resident at the New America Foundation, makes the important point that the metrics used to establish the unrivaled status of these institutions—the research performance of an array of world-class universities—does not correlate with overall excellence in American higher education: "America's perceived international dominance of higher education . . . rests largely on global rankings of top universities . . . . When President Obama has said, 'We have the best universities,' he has not meant: 'Our universities are, on average, the best'—even though that's what many people hear. He means, 'Of the best universities, most are ours.' The distinction is important."[17] We focus on this distinction to underscore the critical imperative for greater accessibility to academic platforms informed by discovery and knowledge production. Because the excellence of our research-grade institutions does not correlate with their accessibility except to a generally privileged fraction of the pool of potential qualified students, the implications for the majority of individuals and the competitiveness of our society in an increasingly knowledge-intensive global economy are obvious.

"Knowledge is our most important business," writes Louis Menand, Harvard professor of English and American literature, referring not only to academia but more broadly to the role of knowledge in contemporary society. "The success of almost all our other business depends on it, but its value is not only economic. The pursuit, production, dissemination, application, and preservation of knowledge are the central activities of a civilization." Menand moves quickly to contextualize its valuation and the inevitable corollary dilemma: "Knowledge is a form of capital that is always unevenly distributed, and people who have more knowledge, or greater access to knowledge, enjoy advantages over people who have less."[18] Economists, of course, speak of human capital, a concept that in its most general sense refers to the measure of the value of the stock of knowledge, skills, and creativity that may be acquired through investment in education and training. Through investment in human capital, the economist Theodore W. Schultz observed in a pioneering article on the concept, "the quality of human effort can be greatly improved and its productivity enhanced."[19] Alan Wilson, a fellow of the British Academy and Royal Society, corroborates the consensus that knowledge in our contemporary society is its principal capital and social resource, which "empowers people in a knowledge-based economy . . . and underpins any kind of critical thinking." Moreover, he observes, "It is *civilizing*. In a phrase, what counts is *knowledge power*"—a correlation he attributes to Francis Bacon, one of whose aphorisms is generally translated "knowledge is power."[20] The observation may seem a mere rhetorical commonplace, but the claim, variously formulated through the centuries, has never been more relevant than in the present knowledge economy.

"We live at the centre of a knowledge explosion," Wilson observes. Yet, in tandem with this assertion, he is compelled to juxtapose a question relevant to our own assessment of the limitations of contemporary knowledge production: "Why doesn't the growth of knowledge sustain progress?" In the midst of so much knowledge, both theoretical and practical, perhaps what is lacking, in his estimation, is the ambition—as well as the "requisite knowledge"—to conceptualize and develop the "knowledge space" and institutional frameworks for addressing the challenges that beset global society. Universities are moving too slowly to accommodate the pace of transformation in the structure of knowledge, he argues,[21] referring in part to the interdisciplinary imperative we consider in chapter 5. Whether the unchecked proliferation of knowledge that has characterized our era can be harnessed toward societal purpose remains a matter of conjecture. The philosopher Robert Frodeman probes in this context the attendant limitations of the "epistemological regime we have been living within, that of infinite, largely laissez-faire knowledge production." As evidence of the scale—if not the efficacy—of contemporary scholarly output, he cites research that estimates that in 2009 more than one and a half million peer-reviewed journal articles were published in some 26,400 academic journals. Another study found that between 2002 and 2006, only 40 percent of articles published in the leading science and social science journals were cited during the first five years following their publication, and as of 2005, according to another estimate, 48 percent of all articles published had never been cited.[22]

The imperative for discovery that distinguishes the research university from other institutional types must be reconciled with other dimensions of the present model. Despite the critical niche these institutions occupy in the knowledge economy, their preponderant commitment to discovery and innovation restricts the potential of their contribution unless some among them embrace a broader societal embeddedness. Knowledge production flourishes within a number of organizational settings, including industrial laboratories and the system of national laboratories that contribute to our national innovation system. But with missions spanning teaching, research, and public service, research universities are uniquely positioned to assume an obligation to construe their purposes in a context of societal engagement. We mistakenly assume that the intellectual objectives of our institutions, especially in terms of scientific research and technological innovation, are automatically and inevitably aligned with our most important goals as a society. But if these institutions are to create knowledge that is as socially useful as it is scientifically meritorious, a deliberate effort will be required by some to integrate their quest to advance discovery, creativity, and innovation with an explicit mandate to assume responsibility for the societies they serve.[23]

The proliferation of increasingly specialized knowledge that research universities produce tends to bring diminishing returns on investment as its impact on the world is measured in smaller and smaller ratios. Prestige will always attach to the pursuit of the unknown, but there is scant reason why research-grade institutions must conform exclusively to the precedent of a historical model that prioritizes the isolation and analysis of increasingly specialized knowledge. In our valorization of basic research, motivated primarily by curiosity rather than in pursuit of a societal goal, we lose sight of the potential for application and outcome when research is use-inspired.[24] This is not to perpetuate a spurious dichotomy between basic and applied research; both are crucial, and in many cases the boundary between them is so permeable as to be meaningless.[25] But in our accustomed effort to produce novel and abstract knowledge, academic culture sometimes overlooks the fact that its institutions possess the capacity to give direction and purpose to scientific discovery and technological application to advance desired outcomes or to create useful products, processes, and ideas.

Although American research universities retain global leadership in discovery and innovation, their capacity to mount responses at scale and in real time is diminished by entrenchment in bureaucratic constructs that often serve primarily to perpetuate existing academic infrastructure and administrative practices. As a consequence, our institutions are internally adaptive when their effort should be directed toward the mediation of societal adaptation to the complexity and ambiguity that has become our default condition. Toward this end, some institutions beyond those already informed by the utilitarian ideals of the land grant system might more fully embrace ambitious and multifaceted public outreach and engagement programs dedicated to societal advancement and regional economic development. No less imperative is a commitment to the production in sufficient numbers of scientists, engineers, artists, philosophers, economists, doctors, and lawyers—in short, the educated citizenry from which we draw our future leaders in every sector.

American higher education can no longer assume that its competitive position in the world is unassailable.[26] Our global economic leadership is challenged by ambitious emerging nations that intend to compete by making massive investments in education and research. Around the world, national leaders understand that university research has been the chief catalyst for America's adaptability and economic dominance during the past century and seek to emulate our model. While nations worldwide are investing strategically to educate broader segments of their populations for the new global knowledge economy, America has allowed its research universities, despite their historical preeminence, to lose their adaptive capacities. If we are to prevail in this era of massively escalating complexity and competition, what will be required from our universities is perpetual innovation on all fronts, including pedagogical design to accommodate talent from a broader demographic cross section. Such innovation is not only the product of advances in knowledge production, but it will require evolution in the structure, practices, and interrelationships of our knowledge enterprises. It is the inherent and fraught complexity of these various interrelated dimensions to the research university, as well as their interaction and interplay, that is the context of the assessment and analysis in the following chapters. Historical perspective on the lineage of antecedent university models, including their conceptualization, structures, operations, and practices, enriches our understanding of contemporary academe. Through an appreciation of the present model of the American research university and some perspective on its historical evolution, we hope to articulate the imperative for a new and differentiated model to complement the set of existing institutions.

## The Public Purposes of the "Higher Learning"

An egalitarian conception of higher education has from the outset of our republic been integral to our collective identity as well as pivotal to the attainment of what would be framed as the American Dream. When John Adams and his colleagues drafted the Constitution of the Commonwealth of Massachusetts, which was ratified in June 1780, the purposes of what was then often termed the "higher learning" were not summarily dismissed. In a document that seven years hence would serve as a prototype for the Constitution of the United States of America, section 2 of chapter 5 begins as follows: "Wisdom and knowledge, as well as virtue, diffused generally among the body of the people, being necessary for the preservation of their rights and liberties; and as these depend on spreading the opportunities and advantages of education in the various parts of the country, and among the different orders of the people, it shall be the duty of legislatures and magistrates, in all future periods of this commonwealth, to cherish the interests of literature and the sciences, and all seminaries of them . . . ." Inasmuch as only one such "seminary" then existed in Massachusetts—namely Harvard College, which welcomed its first class of nine students, presided over by a single master, in 1636—the document specifies "especially the university at Cambridge."[27]

In this passage, one of the leading political thinkers of the American Revolution and second president of the United States—one of possibly not more than a few thousand college graduates then to be found in the fledgling republic—articulated the foundational principle that in a democracy the government must assume responsibility for the education of its citizens. With reference to the imperative for an educated citizenry addressed in the context of his vision for the University of Virginia, Thomas Jefferson, a graduate of the College of William and Mary, expressed a similar conception in 1820: "I know of no safe depository of the ultimate powers of the society, but the people themselves; and if we think them not enlightened enough to exercise their control with a wholesome discretion, the remedy is not to take it from them, but to inform their discretion by education."[28] In the 1780s, he wrote, "I think by far the most important bill in our whole code is that for the diffusion of knowledge among the people. No other sure foundation can be devised for the preservation of freedom and happiness."[29] Elsewhere, regarding the necessary correlation between an educated citizenry and the exercise of democracy, Jefferson had observed, "If a nation expects to be ignorant and free, in a state of civilization, it expects what never was and never will be."[30] James Madison, a graduate of the college that would become Princeton and author of the Bill of Rights, made the same point in 1822 when he wrote, "Knowledge will forever govern ignorance: And a people who mean to be their own governours must arm themselves with the power which knowledge gives."[31] Institutions embody the values of a society, and in chapter 2 we seize on Adams' reference to Harvard to consider the implications of the persistence of an elitist model incommensurate to the demand for higher education in a remarkably diverse nation of nearly 320 million.

The egalitarian tenets intrinsic to the vision of the founders of the republic are embodied in our nation's public universities, which taken together outperform and outproduce their private institutional peers in the scale of their contribution to our nation. Daniel Mark Fogel, president emeritus of the University of Vermont, delineates the extent of their contribution: "They perform more than 60 percent of the academic research and development in the nation. They educate some 85 percent of the students who receive bachelor's degrees at all American research universities, and 70 percent of all graduate students. They award more than 50 percent of the doctorates granted in the United States in eleven of thirteen national needs categories—including between 60 to 80 percent of the doctorates in computer and information sciences, engineering, foreign languages and linguistics, mathematics and statistics, physical sciences, and security."[32] Accordingly, public higher education was conceived with social outcomes in mind and is thus often represented as a social contract or compact, policy scholar John Aubrey Douglass explains: "To a degree perhaps unmatched by any other single institution in our society or by any other nation in the world, America's public universities were conceived, funded, and developed as tools of socioeconomic engineering . . . . These institutions were to benefit the individual not as a goal unto themselves but as a means to shape a more progressive and productive society."[33] Although the republic's founders so valued the purposes of higher education in a participatory democracy that the establishment of a great national university was proposed on more than one occasion during James Madison's presidency,[34] in the absence of such an institution, one might even say that our public universities collectively comprise a de facto national university committed to the public good.

Public sector investment in higher education in the United States during the twentieth century produced a level of educational attainment unmatched anywhere in the world, which served as a springboard to intergenerational economic mobility and catalyst to innovation and thus national economic competitiveness.[35] During the three decades following World War II, a period of expansion for colleges and universities that Louis Menand has termed the "Golden Age" of American higher education, growth in undergraduate enrollments, including community colleges, increased fivefold and nearly 900 percent in graduate schools.[36] Yet, despite the success of this model, public investment in higher education has progressively declined. According to economist Robert J. Gordon, in the decade between 2001 and 2012, funding for higher education from states and municipalities declined by one-third when adjusted for inflation. By way of example, Gordon observes, "In 1985 the state of Colorado provided 37 percent of the budget of the University of Colorado, but last year provided only 9 percent."[37] Research from the Center on Budget and Policy Priorities found that state appropriations for higher education declined 28 percent between fiscal years 2008 and 2013: "Eleven states have cut funding by more than one-third per student, and two states— Arizona and New Hampshire—have cut their higher education spending per student in half."[38] During the past year, funding has been restored by an average of 7.2 percent, but state spending remains 23 percent below prerecession levels: "Per student spending in Arizona, Louisiana, and South Carolina is down by more than 40 percent since the start of the recession."[39]

Such disinvestment in public higher education means increased tuitions and diminished access. It is just one of the many factors stemming the momentum of increased accessibility to our nation's colleges and universities that marked the course of the past century. As a result, many of the students who would most benefit from this obvious avenue of upward mobility—those whom we broadly categorize as "socioeconomically disadvantaged" or "historically underrepresented"—cannot or choose not to seek admission to a research-grade university. The decline comes at a time when more and more Americans of all ages, socioeconomic backgrounds, levels of academic preparation, and differing types of intelligence and creativity seek enrollment in our colleges and universities, overwhelming a set of institutions built to accommodate the needs of our country prior to the Second World War, when the population of the United States was less than half its present level and only 1.14 percent of Americans were enrolled in college. Over the past quarter century, total enrollment in institutions of higher education has grown from under 13 million to more than 21 million (figure 1).[40] Roughly three-fourths of high school graduates now enroll in some form of college, including community colleges and for-profit sector institutions—a fourfold increase since the midcentury. By one estimate, community colleges enroll 45 percent of all U.S. undergraduates, and for-profit schools enroll 10 percent. Although such burgeoning enrollments would suggest progress, degree completion rates have fallen, and the outcomes of attendance vary widely according to institutional type.[41]

### Access to Academic Excellence for a Broad Demographic

Although nations worldwide are investing strategically to educate broader segments of their citizenry for the knowledge economy, America's educational infrastructure remains unable to accommodate projected enrollment demands. America's leading institutions have become increasingly exclusive and define their excellence through admissions practices based on the exclusion of the majority of applicants. In this sense, prestige is attained through the maintenance of scarcity, and meritocratic pretense may be perceived as a defensive posture and abdication

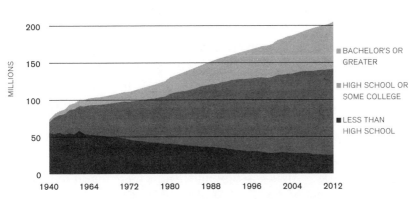

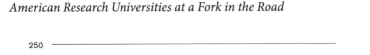

FIGURE 1. Population of the United States by highest educational attainment, 1940–2012. Source: U.S. Census Bureau, Education and Social Stratification Branch, Table A-1: Years of School Completed by People 25 Years and Over, by Age and Sex: Selected Years 1940 to 2012.

of implicit responsibility. Even though our leading universities, both public and private, retain their dominance in global rankings, our success in maintaining excellence in a relative handful of elite institutions does little to ensure our continued prosperity and competitiveness, especially if we stop to consider the disproportionately few students fortunate enough to be admitted to these top schools. Princeton historian Anthony Grafton underscores this point when he refers to the "little group of traditional liberal arts colleges, all of whose students could fit in the football stadium of a single Big Ten school."[42] Another assessment using the same benchmark similarly concludes that the "nation's liberal arts college students would almost certainly fit easily inside a Big Ten football stadium: fewer than 100,000 students."[43] And indeed, by one estimate the total enrollment of undergraduates in the eight traditional Ivies during academic year 2012–2013 was 65,677 while the top fifty liberal arts colleges collectively enrolled 95,496.[44] Michigan Stadium in Ann Arbor seats roughly 110,000.

But the dilemma of access to academic excellence is not limited to the aggregate enrollment numbers of small liberal arts colleges. If we take institutional membership in the Association of American Universities (AAU), which represents sixty leading research universities in the United States, both public and private, as proxy for academic quality, available seats for undergraduates number roughly 1.1 million. AAU public institutions enrolled 918,221, while AAU privates enrolled 211,500. Total undergraduate enrollment at AAU schools thus represents approximately 6 percent of college students in the United States. If we take into account only the thirty-four public AAU member institutions, that figure becomes less than 5 percent. Enrollment at the twenty-six private member institutions totals 1.14 percent of American undergraduates.[45] To frame the dilemma another way, in a nation with roughly 18.2 million undergraduates enrolled in postsecondary education, the combined undergraduate enrollments of the 108 research-extensive universities, which includes all sixty AAU schools, numbers little more than 2 million, or roughly 11 percent of American students.[46] As Charles M. Vest, then president of MIT, observed of the distinctive character of a research-grade academic milieu, which offers opportunities for undergraduates to participate in research with faculty working at the frontiers of knowledge, "Our society will ask much more of these students—and they will ask more of themselves—than just to know what others have accomplished. If they are going to help us expand our knowledge and solve our problems, they are going to have to know how to research, to analyze, to synthesize, and to communicate. They must learn how to gather data, to develop hypotheses, to test and refine them, or throw them out when necessary and start over."[47]

Such limited accessibility to the milieu of knowledge production characteristic of research-grade institutions obtains at a time when workforce experts project a shortfall by 2018 of three million educated workers. Anthony Carnevale, director of the Georgetown University Center on Education and the Workforce, and colleagues estimate that degree production would have to increase by roughly 10 percent each year to prevent that shortfall. For our nation to achieve the ambitious objectives for educational attainment specified by President Barack Obama in his first address to a joint session of Congress in February 2009—the president envisioned an America that by the end of the present decade would again boast the highest proportion of college graduates in the world—by this estimate our colleges and universities would have to produce an additional 8.2 million graduates by 2020.[48] Another study led by Carnevale underscored the ramifications of an "undereducated" society: "The United States has been underproducing college-going workers since 1980.

Supply has failed to keep pace with growing demand, and as a result, income inequality has grown precipitously." Carnevale and colleagues elaborate: "The undersupply of postsecondary-educated workers has led to two distinct problems: a problem of efficiency and a problem of equity." At issue is the loss in productivity that comes with a workforce lacking advanced skills. At the same time, "scarcity has driven up the cost of postsecondary talent precipitously, exacerbating inequality." The upshot of this analysis, according to Carnevale, is that "to correct our undersupply and meet our efficiency and equity goals for the economy and for our society, we will need to add an additional 20 million postsecondary-educated works to the economy by 2025."[49] But when conventional wisdom dictates that enrollment growth comes at the expense of academic quality, few indeed are the institutions willing to pursue strategies to produce the additional graduates our nation needs.

Both in the Ivies and more recently in the so-called public Ivies, the set of "flagship" public universities that rival their private institutional peers in their pursuit of prestige, admissions policies are predicated on exclusion. In the mid-twentieth century the sons and daughters of middle-class families who brought home respectable grades while in high school could reasonably expect to be admitted to the leading public universities of their respective states. During the 1950s and 1960s, for example, California high school graduates who completed a set of required courses and attained a cumulative 3.0 grade point average qualified for admission to the University of California. Prior to the adoption of the 1960 Master Plan for Higher Education in California, roughly the top 15 percent of California high school graduates were eligible to attend the University of California. The implementation of the Master Plan reduced the percentage of eligible students from this historical figure to the top 12.5 percent. Douglass explains that the trajectory toward increasingly selective admissions arrived with the establishment in 1979 of the eligibility index—a sliding scale of grade point average in required courses and SAT scores used to determine eligibility—coupled with slowing of enrollment growth.[50] The announcement by Stanford University in April 2014 that only 5 percent of applicants had been accepted epitomizes the increasing selectivity of top private universities.[51] But leading public universities are becoming increasingly selective as well, and the broad access to a quality education that could once be taken for granted is now flatly denied the majority of qualified applicants. A significant proportion of alumni who graduated from these schools in the 1970s or 1980s—many of whom no doubt attribute their professional success in large measure to the caliber of their education—would be summarily turned away under current admissions protocols. The elitism of our top-tier institutions may appear meritocratic, but their exclusivity suggests nothing so much as the persistence in American higher education of the class prerogatives historically associated with the social patterns of Britain. As Christopher Newfield puts it, "The entrenched practices, the deep culture, the lived ideology, the lifeworld of American higher education all point toward defining excellence through selectivity, and would seek to improve any university regardless of mission by tightening admissions standards."[52] Policy scholar David Kirp frames the dilemma in the following terms:

> In the realms of commerce, when demand exceeds supply, firms are supposed to expand or else jack up their prices, a practice that encourages new entrants. But this isn't at all how higher education operates. While enrollment in postsecondary institutions has increased by more than half since 1970, much of that growth has been absorbed by community colleges . . . and regional public universities. The very idea of expansion is anathema to the elite . . . . Instead these schools set ever-higher standards for admission. The most selective reject seven out of eight applicants, almost all of whom are qualified.[53]

Large-scale enrollment need not be incompatible with academic excellence. The University of Toronto, for example, the largest major research university in Canada and public member institution of the AAU, enrolls 67,128 undergraduates and 15,884 graduate students at three urban campuses and reports research expenditures exceeding $1.2 billion annually. The institution consistently ranks topmost among Canadian universities, twenty-eighth globally in the Academic Ranking of World Universities, and twentieth globally in the most recent *Times Higher Education* World University Report. But whether by design or default, other leading research-grade universities have not similarly scaled up enrollment capacities commensurate to demand or proportionate to the growth of the population. Both the elite private institutions and the set of public research universities continue to raise thresholds for admission. Measures to remediate limited access abound, of course, and nearly all leading colleges and universities offer opportunities to students of exceptional academic ability from underrepresented and socioeconomically disadvantaged backgrounds. It is always possible to recruit academically gifted students from across the spectrum of socio-economic backgrounds in the interest of diversity. This way, a measure of diversity can be achieved without actually drawing more deeply from the broader talent pool of qualified applicants representative of the ethnic and socioeconomic diversity of the nation. Robert J. Gordon observes that "presidents of Ivy League colleges and other elite schools point to the lavish subsidies they provide as tuition discounts for low- and middle-income students, but this leaves behind the vast majority of American college students who are not lucky or smart enough to attend these elite institutions."[54] But intelligence is distributed throughout the population, and admissions policies that merely skim from the top shortchange countless gifted and creative individuals. At issue is not the education of students from the top 5 percent of their high school classes but rather the imperative to educate the top 25 percent to very high levels of achievement.

Economist and former Princeton president William G. Bowen and colleagues have framed this dilemma as a contest between "equity" and excellence in American higher education. They describe a "simmering debate over whether it is better to educate a small number of people to a very high standard or to extend educational opportunities much more broadly—even if this means accepting a somewhat lower standard of performance and, in general, spreading resources more thinly." Equity and excellence are complementary, the authors observe, because talent is distributed throughout the socioeconomic spectrum; national competitiveness in educational attainment depends on extending opportunities to sufficient numbers from all demographic strata; diversity enhances the quality of the educational experience; and the success of our democracy depends on an educated citizenry. With reference to the attainment of equity, which the authors define as the "broad extension of educational opportunity," at issue is the "question of fairness in its provision." In practice, excellence requires compromise if equity is to be attained: "In its most shallow construction, this linkage takes the form of a direct, zero-sum tradeoff between the two ideals."[55] Although their assessment advances our appreciation of the complementarity of these objectives, negotiation between the contesting claims of excellence and equity is inevitable. Accordingly, the New American University model attempts to transcend these constraints. The model brooks no compromise in the quality of knowledge production and assumes that equity is attained only when all academically qualified students are offered an opportunity for access regardless of socioeconomic background. We thus underscore the observation of Bowen and colleagues that "society at large can build the educational scale that it requires only if its institutions of higher education tap every pool of talent."[56] Whereas their assessment focuses on the socioeconomically disadvantaged and historically underrepresented, the New American University model embraces equally students from all demographic strata capable of accomplishment in a research-grade milieu, including the gifted and creative students who do not conform to a standard academic profile.

The crux of the dilemma confronting American higher education in this context has been succinctly framed by Christopher Newfield: systemic inequality, referring to the inherent conflict between "mass scale and top quality." According to Newfield, the inequity behind the "strikingly hierarchical university system" in the United States, with its "ever-richer small elite and an ever-poorer large majority," could only be remediated by "proper financial support for full access to mass quality, to high quality on a mass scale." With reference to the educational outcomes of students attending the myriad of "entry-level" colleges and universities, the assessment Newfield proffers is not unexpected: "Less selective universities have lower status, but does that mean that they are inferior educationally? Unfortunately it does. They are inferior . . . because they are unable to deliver solid academic outcomes" regardless of motivated students and despite the best efforts of committed faculty, staff, and administrators. As evidence that more selective institutions produce better educational outcomes—that selectivity in the conventional model is an index of quality—he cites the data collected by Bowen and colleagues in *Crossing the Finish Line*. As Bowen, Chingos, and McPherson point out, "More selective universities, by definition, enroll students with stronger entering credentials who are more likely to graduate regardless of where they go to college."[57] Newfield paraphrases the major thrust of their conclusion: "The most important factor affecting graduation rates is the university's selectivity: the greater the selectivity, the higher the graduation rate." He identifies the motivations behind increasingly rigorous admissions standards: "The promise is that the outcome of increased selectivity will be both more money and better students who are more likely to succeed and who will produce better work while allowing their professors to do better research and their institution to in turn attract better incoming students and better—wealthier—donors."[58]

Newfield argues for the improvement of overall educational attainment through the improvement of outcomes for socioeconomically disadvantaged students. His strategy is to "improve the quality of the less selective schools without increasing their selectivity." What he terms "egalitarian meritocracy" "focuses equally on obtaining high-quality outcomes and on ensuring their wide distribution in society." In other words, "egalitarian meritocracy rejects the tradeoff between equality and quality." We concur with his assessment of the challenge and the objective of any strategy to remediate this fundamental inequality in our society:

> The educational quality of a society [is] tied to the egalitarian expansion of attainment as much as to the attainment level of an elite. Egalitarian meritocracy rests on an important intuition: it is bizarre that our country's sense of quality depends on our power of rejection, when in fact quality depends on our power to inculcate skill, knowledge, and craft development across the full extent of society. The egalitarian intuition also holds that it is perverse for university faculty, as educators, to prefer selective and vertical over general and horizontal development.[59]

Newfield contends that such expansion of attainment would come as a consequence of a dramatic increase in expenditures at entry-level schools. However, the remediation for systemic inequality that he suggests— "proper financial support for full access to mass quality, to high quality on a mass scale"—is utopian and represents an unattainable societal goal.

By contrast, the strides toward egalitarian meritocracy enabled by the New American University model are necessarily incremental; no single institutional model is a panacea. Yet, the New American University represents an institutional instantiation of the ideal of egalitarian meritocracy and adaptation of the model constitutes a pragmatic strategy to remediate inequity. As a complement to the set of research-grade institutions entrenched in their commitment to the "selective and vertical over general and horizontal development" of society, institutions committed to providing accessibility to environments underpinned by discovery and pedagogical foundations of knowledge production offer the potential to advance the objectives of egalitarian meritocracy that, however subverted, undergird the dynamics of our democracy.

## The American Dream, Meritocracy, and Intergenerational Economic Mobility

"Freedom from the constraints of aristocratic society lured many of our ancestors to cross the ocean to the New World," observes Brookings Institution fellow Julia B. Isaacs. "European visitors such as Alexis de Tocqueville marveled at the economic dynamism and social mobility of American society in the first half of the nineteenth century."[60] From the earliest days of the American republic, assumptions regarding the potential of the meritorious to succeed have shaped the narrative arc of our democratic experiment, engendering the myth of the American Dream. Sociologists Stephen J. McNamee and Robert K. Miller broadly trace the origins of this worldview to the conflation of not unexpected determinants: that strain of individualism in our national character that would find expression in the American Revolution and persist in the settlement of the frontier coupled with the embrace of free market capitalism. The assessment of Tocqueville is aptly invoked in this context, and his contention that with their intrinsic individualism and egalitarianism, Americans "acquire the habit of always considering themselves as standing alone, and . . . are apt to imagine that their whole destiny is in their own hands."[61]

More recently, the confluence of economic, political, and social currents that produced the American Century enabled the American Dream. For millions in the twentieth century, its attainment would prove to be no mere rhetoric. And despite the challenges of the present, America still represents the promise of boundless opportunity for those willing to work hard and sacrifice—effort invariably intended to provide children and grandchildren with more prosperous lives. McNamee and Miller offer the following succinct summary of its implicit assumptions: "Presumably, if you work hard enough and are talented enough, you can overcome any obstacle and achieve success. No matter where you start out in life, the sky is ostensibly the limit. According to the promise implied by the American Dream, you can go as far as your talents and abilities can take you."

Presumably "being made of the right stuff" and "having the right attitude" should ensure success. But McNamee and Miller persuasively deconstruct our various cherished assumptions regarding the "myth of meritocracy," which may be and are indeed often betrayed by the following reality checks: "It takes money to make money (inheritance); it's not what you know but whom you know (connections); what matters is being in the right place at the right time (luck); the playing field isn't level (discrimination); and he or she married into money (marriage).[62] As the prime mover for individual achievement and springboard to intergenerational economic mobility, higher education epitomizes promise for the meritorious, but the drift of societal trends diminishes its potential.

The American economy may be recovering from the fiscal collapse of 2008 but the prosperity we have known during the past seventy years appears increasingly imperiled. Projections suggest that following nearly four centuries of expansive and quantifiable advancement in our standard of living and quality of life, the present generation of younger Americans is very likely to witness the commencement of incipient decline across a spectrum of indicators. Data cited by the National Academies herald interrelated decline in educational outcomes, health indicators, and prosperity: "For the first time in generations," observes the committee that produced the report, "the nation's children could face poorer prospects than their parents and grandparents."[63] Apart from declines in educational attainment, evidence is abundant to corroborate the dismal prognosis. An OECD report, for example, found that life expectancy in the United States ranked twenty-fourth among the member nations despite the highest level of spending on health care both as a share of domestic gross product and per capita.[64] Another report shows that the life spans of the least-educated Americans are contracting.[65] For the first time since the Second World War, key benchmarks of national competitiveness suggest that American leadership in scientific discovery and technological innovation is threatened as well.[66]

A confluence of factors—economic, social, and political—produced the American Century, but increasingly stark inequality in our society has eroded much of that progress, and the economic gains Americans took for granted stalled by the end of the 1970s. Economists Claudia Goldin and Lawrence Katz show that the twentieth century, an era of unprecedented technological advancement and economic growth, must

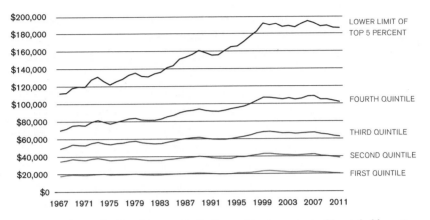

FIGURE 2. Upper limits of income quintiles and top 5 percent of households, 1967–2011, in constant 2011 dollars. Source: U.S. Census Bureau, Current Population Survey, Annual Social and Economic Supplements.

be understood as comprising two distinct phases: "During much of the first three-quarters of the twentieth century, rapidly rising productivity translated into widely shared prosperity and enormous increases in the standard of living, straight across income distribution." Even though prosperity for many increased "monumentally and almost continuously," the correspondingly proportionate distribution of these gains did not persist. Analysis of trends in income inequality since the 1970s show the annual growth rate of family incomes for those in the bottom quintile nearly stagnant while rising sharply for those at the top: "The degree of inequality resulting from these trends is one that the United States has not seen since before the 1940s and has left the country with the most unequal income and wage distributions of any high-income nation" (figure 2).[67] According to Joseph Stiglitz, "As we look out at the world, the United States not only has the highest level of inequality among the advanced industrial countries, but the level of its inequality is increasing in absolute terms relative to that in other countries." He adds, "We are now approaching the level of inequality that marks dysfunctional societies—it is a club that we would distinctly not want to join, including Iran, Jamaica, Uganda, and the Philippines."[68]

The new Gilded Age of dubious notoriety has brought to the most affluent concentrations of income and wealth not seen since the Great Depression, as documented by economists Thomas Piketty and Emmanuel

Saez. The Great Recession associated with the economic collapse of 2008 exacerbated the inequality in our society, but Piketty and Saez show to what extent the recovery has favored those at the top. The *New York Times* offered the following synopsis of their recent updated study: "The top 10 percent of earners took more than half of the country's total income in 2012, the highest level recorded since the government began collecting the relevant data a century ago . . . . The top 1 percent took more than one-fifth of the income earned by Americans, one of the highest levels on record since 1913, when the government instituted an income tax." Saez assesses the extent to which gains in average real income per family were distributed: "Top 1 percent incomes grew by 34 percent, while bottom 99 percent incomes grew only 0.4 percent from 2009 to 2012. Hence, the top 1 percent captured 95 percent of the income gains in the first three years of the recovery." Despite the conclusions Piketty draws from historical data regarding the role of inherited wealth in perpetuating inequality, Saez underscores that those capturing the gains in recent decades are an "extremely small income elite"—the new "working rich" and not the "rentiers" of another generation who derived incomes from inherited fortunes: "The labor market has been creating much more inequality over the last thirty years, with the very top earners capturing a large fraction of macroeconomic productivity gains."[69]

The Great Recession further frayed social cohesion through the polarization of skills and wages, leading to what has been termed a "hollowing out" of the middle class. "Job polarization refers to the increasing concentration of employment in the highest- and lowest-wage occupations, as job opportunities in middle-skill occupations disappear," economists Nir Jaimovich and Henry Siu explain. Although middle-skill occupations tend to be routine, high-wage occupations are invariably nonroutine and demand the sort of cognitive skills acquired through advanced education: "This hollowing out of the middle has been linked to the disappearance of jobs focused on 'routine' tasks—those activities that can be performed by following a well-defined set of procedures." Jaimovich and Siu document growth in both cognitive and manual nonroutine occupations between 1967 and 2011 but a decline in routine occupations.[70] MIT economist David Autor similarly shows that from 2007 through 2009, employment in high-skill, high-wage jobs remained stable, while low-skill, low-wage jobs even showed slight gains. Middle-skill, middle-wage jobs such as those in sales, office and administrative, production, and operations saw job losses of 7 to 17 percent of total employment in those sectors.[71] During recent decades, writes Joseph Stiglitz, "America's middle class has been eviscerated, as the 'good' middle-class jobs—requiring a moderate level of skills, like auto workers' jobs—seemed to be disappearing relative to those at the bottom, requiring few skills, and those at the top, requiring greater skills levels."[72] More recent data from the U.S. Census Bureau confirms the persistence of the hollowing out of the middle-class employment sector. According to their most recent annual report on income and poverty, median household income for 2011 declined to its 1996 level when adjusted for inflation, and income inequality rose to its highest level on record since 1967. In 2011, 46 million Americans, or 15 percent of the population, lived in poverty.[73]

Despite the conventional wisdom that America is a classless society and represents the promise of boundless opportunity for those willing to work hard and sacrifice, stark inequalities in opportunity grounded in socioeconomic disadvantage based on family income and the educational attainment of parents increasingly remain a barrier to intergenerational economic mobility as well as access to higher education.[74] The correlations between socioeconomic status and educational attainment follow a consistent pattern, beginning with college enrollment. According to a new report from the College Board, "In 2012, when about 82 percent of high school graduates from families with incomes above $90,500 enrolled immediately in college, 65 percent of those from the middle-income quintile ($34,060 to $55,253) and 52 percent of those from families with incomes below $18,300 enrolled" (figure 3).[75] An estimate of total enrollment of students from socioeconomically disadvantaged families casts the dilemma in especially stark terms. According to Bowen and colleagues, in 2006, the percentage of first-generation college students from families with incomes in the bottom quartile of distribution comprised no more than 3.1 percent of university enrollment nationwide.[76] The correlation between family income and SAT scores has been documented by the College Board as well (figure 4).[77] Whether Americans are content with a society in which the best predictor of success for admittance to a top university is the zip code of the family home remains to be determined.

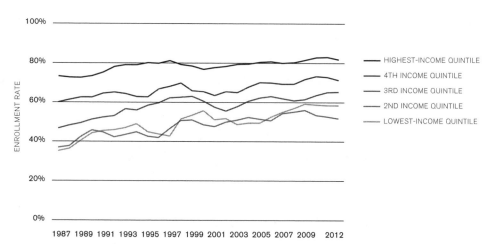

FIGURE 3. Postsecondary enrollment rates of recent high school graduates by income, 1987 to 2012. Source: College Board, *Education Pays, 2013,* figure 2.1. Adapted with permission of the authors.

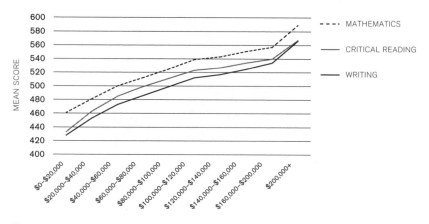

FIGURE 4. Mean SAT component score by annual family income, 2012. Source: College Board, Total Group Profile Report, 2012.

A remarkable disparity between rates of initial enrollment and persistence through graduation underscores the dilemma. Political scientist Suzanne Mettler offers the following summary of outcomes correlated to family income: "Three out of four adults who grow up in the top quarter of the income spectrum earn baccalaureate degrees by age 24, but it's only one out of three in the next quarter down. In the bottom half of economic distribution, it's less than one out of five for those in the third

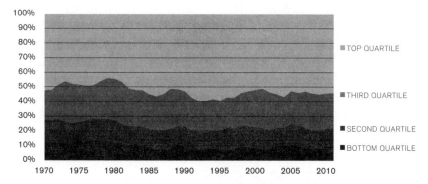

FIGURE 5. Share of total bachelor's degrees by age 24 by family income quartile, 1970–2011. Source: Postsecondary Education Opportunity (Oskaloosa, IA, 2013).

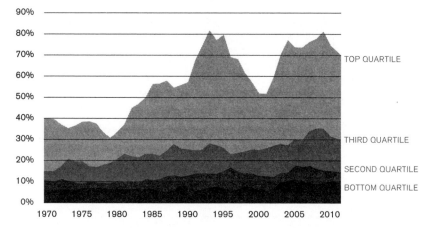

FIGURE 6. Estimated bachelor's degree attainment rate by age 24 by family income quartile, 1970–2011. Source: Postsecondary Education Opportunity (Oskaloosa, IA, 2013).

bracket and fewer than one out of ten in the poorest."[78] Higher-education policy analyst Tom Mortenson corroborates with the similar estimate that 79.1 percent of Americans from the top quartile of family income attain a baccalaureate degree by the age of 24, while only 10.7 percent from the bottom quartile achieve the same degree. He finds the overall baccalaureate attainment rate for this age group to be 30.1 percent (figures 5 and 6).[79] Another study shows that just 9 percent of the oldest millennials from the bottom economic quartile achieve a college degree, compared to 54 percent for their peers from the top quartile.[80]

Although the American Dream remains predicated on the promise of economic mobility across generations, the extremes of the socioeconomic ladder are becoming more and more entrenched, a phenomenon that economists term "stickiness at the ends" of income distribution. Data from the Economic Mobility Project of the Pew Charitable Trusts reveal that 70 percent of Americans reared in the bottom quintile of family income remain below median income, while 63 percent of those from the top quintile remain above the middle. No less dispiriting is the finding that "only 4 percent of those raised in the bottom quintile make it all the way to the top as adults."[81] Observes Isaacs: "All Americans do not have an equal shot at getting ahead, and one's chances are largely dependent on one's parents' economic position . . . . The chances of making it to the top of the income distribution decline steadily as one's parents' family income decreases."[82] Intergenerational economic mobility is correlated with educational attainment, but opportunities for individuals are "starkly different," a recent report from the U.S. Department of Treasury corroborates (figures 7a–b), depending on whether one completes a baccalaureate degree:

> Without a college degree, children born in the lowest-income quintile have a 45 percent chance of remaining in the bottom quintile as adults and a nearly 70 percent chance of ending up in the bottom two quintiles. With a college degree, children born in the bottom quintile have less than a 20 percent chance of staying in the bottom quintile of the income distribution and about an equal chance of ending up in any of the higher-income quintiles.[83]

Put yet another way: "College graduates are more upwardly mobile from the bottom and less likely to fall from the top and middle."[84] Comparisons of intergenerational outcomes with other prosperous industrialized nations reveal evidence of its decline in the United States: "Surprisingly," observes Isaacs, "American children from low-income families appear to have less relative mobility than their counterparts in five northern European countries."[85]

Long heralded as the most effective mechanism for meritocratic advancement and means of economic and social mobility, higher education has in recent decades been perceived to reinforce social stratification. Anthony Carnevale has termed it an "increasingly powerful mechanism for the intergenerational reproduction of privilege."[86] Carnevale and his

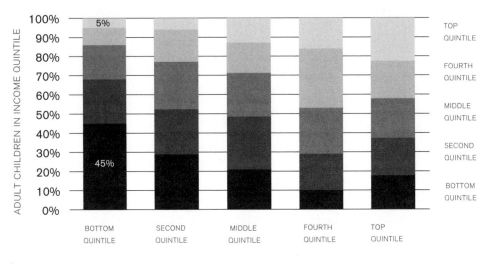

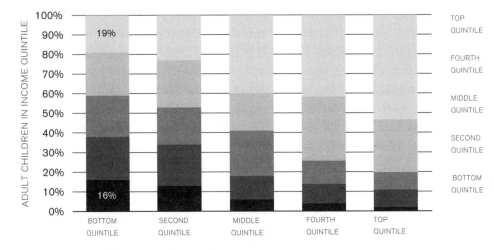

FIGURE 7. Intergenerational mobility for children (a) without and (b) with a college degree from families of varying incomes. Adapted from "Chances of Getting Ahead for Children with and without a College Degree, from Families of Varying Incomes," Ron Haskins, "Education and Economic Mobility," in Julia Isaacs, Isabel Sawhill, and Ron Haskins, *Getting Ahead or Losing Ground: Economic Mobility in America* (Washington, DC: Economic Mobility Project, an Initiative of the Pew Charitable Trusts, 2008).

colleague Jeff Strohl elaborate: "In the postindustrial economy, educational attainment, especially postsecondary educational attainment, has replaced the industrial concept of class as the primary marker for social stratification."[87] David Brooks observed the broad implications of this trend for ethnicity and race as well as class: "We once had a society stratified by bloodlines, in which the Protestant Establishment was in one class, immigrants were in another, and African Americans were in another. Now we live in a society stratified by education."[88] Stanford sociologist Sean Reardon offers precise data on the consequences of the "income achievement gap," which for children from between the 90th and the 10th percentiles is now "more than twice as large as the black-white achievement gap." By contrast, according to Reardon, "Fifty years ago the black-white gap was one and a half to two times as large as the income gap." Moreover, "the achievement gap between children from high- and low-income families is roughly 30 to 40 percent larger among children born in 2001 than among those born twenty-five years earlier."[89]

In an assessment of both the Carnevale and Reardon studies, Thomas Edsall summarizes a number of the broader implications: "Instead of serving as a springboard to social mobility as it did for the first decades after World War II, college education today is reinforcing social stratification, with a huge majority of the 24 percent of Americans aged 25 to 29 currently holding a bachelor's degree coming from families with earnings above median income." And consistent with the findings of Bowen and colleagues, Edsall reports, "Seventy-four percent of those now attending colleges that are classified as 'most competitive,' a group that includes schools like Harvard, Emory, Stanford, and Notre Dame, come from families with earnings in the top income quartile, while only 3 percent come from families in the bottom quartile."[90] In a trend seen at "flagship" public universities across the nation, David Leonhardt reports that during one recent academic year, more entering freshmen at the University of Michigan were products of families with incomes exceeding $200,000 per year than all of their peers originating from families in the bottom half of income distribution.[91] "At the nation's most selective 193 colleges and universities," by one recent estimate, "affluent students (those from the richest socioeconomic quarter of the population) outnumber economically disadvantaged students (those from the bottom quarter) by fourteen to one."[92]

Whether as a society we succeed in addressing the challenges associated with stagnant personal income growth and increasing inequality between the rich and the poor remains a matter for conjecture. Such disparities are inevitable, but the degree of the present inequity betokens neither productive social nor cultural outcomes and raises the specter of social disruption. Income growth is now disproportionately the prerogative of the affluent, while prosperity remains a reasonable expectation for the "creative class" celebrated by Richard Florida: the intelligentsia comprising artists, musicians, writers, designers, architects, engineers, scientists, and other "knowledge workers" for whom creativity is an essential dimension of their livelihood.[93] Yet, for those barred from higher education by cultural, economic, or social circumstances, prospects for advancement may begin to appear futile. And behind the trend of declining enrollment of men in the traditional college age bracket could lay an abandonment of aspiration that signals broader socioeconomic stagnation. Demographic trends suggest that the United States is becoming a nation divided between a vibrant and dynamic upper class, a static and challenged middle class, and a disadvantaged majority increasingly defined by the working poor and those socially and economically unable to realize the American Dream. In assessing the American research university, we imagine an institution with the potential to redress societal inequities and reverse declining indicators of societal well-being.

Indeed, in his celebrated study of inequality, Thomas Piketty deems the diffusion of knowledge the "principal force for convergence," referring to the "reduction and compression of inequalities." He writes, "The main forces for convergence are the diffusion of knowledge and investment in training and skills." Moreover, "knowledge and skill diffusion is the key to overall productivity growth as well as the reduction of inequality both within and between countries." He elaborates, "Historical experience suggests that the principal mechanism for convergence at the international as well as domestic level is the diffusion of knowledge. In other words, the poor catch up with the rich to the extent that they receive the same level of technological know-how, skill, and education." But such remediation of inequality through the diffusion of knowledge "depends in large part on educational policies, access to training, and to the acquisition of appropriate skills, and associated institutions."[94] Yet, in the estimation of Suzanne Mettler, prospects for suitable policies to advance broader access to educational attainment appear dismal, sub-verted by "political polarization, as the parties in Congress have grown more ideological and less willing to work together than at any point in at least a century, and plutocracy, the responsiveness of the political system primarily to the concerns of wealthy and powerful interests."[95] Although such political and social forces are inimical to progress in educational attainment, we contend that new institutional models, including the model we propound in these chapters, offer a workaround to the dilemma posed by lack of accessibility at scale to the milieu of discovery and knowl-edge production.

## Indicators of Decline in Educational Attainment

The trajectory of educational attainment in the United States in the twentieth century can be readily summarized: "During the first three-quarters of the century educational attainment rose rapidly, but during the last quarter of the century it stagnated," write Goldin and Katz.[96] With roughly three-quarters of high school graduates now enrolled in some form of college, including community colleges—which by one estimate enroll 45 percent of all U.S. undergraduates—this fourfold increase in col-lege attendance since the midcentury would suggest progress in educa-tional attainment. But, to the contrary, degree completion rates have fallen, and the outcomes of attendance vary widely according to institu-tional type.[97] The evidence of decline is apparent at all levels of the edu-cational process. By one estimate, one in four ninth-graders nationwide fails to complete high school.[98] A recent report on high school gradua-tion rates in fifty of the largest U.S. cities finds that seventeen had grad-uation rates lower than 50 percent.[99] Only one-third of students who graduate from public high schools possess even the minimum academic prerequisites colleges expect.[100] High school students who are eminently qualified fail to submit applications to suitable colleges and universities for lack of appropriate counseling.[101] In educational outcomes, the United States now ranks twentieth among industrialized nations in its high school graduation rate (figure 8), and over the course of a decade, it fell from first to sixteenth in its tertiary graduation rate.[102] Among the thirty-four member nations of the OECD, U.S. baccalaureate attainment in the so-called STEM fields—the domains of science, technology, engineer-ing, and mathematics—ranked twenty-fourth in a recent assessment.[103]

Evidence of stagnation in educational attainment comes as well from OECD analysis that compares baccalaureate degree completion rates in member nations across generations. Even though younger cohorts in most OECD member nations have outstripped preceding generations in educational attainment, the less than one percentage point difference between the respective American cohorts attests to a worrisome lack of progress (figure 9).[104] "Barely 30 percent of American adults have achieved a higher level of education than their parents did," the economist Eduardo Porter paraphrases the findings of the most recent report. However, "Among 25- to 34-year-olds, only 20 percent of men and 27 percent of women . . . have achieved a higher level of education than their parents." Among Americans in this age bracket whose parents did not finish high school, only one in twenty attain a baccalaureate degree.[105] "Clearly the United States no longer leads the world in the education of young adults," Goldin and Katz remark.[106]

With reference to the decline in degree completion rates,[107] William Bowen and colleagues demonstrate persuasively not only that the benefits associated with educational attainment correlate with degree completion rather than an inconclusive period of enrollment ("getting started") but that academically gifted but socioeconomically disadvantaged students tend to be disproportionately "undermatched" in their choice of institutions. They speak of the "surprisingly large numbers of high school seniors who were presumptively qualified to attend strong four-year colleges but did not do so, instead attending less selective four-year colleges, two-year colleges, or no college at all." Although the researchers blame undermatching on some combination of inertia and lack of information, planning, and encouragement, the consequences for high achievers from socioeconomically challenged backgrounds are certain. The data suggest a "high personal and societal cost associated with failing to take advantage of challenging educational opportunities." Students who attend more selective institutions are more likely to graduate and do so in normative time, and will undeniably benefit from superior institutional resources and the obvious peer effects of interaction with gifted classmates as well as distinguished faculty: "The scale of the undermatch phenomenon among students from modest backgrounds suggests that there is a considerable opportunity to increase social mobility and augment the nation's human capital."[108]

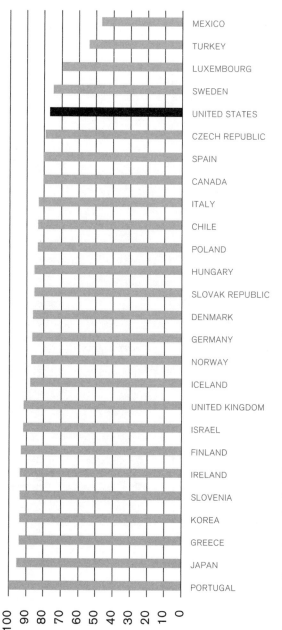

FIGURE 8. Secondary school graduation rates in OECD member nations, 2010. Source: OECD, World Education Indicators Program, Table A2-1: Upper Secondary Graduation Rates (2010).

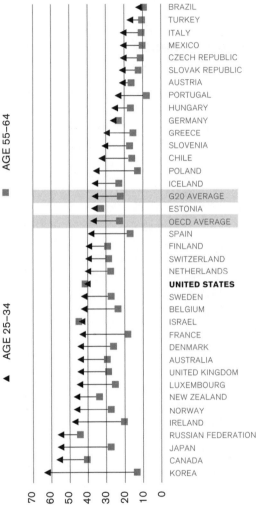

FIGURE 9. Percentages of OECD member nation populations that have attained tertiary education (2009) by age cohorts, in descending order based on the cohorts aged 25 to 34. Adapted from OECD (2011), *Education at a Glance*, Table A1.3a.

Forty-five percent of all U.S. undergraduates attend a community college, according to the American Association of Community Colleges, with 4.6 million attending part-time.[109] Even though community colleges offer affordable instruction and training as well as opportunities for subsequent transfer to four-year institutions, shortcomings in the process corroborate the concerns cited by Bowen and colleagues. At a time when increased enrollment in community colleges is proffered by the Obama administration as well as state and local governments as a solution to the decline in educational attainment,[110] evidence suggests that outcomes for students are sometimes subpar, while the aggregate economic benefit of enrollment may be negligible. Two-year graduation rates for students enrolled in community colleges do not exceed 13 percent, according to Robert J. Gordon, a figure that increases to 28 percent after four years.[111] Other research showed that only 39 percent of students who enrolled with the intent to obtain a degree or certificate had achieved that goal within six years. Of the 61 percent who failed in this objective, only 29 percent reported higher earnings as a result of attendance.[112] With reference to the decline in the rate of baccalaureate degree attainment, another study found that the "shift in the distribution of students' initial college type, largely the shift toward community colleges, explains roughly three-fourths of the observed decrease in completion rates.[113]

Concerns regarding growing income inequality and diminishing economic mobility converge in alarm over prospects for the postsecondary education of academically promising but socioeconomically disadvantaged high school seniors. A recent report on the plight of high-achieving students from low-income families by economists Caroline Hoxby, of Stanford, and Christopher Avery, of Harvard, surveys comprehensive data and has received widespread attention. Hoxby and Avery frame the dilemma of "undermatching" thus: "We show that a large number—probably the vast majority—of very high-achieving students from low-income families do not apply to a selective college or university."[114] Although this tendency is pernicious and clearly warrants intervention, the restricted scope of the study skirts the real challenge, which is far greater. Hoxby and Avery perpetuate the elitist model of higher education, which is incommensurate with the scale and needs of our nation. Implicit in the report is the assumption that the failure to attend one of the 236 colleges and universities identified in the top categories of Barron's *Profiles of*

*American Colleges* represents the kiss of death for the prospects of these low-income high achievers.

We learn from their report that no more than roughly 4 percent of American high school students are high achievers, which in itself should be sufficiently worrisome to provoke a national policy discussion. But Hoxby and Avery focus on the subset of high achievers from families with income in the bottom two quartiles: "We estimate that there are at least 25,000 and probably something like 35,000 low-income high achievers in the U.S."[115] In a nation of 316 million that produces roughly 3 million high school graduates annually, the set of 35,000 students at issue represents a small fraction of prospective college freshmen—roughly 1 percent.[116] The larger challenge of providing access to quality education at scale is not addressed and remains unresolved.

### A College Degree and Access to the Middle Class

"A social chasm is opening up between those in educated society and those in noneducated society," writes David Brooks.[117] At stake is access to the middle class—or better, according to Carnevale and colleagues: "While it is true that the middle class is declining, a more accurate portrayal of the American class dynamic would be to say that the middle class is dispersing into two opposing streams of upwardly mobile college-haves and downwardly mobile college-have-nots." Higher education represents our best hope for the advancement of both individuals and the collective. And indeed, the consequences of stagnation and decline in educational attainment are considerable, both for the individual and society. As the Carnevale report puts it: "The implications of this shift represent a sea change in American society. Essentially, postsecondary education or training has become the threshold requirement for access to middle-class status and earnings in good times or in bad. It is no longer the preferred pathway to middle-class jobs—it is, increasingly, the only pathway."[118] David Autor points out that roughly two-thirds of the growth in the wage premium in the United States between 1980 and 2005 is an outcome of education and especially college: "The earnings gap between college and high school graduates has more than doubled in the United States over the past three decades."[119]

However one parses the estimates of earnings differentials for the educated, the gist is unequivocal. The Department of Treasury reports that median weekly earnings for baccalaureate degree holders in 2011 were 64 percent higher than for high school graduates: "Recent evidence suggests that the earnings differential observed today is higher than it has ever been since 1915, which is also the earliest year for which there are estimates of the college wage gap." The report gives evidence of the rate of growth of the earnings gap, or "skill premium": "In 1980, a college graduate earned 50 percent more than a high school graduate; by 2008, college graduates earned nearly twice as much as those with only a high school diploma." Differentials for those with advanced and professional degrees increase correspondingly, with recipients of master's degrees in 2011 earning almost double and those with professional degrees more than two and a half times what high school graduates earn (figure 10).[120] More than a decade ago, the U.S. Census Bureau estimated that baccalaureate degree holders earn $1.2 million more over the projected course of their working lives than high school graduates. For recipients of doctoral degrees, the estimate is $3.4 million, and for those with professional degrees, $4.4 million.[121] "Moreover," the Treasury report elaborates, "the earnings differential underestimates the economic benefits of higher education since college-educated workers are less likely to be unemployed and more likely to have jobs that provide additional nonwage compensation (e.g., paid vacation, employer-provided health insurance)."[122] And even during the current "jobless recovery," educational attainment correlates with higher rates of employment. According to the Bureau of Labor Statistics, in September 2013, the unemployment rate for those aged 25 and older who held baccalaureate degrees or higher was 3.7 percent, while the comparable rate for those who had only a high school diploma was 7.6 percent (figure 11).[123] "The unemployment rate for individuals with at least a bachelor's degree has consistently been about half the unemployment rate for high school graduates," according to the College Board (figure 12).[124]

Although the array of correlates of educational attainment begins with its intrinsic value to the individual, the list of collateral returns to society is impressive. Well-informed citizens advance the democratic process and enrich their communities and states. A more educated workforce generates greater tax revenues and influences quality-of-place decision making.[125] According to economist Enrico Moretti, an increase in the percentage of college-educated workers in a local workforce raises the predicted wages of the entire workforce, even those who do not have a

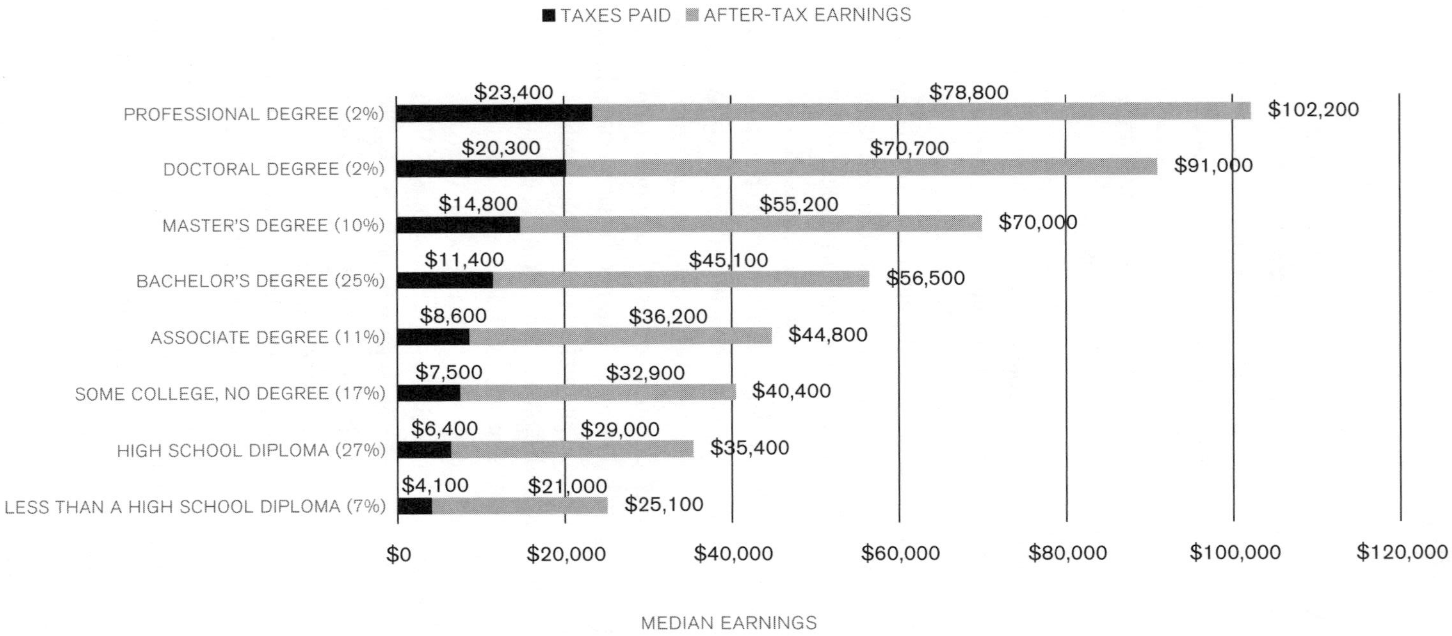

■ TAXES PAID ■ AFTER-TAX EARNINGS

MEDIAN EARNINGS

PROFESSIONAL DEGREE (2%): $23,400 / $78,800 / $102,200
DOCTORAL DEGREE (2%): $20,300 / $70,700 / $91,000
MASTER'S DEGREE (10%): $14,800 / $55,200 / $70,000
BACHELOR'S DEGREE (25%): $11,400 / $45,100 / $56,500
ASSOCIATE DEGREE (11%): $8,600 / $36,200 / $44,800
SOME COLLEGE, NO DEGREE (17%): $7,500 / $32,900 / $40,400
HIGH SCHOOL DIPLOMA (27%): $6,400 / $29,000 / $35,400
LESS THAN A HIGH SCHOOL DIPLOMA (7%): $4,100 / $21,000 / $25,100

$0   $20,000   $40,000   $60,000   $80,000   $100,000   $120,000

FIGURE 10. Median earnings and tax payments of full-time year-round workers ages 25 and older, by education level, 2011. Source: College Board, *Education Pays, 2013*, figure 1.1. The original caption clarifies that the dark segment in each bar represents estimated average federal, state, and local taxes paid at respective income levels. The figures specified parenthetically represent the percentage of full-time workers at each level of educational attainment. Adapted with permission of the authors.

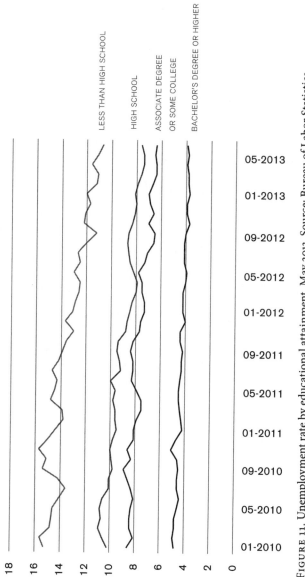

FIGURE 11. Unemployment rate by educational attainment, May 2013. Source: Bureau of Labor Statistics.

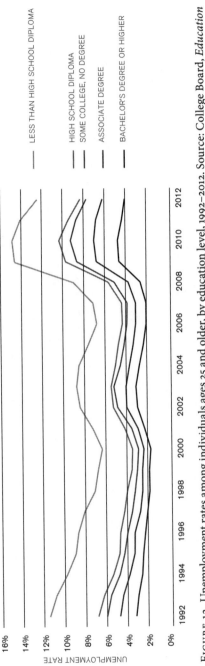

FIGURE 12. Unemployment rates among individuals ages 25 and older, by education level, 1992–2012. Source: College Board, *Education Pays, 2013:* Figure 2.1. Adapted with permission of the authors.

college degree. The rise in wages is greater for those with less education, meaning that high school graduates or even dropouts benefit more from the spillover related to a highly educated workforce than college graduates.[126] In addition to increased opportunities for more meaningful employment, higher education influences lifestyle choices that correlate with better health and greater civic participation. David Brooks offers the following succinct compendium of the behavioral differences and social norms between the two strata: "Divorce rates for college grads are plummeting, but . . . the divorce rate for high school grads is now twice as high as that of college grads . . . . High school grads are twice as likely to smoke as college grads. They are much less likely to exercise. College grads are nearly twice as likely to vote. They are more than twice as likely to do voluntary work. They are much more likely to give blood."[127]

Nearly two-thirds of the jobs coming online during the next decade will require at least some college education, according to Carnevale and colleagues, and one-third will require a bachelor's degree.[128] More and more knowledge inputs are increasingly required to perform almost any job in the ever more complex global knowledge economy, and American research universities are the principal source of the advanced education that produces a skilled workforce. The economic success of individuals that is an outcome of educational attainment contributes to broad prosperity; in fact, it is the main driver. Without it, coming generations in the United States and nations of Western Europe face a reduction in quality of life, something unheard of in the past. As a nation, we are at a critical juncture, as expressed in the following formulation from a report of the National Academies:

> Without a renewed effort to bolster the foundations of our competitiveness, we can expect to lose our privileged position . . . . We owe our current prosperity, security, and good health to the investments of past generations, and we are obliged to renew those commitments in education, research, and innovation policies to ensure that the American people continue to benefit from the remarkable opportunities provided by the rapid development of the global economy and its not inconsiderable underpinning in science and technology.[129]

The effort to spur the competitiveness of our nation depends on a highly educated citizenry, which assumes accessibility for sufficient numbers to the sort of education provided by research-grade institutions. Public disinvestment in higher education is only part of the problem. The dilemma must in part be construed as a consequence of inherent limitations in the effectiveness of these institutions, and especially their lack of scalability. It is incumbent on public research universities, which serve socioeconomically disadvantaged and historically underrepresented students in greater numbers but also advance the economic competitiveness of our nation through their platforms of integrated teaching and research, to scale their enterprises to promote accessibility to milieus of discovery and knowledge production to a demographic representative of the socioeconomic and intellectual diversity of our nation.

## A Design Process for a New American University

Most colleges and universities in the United States define themselves in relation to the set of elite institutions that comprise the putative gold standard in American higher education, which we delineated at the outset of this chapter: the Ivies, the great land-grant universities, and the major research universities constructed on the foundations of private fortunes in the late nineteenth century.[130] For liberal arts colleges and major research universities alike, these institutions constitute a prototype that to a remarkable extent remains impervious to change, aloof from social needs, and, ironically, inaccessible to the majority of Americans with the talent and ability to learn and compete at this level. Rather than extrapolate from or replicate historical models representative of the gold standard, Arizona State University has sought to reconstitute itself as the foundational prototype for the New American University model— an institution predicated on accessibility to an academic platform underpinned by discovery and knowledge production, inclusiveness to a broad demographic representative of the socioeconomic diversity of the region and nation, and, through its breadth of functionality, maximization of societal impact.[131]

The institutional vision statement sets out the basic tenets of the reconceptualization, which are at once egalitarian in terms of accessibility yet express competitive intent regarding the intensity of discovery and knowledge production leading to outcomes commensurate to the needs of society: "To establish ASU as the model for a New American University, measured not by those whom we exclude, but rather by those whom we include and how they succeed; pursuing research and discovery that benefits the public good; assuming major responsibility for the economic, social, and cultural vitality and health and well-being of the community." ASU seeks to provide broad accessibility to a milieu of world-class research and scholarship to a diverse and heterogeneous student body that includes a significant proportion of students from socioeconomically differentiated and historically underrepresented backgrounds, including first-generation college applicants. While America's leading universities, both public and private, have become increasingly exclusive, the approach adopted by ASU has been to expand the capacity of the institution to meet enrollment demand to provide unmatched educational opportunities to the many gifted and creative students who do not conform to a standard academic profile, as well as to offer access to students who demonstrate every potential to succeed but lack the financial means to pursue a four-year undergraduate education at a research university. The model connects academically qualified students from a broad demographic swathe to an academic platform of unrivaled knowledge production commensurate with the scale of enrollment demand.

No less essential are the institution's mission and goals, which reflect the intent of the nation's youngest major research institution and one of the largest universities governed by a single administration to redefine its terms of engagement. The university's four major objectives are to demonstrate leadership in academic excellence and accessibility; to establish national standing in academic quality and impact of colleges and schools in every field; to establish ASU as a global center for interdisciplinary research, discovery, and development by 2020; and to enhance local impact and social embeddedness. The objectives specified correspond to the outputs of the most highly selective public universities and must be evaluated within the context of their accomplishment by a large public university committed to drawing from the broader talent pool of socioeconomic diversity.

These overarching institutional goals are advanced by a set of eight interrelated "design aspirations," which may be understood to represent ideals for institutional culture as well as strategic approaches to the accomplishment of goals and objectives. More general guidelines than precepts, these formulations may appear merely rhetorical but were intended to inspire creativity, spark innovation, and foster institutional individuation. The design aspirations have been variously formulated and in one iteration call for the university to respond to its cultural, socio-economic, and physical setting; become a force for societal transformation; pursue a culture of academic enterprise and knowledge entrepreneurship; conduct use-inspired research; focus on the individual in a milieu of intellectual and cultural diversity; transcend disciplinary limitations in pursuit of intellectual fusion (transdisciplinarity); embed the university socially, thereby advancing social enterprise development through direct engagement; and advance global engagement.

The charter statement for the reconceptualized institution reads as follows: *Arizona State University is a comprehensive public research university, measured not by whom it excludes, but by whom it includes and how they succeed; advancing research and discovery of public value; and assuming fundamental responsibility for the economic, social, cultural, and overall health of the communities it serves.* The formulation expresses the commitment of the academic community to serve the state and nation as a prototype for a New American University—a model for an institution that provides accessibility to an academic platform underpinned by discovery and a pedagogical foundation of knowledge production to a student body representative of the socioeconomic and intellectual diversity of our society; a research enterprise committed to discovery, creativity, and innovation commensurate with the scale, pace, and complexity of the challenges that confront society; public service to advance the common good, including the quality of life and standard of living of the diverse communities of the metropolitan region and state, as well as nationally and internationally; and collaborative engagement construed globally to spur innovation across academia, business and industry, and government. The university seeks the success of each student regardless of socioeconomic background and assumes responsibility for contributing to and being held accountable for the economic, social, and cultural health and well-being of the community.

Rather than extrapolate from existing structure and operations or replicate historical models, the design process has sought to create a distinctive institutional profile by building on existing strengths to produce a federation of unique transdisciplinary departments, centers, institutes, schools, and colleges ("schools") and a deliberate and complementary clustering of programs arrayed across four differentiated campuses. In this "school-centric" conception, academic units compete for status not intramurally but with peer entities globally. In the process, ASU has advanced interdisciplinarity through the consolidation of a number of traditional academic departments, which henceforth no longer serve as the sole institutional locus of respective disciplines.

Our contention that the New American University is a complex and adaptive knowledge enterprise requires some clarification. At some level, discussion of adaptation may be subsumed in the model of organizational change offered by Daniel Katz and Robert L. Kahn. In their classic mid-twentieth-century study *The Social Psychology of Organizations*, Katz and Kahn brought open systems theory and its biological metaphor of the interaction between an organism and its environment to the assessment of organizations. Open systems theory conceptualizes the interdependence of a social structure and its external environment, especially the role of processes of input, throughput, and output in the facilitation of survival and growth.[132] Structure determines the dynamics of the operations, while increasing complexity is a function of adaptation. In knowledge enterprises like universities, information is the principal input and with throughput yields outcomes useful to society. Restructuring is thus key to adaptation and determines output—that is, useful knowledge. Although an adequate effort to frame the model as a complex adaptive system lies outside the scope of this discussion, *adaptation* for our purposes simply refers to the evolution of "fitness" in both individuals and the collective to respond to the scale and complexity of the emergent challenges that confront the global community. For the individual, maximization of the capacity to adapt is an outcome of increasing levels of educational attainment. As Louis Menand observes, "The ability to create knowledge and put it to use is *the* adaptive characteristic of humans."[133] At an institutional level, adaptation assumes institutional evolution, or innovation, which is the aggregate product of interactions between "fit" agents.[134]

The concept of the New American University represents a divergent and differentiated model for the American research university intended to complement this set of remarkable and highly successful institutions. And although we speak of the New American University as if the concept represents a fixed and distinct paradigm, the predication of the model comes with the caveat that institutions, in an attempt to embrace the prototype, should not succumb to a new form of isomorphism: the paradoxical tendency for organizations and institutions within given sectors to emulate one another and become increasingly homogeneous.[135] We do not profess the prescription of a set of design strategies applicable in all contexts because no such algorithm or protocol exists. An institution committed to advancing a differentiated profile must consider its mission and setting; the character of its academic community; the scope of its constituent colleges, schools, and departments; and the extent of its dedication to public service and community engagement. Any comprehensive reconceptualization of an organization or institution must thus proceed according to its own intrinsic logic, especially in the case of an institution as complex as a major research university. To better appreciate the design process undertaken to reconceptualize the curriculum, organization, and operations of Arizona State University, we present a case study in chapter 7. The intervening chapters provide historical and theoretical perspective on various interrelated dimensions of the American research university shaping the evolution of this set of transformative institutions. In these chapters we examine the contours of this highly successful model—the most complex and sophisticated institutional model ever produced. Our survey of its emergence and evolution over the course of more than three centuries from a number of historical and theoretical perspectives serves to introduce the complementary model of the New American University.

## Notes

1. Frank H. T. Rhodes, *The Creation of the Future: The Role of the American University* (Ithaca, NY: Cornell University Press, 2001), xi.

2. Roger L. Geiger, *To Advance Knowledge: The Growth of American Research Universities, 1900–1940* (Oxford: Oxford University Press, 1986), 2–3.

3. Clark Kerr, *The Uses of the University*, 5th ed. (1963; Cambridge, MA: Harvard University Press, 2001), 1.

4. Jonathan R. Cole, *The Great American University: Its Rise to Preeminence, Its Indispensable National Role, and Why It Must Be Protected* (New York: Public Affairs, 2009), 2. In the following, and especially in chapter 4, we enlist arguments to be found in this essential overview.

5. *China Daily*, "Chinese Ivy League" (October 21, 2009). See also Robert A. Rhoads et al., *China's Rising Research Universities: A New Era of Global Ambition* (Baltimore: Johns Hopkins University Press, 2014).

6. For a general discussion of the American research university in comparative context, see Michael M. Crow and William B. Dabars, "Knowledge without Borders: Amer-

ican Research Universities in a Global Context," *Cairo Review of Global Affairs* 5 (Spring 2012): 35–45.

7. For an overview of the economic impact of science-based technological innovation in various national contexts, see Richard C. Atkinson and William A. Blanpied, "Research Universities: Core of the U.S. Science and Technology System," *Technology in Society* 30 (2008): 30–38.

8. For the purposes of this discussion, we follow the most recent classification scheme of the Carnegie Foundation for the Advancement of Teaching, which now designates institutions formerly termed "research-extensive" as either RU/VH ("research university/very high research activity") or RU/H (high research activity). Of these institutions, 108 are currently designated RU/VH, and 99 are classified RU/H. For a discussion of the methodology, involving both aggregate and per capita levels of research expenditures, see http://classifications.carnegiefoundation.org/methodology/basic.php. The total number of accredited degree-granting institutions, including two-year institutions, specified for the academic year 2011–2012 is 4,706. Thomas D. Snyder and Sally A. Dillow, *Digest of Education Statistics 2012* (NCES 2014-015) (Washington, DC: National Center for Education Statistics, Institute of Education Sciences, U.S. Department of Education, 2013), 309.

9. Institute of Higher Education, Shanghai Jiao Tong University, Academic Ranking of World Universities: http://www.shanghairanking.com/ARWU2013.html. *The Economist* called ARWU "the most widely used annual ranking of the world's research universities," and the *Chronicle of Higher Education* termed it "the most influential international ranking." Their methodology evaluates the scientific and scholarly contributions of alumni (10 percent); scientific and scholarly contributions of faculty (20 percent); citations of researchers in twenty-one broad subject categories (20 percent); research output, measured by the number of articles published in leading journals such as *Nature* and *Science* (20 percent); research output, measured by articles in *Science Citation Index Expanded* and *Social Science Citation Index* (20 percent); and size of institution, assessing academic performance with respect to the size of an institution (10 percent).

10. Cole, *Great American University,* 5.

11. Rhodes, *Creation of the Future,* 229.

12. Joseph E. Stiglitz, "Knowledge as a Global Public Good," in *Global Public Goods: International Cooperation in the Twenty-First Century,* ed. Inge Kaul, Isabelle Grunberg, and Marc Stern (Oxford: Oxford University Press, 1999).

13. Joel Mokyr, *The Gifts of Athena: Historical Origins of the Knowledge Economy* (Princeton, NJ: Princeton University Press, 2002).

14. National Academies. Committee on Prospering in the Global Economy of the Twenty-First Century (U.S.), *Rising Above the Gathering Storm: Energizing and Employing America for a Brighter Economic Future* (Washington, DC: National Academies Press, 2007), 1.

15. Apart from the important discussion of this topic by Jonathan Cole, see also Roger L. Geiger, *Research and Relevant Knowledge: American Research Universities since*

*World War II* (Oxford: Oxford University Press, 1993); Geiger, *Knowledge and Money: Research Universities and the Paradox of the Marketplace* (Stanford: Stanford University Press, 2004); James J. Duderstadt, *A University for the Twenty-First Century* (Ann Arbor: University of Michigan Press, 2000); and Atkinson and Blanpied, "Research Universities." For historical perspective in this context, see Nathan Rosenberg and Richard R. Nelson, "American Universities and Technical Advance in Industry," *Research Policy* 23, no. 3 (1994): 323–348. See also Michael M. Crow and William B. Dabars, "University-Based Research and Economic Development: The Morrill Act and the Emergence of the American Research University," in *Precipice or Crossroads: Where America's Great Public Universities Stand and Where They Are Going Midway through Their Second Century,* ed. Daniel Mark Fogel (Albany: State University of New York Press, 2012), 119–158.

16. Joseph A. Schumpeter, *The Theory of Economic Development* (Cambridge, MA: Harvard University Press, 1934). Schumpeter ascribed the innovation intrinsic to "creative destruction" to entrepreneurs: "The function of entrepreneurs is to reform or revolutionize the pattern of production by exploiting invention or, more generally, an untried technological possibility for producing new commodities or producing an old one in a new way" (8).

17. Kevin Carey, "Americans Think We Have the World's Best Colleges. We Don't," *New York Times* (June 28, 2014).

18. Louis Menand, *The Marketplace of Ideas: Reform and Resistance in the American University* (New York: W. W. Norton, 2010), 13.

19. Theodore W. Schultz, "Investment in Human Capital," *American Economic Review* 51, no. 1 (March 1961): 1–17. Another notable usage of the concept of capital—in this case cultural capital, which is in large measure the product of educational attainment and thus directly correlated with social capital—comes from the French sociologist Pierre Bourdieu. See his essay "The Forms of Capital," in *Handbook for Theory and Research in the Sociology of Education,* ed. John G. Richardson (Westport, CT: Greenwood Press, 1986), 241–258.

20. Alan Wilson, *Knowledge Power: Interdisciplinary Education for a Complex World* (London: Routledge, 2010), ix, 1. The aphorism "ipsa scientia potestas est" appears in the collection of Bacon's essays *Meditationes Sacrae* (1597).

21. Wilson, *Knowledge Power,* ix, 1.

22. Robert Frodeman, *Sustainable Knowledge: A Theory of Interdisciplinarity* (Basingstoke: Palgrave Macmillan, 2014), 62, 76, 82, n. 5. Frodeman cites Arif E. Jinha, "Article 50 Million: An Estimate of the Number of Scholarly Articles in Existence," *Learned Publishing* 23: 258–263; Mark Bauerlein, et al., "We Must Stop the Avalanche of Low-Quality Research," *Chronicle of Higher Education* (June 13, 2010).

23. Michael M. Crow, "The Research University as Comprehensive Knowledge Enterprise: A Prototype for a New American University," in *University Research for Innovation,* ed. Luc E. Weber and James J. Duderstadt (London: Economica, 2010); relevant discussions regarding the imperative for universities to serve society include Derek Bok, *Beyond the Ivory Tower: Social Responsibilities of the Modern University* (Cambridge,

MA: Harvard University Press, 1982); Duderstadt, *University for the Twenty-First Century*; Philip Kitcher, *Science, Truth, and Democracy* (Oxford: Oxford University Press, 2001).

24. Donald E. Stokes, *Pasteur's Quadrant: Basic Science and Technological Innovation* (Washington, DC: Brookings Institution Press, 1997); Kitcher, *Science, Truth, and Democracy*.

25. Stokes, *Pasteur's Quadrant*, 6–12, 58–89.

26. A sobering assessment of our competitive position is to be found in John Aubrey Douglass, "The Waning of America's Higher Education Advantage: International Competitors Are No Longer Number Two and Have Big Plans in the Global Economy" (Berkeley: Center for Studies in Higher Education, University of California, 2006).

27. http://www.malegislature.gov/laws/constitution; http://www.harvard.edu/history

28. Thomas Jefferson to William Charles Jarvis, September 28, 1820, in Thomas Jefferson, *The Writings of Thomas Jefferson*, ed. Paul L. Ford (New York: G. P. Putnam's Sons, 1892–1899), vol. 10, 161, cited in William G. Bowen, Martin A. Kurzweil, and Eugene M. Tobin, *Equity and Excellence in American Higher Education* (Charlottesville: University of Virginia Press, 2005); and Jon Meacham, *Thomas Jefferson: The Art of Power* (New York: Random House, 2012), 469.

29. Thomas Jefferson and the University of Virginia Commissioners, The Rockfish Gap Report (August 4, 1818); *The Papers of Thomas Jefferson*, vol. 10, 244–245, quoted in Meacham, *Thomas Jefferson: The Art of Power*, 469.

30. Thomas Jefferson to Charles Yancey, January 6, 1816, cited in Bowen, Kurzweil, and Tobin, *Equity and Excellence in American Higher Education*, 3, who cite from Richard Hofstadter, *Anti-Intellectualism in American Life* (New York: Knopf, 1970), 300.

31. James Madison to W. T. Barry (August 4, 1822), *The Writings of James Madison*, ed. Gaillard Hunt (New York: G. P. Putnam's Sons, 1900–1910) 9: 103.

32. Daniel Mark Fogel, introduction to *Precipice or Crossroads: Where America's Great Public Universities Stand and Where They Are Going Midway through Their Second Century*, ed. Daniel Mark Fogel (Albany: State University of New York Press, 2012), xix–xx.

33. John Aubrey Douglass, *The Conditions for Admission: Access, Equity, and the Social Contract of Public Universities* (Stanford: Stanford University Press, 2007), 7–8.

34. Albert Castel, "The Founding Fathers and the Vision of a National University," *History of Education Quarterly* 4, no. 4 (December 1964): 280–302.

35. Claudia Goldin and Lawrence F. Katz, *The Race between Education and Technology* (Cambridge, MA: Belknap Press of Harvard University Press, 2008), 11–43.

36. Louis Menand, "College: The End of the Golden Age," *New York Review of Books* (October 18, 2001). Menand refers the reader to Roger L. Geiger, "The Ten Generations of American Higher Education," in *Higher Education in the Twenty-First Century: Social, Political, and Economic Challenges*, 3rd ed., ed. Philip G. Altbach, Robert O. Berdahl, and Patricia J. Gumport (Baltimore: Johns Hopkins University Press, 1999), 58–59.

37. Robert J. Gordon, "The Demise of U.S. Economic Growth: Restatement, Rebuttal, and Reflections," NBER Working Paper 19895 (Cambridge, MA: National Bureau of Economic Research, February 2014), 10.

38. Phillip Oliff et al., "Recent Deep State Higher Education Cuts May Harm Students and the Economy for Years to Come" (Washington, DC: Center on Budget and Policy Priorities, March 2013), 1–3, 4, figure 1. For historical perspective on the extent of public disinvestment in higher education, see Donald E. Heller, "State Support of Higher Education: Past, Present, and Future," in *Privatization and Public Universities*, ed. Douglas M. Priest and Edward P. St. John (Bloomington: Indiana University Press, 2006), 11–37; Donald Hossler et al., "State Funding for Higher Education: The Sisyphean Task," *Journal of Higher Education* 68, no. 2 (March/April 1997): 160–190.

39. Michael Mitchell, Vincent Palacios, and Michael Leachman, "States Are Still Funding Higher Education Below Pre-Recession Levels" (Washington, DC: Center on Budget and Policy Priorities, May 2014), 1–3, 4, figure 1.

40. Thomas D. Snyder and Sally A. Dillow, *Digest of Education Statistics 2011.* Table 279: Degrees conferred by degree-granting institutions, by level of degree and sex of student: Selected years, 1869–70 through 2019–20 (Washington, DC: National Center for Education Statistics, Institute of Education Sciences, U.S. Department of Education, 2012); U.S. Department of Treasury with the U.S. Department of Education, "The Economics of Higher Education" (Washington, DC, December 2012).

41. Sarah E. Turner, "Going to College and Finishing College: Explaining Different Educational Outcomes," in *College Choices: The Economics of Where to Go, When to Go, and How to Pay For It,* ed. Caroline M. Hoxby (Chicago: University of Chicago Press, 2004); Anthony P. Carnevale and Jeff Strohl, "How Increasing College Access Is Increasing Inequality, and What to Do about It," in *Rewarding Strivers: Helping Low-Income Students Succeed in College,* ed. Richard D. Kahlenberg (New York: The Century Foundation, 2012), 73.

42. Anthony Grafton, "Can the Colleges Be Saved?" Review of Andrew Delbanco, *College: What It Was, Is, and Should Be* (Princeton, NJ: Princeton University Press, 2012), *New York Review of Books* (May 24, 2012): 24.

43. Michael S. McPherson and Morton Owen Schapiro, "Economic Challenges for Liberal Arts Colleges," in *Distinctively American: The Residential Liberal Arts College,* ed. Steven Koblik and Stephen R. Graubard (New Brunswick, NJ: Transaction, 2000), 49–50.

44. Academic year 2012–2013 data are the most recent available from IPEDS (Integrated Postsecondary Education Data System). Assessment of top fifty liberal arts colleges derived from the 2015 *U.S. News & World Report* ranking excluding military academies. Analysis for University Innovation Alliance by Archer Analytics LLC.

45. According to AAU analysis of IPEDS data, fall 2011 undergraduate enrollment at the sixty member institutions in the United States was 1,129,721. Percentages were calculated based on the total number of undergraduates attending Title IV participating institutions, which in 2011 enrolled 18,497,102. Graduate student enrollment totaled 560,000, which represents 18.8 percent of the national total. The AAU roster includes

two Canadian institutions, enrollments in which were omitted in these calculations. We wish to express our appreciation to Josh Trapani, director of policy analysis, Association of American Universities.

46. Carnegie Foundation for the Advancement of Teaching, Summary Tables: Distribution of institutions and enrollments by classification category, based on IPEDS fall enrollment 2009, http://classifications.carnegiefoundation.org/summary/basic.php; S. A. Ginder and J. E. Kelly-Reid, *Enrollment in Postsecondary Institutions, Fall 2012: First Look (Provisional Data)* (Washington, DC: National Center for Education Statistics, 2013), http://nces.ed.gove/pubsearch. The latter document specifies total undergraduate enrollments at Title IV institutions as 18,236,340. Our tally of fall 2013 enrollments at the 108 RU/VH institutions showed 2,045,667 undergraduates, which represents 11.2 percent of American undergraduates.

47. Charles M. Vest, "The Object of Research, the Object of Education," excerpt from president's letter to the parents of MIT undergraduates, 1994.

48. Anthony P. Carnevale, Nicole Smith, and Jeff Strohl, "Help Wanted: Projections of Jobs and Education Requirements through 2018" (Washington, DC: Georgetown University Center on Education and the Workforce, June 2010), 18; executive summary, 4.

49. Anthony P. Carnevale and Stephen J. Rose, "The Undereducated American" (Washington, DC: Georgetown University Center on Education and the Workforce, June 2011), 1, 8, 10.

50. Douglass, *Conditions for Admission,* 42, 80, 112. Douglass explains that in the late 1950s, the subject area requirement for resident freshman applicants from accredited high schools specified a B average in the last three years in an array of ten high school academic subjects. He quotes from the coursework requirements for freshman applicants, which included a "B average in the last three years, expressed in grade points, in a pattern of ten high school academic subjects: one year in American history and civics, three in English, one in algebra, one in geometry, one in laboratory science, two in foreign language, and one additional in either mathematics, foreign language, or laboratory science." Approximately 10 percent of students were admitted by "exception" or through other means (42).

51. Richard Pérez-Peña, "Best, Brightest and Rejected: Elite Colleges Turn Away Up to 95%," *New York Times* (April 8, 2014).

52. Christopher Newfield, "The End of the American Funding Model: What Comes Next?" *American Literature* 82, no. 3 (September 2010): 621.

53. David L. Kirp, *Shakespeare, Einstein, and the Bottom Line: The Marketing of Higher Education* (Cambridge, MA: Harvard University Press, 2003), 2.

54. Gordon, "Demise of U.S. Economic Growth," 10–11.

55. Bowen, Kurzweil, and Tobin, *Equity and Excellence,* 1–4.

56. Bowen, Kurzweil, and Tobin, *Equity and Excellence,* 3.

57. William G. Bowen, Matthew M. Chingos, and Michael S. McPherson, *Crossing the Finish Line: Completing College at America's Public Universities* (Princeton, NJ: Princeton University Press, 2009), 192.

58. Christopher Newfield, "End of the American Funding Model," 613, 617, 619–621.

59. Newfield, "End of the American Funding Model," 622–623. Newfield elaborates: "My own version of this intuition holds that this preference for rejection and narrow, selective development is the hallmark of a primitive era, and that we bring this prejudicial love of selection into the twenty-first century at our own peril."

60. Julia B. Isaacs, "International Comparisons of Economic Mobility," in *Getting Ahead or Losing Ground: Economic Mobility in America*, ed. Julia B. Isaacs, Isabel V. Sawhill, and Ron Haskins (Washington, DC: Brookings Institution, 2012), 37.

61. Stephen J. McNamee and Robert K. Miller, *The Meritocracy Myth*, 2nd ed. (Lanham: Rowman and Littlefield, 2009), 1–8. The excerpt from Tocqueville is from *Democracy in America* (New York: Schocken, 1967), 120.

62. McNamee and Miller, *Meritocracy Myth*, 1–8.

63. National Academies, *Rising Above the Gathering Storm*, 13.

64. In 2007, the United States spent two and one-half times the OECD average. *OECD Indicators: Health at a Glance* (2009), 1.1: Life expectancy at birth. http://dx.doi .org/10.1787/717383404708

65. Stuart J. Olshanksy et al., "Differences in Life Expectancy Due to Race and Educational Differences are Widening, and Many May Not Catch Up," *Health Affairs* 31, no. 8 (2012), cited in Sabrina Tavernise, "Life Spans Shrink for Least-Educated Whites in the U.S.," *New York Times* (September 20, 2012).

66. National Academies. Committee on Prospering in the Global Economy of the Twenty-First Century (U.S.), *Rising Above the Gathering Storm Revisited: Rapidly Approaching Category 5* (Washington, DC: National Academies Press, 2010); National Science Board, *Science and Engineering Indicators: 2012 Digest*, www.nsf.gov/statistics /digest12.

67. Goldin and Katz, *Race Between Education and Technology*, 3, 44–49.

68. Joseph E. Stiglitz, *The Price of Inequality: How Today's Divided Society Endangers Our Future* (New York: W. W. Norton, 2012), 21–22.

69. Emmanuel Saez, "Striking It Richer: The Evolution of Top Incomes in the United States" (September 3, 2013), http://elsa.berkeley.edu/%7Esaez/saez-UStopincomes-2012. pdf. This is an updated version of the article published by the Stanford Center for the Study of Poverty and Inequality (Winter 2008); see also Thomas Piketty and Emmanuel Saez, "Income Inequality in the United States, 1913–1998," *Quarterly Journal of Economics* 118, no. 1 (February 2003): 1–39; and Annie Lowrey, "The Rich Get Richer through the Recovery," *New York Times* (September 10, 2013).

70. Nir Jaimovich and Henry E. Siu, "The Trend Is the Cycle: Job Polarization and Jobless Recoveries," Working Paper 18334 (Cambridge, MA: National Bureau of Economic Research, August 2012): 2, 7–9.

71. David H. Autor, "The Polarization of Job Opportunities in the U.S. Labor Market: Implications for Employment and Earnings" (Washington, DC: Center for American Progress, April 2010), 9. See also David H. Autor, Lawrence F. Katz, and Melissa S. Kearney, "The Polarization of the Labor Market," *American Economic Review* 96, no. 2 (May 2006): 189–194.

72. Stiglitz, *Price of Inequality*, 9.

73. DeNavas-Walt, Carmen, Bernadette D. Proctor, and Jessica C. Smith, U.S. Census Bureau, Current Population Reports, P60-243, *Income, Poverty, and Health Insurance Coverage in the United States: 2011* (Washington, DC: U.S. Government Printing Office, 2012), cited in Catherine Rampell, "Behind the Decline in Incomes," *New York Times* (September 12, 2012). http://economix.blogs.nytimes.com/2012/09/12/behind -the-decline-in-incomes/

74. See especially the report from the Pew Center for the States, "Pursuing the American Dream: Economic Mobility across Generations" (Washington, DC: Economic Mobility Project, Pew Charitable Trusts, 2012).

75. Sandy Baum, Jennifer Ma, and Kathleen Payea, *Education Pays, 2013: The Benefits of Higher Education for Individuals and Society* (New York: College Board, 2013), 34. The figures specified refer to enrollment in all institutional types, including two-year community colleges.

76. Bowen, Kurzweil, and Tobin, *Equity and Excellence in American Higher Education,* 98–99, figure 5.2.

77. Catherine Rampell, "SAT Scores and Family Income," *New York Times* (August 27, 2009).

78. Suzanne Mettler, "College, the Great Unleveler," *New York Times* (March 1, 2014).

79. Thomas G. Mortenson, "Bachelor's Degree Attainment by Age 24 by Family Income Quartiles, 1970–2010" (Oskaloosa, IA: Pell Institute for the Study of Opportunity in Higher Education, 2010).

80. Martha J. Bailey and Susan M. Dynarski, "Gains and Gaps: Changing Inequality in U.S. College Entry and Completion," NBER Working Paper 17633 (Cambridge, MA: National Bureau of Economic Research, December 2011), 4–5, cited by Jordan Weissmann, *Atlantic* (March 21, 2013).

81. Pew Center for the States, "Pursuing the American Dream," 2.

82. Julia B. Isaacs, "Economic Mobility of Families across Generations," in *Getting Ahead or Losing Ground: Economic Mobility in America,* ed. Julia B. Isaacs, Isabel V. Sawhill, and Ron Haskins (Washington, DC: Brookings Institution, 2012), 19. Analysis reveals that for children born in the bottom quintile of family income, 42 percent remain at the bottom, with an additional 42 percent ascending only to the second or middle quintiles. "Only 17 percent of those born to parents in the bottom quintile climb to one of the top two income groups." Yet, for children whose parents have attained the uppermost quintile, 39 percent remain at the top, and 23 percent more end up in the next quintile.

83. U.S. Departments of Treasury and Education, "Economics of Higher Education," 15; 16, figure 6.

84. Susan K. Urahn et al., *Pursuing the American Dream: Economic Mobility across Generations* (Washington, DC: Pew Charitable Trusts, 2012), 25.

85. Isaacs, "Economic Mobility of Families," 19.

86. Anthony P. Carnevale quoted in Thomas B. Edsall, "The Reproduction of Privilege," *New York Times* (March 12, 2012).

87. Carnevale and Strohl, "How Increasing College Access Is Increasing Inequality," 71.

88. David Brooks, "The Education Gap," *New York Times* (September 25, 2005).

89. Sean F. Reardon, "The Widening Academic Achievement Gap between the Rich and the Poor: New Evidence and Possible Explanations," in *Whither Opportunity? Rising Inequality, Schools, and Children's Life Chances,* ed. Greg J. Duncan and Richard J. Murname (New York: Russell Sage Foundation, 2011), 4–5.

90. Edsall, "Reproduction of Privilege," *New York Times* (March 12, 2012).

91. David Leonhardt, "Top Colleges Largely for the Elite," *New York Times* (May 24, 2011). The figures cited are for fall 2003.

92. Peter Dreier and Richard D. Kahlenberg, "Making Top Colleges Less Aristocratic and More Meritocratic," *New York Times* (September 12, 2014).

93. Richard Florida, *The Rise of the Creative Class: And How It Is Transforming Work, Leisure, Community, and Everyday Life* (New York: Basic Books, 2002).

94. Thomas Piketty, *Capital in the Twenty-First Century,* trans. Arthur Goldhammer (Cambridge, MA: Harvard University Press, 2014), 22, 71.

95. Suzanne Mettler, *Degrees of Inequality: How the Politics of Higher Education Sabotaged the American Dream* (New York: Basic Books, 2014), 5.

96. Goldin and Katz, *Race between Education and Technology,* 22.

97. Turner, "Going to College," 13–16; Carnevale and Strohl, "How Increasing College Access Is Increasing Inequality," 73.

98. Andrew Hacker, "Is Algebra Necessary?" *New York Times* (July 28, 2012); Chris Chapman, Jennifer Laird, Nicole Ifill et al., *Trends in High School Dropout and Completion Rates in the United States: 1972–2009* (U.S. Department of Education, NCES 2012-006) (Washington, DC: National Center for Education Statistics, 2011), 50, table 12.

99. Christopher B. Swanson, "Closing the Graduation Gap: Educational and Economic Conditions in America's Largest Cities" (Bethesda, MD: Editorial Projects in Education, 2009).

100. Jay P. Greene and Greg Forster, "Public High School Graduation and College Readiness Rates in the United States" (Education Working Paper No. 3, Center for Civic Innovation, Manhattan Institute, September 2003). The report found that in 2001 only 20 percent of black students and 16 percent of Hispanic students were academically prepared for college.

101. Caroline M. Hoxby and Christopher Avery, "The Missing 'One-Offs': The Hidden Supply of High-Achieving, Low-Income Students," NBER Working Paper 18586 (Cambridge, MA: National Bureau of Economic Research, 2012).

102. National Academies, *Rising Above the Gathering Storm Revisited,* 49–50.

103. Brookings Institution analysis of OECD data for 2009, cited in Jonathan Rothwell et al., "Patenting Prosperity: Invention and Economic Performance in the United States and Its Metropolitan Areas" (Washington, DC: Brookings Institution, February 2013), 32, table 16.

104. A comparison between cohorts aged 25 to 34 and 55 to 64 in 2011 found that whereas the older generation of Americans ranked fifth globally in baccalaureate attainment, the younger has fallen behind eleven nations. The United States ranked twelfth among member nations in the percentage of 25- to 34-year-olds, a figure of 42 percent.

A comparison between the respective cohorts in 2009 in Korea found that only 13 percent of the older generation had completed college in contrast to 63 percent for the younger generation. While Korea has more than quadrupled its tertiary attainment rate and now leads among industrialized nations, the rate in the United States remains almost stagnant. OECD (2013), *Education at a Glance 2013: OECD Indicators.* http://dx .doi.org/10.1787/eag-2013-en

105. Eduardo Porter, "A Simple Equation: More Education = More Income," *New York Times* (September 10, 2014).

106. Goldin and Katz, *Race between Education and Technology,* 326–327, figure 9.1.

107. Turner, "Going to College and Finishing College": Carnevale and Strohl, "How Increasing College Access Is Increasing Inequality," 73.

108. Bowen, Chingos, and McPherson, *Crossing the Finish Line,* 1, 88, 104, 109–110, 266, n. 5.

109. American Association of Community Colleges, *2014 Fact Sheet.*

110. Barack Obama, "Remarks by the President on the American Graduation Initiative," Macomb Community College, Warren, Michigan, July 14, 2009.

111. Gordon, "Demise of U.S. Economic Growth: Restatement, Rebuttal, and Reflections," 11. See also Gordon, "The Great Stagnation of American Education," *New York Times* (September 7, 2013).

112. Gary Hoachlander, Anna C. Sikora, and Laura Horn, "Community College Students," *Education Statistics Quarterly* 5, no. 2 (2003): 121–128.

113. John Bound, Michael F. Lovenheim, and Sarah Turner, "Why Have College Completion Rates Declined? An Analysis of Changing Student Preparation and Collegiate Resources," *American Economic Journal: Applied Economics* 2, no. 3 (2010): 129–157.

114. Hoxby and Avery, "Missing 'One-Offs,'" 1. For the purposes of the study, the authors explain, "low-income" refers to the bottom quartile of income distribution for families with a high school senior, and "high-achieving" to a "student who scores at or above the 90th percentile on the ACT comprehensive or the SAT I (math and verbal) and who has a high school grade point average of A—or above." Colleges and universities deemed "selective" achieve this status through inclusion in the top categories (Very Competitive Plus, Highly Competitive, Highly Competitive Plus, and Most Competitive) of Barron's *Profiles of American Colleges.* We learn that in the 2008 edition, 236 schools were thus designated (1, n. 1).

115. Hoxby and Avery, "Missing 'One-Offs,'" 11.

116. IPEDS data for 2011 gives the figure of 3.039 million high school graduates in 2008–2009. Snyder and Dillow, *Digest of Education Statistics 2011,* table 35.

117. Brooks, "Education Gap."

118. Carnevale, Smith, and Strohl, "Help Wanted," 3, 13.

119. David H. Autor, "Skills, Education, and the Rise of Earnings Inequality Among the 'Other 99 Percent,'" *Science* 344, no. 6186 (May 23, 2014): 843.

120. U.S. Departments of Treasury and Education, "Economics of Higher Education," 3, 5, 13.

121. U.S. Census Bureau, "The Big Payoff: Educational Attainment and Synthetic Estimates of Work-Life Earnings" (Current Population Survey P23-210) (July 2002), 4. The estimates are derived from calculations based on 1999 dollars over a hypothetical working life of forty years (8).

122. U.S. Departments of Treasury and Education, "Economics of Higher Education," 3.

123. Bureau of Labor Statistics, Table A-4: Employment status of the civilian population 25 years and over by educational attainment.

124. Baum, Ma, and Payea, *Education Pays*, 19.

125. Thomas G. Mortenson et al., "Why College? Private Correlates of Educational Attainment" *Postsecondary Education Opportunity: The Mortenson Research Seminar on Public Policy Analysis of Opportunity for Postsecondary Education* 81 (March 1999).

126. Enrico Moretti, "Estimating the Social Return to Higher Education: Evidence from Longitudinal and Repeated Cross-Sectional Data," *Journal of Econometrics* 121 (2004): 175–212. Moretti estimates that all wage earners in a local workforce benefit from an increase in the proportion of baccalaureate degree holders. He reports that a "one percentage point increase in the supply of college graduates raises high school dropouts' wages by 1.9 percent, high school graduates' wages by 1.6 percent, and college graduates wages by 0.4 percent" (175).

127. Brooks, "Education Gap."

128. Carnevale, Smith, and Strohl, "Help Wanted," 13: "By 2018, the economy will create 46.8 million openings—13.8 million brand-new jobs and 33 million 'replacement jobs,' positions vacated by workers who have retired or permanently left their occupations." See also Anya Kamenetz, "Dropouts: College's 37-Million-Person Crisis—And How to Solve It," *Atlantic* (December 5, 2012).

129. National Academies, *Rising Above the Gathering Storm*, 13. The issue of decline in our national standard of living as a consequence of lack of investment in educational infrastructure is addressed in this and a number of other recent reports.

130. Geiger, *To Advance Knowledge*, 2–3.

131. Michael M. Crow articulated the vision for a New American University when he became the sixteenth president of Arizona State University in July 2002. For a prior discussion of the New American University model, see, for example, Crow, "Research University as Comprehensive Knowledge Enterprise."

132. Daniel Katz and Robert L. Kahn, *The Social Psychology of Organizations* (New York: Wiley, 1966).

133. Menand, *Marketplace of Ideas*, 13.

134. A more recent discussion of the concept is to be found in John Holland, "Complex Adaptive Systems," *Daedalus* 121, no. 1 (1992): 17–30.

135. Paul J. DiMaggio and Walter W. Powell, "The Iron Cage Revisited: Institutional Isomorphism and Collective Rationality in Organizational Fields," *American Sociological Review* 48, no. 2 (1983): 147–160.

# TWO

# The Gold Standard
# in American Higher Education

When, in 1636, Harvard College welcomed its first class of nine students, presided over by a single master, the entire European population of the colonies likely did not exceed ten thousand settlers. The Charter of 1650 specified its purposes: "The advancement of all good literature, arts, and sciences; the advancement and education of youth in all manner of good literature, arts, and sciences; and all other necessary provisions that may conduce to the education of the ... youth of this country."[1] These purposes endure more than three centuries later, as we are assured on Harvard's website. The nonpareil elite private research university, Harvard University observed its 375th anniversary in 2011, and among its claims to distinction is its precedence as both the oldest corporation and institution of higher learning in the United States. But in the course of the emergence of the American research university, Harvard and the other colonial colleges that would comprise the Ivy League, modeled on Oxford and Cambridge and focused on the teaching of undergraduates in residential colleges, would come to represent only one strand in American higher education.[2]

In the standard account of the emergence of the American research university, the model would be determined not solely by Harvard and its institutional peers but rather by the conflation of this colonial replication of the "Oxbridge" model with the framework of the German university epitomized in the exemplar of the University of Berlin, established in 1809. The prototype for the American research university would appear more or less fortuitously in 1876 with the establishment of Johns Hopkins University. The consensus of scholarship holds that this institution constitutes the definitive prototype for the American research university. Following the death of railroad magnate, financier, and philanthropist Johns Hopkins in 1873, the trustees of his estate were charged with establishing a university and a hospital from the resources of what was then the largest bequest in U.S. history. Their decision to focus on research and graduate education would determine the course of American higher education.[3] Johns Hopkins would conjoin in a single institution the Oxbridge model of residential undergraduate education, epitomized and already well established on these shores by such elite colonial colleges as Harvard, Yale, Princeton, and Dartmouth, with the advanced scientific research characteristic of German academic institutions. In the estimation of one scholar of American higher education, the establishment of Johns Hopkins would thus prove to be "perhaps the single most decisive event in the history of learning in the Western hemisphere," a claim that historian Roger Geiger concedes may be "extravagant" but not unreasonable.[4]

At Johns Hopkins, former University of California president Daniel Coit Gilman introduced into American higher education the pattern of specialized graduate study modeled on the practices of German scientific research institutes and thus an emphasis on the reciprocity of learning and research.[5] Until research achieved the status accorded it there, and through this influence at other elite institutions, this sector that we regard as intrinsic to the purposes of higher education, Geiger explains, was "largely adventitious in the scheme of things."[6] Nannerl Keohane, former president of Duke University, elaborates on the impact of this prototype: "Established universities such as Harvard and Yale, and new institutions such as Stanford or Chicago, adapted the Johns Hopkins/ Germanic model by grafting it onto the traditional undergraduate liberal arts training by a collegiate structure within the larger university context."[7] Clark Kerr, then University of California president emeritus, provides a useful synopsis of the innovations to American higher education introduced by Johns Hopkins:

> The Hopkins idea brought with it the graduate school with exceptionally high academic standards in what was still a rather new and raw civilization; the renovation of professional education, particularly in medicine; the establishment of the preeminent influence of the department; the creation of

research institutes and centers, or university presses and learned journals and the "academic ladder"; and also the great proliferation of courses.[8]

But to more fully appreciate the significance of this new prototype, we might look more closely for its source in the confluence of two distinct national academic traditions. The English model, elitist and "collegiate," with reference to its focus on the teaching of undergraduates in residential colleges, is represented by Oxford and Cambridge. For roughly seven centuries—until a royal charter from King William IV established the University of London in 1836—these two institutions remained the only universities in England.[9] The German model, which emphasized scientific research, is represented in the founding vision for the University of Berlin, which was established through the influence of the philologist, philosopher, and liberal Prussian minister of education Wilhelm von Humboldt. "If the Germans provided us with a blueprint for advanced research, the British provided us with an outline for organizing undergraduate collegiate education," Jonathan Cole explains.[10] "Across the United States," observes Arthur M. Cohen, "science and research, along with advanced training—the German model—was appended to preexisting institutions that more closely resembled English boarding schools for adolescent boys."[11] As historian William Clark puts it, "At American universities, the undergraduate college remained essentially a descendant of the Oxbridge college, while the graduate schools emerged as a superstructure of German faculties or departments that were added on to the undergraduate college. After the 1870s, the new graduate schools cultivated research, while the college had a traditional pedagogical mission."[12]

As a consequence of this conflation, Clark Kerr has pointed out, the American research university would in a single institution combine the signature characteristics of two great academic traditions: the "academic cloister of Cardinal Newman," referring to John Henry Newman, and the vaunted research aspirations of the nineteenth-century German university. But this American institution would become neither Oxford nor Berlin, Kerr asserts: it is instead a "new type of institution in the world."[13] The influence of these nineteenth-century models would endure, we are reminded by the Canadian literary scholar Bill Readings, an astute observer of the American university: "Most projects for the university of the

twenty-first century bear a striking resemblance to the university projects of the nineteenth century . . . . The vast majority of contemporary
'solutions' to the crisis of the university are, in fact, no more than restate-
ments of Humboldt or Newman, whose apparent aptness is the product
of ignorance of these founding texts on the history of the institution. So
we hear a great deal about the need to value both teaching and research,
or the indirect utility of pure research, as if these were new ideas."[14]

The inherent focus on discovery in the American research university,
which we take for granted as one of its overarching purposes, was not inevitable, especially given the authority accorded the "academic cloister"
model propounded by Cardinal Newman. As Hanna Holborn Gray, president emerita of the University of Chicago, points out, Newman articulated a "set of beliefs about the knowledge most worth having, and the
kind of person education should seek to develop," thus underscoring the
role of a broad general education grounded in the liberal arts in the formation of what he termed "good members of society." Although characteristic of the period, this sort of high-minded verbiage today appears
quaint: "He proposed an idea of a university founded in a largely traditional conception of the liberal arts with the humanities at their center,
one that excluded research, locating the discovery and advancement of
knowledge in separate academies and confining the university to the
function of teaching."[15] In the preface to his influential volume *The Idea
of a University*, which is based on a set of lectures, some of which he delivered in Dublin in 1852, Newman makes the astonishing assertion that
"it is the diffusion and extension of knowledge rather than the advancement" that defines the "essence" of the university: "If its object were scientific and philosophical discovery, I do not see why a university should
have students."[16] Cole observes that although Newman's nostalgic conception informed the debate regarding the purposes of a university for
decades to follow, "it did not, fortunately, influence the actual evolution
of universities—at least in the United States."[17] Frank Rhodes remarks
of Newman's pronouncements, "It is the idea of a college; it is not the
idea of a university."[18]

The German model, by contrast, more or less consolidated with the
establishment of the University of Berlin, underscored the unity of research and teaching. Gray characterizes the scope of Humboldt's concep-

tion as "breadth of basic scholarship whose different parts together illu-
minated a coherent universality of thought and learning to be expanded
and pursued for their own sake at the highest intellectual level." This was
a conception that "celebrated an ideal of *Wissenschaft*, of a learning and
cultivation both broad and deep, with research carried out to extend
knowledge itself through new discovery and interpretation." Menand
parses *Wissenschaft* as "pure learning—the idea of knowledge for its own
sake," and comparative literature scholar Elinor Shaffer explains that even
though the term may explicitly refer to the natural sciences, more broadly
it designates knowledge or scholarship.[19] The institution would be predicated on "academic freedom for professor and student alike, so that the
goal of intellectual creativity, the following of rigorous investigation and
analysis wherever these might lead, could be fully encouraged and
realized."[20]

No less crucial for Humboldt and his advisors were lofty aspirations
for the role of education in the formation of the individual. As an intellectual as well as a government functionary, Humboldt drew inspiration
and even practical guidance from the circle of philosophers associated
with the German idealist tradition, including, most notably, Johann Got-
tlieb Fichte and F. W. J. Schelling.[21] At the crux of their romantic conception of the influence of education on the individual lies the concept
of *Bildung*, which refers broadly to education or culture but more precisely to the development or "cultivation" of the individual. According
to Josef Bleicher, the concept "transcends mere acquisition of knowledge"
and thus implies "bringing all the potentials contained within us to full
expression." The process engages not only the individual but also embraces the dimension of the ethical citizen in society and thus service to
the community.[22] Informed by a series of essays and occasional papers
produced by Schelling and his peers, Humboldt argued that only an institution that unites teaching with research could produce such an individual.[23] As Jeffrey Peck put it, "*Bildung* through *Wissenschaft* was to become the cornerstone of the university."[24]

The importance for the American research university of the prototype established by the conjunction of these various functions in a single institution cannot be overstated. It is this integrated platform for research and learning that is predominant in the American research

university and that the New American University seeks to leverage. The objective of the new model is to produce not only knowledge and innovation but also students who are adaptive master-learners empowered to integrate a broad array of interrelated disciplines and adapt over their lifetimes to changing workforce demands and shifts in the global knowledge economy.

Although the preeminence of Oxford and Cambridge render them obvious, if flawed, prototypes for the American research university, the relative obscurity for Americans of the institution known since 1949 as Humboldt-Universität justifies a digression to assess more closely its stature and influence in the German states prior to their unification in 1871, as well as its persistence as a benchmark of academic culture.[25] "It was in Germany that the rebirth of the university took place," writes Clark Kerr. "It was the establishment of Berlin . . . that was the dramatic event. The emphasis was on philosophy and science, on research, on graduate instruction, on the freedom of professors and students (*Lehrfreiheit* and *Lernfreiheit*). The department was created and the institute. The professor was established as a great figure within and without the university."[26] In the estimation of Kerr, "The modern German research university, beginning with the founding of the University of Berlin in 1809, approached the discovery of truth and knowledge in all fields on the basis of scientific principles, joining the rational and empirical traditions to form the basis of modern scientific research." The new model would moreover contribute significantly to the economic ascent of Germany during the late nineteenth century, as well as anticipate the American model of agency-sponsored research.[27]

Although remarkable from our accustomed perspective on the limited influence of intellectuals on the public sphere, Humboldt apparently enjoyed the prerogative of proffering position papers on academic reform to the king.[28] Counsel from the circle of philosophers associated with Fichte and Schelling, whose commitment to higher education represented a confluence of ideals and values from the Enlightenment and the romantic movement, is held to have secured the unity of teaching and research in the German universities. "At no time in the eighteenth century or the later nineteenth were so many reform ideas produced by members of the German professoriate," historian Charles McClelland explains. "The bureaucracy, in contrast to that of other periods, was willing to listen and even act on ideas."[29] Shaffer contends that the potency of this influence stems from the conviction that implicit within philosophical speculation was the demand for a "complete overhaul of the practical sphere." She observes that an "indissoluble connection between theory and practice was a central plank in their philosophy and thus built into the structures of the new university."[30]

Humboldt and his counselors on pedagogical reform articulated a number of tenets that would come to be deemed intrinsic to the academic culture of the contemporary American research university. In his lectures, Schelling, for example, insisted on institutional autonomy and independence from any measure of state control, as well as the principle of academic freedom, which must be held sacrosanct if universities were to be "scientific" institutions. And because universities must do more than just transmit knowledge, teachers must themselves be researchers: a "teacher who has not carried out research is by definition incapable of teaching its methods or results." According to Schelling, a teacher who is "incapable of reconstructing the totality of his science for himself, or reformulating it from his own inner vision, will never go beyond the mere historical exposition of the science." The process of inquiry, moreover, is "more valuable than the results; it is the process that the educated man learns, and can apply in whatever sphere he finds himself." This conviction regarding the unity between research and teaching was held by all of Humboldt's advisors.[31]

A host of other innovations realized in Berlin would similarly strike us as consonant with our contemporary conception of academic culture. These include self-determination for each institution, competition among universities, and a model of pluralism—conceived in defiance of Napoleonic bureaucratic centralization, Shaffer reminds us, as well as the recommendation that the state provide financial aid to qualified students regardless of their backgrounds. An introductory curriculum preparatory to specialization anticipates the general education requirements in the liberal arts common to American colleges and universities. Scholars were expected to contribute knowledge that leads to the advancement of society. Shaffer summarizes: "There is no antithesis between knowledge and action: good science will also serve practical ends." Moreover, "the university should have a wider function in the community."[32]

America's research universities achieved preeminence following World War II, but throughout the nineteenth century and for three decades to follow, German academic culture represented the vanguard: "Of all the universities in Western society, those of Germany have probably had the greatest significance in modern times," writes McClelland. "They were the first to fuse teaching with research functions and thereby to create the very model of the modern university. They were the fountainheads of a large part of modern scholarship and science." The conception of the reciprocity of research and teaching envisioned by Humboldt represented an innovation of the first order. Indeed, the ideal of *Wissenschaft* institutionalized by Humboldt at Berlin consolidated the concept of the "teacher-scholar," McClelland points out, producing an individual who "excels in both the discovery and transmission of knowledge."[33] "Berlin was the first university in the world where research and not only instruction was regarded as a primary duty of its professors," another scholar observes.[34]

Even though the formation of the University of Berlin represents a critical episode in the evolution of the modern research university, some historians have begun to question the suppositions of what is called the "Humboldt myth." Mitchell G. Ash, for example, points out that many of the structures and practices consolidated with Berlin derived from eighteenth-century institutions, especially the universities of Halle and Göttingen, established respectively in 1694 and 1737.[35] Unlike medieval universities, which conceived of education as training in received doctrine, Halle and Göttingen embraced the practices of the scientific academies of the sixteenth and seventeenth centuries.[36] Peter Weingart observes that by the end of the eighteenth century, "research had moved out of the academies into the universities" because these latter institutions more readily accommodated the plurality of disciplinary cultures that arose as a consequence of increasing specialization.[37] In the estimation of Ash, moreover, the conception for Berlin was the product of collective effort and less likely to be associated by contemporaries with Humboldt than such figures as Kant, Schleiermacher, and Fichte.[38]

Such was the acclaim of German academic culture during the nineteenth century that more than nine thousand Americans studied at German universities, according to Menand, drawn not only by internationally renowned scientists and scholars but also the promise of academic freedom and the ethos of *Wissenschaft*.[39] Following its institutionalization at Johns Hopkins, however, the German model would be Americanized in short order, according to historians Hugh Davis Graham and Nancy Diamond, as graduate schools were superimposed on the existing departmental configurations of some major universities. The orientation of the German model toward research and graduate education assumed prominence in American higher education, but "by the early twentieth century even Johns Hopkins looked more like Yale, or like the University of North Carolina, than like von Humboldt's model in Berlin."[40] Beginning in the 1890s, graduate schools modeled on Johns Hopkins were thus created with the establishment of the University of Chicago, for example, and the transition of Harvard and Columbia from colleges into universities. "Transmitting knowledge to younger students would not be sufficient to match what the European universities were accomplishing," Cole observes regarding the competitive intent of leading American universities. Thus, "by the turn of the twentieth century Harvard, Columbia, Chicago, Hopkins, Michigan, Wisconsin, and Yale were being transformed into research institutions." The objective was broader than the discovery of new knowledge, however: "The new American model had two main goals: producing cutting-edge discoveries and using that knowledge to serve the needs of American society."[41]

### The Land-Grant Institutions Inform the Emergence of the American Research University

Another strand in the emergence of the American research university would come in the midst of national crisis when in July 1862, President Abraham Lincoln signed into law the Morrill Act. The statute provided funding derived from the sale of federal lands to state governments to build new colleges and universities or transform existing schools to provide instruction in practical fields to the sons and daughters of the working and middle classes. The originating legislation for the land-grant system came only fourteen years prior to the establishment of Johns Hopkins University. The American research university thus assumed its defining structure and characteristics contemporaneously and in interrelationship with the formation of the land-grant colleges and universities during the final quarter of the nineteenth century. Among the institutions that were established as a consequence of the Morrill Act, and those already established that became its beneficiaries, a considerable number emerged in the decades following the Civil War as research universities. Nearly three dozen land-grant schools were founded within the decade following the enabling legislation. Seventeen of them had already been established as public colleges or universities but would thereafter become designated land-grant institutions.[42] The contemporaneity of their emergence as well as their attendant reciprocal influence marks an important chapter in the history of American higher education. The legislation moreover set a precedent for federal support for higher education as well, and as a consequence of its mandate, the land-grant institutions shaped the research enterprises of the emerging American research universities through an emphasis on scientific inquiry and technological innovation.[43] Indeed, in the estimation of former University of California president Richard C. Atkinson and colleague William Blanpied, the land-grant colleges were the "first quasi-research universities in the United States."[44]

Of the fifteen institutions singled out by Geiger as foundational to the American research university, six are land-grant institutions, both public and private: California, Cornell, Illinois, Minnesota, MIT, and Wisconsin. Although in general usage the designation "land-grant" is often regarded synonymous with state colleges and universities, a notable few are private, such as the Massachusetts Institute of Technology, or private with public colleges, such as Cornell University.[45] Of the seventy-six land-grant institutions that comprise the roster maintained by the Association of Public and Land-Grant Universities, forty-two, including eight campuses of the University of California system, emerged as major research universities, with the majority in this category representing the definitive type of the flagship public research university. Twenty land-grant schools, including six University of California campuses, are member institutions of the Association of American Universities (AAU).[46]

The Morrill Act, with its provisions for the distribution of as many as 90,000 acres of federal land to each state, would fund the establishment of collegiate institutions to provide instruction in agriculture and the "mechanical arts" to the children of the working and middle classes.[47] The legacy of the utilitarian and egalitarian tenets specified in the Morrill Act, epitomized by curricula in the "useful arts"—identified by historian John Thelin as agriculture, mechanics, mining, and military instruction[48]—would play an important role in the ascendancy of the scientific disciplines and fields of engineering in American research universities, thus shaping the research enterprises of the emerging set of American research universities.[49] The legislation would produce a diverse and heterogeneous set of colleges and universities that have exerted a broad impact disproportionate to their actual number. By one estimate, land-grant institutions have educated one-fifth of all Americans with college degrees.[50] In setting a precedent for federal support for higher education, the impact of the legislation would burgeon exponentially following World War II. [51] According to some assessments of American higher education, the global preeminence attained by American research universities in the postwar era is a direct consequence of federal patronage, beginning with the seed funding provided to many of the land-grant schools.[52] The federal precedent moreover encouraged state legislatures to provide annual appropriations for universities and colleges.[53]

The entrepreneurial dimension of the American research university, considered more fully in chapter 4, has been correlated with the Morrill Act by scholars who perceive in its utilitarian provisions the seed for teaching and research with the potential for contributions to economic development. Indeed, economist Nathan Rosenberg deems the responsiveness of American universities to regional economic conditions the "most distinctive feature of American universities, at least as far back as the passage of the Morrill Act of 1862." Such institutions, comparatively autonomous and operating in a competitive environment devoid of centralized federal authority, have historically been "heavily beholden to the needs of local industries and to the priorities established by state legislatures." The attendant focus on economic relevance thus stems from their willingness to accommodate the requirements of agriculture, business, and industry: "America's decentralized higher education system can be fairly described as 'market-driven,' rather than locked into a centralized system in which the reallocation of budgets and personnel is severely restricted by political and bureaucratic considerations, as well as by the constraints of past history."[54]

## The Utilitarian Predication of the Land-Grant Institutions

The fellows of Yale College commissioned a report in 1828 to consider the "expediency of so altering the regular course of instruction . . . as to leave out of said course the study of the dead languages." The report, however, concluded that because the purposes of a college education were to "form the taste and discipline the mind," the study of classics should continue because such a curriculum both "lays the foundations of correct taste" and "forms the most effectual discipline of the mental faculties."[55] Although the elite colleges of colonial New England had deemed the "education of Christian gentlemen essentially synonymous with classical learning," writes Caroline Winterer,[56] in the decades following the Civil War, a groundswell of sentiment in favor of utilitarian instruction would eclipse the model inherited from Britain and the Continent, consistent with the mandate of the land-grant institutions. As noted by Laurence Veysey, "During the ten years after 1865, almost every visible change in the pattern of American higher education lay in the direction of concessions to the utilitarian type of demand for reform." General societal approbation for instruction deemed applicable to daily life fueled the demand for practical instruction.[57] By this time, the American public held a generalized conception of the knowledge disseminated at colleges and universities as a means for "improvement," whether practical or spiritual.[58]

The Morrill Act reflected the practical ethos intrinsic to our national culture from the earliest days of the American Republic. With its provisions for the distribution of federal lands to enable states to fund programs of instruction in agriculture and the industrial arts for the children of the middle class, the legislation embodied what one scholar termed "practical people doing practical things, whether the practicalities of the earlier colleges of agriculture and mechanical arts or the advanced research of a Massachusetts Institute of Technology or Cornell."[59] Not only did the Morrill Act legitimize the utilitarian ideals that would shape the American university throughout the rest of the nineteenth century, but it also encouraged the perception that one of the primary purposes of an undergraduate education is preparation for professional life or direct entry into the workforce. To aid citizens of more modest social strata then entering universities in increasing numbers, instruction would stress application in everyday life. Unlike their British and European counterparts, Rosenberg and Richard R. Nelson observe, American universities would be "perceived as a path to commercial as well as personal success."[60] The utilitarian conception of higher education encouraged ambivalence toward privilege, but because of its association with the common good, it was also deemed to be more democratic.[61]

General enthusiasm for norms of practical utility would find expression in the utilitarian tenets formulated by Ezra Cornell, whose specifications for the establishment of the university that would bear his name include the oft-cited formulation "I would found an institution where any person can find instruction in any study."[62] With its novel integration of the traditional humanities curriculum with science and practical fields, especially engineering and agriculture, Cornell University, established in 1865, represented a new vision for a "modern" university. According to Veysey, Cornell was the "first spectacular visible fruit of the Morrill Act."[63] The utilitarian predilection of the land-grant universities was perhaps the primary impetus for the dispersion of scientific and engineering skills following the Civil War and in important respects contributed to the role of science and engineering in the nascent American research university.[64] The emergence of instruction in these fields, however, was by no means exclusively an outcome of the Morrill Act: Harvard had established the Lawrence Scientific School in 1846, followed by the Jefferson Physical Laboratory in the 1870s; the Yale Scientific School was established in 1847 and in 1861 renamed the Sheffield Scientific School; and Dartmouth had established the Chandler Scientific School in 1852.[65] Nevertheless, in the estimation of experts in university-industry relations, public universities and "especially those established under the Morrill Act affected the direction of the academic research enterprise during this period to a greater extent than the private Ivy League institutions."[66]

The utilitarian predication of the nascent American research university model would prove to be especially conducive to the persistence of what Rosenberg and Nelson term "hands-on problem-solving" coupled with ambivalence toward the abstract and theoretical, an orientation expressed in the 1830s by Alexis de Tocqueville, whom the economists quote as follows: "In America the purely practical part of science is admirably understood and careful attention is paid to the theoretical portion, which is immediately requisite to application . . . . But hardly anyone in the United States devotes himself to the essentially theoretical and abstract portion of human knowledge." Tocqueville concludes that the motivation for scientific investigation is the pursuit of "every new method that leads by a shorter road to wealth, every machine that spares labor, every instrument that diminishes the cost of production, every discovery that facilitates pleasure."[67]

As an expression of the social and cultural milieu of mid-nineteenth-century America, the Morrill Act engendered institutions in which teaching and research consistent with its purposes—as specified in its provisions, "without excluding other scientific and classical studies, and including military tactics, to teach such branches of learning as are related to agriculture and the mechanic arts"[68]—would prove conducive to the emergence of scientific discovery and technological invention. What we would term "applied science and engineering" did not generally appear in the curricula of American universities until the 1840s because deemed both "too practical and plebeian."[69] Although this orientation would persist into the 1920s, according to Rosenberg and Nelson, the practical inclinations of the republic perceived by Tocqueville would encourage the rise of engineering education in the United States, beginning in 1802 at the U.S. Military Academy at West Point. Its graduates would go on to lend their expertise to the scientific exploration of the continent undertaken in association with the Lewis and Clark expedition and the construction of vast national infrastructure projects such as the transcontinental railroad and the system of locks and dams erected on the Mississippi River. Demand for trained engineers would lead to the establishment of Rensselaer Polytechnic Institute in 1824 and the Massachusetts Institute of Technology in 1865. In that same decade, institutions such as Yale and Columbia would introduce courses of engineering.[70] Veysey has deemed Cornell the first institutional reification of the ideals of the Morrill Act, but economist Henry Etzkowitz identifies two key inflection points that epitomize the transformation of research universities into "economic development enterprises." According to Etzkowitz, the expansion of the academic model to embrace industry commenced with the establishment of MIT, followed by the introduction of the entrepreneurial dimension into the academic culture of a liberal arts curriculum at Stanford in the early twentieth century.[71]

## An "Institutional Revolution": Toward Accessibility and Accountability

The egalitarian values of the American republic would produce a set of institutions poised to veer away from the historical class prerogatives characteristic not only of the "ancient universities" of Britain but the Humboldtian model as well. The elitism of our top-tier institutions may masquerade as meritocratic, but the exclusivity of Oxford and Cambridge by most accounts represented an unabashed display of social privilege: "Few countries have had universities as confined to the élite as England in 1800," observes the University of Edinburgh historian R. D. Anderson. Oxbridge students were "sons either of the aristocracy and gentry, for whom the university was a social finishing school as much as an intellectual experience, or of the clergy."[72] The model enshrined by Cardinal Newman has been characterized as a "university for aristocrats and scholars, unscientific, undemocratic, highly personalized, gloriously impractical."[73] Connotations of aristocratic privilege in this milieu are not without basis inasmuch as University College London, established in 1826—seven centuries after the founding of Oxford and Cambridge— became the first university in the United Kingdom to admit students regardless of race, class, or religion, and the first to admit women. [74] A similar elitism apparently obtained on the Continent: by one estimate no more than 1 percent of each given cohort of applicants would have been admitted to the handful of leading German universities in the first decades of the nineteenth century.[75]

The increasing rationalization, bureaucratization, and secularization of late-eighteenth-century society, however, brought skepticism of the framework of privilege and authority historically sanctioned by the social institutions of early modern Britain, referring broadly to the rules, laws, and relationships that govern society. The economist Douglas Allen argues that the technological innovation, sustained economic growth, and nexus of market relations generated in the wake of the Industrial Revolution encouraged society to entertain new expectations not only for the reliability and standardization of industrial products and consumer goods but also accountability, productivity, and performance in interpersonal conduct. Allen terms this transformation in social expectations the "institutional revolution." Because technological innovation reduced the variability and contingency visited on daily life by the vicissitudes of nature, he contends, society could better appreciate variance in human inputs and thus the impact of conduct, especially with regard to merit, productivity, and performance: "When nature played a large role, and when one could not separate this role from other inputs, then measurement could not cost-effectively distinguish input contributions and therefore had little meaning." The advent of modern science promoted the development of statistical analysis in the nineteenth century, but improvements in the measurement of productivity and performance motivated by the transformation of social institutions in the wake of industrialization found broader application.[76]

Whereas Allen focuses selectively on the economic implications of measurement for such institutions as the aristocracy, naval administration, and criminal law, for example, we underscore its significance for higher education and especially for research universities. Despite the prerogatives of authority and privilege historically exercised by universities, the institutional revolution brought expectations for the objective assessment and reward of merit, whether for the individual or a given collective, which assumed the direct measurement of performance. The administrative apparatus of British universities consolidated during the nineteenth century to an extent sufficient to standardize the granting of degrees, for example, but improvements in the measurement of merit, productivity, performance, and outcomes in higher education would not attain standards of precision until the twentieth century and then especially in the United States. The significance of the institutional revolution for colleges and universities in the present century becomes obvious. Meaningful assessment of merit allows institutions to reward accomplishment, while the accurate measurement of productivity, performance, and outcomes allows them to enter into productive collaborative as well as competitive relationships.

The gold standard for the American research university coalesced in the decades between 1876 and 1915. Although America was less populous and the world arguably less complex a century ago, ambitions for social progress apparently flourished because this era witnessed an unprecedented spurt in the establishment of four-year colleges, both public and private. The motivations for their establishment were primarily regional and in many instances even municipal, determined by the aspirations of citizens who simply wanted a local college. Most were built on some variation of the traditional model and continue to serve generations of Americans. Nevertheless, whether we consider the citizens of Slippery Rock, Pennsylvania, who organized to convert a normal school into a state college, or tycoons and industrialists like Johns Hopkins and Leland

Stanford, their forward-looking ambition appears remarkable given the apparent lack of motivation to build new institutions in our own era.

## A Trajectory toward a Decentralized and Competitive "Academic Marketplace"

During the Constitutional Convention in Philadelphia in 1787, James Madison called for the establishment of a national university and the legislative authority to "offer premiums to encourage the advancement of useful knowledge and discoveries." The founders of the republic were motivated not by their dedication to the ideals of the Age of Reason, Albert Castel explains, or their "conviction that our experiment in republican government could not succeed unless the people and their officials were properly educated." At a point in time still rife with sectionalism, statesmen sought to advance a great national university that would "combat divisive tendencies by bringing together at a central seat of learning the choice young men of all the states" to "give to America that unity of purpose and policy which would enable it to fulfill its glorious destiny in the world."[77] The rejection of the proposal, which may have led to the formation of a federal ministry of higher education, has been attributed to its conflict with the doctrine of states' rights.[78] But, as it happens, the failure to enact the legislation would yield extraordinary outcomes, setting the course for the decentralized configuration of American higher education, which would fortuitously unleash competition between institutions and contribute to this defining attribute of American higher education.[79]

The organization and objectives of the contemporary American research university may at first glance appear so self-evident as to have been inevitable from the outset, but in reality the institution in its present form represents the culmination of a trajectory marked by the interplay of sometimes fraught cultural, societal, and economic forces shaped by more than two centuries of what has been termed "haphazard evolution" rather than planning. Yet, according to Graham and Diamond, historical circumstance would remarkably turn "fragmentation, incoherence, qualitative unevenness, and economic vulnerability" into assets. The emergence of a set of heterogeneous institutions competitively engaged and possessed of the capacity to contribute to national prosperity—a scenario aptly characterized as a competitive "academic marketplace"—was by no means foreseen during the formative years of the early republic. Decentralization in this context refers to the absence of a centralized national ministry, or even regional ministries, of higher education. "Decentralization was accelerated by a colonial and revolutionary environment in America that combined community isolation, entrepreneurial incentives for upward mobility, fractious Protestant denominationalism . . . and revolutionary egalitarianism." Moreover, the authors attribute the aversion to centralized authority in part to the U.S. Constitution, which, "shaped by classical liberalism's respect for contract and fear of centralized state power, created a federal system that limited and fragmented national authority and reserved education policy for state and local governments."[80] "The Tenth Amendment reserves all powers not delegated to the central government to the states," another assessment explains. "Since education is not explicitly mentioned in the Constitution, the states have taken the lead in this area, with the federal government playing a secondary role."[81] Federal intervention has nevertheless been fundamental to the development of American higher education and has played a pivotal role in the evolution of the set of major research universities, a point we take up in the following section of this chapter.

Since the late nineteenth century, European national systems of higher education by contrast have typically been subject to a marked degree of state control, characterized by centralized planning and policy making, including allocation of funding and determination of institutional specialization with an emphasis on advanced study, professional training, and research.[82] Whereas American research universities, both public and private, compete openly for federal research dollars and private investment, education ministries elsewhere exert centralized control over the allocation of resources to institutions. The Higher Education Funding Council for England (HEFCE), for example, determines priorities for expenditure each year and apportions total funds accordingly. Atkinson and Blanpied underscore the extent to which the competitive process in the United States has engendered quality in its research universities and contend that efforts to replicate the model in other national contexts inevitably falter if participants are culturally averse to competition. And while American research universities integrate undergraduate and graduate instruction with research, various national systems maintain parallel and differentiated research sectors that compete with universities.

The examples of Germany and France are cited, where the eighty institutes of the Max Planck Society and the Centre National de la Recherche Scientifique (CNRS) respectively constitute each nation's foremost research organization.[83]

## The Compact between the Federal Government and America's Research Universities

Seventy-five years of protracted debate regarding the role of the federal government in higher education would follow the initial deliberations of the Constitutional Convention, culminating with the Morrill Act, which set a precedent for federal support for higher education. But the ascension of American research universities to global preeminence may be correlated most directly with federal investment in research in the decades following World War II.[84] The postwar era set the stage for unprecedented federal support of scientific research conducted by our nation's research universities focused primarily on national defense, economic prosperity, and public health. The terms of the "social contract for science" have been defined thus: "Government promises to fund the basic science that peer reviewers find most worthy of support, and scientists promise that the research will be performed well and honestly and will provide a steady stream of discoveries that can be translated into new products, medicines, or weapons."[85] This remarkably productive symbiosis produced what has been characterized as a "decentralized, pluralistic, and intensely competitive academic marketplace fueled by federal research dollars." Fierce competition for federal and industry support and private investment has encouraged innovation and risk-taking and led a number of ambitious universities to emerge as major research institutions.[86]

Federal investment in academic research was hardly novel. Support for agricultural research may be traced to the Hatch Act of 1887, for example, initiating what Roger Geiger terms a "tangled skein of relationships" that would prove incalculably beneficial to our collective well-being and the academic sector alike. But it was chiefly as a consequence of national defense interests that federal investment assumed its present contours. Thus was established the sometimes fraught relationship between American research universities and the defense establishment, or what President Dwight D. Eisenhower in his famous 1961 farewell address to the nation would term the "military-industrial complex."[87] Although federal investment for university-based research has been a defining characteristic of the compact, the interrelationship between the federal government and the academic sector has been crucial to the ascendancy of the American research university in other respects. The Works Progress Administration (WPA), for example, created by the Franklin Delano Roosevelt administration and funded by Congress to address the economic downturn of that era, allowed for the construction of important academic infrastructure, much of it still in use today. The Servicemen's Readjustment Act of 1944, known as the G.I. Bill, contributed to broad accessibility to major research universities through its impact on millions of returning veterans. Federal support of financial aid programs, including the Pell Grant, continues to exert impact for millions of students.[88]

The terms of the compact between the federal government and America's research universities were defined by the policy manifesto *Science— The Endless Frontier: A Report to the President on a Program for Postwar Scientific Research,* issued in July 1945 by Vannevar Bush, the founding director of the Office of Scientific Research and Development (OSRD) under Presidents Roosevelt and Truman. The report initiated peacetime federal investment in a national science enterprise led by a handful of elite research universities and the nascent system of national laboratories. The charge to academic science implicit in the report propounded the perception of science as a wellspring that would not only maintain American military preeminence but also drive economic growth and improve the quality of life through the production of science-based technologies for the benefit of all humankind. Gregg Zachary makes the point that the image of the frontier evoked in the title of the report was especially felicitous: thus the "quest for knowledge could replace the vanishing geographical frontier as the new source of American freedom and creativity."[89]

Inasmuch as the report codified the argument for continued government sponsorship of research and development, it led to the establishment of federal agencies such as the National Science Foundation (NSF), National Institutes of Health (NIH), and National Aeronautics and Space Administration (NASA), as well as the system of national laboratories, such as Los Alamos National Laboratory and Lawrence Livermore National Laboratory.[90] A significant amount of the research undertaken by academically affiliated scientists and engineers is conducted within the system of national laboratories, which are funded by federal agencies such as the U.S. Department of Energy but administered by industrial contractors or universities.[91] Although the status of American research universities as the principal locus for research and development appears in hindsight to have been inevitable, funding for research could just as well have been apportioned to industrial laboratories or independent research institutes. But the success of the Manhattan Project demonstrated the potential and economic benefit of university-based research, and the Bush report consolidated the formal relationships between the federal government and research universities.[92] The focus on science and technology, however, overlooked the social sciences and humanities, which, Jonathan Cole explains, "seriously damaged the future of both sets of disciplines, slowing down their development and reducing appreciation for interdisciplinary research." The omission would not be redressed until the 1960s, when the National Science Foundation began to support the social and behavioral sciences.[93]

Federal investment in knowledge production is essential because the private sector generally lacks sufficient incentive to conduct basic research. Vannevar Bush observed that because "basic research is essentially noncommercial in nature, . . . it will not receive the attention it requires if left to industry."[94] Economists have long noted this lack of incentive for business and industry to invest in basic research. The classic account of this dilemma comes from Richard R. Nelson, who observed in a 1959 paper that although scientific research has both social benefits and economic value, "private-profit opportunities alone are not likely to draw as large a quantity of resources into basic research as is socially desirable." The private sector is unlikely to invest sufficiently in basic research because "few firms operate in so wide a field of economic activity that they are able themselves to benefit directly from all the new technological possibilities opened by the results of a successful basic research effort."[95] Economist Kenneth Arrow observed in a 1962 paper that because basic research is "especially unlikely to be rewarded, . . . it would be necessary for the government or some other agency not governed by profit-and-loss criteria to finance research and invention."[96] Nathan

Rosenberg identifies two key factors: "Market incentives are insufficiently strong to generate the socially optimal amount of investment in research—because of nonappropriabilities and uncertainties." Because knowledge—once "on the shelf"—is regarded as a commodity even though its appropriation remains uncertain, investment in knowledge production presumes a degree of risk the private sector may be unwilling to undertake. Thus, "market forces do not provide strong incentives for the performance of research, especially basic research."[97] "Research costs money—lots of money," observes economist Paula Stephan, and the allocation of federal support for basic research comes with the recognition that scientific research is a public good. A baker makes money by selling his cakes, she explains, and symphony orchestras charge admission for their performances, but scientific researchers cannot readily appropriate the benefits of their work because once disseminated, knowledge may be shared: "It is particularly difficult to appropriate the benefits arising from basic research, which at best is years away from contributing to products that the market may or may not value," she elaborates. "Equally, if not more important, it is virtually impossible to appropriate the benefits that arise from the contribution that basic research makes to future fundamental research."[98]

With the onset of the Cold War, renewed emphasis on American competitiveness through scientific discovery and technological innovation underscored the imperative for continued federal investment in academic research. The terms of the relationship arguably entrenched the American research university in a set of objectives and values defined by the nexus of interests associated with the military-industrial complex, which has been characterized as the Cold War university. Federal investment in scientific research would lead to what historian Stuart W. Leslie termed a "university polarized around the military." With reference to what Senator J. William Fulbright called the "military-industrial-academic complex," Leslie writes, "The 'golden triangle' of military agencies, the high-technology industry, and research universities created a new kind of postwar science, one that blurred traditional distinctions between theory and practice, science and engineering, civilian and military, and classified and unclassified, one that owed its character as well as its contracts to the national security state."[99] The new scientific enterprise—what has been termed "Big Science"—is thus sometimes framed as a sort of Faustian bargain. It is alleged these institutions became "federalized," and the federalization process contributed to the narrowing of their research enterprises and the bureaucratization of science. A call for the reinvention of the American research university thus presumes negotiation of limitations imposed by the Cold War university model.

## Historical Perspective on the Scale of Higher Education in America

As both the oldest corporation and institution of higher education in the United States, Harvard epitomizes the legitimacy and authority that the sociologist J. Douglas Toma ascribes to prestigious colleges and universities in his discussion of institutional isomorphism: the paradoxical tendency for organizations and institutions to emulate one another and become increasingly homogeneous. Harvard is indeed prestigious, and inasmuch as prestige in academe correlates with profit in the corporate sector,[100] Harvard's wealth far exceeds its endowment and vast holdings. Beyond its redoubtable legacy of scientific and scholarly accomplishment, however, the extent of its worldly assets, unrivaled among American institutions, suggests the extent of the resources at the disposal of some of the institutions that represent the gold standard in American higher education. "The magnitude of the endowments that some institutions have is truly mind-boggling," writes economist Ronald G. Ehrenberg.[101] With an endowment recently valued at $36.4 billion, diminished from its pre-recession peak of $38.4 billion, Harvard is the most heavily endowed university in the nation and the wealthiest academic institution in the world. Its endowment trumps those of Yale ($20.8 billion), Princeton ($18.2 billion), and Stanford ($18.7 billion) by a comfortable margin,[102] and by one estimate exceeds the gross domestic product of Jordan.[103] "Wealth, like age, does not make a university great. But it helps." The insight comes from a 1963 Harvard admissions brochure.[104]

With 25 million square feet of academic and administrative quarters and research infrastructure, Harvard owns and operates more than 600 buildings that spill across more than 5,000 acres in Cambridge, surrounding areas in Boston, and elsewhere, including Dumbarton Oaks, in Washington, DC, and Villa I Tatti, near Florence and Fiesole. Harvard's libraries are repositories for over 17 million volumes, and its renowned collections in the visual arts, which total more than a quarter million objects, occupy three distinct museums—the Fogg, Busch-Reisinger, and Arthur M. Sackler—that, along with four research centers, operate collectively as the Harvard Art Museums. The Harvard Museums of Science and Culture comprise a consortium of world-class institutions, including the Peabody Museum of Archaeology and Ethnology and the Museum of Comparative Zoology.[105]

The Faculty of Arts and Sciences, one of eleven academic divisions, comprises Harvard College, which now offers undergraduates more than 3,000 courses in more than forty undergraduate areas of concentration, and the Graduate School, which offers fifty programs of study. The preeminence of the other divisions of the university—from business to design to divinity to engineering to government to law to medicine to public health and more—may be taken for granted. Academic centers, research institutes, and learned societies proliferate. Roughly 2,400 faculty members are recipients of countless international honors, and the roster of current and former faculty includes forty-four Nobel laureates. Twenty-nine heads of state have graduated from Harvard throughout its history, including eight U.S. presidents from John Adams to Barack Obama. Even though federally sponsored research expenditures at Harvard lag behind Johns Hopkins, which has led the nation in this regard for more than three decades, as well as more than two dozen other universities, during fiscal year 2013, these nevertheless totaled $639 million while nonfederal expenditures exceeded $182 million. University income exceeded $4.2 billion, which figure neatly matches reported university expenses.[106]

As the oldest and wealthiest university in America, Harvard may not be unequivocally representative of its institutional type, but we undertake this survey of its resources merely to suggest the scope and breadth of the set of American research universities. It is an immensely successful model that has produced institutional platforms that invariably combine world-class teaching and research with modest levels of enrollment. During the current academic year, for example, undergraduate enrollment numbers roughly 6,700.[107] At its 363rd commencement, which was observed in May 2014, Harvard College awarded 1,662 baccalaureate degrees.[108] In March 2014, Harvard College offered admission to 2,023 prospective students, which represents 5.9 percent of the pool of 34,295 applicants.[109] Of these, we estimate that approximately 1,600 were likely to enroll, based on the pattern of yields obtained during the preceding three academic years.

Harvard is by no means alone in modest levels of enrollment. We have corroborated the observation by Anthony Grafton that all of the students enrolled in all of the traditional liberal arts colleges combined would not fill the football stadium of a single Big Ten university, but the enrollments of some of our leading institutions bear further consideration. The Massachusetts Institute of Technology in fall term 2013 enrolled 4,528 undergraduate and 6,773 graduate students.[110] A three-to-one student-faculty ratio at Caltech comes by dint of enrollment of 997 undergraduates during the academic year 2012–2013, along with 1,253 graduate students.[111] Bard College enrolls roughly 2,000 undergraduates; Williams College about the same number; Bowdoin roughly 1,750; Swarthmore approximately 1,500. The drift for highly selective liberal arts colleges is obvious. Enrollments in public colleges and universities are normally far higher, of course. The entire student body of Harvard College corresponds roughly in number to the total of undergraduate degrees conferred yearly at the University of California, Berkeley,[112] for example, or the number of undergraduates enrolled in the School of Engineering at the University of Texas at Austin.[113] Research-grade universities generally count among their academic units undergraduate colleges of liberal arts and sciences that exceed in their enrollments the entire student bodies of most independent liberal arts colleges. Yet, even these institutions, public as well as private, have not scaled up their enrollment capacities commensurate to the demands of population growth. To some extent the entrenchment of the present model is a function of its success. Because the prestige of these institutions remains unrivaled, there is little incentive to seek change. As a consequence, these institutions have become so highly selective that the vast majority of academically qualified applicants are routinely excluded. The number of bachelor's degrees awarded by the eight institutions of the Ivy League during the academic year 2012–2013 totaled 15,541, while the top fifty liberal arts colleges awarded 23,672. In the same academic year, the Ivies rejected 222,279 applicants while the liberal arts colleges turned away 190,954.[114] If our leading research-grade universities deem it appropriate to maintain such limited enrollments, other institutional models must emerge that offer accessibility to academic platforms that promote knowledge production. At issue is a lack of scalability, especially for our public research universities, which serve greater numbers of first-generation and socioeconomically disadvantaged students but also advance the economic competitiveness of our nation through their integrated teaching and research enterprises.

When Harvard College enrolled its first class, the entire European population of the colonies numbered roughly 10,000. By the outbreak of the American Revolution, the population would reach 2.5 million, and by one estimate no more than 750 students were enrolled in nine colleges, which, apart from Harvard, were the institutions that would become Yale, Penn, Princeton, Columbia, Brown, and Dartmouth, as well as William and Mary and Rutgers. By 1800, the number of colleges had increased to eighteen, with enrollments totaling 1,150.[115] According to the census of 1840, 173 colleges in the nation enrolled roughly 16,000 students. With reference to the average enrollment per institution, one observer remarked: "It can be left to the imagination what kind of a faculty could be supported by ninety-three students or fewer."[116] Following the Civil War, the population of the nation soared to 39,818,000, and an estimated 52,286 students enrolled in 563 degree-granting institutions, which represented 0.13 percent of the population. By the end of the decade following the establishment of Johns Hopkins, the population numbered 50,189,000, and postsecondary enrollments in 811 institutions had more than doubled, totaling 115,817, which nevertheless still represented only 0.23 percent of the nation.[117]

Between 1890 and World War I, enrollments increased, while the number of new colleges established roughly matched the number that failed. The largest institutions dominated growth, with enrollments more than doubling during this period.[118] At the turn of the twentieth century, 977 institutions enrolled 238,000 students and by 1930 roughly 1,400 schools enrolled 1.1 million students.[119] The period between the World Wars has been termed the onset of mass higher education. Enrollments had doubled to 1.5 million by the outbreak of World War II, and for the first time, enrollment in public institutions exceeded the private sector. Yet, in 1939, still no more than 1.1 percent of the population was enrolled in college.[120] The postwar era may be divided neatly into two periods, as suggested by Menand: a period of expansion from 1945 to 1975 termed the Golden Age, and a period of diversification from 1975 to the present.[121] Undergraduate enrollment, including community colleges, increased fivefold from 1940 to 1970. Enrollments in graduate programs increased by nearly 900 percent: "The proportion of young people attending college tripled, from 15 to 45 percent," Geiger elaborates. "Beginning with the flood of returning soldiers . . . and concluding with the tidal wave of community college students in the early 1970s, this period was the most expansive in the American experience."[122] The scale of growth is neatly summarized by Menand: "In 1870, one out of every sixty men between eighteen and twenty-one years old was a college student; by 1900, one out of every twenty-five was in college . . . . In 1940, it was one out of every 6.5 . . . . Today, half of all Americans have some experience of college; 25 percent earn college degrees (associate's or bachelor's)."[123] Over the past quarter century, total enrollments in institutions of higher education has grown from under 13 million to more than 21 million.[124]

The "higher learning" in America may have begun with nine students and a single master at Harvard College in 1636, but postsecondary enrollment nationwide, including community colleges, exceeded 21 million in fall 2012, with 18.2 million undergraduates and 2.9 million graduate students.[125] Forty-five percent of all U.S. undergraduates attend a community college, according to the American Association of Community Colleges, with 4.6 million attending part-time.[126] Seventy-three percent of students attend public institutions. According to the U.S. Treasury report cited, the balance is apportioned accordingly: "Approximately 18 percent attend a private nonprofit college, a sector that ranges from research universities to small liberal arts colleges and specialized religious institutions. Approximately 9 percent attend a private for-profit (i.e., 'proprietary') institution." The report notes that enrollment in this latter sector has soared from 200,000 students at the end of the 1980s to more than 2 million.[127] The trajectory we have delineated suggests the incommensurability of the elitist model with the scale of the demand for higher education. This is especially the case if the objective is to provide the sort of competitive world-class education offered by research-grade institutions. In a nation with 18.2 million undergraduates, available seats in member institutions of the Association of American Universities is limited to 1.1 million students, as we observed in chapter 1, while the combined undergraduate enrollment of the 108 research-extensive universities, which includes all sixty AAU schools, numbers little more than 2 million.[128] With projections for shortfalls in the number of educated workers coupled with estimates that population growth will likely exceed 100 million by mid-century, limitation in the scalability of American higher education is not an issue to be relegated to the back burner.

Every institution is embedded in and contingent on a particular juncture in the historical continuum of a society. Our contemporary colleges and universities are heirs to a venerable lineage, which in the West may be traced to the eleventh or twelfth centuries and earlier to antecedent institutional forms such as the monastery and cathedral schools of the Middle Ages and even the academies of classical antiquity.[129] The platforms or frameworks for these knowledge formations have been characterized both by periods of stasis and episodes of incremental evolution. Organizations adapt to environments according to proponents of ecological theories of institutional or organizational change. Natural selection models of institutional evolution focus on contingencies of fitness to environments to explain change. Corollary theories attempt to explain structural inertia and resistance to change.[130] The process of institutional evolution is ongoing, and the point is that colleges and universities operate in an evolutionarily complex arena, just like any other organizational type. At the same time, there are schools that even today resemble the elite colleges of colonial New England and others that remain entrenched in their nineteenth-century configurations. But institutional evolution must be appreciated in the broader context of the democratic experiment still underway following more than two centuries of tumultuous progress.

To the extent that a research university embraces an explicit commitment to innovation and thus evolves into an academic enterprise, the institution expands its objectives beyond the traditional roles of knowledge production (research) and dissemination (teaching). It is in this sense that we refer to the New American University model as a comprehensive knowledge enterprise. Henry Etzkowitz captures something of the sense of this model with his concept of an "entrepreneurial university" and in the following formulation alludes to the reorganization requisite to the accommodation of its expanded mission: "As the university takes on a new role in society, it undergoes internal changes to integrate new functions and relationships. The 'inner logic' of the original academic mission has been widened from knowledge conservation (education) to include also knowledge creation (research) and then application of this new knowledge (entrepreneurship)." Application of knowledge in this sense assumes academic engagement with industry and government—what Etzkowitz terms the "triple helix" of innovation, which we consider more fully in chapter 4 and again in the case study in chapter 7. Moreover, to the extent that a public university redefines itself as an academic enterprise, it rejects designation as an agency, a bureaucratic category, the implications of which we consider in the following chapter. In this context, Etzkowitz elaborates: "Each successive academic organizational innovation has given the university an enhanced ability to set its own strategic direction.[131]

The evolutionary trajectory of universities in the Western world can be modeled as a set of hypothetical coordinates spanning four quadrants (figure 13). Movement along the $x$-axis represents expansion in the scale of the institution, referring to its breadth of functionality. If an institution embraces the scope of a comprehensive knowledge enterprise, its commitment to innovation will complement its traditional roles and underscore its focus on the public good. Scale thus refers both to intellectual, or pedagogical, and functional breadth. The movement described by the $y$-axis, meanwhile, reflects the orientation of the institution toward academic enterprise. At the bottom of the $y$-axis, one finds what organizational theorists call conserving institutions: inwardly focused, risk-averse, and concerned primarily with self-preservation. Innovation is unlikely to flourish in an institutional culture steeped in orthodoxy, which may flounder in a competitive academic landscape rife with the forces of creative destruction. Their entrepreneurial counterparts—institutions willing to adapt, innovate, and take risks in rethinking their identities and roles—are represented in the upper quadrants.

The New American University thus appears in the upper right quadrant, which is reserved for vanguard institutions explicitly committed to innovation.[132] The parabolic segment represents the various points such an institution may occupy. The upward trajectory represents research-grade universities that focus on facilitating innovation, while the horizontal trajectory those committed to increasing their scale and accessibility. The objective in propounding this new and differentiated model for the American research university is to offer an alternative—a complement—to the set of traditional gold standard institutions. The new model establishes the conditions for substantive and

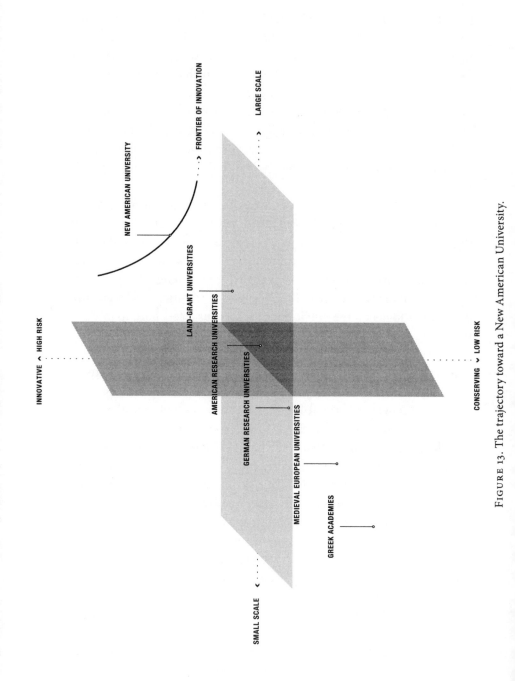

FIGURE 13. The trajectory toward a New American University.

rapid rather than incremental and cumulative change. Because the new model disrupts inertia and stasis, its implementation offers the potential to unleash the revolutionary change characteristic of punctuated equilibrium.[133]

## Notes

1. http://www.college.harvard.edu/icb/icb.do?keyword=k61161&tabgroupid=icb.tabgroup84748

2. Chapter 2 contains revised and expanded sections from our coauthored book chapter, Michael M. Crow and William B. Dabars, "University-Based Research and Economic Development: The Morrill Act and the Emergence of the American Research University," in *Precipice or Crossroads: Where America's Great Public Universities Stand and Where They Are Going Midway through Their Second Century*, ed. Daniel Mark Fogel (Albany: State University of New York Press, 2012), 119–158.

3. For background on the intellectual milieu of Baltimore in this era, see Louis Menand, *The Metaphysical Club: A Story of Ideas in America* (New York: Farrar, Straus and Giroux, 2001), 255–284.

4. Edward Shils, "The Order of Learning in the United States: The Ascendency of the University," in *The Organization of Knowledge in Modern America, 1860–1920*, ed. Alexandra Oleson and John Voss (Baltimore: Johns Hopkins University Press, 1979), 28–29; Roger L. Geiger, *To Advance Knowledge: The Growth of American Research Universities, 1900–1940* (Oxford: Oxford University Press, 1986), 7.

5. Roger L. Geiger, "Milking the Sacred Cow: Research and the Quest for Useful Knowledge in the American University since 1920," *Science, Technology, and Human Values* 13, no. 3 and 4 (Summer and Autumn, 1988): 332.

6. Geiger, "Milking the Sacred Cow," 333–334.

7. Nannerl O. Keohane, "The American Campus: From Colonial Seminary to Global Multiversity," Wolfson College Lectures ("The Idea of a University"), Oxford University (February 3, 1998), 5.

8. Clark Kerr, *The Uses of the University*, 5th ed. (1963; Cambridge, MA: Harvard University Press, 2001), 10–11.

9. University College London and King's College London, established respectively in 1826 and 1829, conjoined in 1836 to form the federated University of London. For a historical overview of the practice of federation, see Sheldon Rothblatt, "Historical and Comparative Remarks on the Federal Principle in Higher Education," *History of Education* 16, no. 3 (1987): 151–180. Although many colleges and other institutions of higher learning obviously flourished prior to the nineteenth century in England, only a royal charter permitted the new university to confer degrees, and thus its claim to be the third oldest university in the realm must be understood in this administrative context. Nineteen institutions today comprise the University of London federation, which apart from University College London and King's College London includes such heterogeneous and differentiated institutions as the London School of Economics, London School of

Hygiene and Tropical Medicine, School of Oriental and African Studies, and Royal Academy of Music. For an overview of the federated London system, see Negley Harte, *The University of London, 1836–1986* (London: Athlone Press, 1986).

10. Jonathan R. Cole, *The Great American University: Its Rise to Preeminence, Its Indispensable National Role, and Why It Must Be Protected* (New York: Public Affairs, 2009), 18.

11. Arthur M. Cohen, *The Shaping of American Higher Education: Emergence and the Growth of the Contemporary System*, 2nd ed. (San Francisco: Jossey-Bass, 2010), 70.

12. William Clark, *Academic Charisma and the Origins of the Research University* (Chicago: University of Chicago Press, 2006), 28.

13. Kerr, *Uses of the University*, 1.

14. Bill Readings, *The University in Ruins* (Cambridge, MA: Harvard University Press, 1996), 62.

15. Hanna Holborn Gray, *Searching for Utopia: Universities and Their Histories* (Berkeley: University of California Press, 2012), 39–40.

16. John Henry Newman, *The Idea of a University* (Notre Dame: University of Notre Dame Press, 1982), xxxvii. Reprint of the so-called "definitive edition" published by Longmans, Green, and Company, 1873.

17. Cole, *Great American University*, 17.

18. Frank H. T. Rhodes, *The Creation of the Future: The Role of the American University* (Ithaca, NY: Cornell University Press, 2001), 43.

19. Menand, *Metaphysical Club*, 256; Elinor S. Shaffer, "Romantic Philosophy and the Organization of the Disciplines: The Founding of the Humboldt University of Berlin," in *Romanticism and the Sciences*, ed. Andrew Cunningham and Nicholas Jardine (Cambridge: Cambridge University Press, 1990), 38.

20. Gray, *Searching for Utopia*, 40–41.

21. Shaffer, "Romantic Philosophy and the Organization of the Disciplines," 38–39.

22. Josef Bleicher, "Bildung," *Theory, Culture, and Society* 23 (2006): 364–365.

23. Shaffer, "Romantic Philosophy and the Organization of the Disciplines," 38–39.

24. Jeffrey M. Peck, "Berlin and Constance: Two Models of Reform and Their Hermeneutic and Pedagogical Relevance," *German Quarterly* 60, no. 3 (Summer 1987): 392.

25. In 1949, the University of Berlin was renamed Humboldt-Universität in recognition of Wilhelm von Humboldt and his brother, the naturalist Alexander von Humboldt. According to Mitchell G. Ash, because the name Humboldt is associated with academic ideals, its invocation was in part motivated by a professoriate asserting the values of "socialist humanism" in the German Democratic Republic. See Ash, "Bachelor of What, Master of Whom? The Humboldt Myth and Historical Transformations of Higher Education in German-Speaking Europe and the United States," *European Journal of Education* 41, no. 2 (2006): 253.

26. Kerr, *Uses of the University*, 8–9.

27. Clark Kerr, *Higher Education Cannot Escape History: Issues for the Twenty-First Century* (Albany: SUNY Press, 1994), quoted by Frank Albritton, "Humboldt's Unity of

Research and Teaching: Influence on the Philosophy and Development of U.S. Higher Education" (October 2006), available at SSRN: http://ssrn.com/abstract=939811 or http://dx.doi.org/10.2139/ssrn.939811.

28. Shaffer, "Romantic Philosophy and the Organization of the Disciplines," 38–39.

29. Charles E. McClelland, *State, Society, and University in Germany, 1700–1914* (Cambridge: Cambridge University Press, 1980), 105.

30. At issue were administrative concerns but also new conceptions of the unity of knowledge put forth by Schelling and his peers. Reform entailed the imperative to reconceptualize universities to reflect what Shaffer describes as a "Romantic idealist conception of knowledge and the relations among the disciplines." Schelling thus intended that the "ultimate unity of knowledge" inform the practical arrangements of the new university in Berlin. In a series of lectures he presciently contended that this organicist conception should determine the "actual structure of our universities today, in order that the unity of the whole may reemerge amid the widespread specialization." Shaffer, "Romantic Philosophy and the Organization of the Disciplines," 41.

31. Shaffer, "Romantic Philosophy and the Organization of the Disciplines," 41–48; quotation from F. W. J. Schelling, *Lectures on the Method of Academic Studies,* trans. E. S. Morgan, ed. Norbert Guterman (Athens, OH, 1966).

32. Shaffer, "Romantic Philosophy and the Organization of the Disciplines," 41–48.

33. McClelland, *State, Society, and University in Germany,* 2, 122–124.

34. Sven-Eric Liedman, "General Education in Germany and Sweden," in *The European and American University since 1800: Historical and Sociological Essays,* ed. Sheldon Rothblatt and Björn Wittrock (Cambridge: Cambridge University Press, 1993), 82, 123–124.

35. Ash, "Bachelor of What, Master of Whom?," 245–253. See also R. D. Anderson, "Before and After Humboldt: European Universities between the Eighteenth and Nineteenth Centuries," *History of Higher Education Annual* 20 (2000): 5–14.

36. Wolfram W. Swoboda, "Disciplines and Interdisciplinarity: A Historical Perspective," in Joseph J. Kockelmans, ed., *Interdisciplinarity and Higher Education* (University Park: Pennsylvania State University Press, 1979), 56–59. Swoboda contends that until the advent of the new scientific academies, which were deliberately organized to pursue new knowledge, research was deemed "extracurricular."

37. Peter Weingart, "A Short History of Knowledge Formations," in *The Oxford Handbook of Interdisciplinarity* (Oxford: Oxford University Press, 2010), 7.

38. Ash, "Bachelor of What, Master of Whom?," 246–247.

39. Menand, *Metaphysical Club,* 256.

40. Hugh Davis Graham and Nancy Diamond, *The Rise of American Research Universities: Elites and Challengers in the Postwar Era* (Baltimore: Johns Hopkins University Press, 1997), 19.

41. Cole, *Great American University,* 29–30.

42. Allen Nevins, *The State Universities and Democracy* (Urbana: University of Illinois Press, 1962), 26, nn. 3, 27, cited in Eugene M. Tobin, "The Modern Evolution of

America's Flagship Universities," Appendix A in William G. Bowen, Matthew M. Chingos, and Michael S. McPherson, *Crossing the Finish Line: Completing College at America's Public Universities* (Princeton, NJ: Princeton University Press, 2009), 320, n. 3. Nevins offers the following account of the establishment of the land-grant institutions: "Of the institutions benefited by the Morrill land grants, seventeen had been founded (often feebly) before 1862; eighteen more before the end of 1865; and sixteen others before the end of 1870." The Morrill Act is officially designated the Act of July 2, 1862, ch. 130, 12 Stat. 503, 7 U.S.C. 301 et seq.

43. Nathan Rosenberg and Richard R. Nelson, "American Universities and Technical Advance in Industry," *Research Policy* 23, no. 3 (1994): 323–348.

44. Richard C. Atkinson and William A. Blanpied, "Research Universities: Core of the U.S. Science and Technology System," *Technology in Society* 30 (2008): 33.

45. Tobin, "Modern Evolution of America's Flagship Universities," 320.

46. Association of Public and Land-Grant Universities (APLU), "Land-Grant Heritage," http://www.aplu.org. For a list of member institutions in the Association of American Universities (AAU), comprising sixty-one leading research universities in the United States and Canada, see http://www.aau.edu/about/.

47. John R. Thelin, *A History of American Higher Education* (Baltimore: Johns Hopkins University Press, 2004), 75–77. Thelin explains that the distribution of federal land, widely misunderstood to be "literal gifts of land on which a state government would build a college" in reality represented a "complex partnership in which the federal government provided incentives for each state to sell distant Western lands," with the obligation to apply profits realized toward the establishment of collegiate institutions.

48. Thelin, *History of American Higher Education,* 76. The focus on agriculture, mechanics, mining, and military instruction would lead to the designation A&M in the names of a number of such institutions, Thelin explains.

49. Rosenberg and Nelson, "American Universities and Technical Advance in Industry," 323–348.

50. Enrico Moretti, "Estimating the Social Return to Higher Education: Evidence from Longitudinal and Repeated Cross-Sectional Data," *Journal of Econometrics* 121 (2004): 190. Additional perspective comes with the estimate that the public research universities of our nation taken together have produced more than 70 percent of all baccalaureate degree recipients and conduct two-thirds of all funded research. See Peter McPherson et al., "Competitiveness of Public Research Universities and Consequences for the Country: Recommendations for Change," NASULGC Discussion Paper Working Draft (2009).

51. Alexandra Oleson and John Voss, eds., introduction to *The Organization of Knowledge in Modern America, 1860–1920* (Baltimore: Johns Hopkins University Press, 1979), xii.

52. A concise discussion of federal support for American higher education is to be found in Atkinson and Blanpied, "Research Universities: Core of the U.S. Science and Technology System," 30–48. See also Roger L. Geiger, *Research and Relevant Knowl-*

*edge: American Research Universities since World War II* (Oxford: Oxford University Press, 1993).

53. Thelin, *History of American Higher Education*, 76; Oleson and Voss, *Organization of Knowledge in Modern America*, xii.

54. Nathan Rosenberg, "America's Entrepreneurial Universities," in *The Emergence of Entrepreneurship Policy: Governance, Start-ups, and Growth in the U.S. Knowledge Economy*, ed. David M. Hart (Cambridge: Cambridge University Press, 2003), 113–114, 116; Rosenberg and Nelson, "American Universities and Technical Advance in Industry," 326.

55. *Reports on the Course of Instruction in Yale College, by a Committee of the Corporation and the Academical Faculty* (New Haven, CT: Hezekiah Howe, 1828), quoted by David L. Kirp, *Shakespeare, Einstein, and the Bottom Line: The Marketing of Higher Education* (Cambridge, MA: Harvard University Press, 2003), 256.

56. Caroline Winterer, *The Culture of Classicism: Ancient Greece and Rome in American Intellectual Life, 1780–1910* (Baltimore: Johns Hopkins University Press, 2002), 10.

57. Laurence R. Veysey, *The Emergence of the American University* (Chicago: University of Chicago Press, 1965), 61–66.

58. Shils, "Order of Learning in the United States," 28.

59. Henry Steck, "Corporatization of the University: Seeking Conceptual Clarity," *Annals of the American Academy of Political and Social Science* 585 (2003): 73.

60. Rosenberg and Nelson, "American Universities and Technical Advance in Industry," 325.

61. By 1901, University of California president Benjamin Ide Wheeler could thus proclaim, "A university is a place that rightfully knows no aristocracy as between studies, no aristocracy as between scientific truths, and no aristocracy as between persons." Wheeler, "University Democracy," *University Chronicle* XV (Berkeley, 1901), 2, cited in Veysey, *Emergence of the American University*, 66.

62. Rosenberg and Nelson, "American Universities and Technical Advance in Industry," 324–325.

63. Veysey, *Emergence of the American University*, 82–86, cited by Geiger, *To Advance Knowledge*, 6.

64. Earle D. Ross, *Democracy's College: The Land-Grant Movement in the Formative Stage* (Ames: Iowa State College Press, 1942).

65. Veysey, *Emergence of the American University*; Atkinson and Blanpied, "Research Universities: Core of the U.S. Science and Technology System," 33.

66. David C. Mowery et al., *Ivory Tower and Industrial Innovation: University-Industry Technology Transfer Before and After the Bayh-Dole Act* (Stanford: Stanford University Press, 2004), 9.

67. Alexis de Tocqueville, *Democracy in America* (Boston: John Allyn, 1876), vol. 2, 48, 52–53, cited in Rosenberg and Nelson, "American Universities and Technical Advance in Industry," 324.

68. Morrill Act of 1862, sect. 4, cited in National Association of State Universities and Land-Grant Colleges, "The Land-Grant Tradition" (Washington, DC: NASULGC, 2008), 5.

69. Walter P. Metzger, "The Academic Profession in the United States," in *The Academic Profession: National, Disciplinary, and Institutional Settings*, ed. Burton R. Clark (Berkeley: University of California Press, 1987), 129.

70. Rosenberg and Nelson, "American Universities and Technical Advance in Industry," 327.

71. Henry Etzkowitz, "Research Groups as Quasi-Firms: The Invention of the Entrepreneurial University," *Research Policy* 32 (2003): 110.

72. R. D. Anderson, *Universities and Elites in Britain since 1800* (Cambridge: Cambridge University Press, 1995), 4–5.

73. Nicholas Lemann, "The Soul of the Research University," *Chronicle of Higher Education* (April 28, 2014).

74. Harte, *The University of London, 1836–1986*. The entrenchment of elitism in British higher education is apparent even in the distinction historically observed between a "college" and a "university," Sheldon Rothblatt explains. While the undergraduate experience is associated with affiliation with "private" residential colleges—thirty-eight colleges comprise Oxford University, for example—only "public" bodies such as universities are chartered with the authority to grant degrees. Rothblatt is eloquent regarding the implications of privilege inherent in this distinction: "The first was that the essence of a university in England was the experience of a college, and the essence of a college was the private relationships and friendships that were formed within it—examinations, degrees, and all other such means of self-promotion being crass, illiberal, and denaturing. The second was that a university was impersonal, distant, and vaguely administrative: its task was to collect fees, publish calendars, set examinations, [and] award degrees." Moreover, degrees in this milieu were regarded as mere certificates of competence essential only to those seeking to enhance their social position and career prospects: "It therefore followed that a gentleman had an obligation to resist any external attempt to alienate his personality, such as the introduction of competitive examinations into the university curriculum in the late eighteenth and early nineteenth centuries." Rothblatt, "Historical and Comparative Remarks on the Federal Principle in Higher Education," 152–154.

75. Ash, "Bachelor of What, Master of Whom?," 248.

76. Douglas W. Allen, *The Institutional Revolution: Measurement and the Economic Emergence of the Modern World* (Chicago: University of Chicago Press, 2012), 13. For an assessment of the development of statistical analysis, see Theodore M. Porter, *The Rise of Statistical Thinking, 1820–1900* (Princeton, NJ: Princeton University Press, 1986).

77. Albert Castel, "The Founding Fathers and the Vision of a National University," *History of Education Quarterly* 4, no. 4 (December 1964): 281–282.

78. David Madsen, *The National University: Enduring Dream of the United States* (Detroit: Michigan State University Press, 1966): 15–24. During his presidency, Madison urged the establishment of a national university during four annual addresses, according to John R. Thelin. A bill to create such an institution brought before Congress in 1817 was defeated, however, by the House of Representatives. See Thelin, *History of American Higher Education*, 42.

79. Graham and Diamond, *Rise of American Research Universities*, 9.

80. Graham and Diamond, *Rise of American Research Universities*, 9, 12–15.

81. Michael Mumper et al., "The Federal Government and Higher Education," in *American Higher Education in the Twenty-First Century: Social, Political, and Economic Challenges*, 3rd ed., ed. Philip G. Altbach et al. (Baltimore: Johns Hopkins University Press, 2011), 113–138.

82. A useful overview of European systems of higher education is to be found in the volume *University Governance: Western European Comparative Perspectives*, ed. Catherine Paradeise et al. (Dordrecht: Springer, 2009).

83. Atkinson and Blanpied, "Research Universities: Core of the U.S. Science and Technology System," 41–43.

84. Atkinson and Blanpied, "Research Universities: Core of the U.S. Science and Technology System," 30–48. See also Geiger, *Research and Relevant Knowledge*, 3–29; Graham and Diamond, *Rise of American Research Universities*, 9.

85. David H. Guston and Kenneth Keniston, "The Social Contract for Science," in *The Fragile Contract: University Science and the Federal Government*, ed. Guston and Keniston (Cambridge, MA: MIT Press, 1994), 1–2.

86. Graham and Diamond, *Rise of American Research Universities*, 9–25.

87. Roger L. Geiger, "Science, Universities, and National Defense, 1945–1970," *Osiris* 2nd series, 1992, no. 7: 26–27; Dwight D. Eisenhower, "Farewell Address to the Nation" (January 17, 1961), Public Papers of the Presidents (1960): 1035–1040.

88. Mumper et al., "The Federal Government and Higher Education," 113–118.

89. G. Pascal Zachary, *Endless Frontier: Vannevar Bush, Engineer of the American Century* (Cambridge, MA: MIT Press, 1999), 223. "The popularity of Frederick Jackson Turner's 'frontier' thesis—that the ability to expand into new geographical frontiers sustained American democracy—meant that opinion leaders were acutely susceptible to Bush's argument," Zachary observes (442, n. 14).

90. For a comprehensive overview and history of the origins and development of the system of federal laboratories, see Peter J. Westwick, *The National Labs: Science in an American System, 1947–1974* (Cambridge, MA: Harvard University Press, 2003). See also Michael M. Crow and Barry Bozeman, *Limited by Design: R&D Laboratories in the U.S. National Innovation System* (New York: Columbia University Press, 1998).

91. Atkinson and Blanpied, "Research Universities: Core of the U.S. Science and Technology System," 38.

92. Roger L. Geiger, "Organized Research Units: Their Role in the Development of University Research," *Journal of Higher Education* 61, no. 1 (January/February 1990): 1.

93. Cole, *Great American University*, 100.

94. Vannevar Bush, *Science—The Endless Frontier: A Report to the President on a Program for Postwar Scientific Research* (Washington, DC: U.S. Government Printing Office, 1945), ch. 3.

95. Richard R. Nelson, "The Simple Economic of Basic Scientific Research," *Journal of Political Economy* 67, no. 3 (1959): 302.

96. Kenneth J. Arrow, "Economic Welfare and the Allocation of Resources for Invention," in *The Rate and Direction of Inventive Activity: Economic and Social Factors*,

ed. Richard R. Nelson (Cambridge, MA: National Bureau of Economic Research, 1962), 618, 623.

97. Nathan Rosenberg, "Why Do Firms Do Basic Research (with Their Own Money)?" *Research Policy* 19 (1990): 165–174.

98. Paula Stephan, *How Economics Shapes Science* (Cambridge, MA: Harvard University Press, 2012), 111–112.

99. Stuart W. Leslie, *The Cold War and American Science: The Military-Industrial-Academic Complex at MIT and Stanford* (New York: Columbia University Press, 1993), 2. See also Rebecca S. Lowen, *Creating the Cold War University: The Transformation of Stanford* (Berkeley: University of California Press, 1997); and the collection of essays edited by Noam Chomsky, *The Cold War and the University: Toward an Intellectual History of the Postwar Years* (New York: New Press, 1997).

100. J. Douglas Toma, "Institutional Strategy: Positioning for Prestige," in *The Organization of Higher Education: Managing Colleges for a New Era*, ed. Michael N. Bastedo (Baltimore: Johns Hopkins University Press, 2012).

101. Ronald G. Ehrenberg, *Tuition Rising: Why College Costs So Much* (Cambridge, MA: Harvard University Press, 2000), 36. Ehrenberg offered his appraisal based on market values of endowments on June 30, 1997, when the figure for Harvard approached $11 billion.

102. *Chronicle of Higher Education*, "Year-by-Year Comparison of College and University Endowments, 2007–2012" (February 1, 2013), http://chronicle.com/article/Year -by-Year-Comparison-of/136935/; National Association of College and University Business Officers and Commonfund Institute, "U.S. and Canadian Institutions Listed by Fiscal Year 2013 Endowment Market Value and Change in Endowment Market Value from FY 2012 to FY 2013."

103. "America's Ten Richest Universities Match These Countries' GDPs," *New Republic* (April 30, 2014).

104. *Information about Harvard College for Prospective Students* 60 (September 5, 1963), 1–2, quoted in Thelin, *History of American Higher Education*, xxi.

105. Harvard University, Office of Institutional Research, *Harvard University Fact Book* 2010–2011 and 2011–2012, http://www.provost.harvard.edu/institutional_research /factbook.php; "Harvard at a Glance," http://www.harvard.edu/harvard-glance; http:// www.harvardartmuseums.org/; http://hmsc.harvard.edu/.

106. *Harvard University Fact Book*, http://oir.harvard.edu/fact-book/sponsored_ research; "Harvard at a Glance," http://www.harvard.edu/harvard-glance.

107. "Harvard at a Glance," http://www.harvard.edu/harvard-glance. Graduate and professional students attending Harvard currently number approximately 14,500, or more than twice its undergraduate population and about the same as the number of graduate students attending the University of Michigan. University of Michigan Office of Budget and Planning, "Common Data Set 2012–2013," 1, http://sitemaker.umich.edu /obpinfo/files/umaa_cds_2013.pdf.

108. *Harvard Gazette*, "7,334 Degrees, Certificates Awarded at Harvard's 363rd Commencement" (May 29, 2014).

109. *Harvard Gazette,* "College Admits Class of '18" (March 27, 2014).

110. http://web.mit.edu/registrar/stats/yrpts/index.html

111. http://www.caltech.edu/content/glance

112. http://opa.berkeley.edu/statistics/UndergraduateProfile.pdf

113. "Cockrell School of Engineering Facts & Figures, 2012–2013," http://www.engr.utexas.edu/about/facts.

114. Academic year 2012–2013 data is the most recent available from IPEDS (Integrated Postsecondary Education Data System). Assessment of top fifty liberal arts colleges derived from the 2015 *U.S. News & World Report* ranking excluding military academies. Analysis for University Innovation Alliance by Archer Analytics LLC.

115. William G. Bowen, Martin A. Kurzweil, and Eugene M. Tobin, *Equity and Excellence in American Higher Education* (Charlottesville: University of Virginia Press, 2006), 13.

116. Richard Hofstadter and C. DeWitt Hardy, *The Development and Scope of Higher Education in the United States* (New York: Columbia University Press for the Commission on Financing Higher Education, 1952), 119, quoted in Cohen, *Shaping of American Higher Education,* 69. Cohen makes the points that such estimates are imprecise because institutions often reorganized, changed names, or folded (63).

117. U.S. Department of Education, National Center for Education Statistics, Table 197: Historical summary of faculty, students, degrees, and finances in degree-granting institutions: selected years 1869–1870 through 2009–2010.

118. Roger L. Geiger, "The Ten Generations of American Higher Education," in *Higher Education in the Twenty-First Century: Social, Political, and Economic Challenges,* 3rd ed., ed. Philip G. Altbach, Robert O. Berdahl, and Patricia J. Gumport (Baltimore: Johns Hopkins University Press, 1999), 52. Geiger observes that the ten largest institutions averaged 2,000 students in 1895, and two decades later, that figure had grown to 5,000.

119. Louis Menand, *The Marketplace of Ideas: Reform and Resistance in the American University* (New York: W. W. Norton, 2010), 100. The trend is corroborated by the growth of the professoriate. Menand reports: "There were 5,553 professors in the United States in 1870; in 1890, there were 15,809; in 1930, there were 23,868."

120. Paul E. Lingenfelter, "The Financing of Public Colleges and Universities in the United States," in *Handbook of Research in Education Finance and Policy,* ed. Helen F. Ladd and Edward B. Fiske (New York: Routledge, 2008), 651–654.

121. Menand, *Marketplace of Ideas,* 63–64.

122. Geiger, "The Ten Generations of American Higher Education," 58–59, cited by Menand, *Marketplace of Ideas,* 64.

123. Menand, *Marketplace of Ideas,* 48, n. 26.

124. Thomas D. Snyder and Sally A. Dillow, *Digest of Education Statistics 2011,* table 279: Degrees conferred by degree-granting institutions, by level of degree and sex of student: Selected years, 1869–70 through 2019–20 (Washington, DC: National Center for Education Statistics, Institute of Education Sciences, U.S. Department of Education, 2012); U.S. Department of Treasury with the U.S. Department of Education, "The Economics of Higher Education" (Washington, DC, December 2012).

125. S. A. Ginder and J. E. Kelly-Reid, *Enrollment in Postsecondary Institutions, Fall 2012: First Look (Provisional Data)* (Washington, DC: National Center for Education Statistics, 2013), http://nces.ed.gove/pubsearch, table 1.

126. American Association of Community Colleges, *2014 Fact Sheet.*

127. Snyder and Dillow, *Digest of Education Statistics 2011*, table 279: Degrees conferred by degree-granting institutions, by level of degree and sex of student: Selected years, 1869–70 through 2019–20; U.S. Department of Treasury with the U.S. Department of Education, "The Economics of Higher Education;" Ginder and Kelly-Reid, *Enrollment in Postsecondary Institutions, Fall 2012*, table 1.

128. Association of American Universities, "AAU by the Numbers" (April 2013), https://www.aau.edu/WorkArea/DownloadAsset.aspx?id=13460; Carnegie Foundation for the Advancement of Teaching, Summary Tables: Distribution of institutions and enrollments by classification category, based on IPEDS fall enrollment 2009, which remains the most recent available data, http://classifications.carnegiefoundation.org/summary /basic.php.

129. "Our universities are an original creation of the Middle Ages," writes the philologist Ernst Robert Curtius. "Nowhere in the antique world were there any such associations, with their privileges, their established curriculum, their hierarchy of degrees (bachelor, licentiate, master, doctor)." Curtius, *European Literature and the Latin Middle Ages*, trans. Willard R. Trask (1952; Princeton: Princeton University Press, 2013), 54. The classic account of the earliest universities is still to be found in Hastings Rashdall, *The Universities of Europe in the Middle Ages* (Oxford: Oxford University Press, 1895).

130. See, for example, Michael T. Hannan and John Freeman, "Structural Inertia and Organizational Change," *American Sociological Review* 49 (April 1984): 149–164; Howard E. Aldrich and Jeffrey Pfeffer, "Environments of Organizations," *Annual Review of Sociology* 2, no. 1 (1976): 79–105.

131. Henry Etzkowitz, *The Triple Helix: University-Industry-Government Innovation in Action* (New York: Routledge, 2008), 33.

132. Michael M. Crow, "The Research University as Comprehensive Knowledge Enterprise: A Prototype for a New American University," in *University Research for Innovation*, ed. Luc E. Weber and James J. Duderstadt (London: Economica, 2010).

133. For discussions of the theory of punctuated equilibrium applied to organizational change, see Elaine Romanelli and Michael L. Tushman, "Organizational Transformation as Punctuated Equilibrium," *Academy of Management Journal* 37, no. 5 (1994): 1141–1166; C. J. G. Gersick, "Revolutionary Change Theories: A Multilevel Exploration of the Punctuated Equilibrium Paradigm," *Academy of Management Review* 16, no. 1: 10–36; Karl E. Weick and Robert E. Quinn, "Organizational Change and Development," *Annual Review of Psychology* 50 (1999): 361–386.

# THREE

# The Varieties of Academic Tradition

"College is our American pastoral," muses literary scholar Andrew Delbanco in his defense of elite liberal arts colleges—notwithstanding, as he concedes, that today "only a small fraction will attend college in anything like the traditional sense of the word."[1] And indeed, both the profiles of the American undergraduate and institutions themselves have undergone more than incremental change with the demographic reconfiguration of contemporary society. Tradition nevertheless endures in our colleges and universities, and when Delbanco speaks of the "traditional sense" of college, one may assume he is referring to the organization and practices of a particular sector of American higher education: the selective liberal arts colleges and major research universities that represent the gold standard in American higher education. An anecdote about President Dwight D. Eisenhower recounted by historian John Thelin captures the sense of nostalgia evoked by academic tradition. When he visited the idyllic Georgian campus of Dartmouth College in 1953, Eisenhower is said to have exclaimed, "Why, this is how I always thought a college should look!"[2]

Reverence for tradition has been integral to human consciousness across cultures over the course of civilization. Even though concern for survival is what brought together our forebears into settlements roughly fifteen thousand years ago, historian David Gross observes that "what bound them together culturally and emotionally . . . was the glue of tradition." Across six hundred generations, by his estimate, these "constellations of beliefs . . . defined values, established continuities, and codified patterns of behavior." But inasmuch as this mode of thinking is perpetually oriented toward the past, its potential to become an impediment to

the production of knowledge becomes readily apparent: "Tradition encouraged attitudes of piety and reverence toward what was inherited from
the past, . . . produced respect for authority (with the authoritative always
understood as the accumulated wisdom of the past), . . . . and helped af-
firm the notion that one had to look backward toward some distant origin to find the source of all value." Inasmuch as received ideas represent
dogma and doctrine, Gross points out, tradition may be pernicious to the
exercise of reason and the advancement of science. As a champion of the
empiricism that would come to define scientific method, Francis Bacon
thus inveighed against its "insidious preconceptions."[3]

"Our age is retrospective," Ralph Waldo Emerson famously observed.
"It builds the sepulchres of the fathers." To this he added the pertinent
question "Why should not we also enjoy an original relation to the universe?" Emerson thus demanded a "poetry and philosophy of insight and
not of tradition" and asked, "Why should we grope among the dry bones
of the past?"[4] But tradition does not refer merely to constraint, especially
if one thinks of the emergence of new knowledge as grounded in or contingent on its production and dissemination across the centuries. In this
sense, tradition represents the intellectual lineage or genealogy of knowledge passed down across successive generations, which constitutes the
vital genetic code of the academy. Any scholar or scientist has inevitably "seen farther than others" because he or she is always "standing on
the shoulders of giants," to cite the celebrated observation of Sir Isaac
Newton to his colleague in the Royal Society, Robert Hooke, from a letter dated February 5, 1676.[5] Nor does tradition necessarily imply consensus: "Traditions are not unified, but sites of contestation," the philosopher Michael Bacon observes. Thus, the advancement of knowledge
comes "through critical engagement with competing and even incompatible elements within traditions."[6]

But tradition has a dark side as well, and unquestioning conformity
to its thrall has every potential to become pernicious. There is a term for
this sort of excessive veneration of tradition, and it is *filiopietism*. The
word derives from the adjective *filial* and the noun *piety* and remarkably
appears only in adjectival form in the *Oxford English Dictionary*, where
*filio-pietistic* is defined as "marked by an excess of filial piety."[7] Filiopietism could manifest, for example, as an uncritical approach to the sort

of "great books" survey of knowledge advocated by Robert Maynard
Hutchins, which, as Clark Kerr pointed out, assumes that the "great ideas
have already been discovered and written down, and that the main purpose of education is to pass on the traditional wisdom to future generations."[8] But, more broadly, we succumb to filiopietism when we assume
we have no choice but to accept the status quo because that is just the way
things are done. Louis Menand gets at what we mean here with reference
to the present context with the following observation:

> One thing about systems, especially systems as old as American higher ed-
> ucation, is that people grow unconscious of them. The system gets internal-
> ized. It becomes a mind-set. It is just "the way things are," and it can be hard
> to recover the reasons *why* it is the way things are. When academic prob-
> lems appear intractable, it is often because an underlying systemic element
> is responsible. People who work in the academy, like people in any institu-
> tion or profession, are socialized to operate in certain ways, and when they
> are called upon to alter their practices, they sometimes find that they lack
> a compass to guide them.[9]

Because this is a book that advocates a new model for the American
research university, we bring up filiopietism to assess the impact of the
status quo on knowledge production and dissemination. And because we
underscore the reflexive relationship between knowledge and its institutional setting, our usage of the status quo often refers to institutional design. Academics are trained to question the status quo but tend to assume
that our colleges and universities have, as a matter of course, already long
ago been optimally configured to facilitate knowledge production and
dissemination. There is much more that could be said about the impact
of filiopietism on cognitive or epistemological processes (we allude to
some of these arguments in the following), but here, for the most part,
we tend to focus on the impact of the bureaucratic underpinnings of our
knowledge formations. Because knowledge is at once epistemological,
administrative, and social—a point made by the sociologist Immanuel
Wallerstein,[10] whose assessment of disciplinary knowledge we consider
in chapter 5—the design of a knowledge enterprise should never be considered finished business, nor is design arbitrary or merely adventitious
to the production of knowledge. In this context we concur with the

assessment of organizational and learning theorists John Seely Brown and Paul Duguid: "In a society that attaches particular value to 'abstract knowledge,' the details of practice have come to be seen as nonessential, unimportant, and easily developed once the relevant abstractions have been grasped."[11]

At the administrative or institutional level in colleges and universities, filiopietism often manifests as an entrenchment in organizational structures and practices that have come to seem mere backdrops to knowledge production. These constraints could be said to constitute the institutional historical a priori, which, philosopher Ian Hacking points out, functions something like the paradigms of "normal science" described by Thomas Kuhn.[12] But recognition of limitation carries with it an implicit invitation to initiate change, as philosopher Simon Critchley contends: "If human experience is a contingent creation, then it can be recreated in other ways." This transformative imperative in philosophy— or art or poetry or thinking of whatever type, Critchley elaborates— prevents us from becoming mired in the "slow accumulation of the deadening sediment of tradition." And tradition becomes especially insidious when it passes unrecognized in the absence of critique: "Crisis? What crisis?" quips Critchley.[13] We conduct business as usual on the quad because conventional wisdom holds that when it comes to the organization of our universities, all of the boxes have already been checked. Historical amnesia subverts the realization that our colleges and universities are simply the sort of contingent creations that Critchley ascribes to sedimented tradition, and thus amenable to change. For our purposes, then, recognition of the limitations imposed by excessive veneration of tradition is the first step toward maximizing the potential of our knowledge enterprises.

Filiopietism moreover contributes to isomorphism—the paradoxical tendency for organizations and institutions to emulate one another and become increasingly homogeneous.[14] Isomorphism, in turn, correlates with the academic obsession with prestige.[15] (We turn to these concepts shortly.) An assessment of tradition in the American research university is thus not merely rhetorical. Its manifestation may variously be constructive or destructive—constitutive and foundational—as in the case of such great "traditions" as the liberal arts, or insidious and pernicious, as in a bad case of the affliction we term Harvardization or Berkeley envy.

While we may inveigh against filiopietism, we do not propose to throw tradition under the bus.

## The Trappings and Substance of Academic Tradition

With the possible exception of organized religion and the courts, few institutions of modern society so rigidly adhere to tradition as academe. From the initiation rites of fraternities to the arcana of commencement regalia, American academe leverages the vestiges of centuries of ritual, pomp, and ceremony that derive from ecclesiastical and juridical practices and, more directly, from Oxbridge and the great Continental European universities. The historian William Clark provides a compendium of academic tradition in his remarkable survey *Academic Charisma and the Origins of the Research University*. Here, through the microanalysis of the material culture and academic practices of the institution—ceremonies, rituals, manners, forms, and fashions—we learn of the obscure origins of lectures and seminars, examinations and grading, seminar papers and dissertations, academic degrees, processions and costumes, chairs, titles, and appointments, the collecting practices and classification schemes of university libraries, and the vicissitudes of such conventions as "publish or perish." Both material practices and symbolic processes serve to "uphold authority by sanctifying traditions and differentiating academics as a group from other groups in society," Clark observes.[16]

But Clark does not limit his interrogation of academic tradition to mortarboards and hazings. More broadly, through an examination of the concept of charisma developed by the sociologist Max Weber, he parses the distinctions among charismatic, traditional, and rational authority in academic culture. For Weber, charismatic authority governs the earliest stages of culture and is associated with what he termed "natural leaders"—"holders of specific gifts of the body and spirit"—such as shamans, warriors, generals, and priests.[17] Subsequent stages intermingled charismatic with traditional authority and, only more recently, culminating in the values of the Enlightenment, rational authority. Weber had much to say about charismatic authority and its role in building institutions,[18] and Clark underscores the extent to which legitimate authority in academe remains informed by this more or less ineffable characteristic associated with certain extraordinary individuals. Charisma in this sense is essentially manifest as individual "genius," a quality that transcends rational authority and elevates those who possess it above mundane expectations of mere bureaucratic efficiency, productivity, and routinization.[19]

Scientists and scholars embody rational authority, and academic culture epitomizes rationality, which reflects the progressive rationalization of Western society that Weber perceived. But for Clark, the research university consolidated its influence through its maintenance of figures possessed of charismatic authority—"through the cultivation of charismatic figures within a broader sphere of rationalization." Rationality can be charismatic, Clark explains, and thus charismatic authority inheres in academic superstars, just as the quality once marked shamans and priests. In the academic enterprise—the "entrepreneurial domain of activity within a bureaucratic superstructure," as he aptly puts it—individual genius, if it is to make its mark, must perpetually topple the existing canon: "To assail it and succeed makes one a hero of knowledge, founder of a new canon. A charismatic figure succeeds . . . by finding disciples, who establish a new tradition or canon."[20] In the absence of pretensions to transcendental truth, or at least the claims of scientific method, as historian Martin Jay points out, the most common mode of legitimation in scholarly discourse, especially in the humanities, is name-dropping—that is, citing the authority of "charismatic legitimators."[21]

Academic culture valorizes the discovery of new knowledge and even more so its progenitor when new work overtakes or overturns the status quo in any given field. In literature, for example, the vision of "strong poets" overcomes the "anxiety of influence" in the process memorialized by Harold Bloom.[22] In scientific discovery, to cite the seminal Kuhnian formulations, a novelty disrupts "normal science" and threatens to "subvert the existing traditions of scientific practice" despite strenuous resistance from within the academy. The "tradition-shattering complements to the tradition-bound activity of normal science" shift our shared assumptions—"paradigms"—to produce scientific revolution.[23] We may stand on the shoulders of giants but only those who "break the vessel"— to cite a metaphor enlisted by Bloom—ensure themselves academic superstardom.[24] The entrepreneurial culture of the American research university advances discovery and innovation precisely through such processes of creative destruction.[25]

But Clark recognizes the dark side of tradition and the grievous limitations of traditional authority: "To put it crudely," he says, tradition "most resembles the patterned behavior of animals: progeny or descendents behave the way they do because their progenitors or ancestors behaved that way." By contrast, he contends, both the charismatic and the rational represent "disruptive or revolutionary forces."[26] This would be consistent with the admonition from the Apple advertising campaign introduced in 1997 to "think different." And to an unprecedented extent, many Americans from the earliest days of our republic have done just that and in the process changed the world. As we elaborate in chapter 4, during the preceding century, the United States assumed the mantle of leadership in scientific discovery and technological innovation, which economists correlate with the majority of economic growth since World War II. And most of this discovery and innovation may be attributed either directly or indirectly to the knowledge production of the set of research universities.

Filiopietism inspires the lockstep thinking that produces the set of undifferentiated institutions we might term the Generic Public University and the "Harvard envy" that is endemic to private universities. Despite the plethora of institutional types in American higher education—research universities, liberal arts colleges, regional public and community colleges, and so on—institutions in each category bear a striking resemblance to one another, and less prestigious institutions seem invariably intent on replicating the organization and practices of their aspirational peers. Thus, public research universities tend to model themselves on the University of Michigan or the University of California, Berkeley, for example, and their private counterparts strive toward Harvardization. Similarly, selective private colleges endeavor to become more and more like Bowdoin, Swarthmore, or Williams. Institutional rankings, such as those proffered by *U.S. News & World Report*, only exacerbate this compulsion toward replication, as do the practices of foundations and government agencies. Simplistic ratings methodologies, which pretend that the criteria for evaluation across all institutional types are consistent and immutable, purport to establish precise numerical rank orders.[27] But indicators of quality are often either arbitrary or subjective, and precedence in hierarchies inevitably corresponds to the variables of age and wealth. Not surprisingly, the institution frequently deemed to be preeminent in the United States or even worldwide (also known as Harvard University) just happens to be the nation's oldest and wealthiest, as well as one of the least accessible.

## Filiopietism Fuels Isomorphism and Obsession with Prestige

The paradoxical tendency for organizations and institutions in a given domain to emulate one another and become increasingly homogeneous has not escaped the attention of sociologists. And although much of the literature on organizational theory has been devoted to explications of competitive pressure leading to institutional differentiation and diversity, sociologists Paul J. DiMaggio and Walter W. Powell have focused instead on institutional isomorphism. The process is nowhere more evident than in our colleges and universities, we contend, and reiterate the classic definition cited by the authors: "Isomorphism is a constraining process that forces one unit in a population to resemble other units that face the same set of environmental conditions." The "inexorable push" of isomorphic change leading to the emergence of dominant organizational models is counterintuitively the outcome of competition "not just for resources and customers, but for political power and institutional legitimacy, and for social as well as economic fitness." Institutions take their cues from other institutions because "the major factors that organizations must take into account are other organizations," DiMaggio and Powell explain.[28]

Although counterproductive, the momentum of isomorphism may be considered entirely rational, as institutions succumb to various pressures: coercive, mimetic, and normative. Coercion may arise from governmental regulation or budget cycles, for example. Mimetic isomorphism occurs when uncertainty leads organizations to model themselves on others that are regarded as "more legitimate and successful." Such "isomorphic modeling" is most likely when legitimacy is sought, which certainly accounts for the Berkeley and Harvard envy. Normative modeling is the outcome of professionalization, which DiMaggio and Powell associate with organizational norms inculcated in professionals in their struggle for legitimation: "Professions are subject to the same coercive and mimetic pressures as are organizations," they explain. The struggle for professional legitimation produces a "pool of almost interchangeable individuals who occupy similar positions across a range of organizations and possess a similarity of orientation and disposition that may override variations in tradition . . . that might otherwise shape organizational behavior."[29] This calls to mind the disciplinary socialization we consider more fully in our discussion of interdisciplinarity in chapter 5.

Isomorphism is endemic in our colleges and universities, and J. Douglas Toma focuses the analysis of DiMaggio and Powell on the hothouse of academe, where he finds the objective of much institutional strategy to be "positioning for prestige." This assertion may seem implausibly reductionistic, or at the very least simplistic, but the unceasing efforts of institutions to replicate Berkeley and Harvard down to the last Ionic entablature or Georgian portico is no mere idle diversion. The struggle is deemed worthwhile because, as Toma contends, "prestige is to higher education as profit is to corporations." Since "status serves as a proxy for profit," it should come as no surprise that "legitimacy through enhanced prestige" has become an obsession.[30] Anthony Carnevale and Jeff Strohl similarly observe that although prestige may seem an intangible asset in the "rat race for status," selective institutions regard the allocation of resources "based on prestige and reputational value" worthwhile even as investment to advance academic quality suffers. Prestige may be intangible but it remains an "insatiable target for postsecondary investment."[31]

Institutions become "eerily similar in vision," Toma writes, and "seemingly obsessed with 'moving to the next level.'" Ascent in rank brings with it not only enhanced legitimacy but also the promise of greater autonomy and perceived access to more abundant financial resources because the "most prestigious institutions also tend to be the wealthiest." Toma points out that nothing deters schools in this pursuit: "Even significant differences in prestige or resources among institutions do not seem to matter, as they seemingly all endeavor so purposefully to become more like those directly above them on the prestige hierarchy." Despite claims to be distinctive, institutions seek the "security of isomorphism," which promises conformity and "following standard approaches and pursuing similar goals in roughly the same manner." Rather than differentiate—a competitive strategy common to the corporate sector—colleges and universities pursue "common aspirations and generic approaches toward enhancing prestige." After all, Toma points out, "there are only so many realistic ways to reposition an American institution."[32]

Such competitive positioning obtains even for institutions with "few claims to prestige and little to differentiate themselves." Each is nevertheless compelled to present a more or less "plausible set of assertions as they position within a market segment." As set forth in branding campaigns, the options could be reduced to a checklist, Toma observes. And despite the plurality of institutional types, institutions become more homogeneous through mission creep, which occurs when institutions "seek the advantages that they perceive at the 'next level.'" Jockeying for position often amounts less to substantive differentiation than to investments in the notorious "construction arms race" of academic infrastructure and campus amenities intended to enhance curb appeal. Toma finds claims regarding student body diversity no less competitive. What is worse, because claims regarding the quality of the faculty and curriculum are difficult for prospective students and their parents to corroborate, institutions succumb to the pursuit of revenues at the peripheries—"student residences, dining commons, fitness centers, and even shopping districts"—rather than investment in the academic core.[33]

Claims regarding the administrative bloat of large universities are often misinformed and exaggerated, but their complex organizational structures are inevitably likened to bureaucracies. DiMaggio and Powell remind us that institutional isomorphism is intrinsic to bureaucracies, which Weber perceived as the irreversible but efficient organizational manifestation of the rationalist order—the "iron cage" to which humanity is consigned "perhaps until the last ton of fossilized coal is burnt." Bureaucratization, DiMaggio and Powell point out, makes institutions "more similar without making them more efficient."[34] Although bureaucracies deliver goods and services and perform critical functions that facilitate the operations of society, the bureaucratic mind-set we associate pejoratively with large impersonal public agencies that perform standardized and repetitive tasks efficiently is not normally conducive to discovery, creativity, and innovation.

However we conceive the purposes and functions of our colleges and universities, we tend to assume that their organizational structures inherently facilitate the production and diffusion of knowledge. But if the structure of an institution is inimical to its purposes and functions, its design must be reconsidered lest we observe the triumph of bureaucratization. For the present, we underscore the tendency for large research universities to succumb to the bureaucratic tendencies of routine, standardization, and inertia, which the economist and policy scholar Anthony Downs identified as hallmarks of bureaucracies in his *locus classicus* discussion of the concept. The routine, standardization, and inertia Downs perceived in bureaucracies are nowhere more evident than in generic public universities that conform with the obsolete service model that values universities principally for the basic task of undergraduate education: "Once the users of the bureau's services have become convinced of their gains from it, and have developed routinized relations with it," Downs explains, "the bureau can rely upon a certain amount of inertia to keep on generating the external support it needs."[35] Routine is certainly essential, however, and society favors organizations that exhibit high degrees of competency, productivity, and accountability, traits that are fostered through well-defined and transparent routines. But as organizational theorists point out, excessive reliance on routine can also be a correlate of resistance to change. Along with the sunk costs of organizing labor and capital, institutionalized routines tend to fix direction and set momentum, leading to what has been termed structural inertia. This sort of inertia does not necessarily preclude organizational change but tends to favor merely incremental adjustments in a direction already charted.[36]

Academic culture is conducive to bureaucratic entrenchment: "As bureaus grow older, they tend to develop more formalized rule systems covering more and more of the possible situations they are likely to encounter," Downs elaborates. "These rules . . . tend to divert the attention of officials from achieving the social functions of the bureau to conforming to its rules—the 'goal displacement' described by sociologists . . . . They increase the bureau's structural complexity, which in turn strengthens its inertia because of greater sunken costs in current procedures. The resulting resistance to change further reduces the bureau's ability to adjust to new circumstances."[37] Routine, standardization, and inertia. Conformity to rules. These characteristics may be justifiable in the institutional cultures of our county courthouses and divisions of motor vehicles, but they are less appropriate for institutions dedicated to the production of knowledge and diffusion of innovation.

Various explanations are offered for academic entrenchment in fili-opietism, some of which pin blame on academic leaders. Richard De-Millo cites the innovator's dilemma propounded by Clayton Christensen. From the perspective of Harvard Business School case studies, Christensen argues that only the abandonment of traditional business practices allows managers to negotiate and leverage unanticipated disruptive technologies.[38] But DeMillo identifies an even more fundamental dilemma, which is that "university presidencies are for the most part held by a remarkably homogeneous group of people who tend to pass the same concepts, biases, and views of the future around a tribal campfire where the next generation of leaders submits to review by its elders."[39] Similarly, the professoriate, whose disciplinary socialization is held to encourage orthodox thinking, is unlikely to chafe at aspirational appeals to make sociology at Purdue more like the department at Chicago.[40] More often than not, filiopietism stokes resistance to institutional reform.

### Resistance to Reform in the Academy

For those who believe that the university is "fundamentally sound," John Lombardi contends, critique "invokes tradition and values and attempts to adjust those to the practical realities of contemporary economic circumstances." The alternative he posits is the "replacement of existing university structures with much different learning organizations" or acquiescence to "radical or reformist proposals that would clean house, change standards, and impose new ones." Although we argue that these approaches are not mutually exclusive and that American research universities are capable of accommodating within their complex organizational structures the "much different learning organizations" that Lombardi's revolutionary critics demand, as well as all manner of "reformist proposals,[41] a number of episodes in the history of American higher education epitomize the remarkable recalcitrance of the academy to change.

Resistance to reform is common enough in any sector of human endeavor, but it seems peculiarly endemic to academe. From a spoof compiled during the Edwardian era, Louis Menand singles out some advice that captures this aspect of academic culture: "In 1908, the Cambridge classicist F. M. Cornford, in his satirical guide for young academics, *Microcosmographia Academica*, advised that the basic rule of faculty governance is, 'Nothing should ever be done for the first time.'" Menand frames this excerpt as an illustration of the "tension between the state of knowledge and the system in which learning and teaching actually take place." He aptly observes, "The state of knowledge changes much more readily than the system. Institutions are recalcitrant, and the professional conservatism of professors is an ancient source of ridicule."[42] But as Jonathan Cole points out, institutional evolution is a process: "Truly distinguished American universities are not built overnight or over a decade." And the most committed efforts by academic leaders to transform the status quo have on more than one occasion met with opposition intramurally as well as from external constituencies and the general public alike: "In every era, there have been skeptics and critics who have viewed either the expansion of the university mission or the sheer growth of the university in complexity and size as part of its likely undoing," he observes.[43]

Not all resistance to reform is without merit, of course. The system of electives that most of us who are products of American colleges and universities probably took for granted serves as a case in point. The freedom to declare majors and minors and choose from a remarkably diverse array of courses is a prerogative unknown to many students abroad. The elective system, which is one among many innovations attributed to Thomas Jefferson in his conception of the University of Virginia, would become nearly ubiquitous by the end of the nineteenth century but at the time represented a departure from the prescribed curriculum focused on the classics. Although the number of electives may have been limited when the institution enrolled its first class in March 1825, its adaptation by other schools would expand curricula nationwide, especially following its introduction at Harvard soon after the Civil War by Charles William Eliot, president of Harvard for four decades beginning in 1869. The implementation of the elective system was an overarching concern for Eliot, and by one account, "on the level of academic strategy, he had no master plan in mind in 1869 beyond the single concrete desire to adopt the elective system."[44]

Despite its widespread adaptation and subsequent ubiquity in American higher education, however, the system of electives conceived by Jefferson and promulgated by Eliot remains contested even to the present day. Frank Rhodes, for example, likens electives to curricular "potpourri" and laments the "daunting freedom of choice but precious little guidance" available to undergraduates: "It suggests to the student that one thing is as good as another; that there is no hierarchy of importance or value." In this context he quotes David P. Gardner, then president emeritus of the University of California, who deemed the system of electives a "cafeteria with little indication of which are the entrees and which the desserts." More eloquently, Vartan Gregorian, then president emeritus of Brown University, pronounced such a curriculum "Dante's definition of hell, where nothing connects with nothing." In contrast to such "uncritical accumulation of information," Rhodes suggests that the professoriate attempt to "constitute the blueprint of essential knowledge and common discourse."[45] The extent of general education requirements imposed by faculty committees convened by many of our nation's leading universities serves as evidence of the perceived need to exert guidance through imposed constraints. These take the form of either the distribution model or the core model, Louis Menand explains in his elaborate delineation of the issues surrounding the implementation of general education.[46]

But at least some of the opposition Eliot encountered in his implementation of the system of electives was apparently provoked by currents altogether extraneous to the values of academic freedom that we take for granted: resistance to science in an academic milieu dedicated to classical education and the perpetuation of the New England social elite. Although today Eliot is regarded as a transformational figure in the emergence of the modern research university, the values of science he professed set him at odds with a society ambivalent toward its claims. As a chemist, Eliot represented a departure from type in the presidency, the historian Hugh Hawkins informs us, because four of his five immediate predecessors had been Unitarian ministers, and among his competitors for the presidency was the Professor of Christian Morals and Preacher to the University. His intent to implement such key reforms as the elimination of compulsory chapel and even sectarian affiliation met with resistance from what Hawkins has identified as the "forces of religious orthodoxy"— constituencies accustomed to denominational collegiate affiliation. His efforts at reform were sufficiently controversial to initiate a series of public debates on the mission of higher education with Princeton president James McCosh, a renowned Scottish metaphysician. McCosh deemed it absurd that a student might study "music, French plays, and novels, or whatever captured his fancies," according to historian George Marsden. "Particularly he was alarmed that one could gain a Harvard education without being taught anything of either morality or religion."[47] Hawkins elaborates: "One of McCosh's criticisms of Eliot's free elective system was that it made the colleges less fit to prepare ministers . . . . Aside from its failure to guarantee future ministers with sound classical backgrounds, Eliot's 'new departure' threatened general moral development." The departure in question was the ability of a Harvard student to specialize in science.[48]

As a skeptic regarding the value of limitless proliferation of electives, Frank Rhodes follows the lead of one of the most ambitious, if not the most controversial, academic reformers in American higher education, as well as the very type of university president as public intellectual epitomized by Woodrow Wilson. Robert Maynard Hutchins served as president of the University of Chicago and later its chancellor for more than two decades beginning in 1929. Hanna Holborn Gray, herself president emerita of the University of Chicago, informs us that Hutchins regarded the elective system as the "emblem of higher education's fall from the grace of a required liberal curriculum incorporating a hierarchy of truth."[49] His opposition led him to propose curricular reform repeatedly, which in each case met with rejection from the faculty.

But Hutchins' efforts to reform the curriculum were only the beginning of his comprehensive critique of the modern university, which in retrospect met with wholly justified resistance from the professoriate. By today's standards of academic shared governance, his program of reform appears startlingly autocratic; he sought sweeping authority for the presidency that Gray concedes was "overreaching." Gray quotes from the draft of a confidential memo from Hutchins to the Board of Trustees from July 1942: Hutchins sought nothing less than "full responsibility for and full authority over the educational and scholarly work of the University, its course of study, publications, appointments to its faculty, and all other matters relating to its activities in education and research."[50] Hutchins believed that what he termed his "crusade" would actually produce a more democratic institution, Gray explains, by "reducing the preponderant power of the senior faculty and extending the same rights to those previously excluded from the faculty senate." His intent was to realize the purpose of the university, which Hutchins explained, "is nothing less than to procure a moral, intellectual, and spiritual revolution throughout the world." He contended that the "democratic academic community" he envisioned would "multiply the power which the University can bring to bear upon the character, the mind, and the spirit of men." Gray explains that resistance to reforms proposed by Hutchins came from an academic community that regarded his vision an effort to "impose an ideological conformity threatening to the intellectual freedom at the core of the university."[51]

Not all efforts at academic reform hinge on issues as fundamental as those contested at the University of Chicago. An acrimonious dispute at Dartmouth in the nineteenth century, for example, apparently erupted over seating arrangements for undergraduates when in chapel: "The issues were myriad, they were interrelated in arcane ways, and they were fantastically petty," Louis Menand recounts.[52] As Clark Kerr observed with reference to the University of California, "Hutchins once described the modern university as a series of separate schools and departments held together by a central heating system. In an area where heating is less important and the automobile more, I have sometimes thought of it as a series of individual faculty entrepreneurs held together by a common grievance over parking."[53]

Woodrow Wilson brought great ambitions for reform to his presidency of Princeton University. An entry in the diary of his foreign policy advisor recounts that while in the White House, the twenty-eighth president of the United States suffered from nightmares about his tenure at Princeton. Historian James Axtell quotes an observation by Colonel Edward House from December 1913: "He thought he was seeing some of his Princeton enemies. Those terrible days have sunk deep into his soul and he will carry their marks to his grave." Following his resignation from Princeton in 1910, Axtell recounts, Wilson was "discouraged and emotionally bruised."[54] His tenure, beginning in 1902, was characterized by ambitious efforts at reform both of the culture and structure of the institution, but opposition from administrators, faculty, students, and influential alumni foiled his progressive vision for the university.[55] Fueling this enmity were his efforts to undermine an elitist social hierarchy on campus, reinforced by so-called eating clubs, and his advancement of graduate education.[56] Termed the Quad Plan for the manner in which it reorganized student housing, his initiative to foster inclusiveness and social integration represented an insufferable challenge to entrenched constituencies, and its announcement at the June 1907 commencement elicited a groundswell of opposition.[57]

Wilson's confrontation with senior administrators over the disposition of the Graduate School, which had been formally established in 1900, would prove to be more pernicious. While he sought to situate it centrally on campus where it could inform interaction among students, faculty, and the university at large, Andrew F. West, dean of the Graduate School, contended that the new entity should remain relatively insular. A number of trustees who had bequeathed monies for the Graduate School made their gifts contingent upon its location. The issue came to a head when a prominent Massachusetts alumnus, Isaac Wyman, left his estate to the university but named Dean West as one of his executors. Owing to the size of the grant and Wyman's influence, Wilson capitulated. Disheartened by the setback, Wilson resigned from the presidency to run for governor of New Jersey.[58] Despite his accomplishments over the course of eight years in revising aspects of the curriculum and academic standards, successes in departmental reorganization and faculty recruitment, and impacts on the subsequent formation of distinguished graduate programs in the arts and sciences, Jonathan Cole explains, Wilson would remain checked in his effort to promote the establishment of graduate schools in the mold of institutional peers such as Harvard and Columbia: "Some alumni who wanted Princeton's focus to remain principally on undergraduate education considered the failure to expand to be a blessing in disguise," Cole observes.[59] Axtell assesses the toll exacted on Wilson from these frustrated initiatives for reform: "His failure to determine the location and character of the nascent graduate school and his inability to win support for building residential colleges, or 'quads,' for all of the college's classes, which he hoped would 'democratize' if not eliminate the socially restrictive upper-class eating clubs, had wounded him deeply."[60]

Another thwarted effort at reform comes with the contested vision for the University of Wisconsin propounded by progressives in the early twentieth century, which turned legislators against Charles Van Hise, president from 1903 to 1918. Van Hise focused his efforts concerning the relation of the university to its community with the intent that the "beneficent influence of the university reaches every home in the state."[61] The Wisconsin Idea is characterized by the conviction that the "boundaries of the University are the boundaries of the state" and a sense of obligation to be accessible to the community.[62] Van Hise pursued this goal relentlessly by expanding access and pursuing direct ties to communities through research and service. But partisans in the state legislature opposed the Wisconsin Idea, contending that the institution should maintain a less public profile. The Allen Report of 1913, commissioned by the Wisconsin State Legislature, attacked the initiative propounded by Van Hise. Directing criticism at its champion, partisans in the legislature introduced bills to "remove the president from the Board of Regents, abolish the Board of Regents, discontinue the property tax that was allocated to the University, and lower the entrance requirements for the Law School and the Medical School." Though opposition efforts were unsuccessful, the legislatorial assault on the operation, mission, and purposes of the university continued throughout the end of his term. The Wisconsin Idea, however, continues to shape the values of the University of Wisconsin system despite skepticism from various quarters regarding the purposes of university research and initiatives to advance access and service, manifest in the recent controversy regarding the privatization of the University of Wisconsin at Madison.[63]

The transformation of the University of California into the nation's first multiple-campus university, initially governed by a single administration, represents a suitable chronicle of demands for reform countered by episodes of resistance from entrenched constituencies. Despite initial skepticism from then University of California president Benjamin Ide Wheeler, as well as opposition from UC regents and Berkeley faculty and students, Edward A. Dickson, a regent from Los Angeles, persuaded Wheeler during the final year of his presidency, in 1919, to establish a "southern branch," which preceded the opening of the Westwood campus, in 1929. The university already operated programs in medicine and law in San Francisco, in agriculture at Davis and Riverside, and in marine biology in San Diego, but apparently the prospect of a second major campus proved worrisome to the academic community in Berkeley. In response to public demand for access to higher education during the Great Depression, university officials sought to accommodate surges in enrollment, despite the historic fiscal crisis, through an expansion of academic programs beyond Berkeley and Los Angeles. Robert Gordon Sproul, UC president from 1930 until 1958, initially sought to limit expansion to Los Angeles. When he later supported the establishment of other campuses, faculty and alumni from both Berkeley and Los Angeles opposed his efforts. John Aubrey Douglass writes, "The university's transformation into a multicampus system remained a source of consternation within the academy." Regents repeatedly opposed the efforts of Sproul to transform Santa Barbara State College into a campus of the UC system. Nevertheless, during his tenure, the university established campuses in Santa Barbara (1944) and Riverside (1954), and campuses in Davis (1959), San Diego (1959), Irvine (1960), and Santa Cruz (1962) followed soon thereafter.[64] The Sproul presidency spanned nearly three decades, but it would be the tenure of his successor that more strikingly epitomizes resistance to reform.

Although the tenure of Clark Kerr as president of the University of California from 1958 through 1967 would be associated with the political upheaval of the era, including the Loyalty Oath controversy and student activism that culminated in the Free Speech Movement, his efforts to transform higher education in California in response to changing societal needs in the postwar era have earned him accolades as one of the great academic leaders of the twentieth century.[65] Kerr was initially appointed the first chancellor of UC Berkeley in 1952 when, in recognition of the attainment by UCLA of status coequal to Berkeley, the regents decentralized University of California administration. Prior to decentralization, the chief administrative officer at UCLA had been the provost.[66] But his administrative and political acumen is most closely associated with the development of the California Master Plan for Higher Education, which in 1960 established a tripartite hierarchical differentiation of roles for the University of California system, California State University (CSU) system, and California Community Colleges system.

The general outlines of the plan are too well known to delineate here, but in brief and reduced to its most basic intent, the University of California campuses were to assume responsibility for research and the education of the top 12.5 percent of resident high school graduates; the state college campuses would educate the second tier of students but conduct no research; and the remaining students would attend community colleges primarily focused on preparation of students for the workforce. Cole elaborates: "A principal component of the Master Plan was the opportunity for students who succeeded at one of the lower-tier schools to transfer to a higher-tier school. Another principle was that no student should be denied a college education for lack of financial resources . . . . In short, he wanted to build a state system that was designed for both access and excellence."[67] The lineage of one of the fundamental tenets of the New American University model is here plainly evident.

But the Master Plan represented the culmination of a series of complex negotiations that attempted to balance the demands of various constituencies. According to Kerr, during the development of the plan between June and December 1959, he had to negotiate demands from leaders of state colleges for university status; efforts by the state legislature to seize control of higher education; efforts by certain regents to combine state colleges and UC campuses under a single board ("The system would be too large and too diverse for effective governance, and its internal dynamics would lead, I thought, to a homogenization in a downward direction"); and the unexpected reversal of position by some UC chancellors regarding the right of state colleges to award the PhD. At a joint meeting of the Board of Regents and Board of Education in December 1959, presidents of state colleges appeared in open revolt over demands to offer PhD programs: "I made one last concession: the university would be willing to offer joint PhD programs on a case-by-case basis." Nevertheless, the state college faculty presented "nearly unanimous rejection of the differentiation of research functions as between the state colleges and University of California."[68]

The obstacles Kerr encountered in his efforts to guide the implementation of the Master Plan epitomize resistance to reform in American higher education. The various episodes chronicled are intended to suggest the extent of the tenacity with which conventional wisdom and filiopietism may claim the minds of the informed and uninformed alike. Academic leaders themselves have on more than one occasion championed resistance to reform.[69] For the contemporary research university, historian and pundit Robert Zemsky points out, reform must address access, accountability, affordability, and quality, which he terms the "four horsemen of academic reform."[70] Yet, efforts to address even these issues may be limited by obedience to tradition and obsession with prestige.

## Negotiating "Cost Disease" in Academic Platforms of Discovery

The routine, standardization, and inertia typical of bureaucracies is inimical to discovery, creativity, and innovation, and conformity to rules does not produce great art. Moreover, there is no efficient way to discover the origins of the universe. The purposes of the research university that distinguish this category of institution from those concerned primarily with the dissemination of existing knowledge may thus appear inherently at odds with legitimate societal demands for greater efficiency—and cost savings—in higher education. What is worse, costs associated with efforts to resuscitate and revive an anachronistic model continue to escalate. Much of the invective leveled at academia, excerpts of which we surveyed in the introduction, has been provoked by increases in tuition deemed stratospheric by historical standards. The economist William J. Baumol offers the following perspective in 2012: "Since the early 1980s, the price of college tuition in the United States has increased by a much greater percentage (up 440 percent) than the average rate of inflation (110 percent), median family income (150 percent), and even medical care (250 percent)."[71]

A standard explanation for the putative inevitability of escalating costs in higher education is to be found in the concept of the "cost disease," introduced by Baumol and fellow economist William G. Bowen, former president of Princeton University, in a seminal 1965 article and subsequent book on the economic challenges of the nonprofit sector.[72] Baumol and Bowen focused on the performing arts to examine the implications of lack of productivity gains in labor-intensive "industries" such as higher education. Because increases in productivity generally correlate with improved technologies, the potential for productivity gains in the performing arts was limited. The sector constrained by stagnant levels of productivity was thus contrasted with the sector characterized by the potential for increasing productivity through technological innovation:

> It is apparent that the live performing arts belong to the stable productivity sector of our economy. The legitimate theater, the symphony orchestra, the chamber group, the opera, the dance—all can serve as textbook illustrations of activities offering little opportunity for major technological change.

The output per man-hour of the violinist playing a Schubert quartet in a standard concert hall is relatively fixed, and it is fairly difficult to reduce the number of actors necessary for a performance of *Henry IV*, Part II.[73]

In their 1966 book *Performing Arts: The Economic Dilemma*, Baumol and Bowen elaborate regarding differential productivity growth:

> Whereas the amount of labor necessary to produce a typical manufactured product has constantly declined since the beginning of the industrial revolution, it requires about as many minutes for Richard II to tell his 'sad stories of the death of kings' as it did on the stage of the Globe Theatre. Human ingenuity has devised ways to reduce the labor necessary to produce an automobile, but no one has yet succeeded in decreasing the human effort expended at a live performance of a 45-minute Schubert quartet.[74]

The omission of the violist or cellist is not an option, nor can the performers double the tempi to increase output per man-hour: "The conditions of production themselves preclude any substantial change in productivity," economist James Heilbrun elaborates. Moreover, Baumol and Bowen point out, "The work of the performer is an end in itself, not a means for the production of some good." As Heilbrun elaborates, "Since the performer's labour is the output—the singer singing, the dancer dancing, the pianist playing—there is really no way to increase output per hour."[75] Efforts to cut unit costs through "fewer rehearsals, the use of more poorly trained performers, and shoddy costumes and scenery" would only prove to be counterproductive, Baumol and Bowen explain, inasmuch as the deterioration of aesthetic standards would lead to declining audiences and community support.[76]

More recently, Baumol has likened the approaches and methods of the sector constrained by stagnant productivity—health care and education, in their assessment—to "handicraft" industries. While costs in this sector continue to escalate, he explains, the cost of computers, for example, will continue to lag behind the average rate of inflation: "The reason is not difficult to identify. The items in the rising-cost group generally have a *handicraft* element—that is, a human element not readily replaceable by machines—in their production process, which makes it difficult to reduce their labor content."[77] We might thus term this handicraft component to teaching and research in the top echelons of higher education "artisanal." The bleeding edge of scientific discovery and technological innovation is to be found in American research universities, but there remains something fundamentally artisanal to the methods of knowledge production and dissemination. John Lombardi thus speaks of faculties as guilds, and Paul Duguid points out that apprenticeship is "not merely the preferred method of 'manual' trades, but also of the higher reaches of academic disciplines."[78]

The lack of productivity gains in the performing arts sector thus appears inevitable. And costs would be projected to rise indefinitely for industries in which the basic methods of providing goods or services cannot be improved by technology. Absent technological innovation, so goes the argument, the costs of labor-intensive "services" in the arts, health care, and education—from the performance of a string quartet to kidney transplantation to the production of algae-derived jet fuel in a campus lab—will only ever spiral upward. Economist Gregory Besharov elaborates:

> With wages based on output, the rising productivity in the growth sector results in a rising wage in both sectors. Since the wage goes up and productivity remains constant in the arts sector, its cost of production rises relative to the manufacturing sector. With the further assumption of prices proportional to costs, the relative price of output in the arts sector will increase relative to the other. Hence the "cost disease."[79]

Because research universities are inherently dedicated to discovery, creativity, and innovation, as well as myriad social purposes, the goal of simple profit maximization that motivates other industries would be irrelevant. The comparison is meaningless, according to John Lombardi: "While it is surely possible to reduce cost, and while some inefficiency remains in university and college operations, the scale of cost reduction possible without damaging the product is small." He elaborates: "Many point to the dramatic reduction in the price of such things as consumer electronics and demand similar efficiencies from higher education." But service-intensive sectors such as health care and higher education incur the "double commitment to high-cost specialized professional staff and complex, expensive physical facilities." Moreover, "personal service industries using highly skilled professionals cannot readily increase the scale of their operations because the products they sell are, by definition of the marketplace and the consumers, individualized."[80] The methods of face-to-face instruction and mentored research cannot be automated without sacrificing quality. Despite the mobilization of virtual invisible colleges and epistemic communities, and the implementation of distance learning, there remains something fundamentally artisanal to the production and dissemination of new knowledge.

Proponents of online instruction as a remedy to the cost disease and panacea to accessibility invariably treat higher education with broad strokes, as if the undergraduate experience offered by institutions concerned primarily with access could ever match those characteristic of academic platforms underpinned by discovery and knowledge production. For students fortunate enough to attend research-grade universities and liberal arts colleges, the undergraduate experience is characterized by a focus on the individual in a pedagogical milieu of learning immersion. When conceived and executed properly, distance learning provides an important complement, and, certainly for increasing numbers of students, an alternative to the traditional undergraduate experience. But its potential may lead the uninformed to assume mistakenly that sufficient alternative capacity for higher education, secured by market forces, is already in place. This in turn suggests that mere access to some or any form of higher education is sufficient. It is not. As we contend in chapter 7, online learning is optimally operationalized within the context of research universities.

New models for the American research university are imperative. And notwithstanding the artisanal component to teaching and research in academic platforms committed to discovery, fiscal constraints impose the need to institute more rigorous cost efficiencies. The academy might even learn from the Cheesecake Factory, the successful restaurant chain that Harvard physician Atul Gawande has proposed as a prototype for an alternative model for health care. The escalating costs and notorious inefficiencies of the health care system are well documented: "Our costs are soaring, the service is typically mediocre, and the quality is unreliable," Gawande summarizes. "Every clinician has his or her own way of doing things, and the rates of failure and complication (not to mention the costs) for a given service routinely vary by a factor of two or three, even within the same hospital." Gawande likens the historical model—self-employed physicians in private or small-group practice and community-based hospitals—to the standard of "fork-and-knife" dining in a "linen-napkin-and-tablecloth sort of place." In contrast to more upscale options in the "ecosystem of eating," the casual sector has in recent decades brought heretofore unaffordable and inaccessible cuisine to the general public. Chains such as the Cheesecake Factory have reengineered the gourmet culinary experience for "affordable delivery to millions." To the question proposed by Gawande—"Does health care need something like this?"—one might add, does higher education?[81]

Setting aside for subsequent consideration distinctions to be observed lest the analogy be too hastily drawn, the economies of scale Gawande describes are nonetheless relevant to colleges and universities as well as systems of higher education: "Big chains thrive because they provide goods and services of greater variety, better quality, and lower cost than would otherwise be affordable. Size is the key. It gives them buying power, lets them centralize common functions, and allows them to adopt and diffuse innovations faster than they could if they were a bunch of small, independent operations." And even though the judicious application of such scaling need not impose pernicious standardization in academe, the professoriate is indeed likely to conform to the response Gawande anticipates, which is to "bristle at the idea of chains and mass production, with their homogeneity, predictability, and constant genuflection to the value-for-money god."[82] Assessment of models such as the Cheesecake Factory for higher education may be more or less rhetorical and upon closer inspection would inevitably disclose obvious limitations. But given the challenges confronting American higher education, our nation can no longer merely tweak the status quo in an effort to sustain the present model for another generation.

Costs continue to soar in part because universities often lack sufficient adaptive capacity to innovate and explore alternatives to existing and often obsolete organizational structures, practices, and processes. Universities generally conform to a homogeneous model and lack differentiation. Vast institutional resources are thus devoted to competition with peer institutions in the futile effort to replicate and outperform perceived top-tier schools. Innovation must not only facilitate the advancement of knowledge but also reduce administrative costs. Transinstitutional collaboration in synergistic networks involving universities, industry, and government, for example, both aggregates knowledge and prevents unnecessary replication. Every effort must be undertaken to increase levels of access to world-class teaching, learning, and discovery even as we reduce costs to degree attainment.

## A Tradition Worth Defending Robustly

A liberal arts curriculum has served as the traditional core of American undergraduate education from the outset of our republic and includes the natural sciences as well as the arts, humanities, and social sciences—an important point that is often missed in their discussion. But during recent decades, detractors who view the tradition with increasing skepticism question its value. Policy makers seeking a return on investment from public colleges and universities attempt to frame higher education in narrowly utilitarian terms as workforce development. Proponents of efficiency and thrift in higher education allege that the liberal arts have become or always were irrelevant. Commentators who question the point of a college degree single out the liberal arts as superfluous. But in many respects, to question the value of the liberal arts is to dismiss the purposes of a college education. And in some cases, the perception that the liberal arts are under threat is justified given the interventions of elected officials who seek to regulate the curriculum.

An assessment of the concept warrants digression: In antiquity the liberal arts were termed "liberal" because they were deemed worthy of a free man. The seven traditional liberal arts constitute the three categories or branches of the trivium and the four branches of the quadrivium. The trivium comprises logic, grammar, and rhetoric, while the quadrivium comprises arithmetic, music, geometry, and astronomy.[83] The division into seven branches of learning was not codified until the medieval period, although the philologist Ernst Robert Curtius traces the pedagogical system of medieval learning to the sophist Hippias of Elis, who termed it the "customary, ordinary education."[84] A liberal arts education was customary and ordinary in the sense that it was recognized as the prerequisite for all subsequent study, as well as participation in civic and professional life and service to others.[85]

Even for schools that prioritize workforce preparation, students are invariably shortchanged by the absence of the liberal arts. And apart from considerations of substance in the curriculum, the point has been persuasively argued that socioeconomically disadvantaged students benefit more than most from the sort of liberal arts education historically reserved primarily for the privileged classes. William Durden, then president of Dickinson College, lamented that "every time poor, minority, immigrant, first-generation, or otherwise disadvantaged students in the United States stand to benefit from a liberal arts education, the rules of the game change. Education is suddenly redefined. The liberal arts are devalued, and 'modern' educational theories—usually anti-intellectual, practical, student-centered, and vocational—are trumpeted."[86]

Skepticism regarding the value of the liberal arts is reflected in efforts of elected officials to contravene the autonomy of colleges and universities. Florida Governor Rick Scott achieved a degree of notoriety in October 2011, for example, when he called for reductions in state appropriations for particular academic disciplines in the social sciences. For some reason he seemed especially concerned that Florida universities might be producing too many anthropologists. He explained, "We don't need a lot more anthropologists in the state. It's a great degree if people want to get it, but we don't need them here. I want to spend our dollars giving people science, technology, engineering, and math degrees. That's what our kids need to focus all their time and attention on, those types of degrees, so when they get out of school, they can get a job."

Although Scott sought to eradicate anthropology as a way for public universities to focus resources on the production of graduates in the STEM fields—science, technology, engineering, and math—his attempt to diminish the liberal arts curriculum was both shortsighted and counterproductive. The governor was not mistaken in his assessment that it is imperative to advance the STEM fields, but the notion that to enhance workforce development, legislators must strip away academic programs deemed not immediately applicable reflects a simplistic view of the role of higher education in the economy. Given the importance of scientific discovery and technological innovation to our national competitiveness, American higher education should indeed focus on increasing the quantitative, scientific, and technological literacy of all our students. But the potential for an educated citizenry to contribute to the resolution of the complex challenges that confront society depends on more than science and technology.

The potential for graduates in any field to achieve professional success and thus contribute to our economy depends on their capacity to become adaptive master learners. And a balanced and integrated liberal arts education is a prerequisite to this accomplishment. The significance of a liberal arts curriculum for engineering students, for example, has been underscored by James Duderstadt. He has argued that the "nonlinear nature of the flow of knowledge between fundamental research and engineering application, the highly interdisciplinary nature of new technologies, and the impact of cyberinfrastructure demand new paradigms in engineering research and development." His recommendation is that like the other learned professions—law, medicine, business, and architecture—engineering education requires a "broad liberal arts baccalaureate education as a prerequisite for professional education at the graduate level." He argues that engineering should be construed as a "true liberal arts discipline, similar to the natural sciences, social sciences, and humanities (and the trivium, quadrivium, and natural philosophy of earlier times), by imbedding it in the general education requirements of a college graduate for an increasingly technology-driven and -dependent society."[87]

Citizens and policy makers around the world, and especially in developing economies, model their colleges and universities on American higher education. Early efforts to build research-grade institutions in these nations focused exclusively on science and technology as a mechanism for economic development. But policy makers soon discovered that the exclusion of the humanities and social sciences proved an insurmountable shortcoming in efforts to produce competitive graduates—a realization apparently lost to some elected officials. A recent report from the American Academy of Arts and Sciences thus observed, "At the very moment when China and some European nations are seeking to replicate our model of broad education in the humanities, social sciences, and natural sciences—as a stimulus to innovation and a source of social cohesion—we are instead narrowing our focus and abandoning our sense of what education has been and should continue to be—our sense of what makes America great."[88] As former *Newsweek* editor Jon Meacham points out, "It is inarguably hard to monetize a familiarity with Homer or an intimacy with Shakespeare. It is just possible, though, that the traditional understanding of the liberal arts may help us in our search for new innovation and new competitiveness. The next chapter of the nation's economic life could well be written not only by engineers but by entrepreneurs who, as products of an apparently disparate education, have formed a habit of mind that enables them to connect ideas that might otherwise have gone unconnected."[89]

Arguments on behalf of the liberal arts tend toward the utilitarian, as eloquently articulated by Daniel Mark Fogel, not only president emeritus of the University of Vermont but also a leading Henry James scholar. Fogel writes:

> When the case for higher education touches at all on the arts and humanities (or, for that matter, on such traditional social sciences as political theory and anthropology), it is almost always to attribute to them some marketable utility. Typically, communication skills and a capacity for critical thinking are valued as prerequisites for business success, or modern language and area studies as handmaidens of global commerce. With a little more flair, the arts may be invoked as drivers of the "creative economy," or, alternatively, liberal education may get a perfunctory nod as important to citizenship in a democracy.[90]

Fogel brilliantly surveys further nuances in arguments for the arts and humanities, most of which would resonate only within the precincts of the academy. But one argument in particular bears broadly on the liberal arts and thus the purposes of the American research university. He quotes the philosopher Martha Nussbaum regarding the potential for harm to all of the academic disciplines that comes from the decline in student interest in the arts and humanities: "What we might call the humanistic aspects of science and social science—the imaginative, creative aspect, and the aspect of rigorous critical thought—are also losing ground as nations prefer to pursue short-term profit by the cultivation of the useful and highly applied skills suited to profit-making." More broadly, Fogel paraphrases her contention that an "education that reduces everything to use-value, that sees students only as production units, and that values only work that can be commoditized and only relationships that can be monetized, is profoundly dehumanizing."[91]

It would be superfluous here to rehearse rationales for the liberal arts. But it may be worthwhile to consider the implications of one further claim for the societal benefit of the humanities. Fogel cites an argument from the scholar of English literature M. H. Abrams regarding the imperative significance of critical discourse, which he points out, operates more broadly than the "simplified calculi" of logic and scientific method and is thus "designed for use in the human predicament." Even in our daily routines, Abrams observes, "valid knowledge and understanding are essential, but certainty is impossible." The "rules are uncodified and elusive and there is room for the play of irreducible temperamental differences, yet decisions and judgments are not arbitrary." Absent the critical insight that is the product of a liberal education, Fogel elaborates, how "might we expect those burdened with the power for good and for ill of scientific and technological knowledge to make wise decisions in . . . the domains of policy and ethics, of competing choices and conflicting goods, and of human costs and benefits?"[92]

If reason is to prevail in human affairs, to paraphrase Herbert Simon, then we must confront uncertainty. "When an issue becomes highly controversial—when it is surrounded by uncertainties and conflicting values—then expertness is very hard to come by, and it is no longer easy to legitimate the experts," Simon observes. In these circumstances, we find that there are proponents for the affirmative as well as the negative. The confrontation with uncertainty demands a critical analytical perspective—not so much immediately to decide who is right and who is wrong as to understand the particular combination of facts and values that each side might muster to seek equilibrium between them. Simon continues, "We cannot settle such issues by turning them over to particular groups of experts. At best, we may convert the controversy into an adversary proceeding in which we, the laymen, listen to the experts but have to judge between them."[93] If nothing else, the tradition of the liberal arts produces citizens who sometimes exercise the option to think for themselves and ask tough questions, and this in itself is no small beer. Colleges and universities, and especially our major research universities, are the nonpareil institutional platforms to advance this project, which Plato and some of his contemporaries initiated two thousand four hundred years ago in the hills above Athens. The point then was to frame the right questions and seek the answers, and this approach continues to shape our thinking and our institutions whether we realize it or not. As philosopher Rebecca Goldstein reminds us, this tradition endures not only in our seminar rooms but also at the Googleplex.[94]

## Notes

1. Andrew Delbanco, *College: What It Was, Is, and Should Be* (Princeton, NJ: Princeton University Press, 2012), 11–12.

2. John R. Thelin, *A History of American Higher Education*, 2nd ed. (Baltimore: Johns Hopkins University Press, 2011), 9.

3. David Gross, *The Past in Ruins: Tradition and the Critique of Modernity* (Amherst: University of Massachusetts Press, 2009), 8, 20–21, 24.

4. Ralph Waldo Emerson, "Nature" (1836).

5. Sir Isaac Newton to Robert Hooke (February 5, 1676): "If I have seen farther than others, it is because I was standing on the shoulders of giants." Cited in Matei Calinescu, *Five Faces of Modernity: Modernism, Avant-Garde, Decadence, Kitsch, Postmodernism* (Durham, NC: Duke University Press, 1987), 15–17. Calinescu traces what he terms the "rhetorical commonplace" to the twelfth-century humanist and philosopher Bernard of Chartres (d. 1126), first recorded by John of Salisbury in the *Metalogicon* (1159): "Bernard of Chartres used to compare us to puny dwarfs perched on the shoulders of giants. He pointed out that we see more and farther than our predecessors, not because we have keener vision or greater height, but because we are lifted up and borne aloft on their gigantic stature." For further perspective on this aphorism, see Robert K. Merton, *On the Shoulders of Giants: A Shandean Postscript* (Chicago: University of Chicago Press, 1993).

6. Michael Bacon, "Rorty and Pragmatic Social Criticism," *Philosophy and Social Criticism* 32, no. 7 (2006): 864.

7. *Oxford English Dictionary*, 3rd ed. (Oxford: Oxford University Press, 2012), online version March 2012.

8. Clark Kerr, introduction to José Ortega y Gasset, *The Mission of the University*, ed. and trans. Howard Lee Nostrand (1944; New Brunswick, NJ: Transaction, 1992).

9. Louis Menand, *The Marketplace of Ideas: Reform and Resistance in the American University* (New York: W. W. Norton, 2010), 17.

10. Immanuel Wallerstein, "Anthropology, Sociology, and Other Dubious Disciplines," *Current Anthropology* 44, no. 4 (August–October 2003): 453–465.

11. John Seely Brown and Paul Duguid, "Organizational Learning and Communities-of-Practice: Toward a Unified View of Working, Learning, and Innovation," *Organization Science* 2, no. 1 (February 1991): 40.

12. Ian Hacking, *Historical Ontology* (Cambridge, MA: Harvard University Press, 2002), 5.

13. Simon Critchley, "What Is Continental Philosophy?" *International Journal of Philosophical Studies* 5, no. 3: 357–358. The context for this explication is his discussion of Edmund Husserl's distinction between a "sedimented" and a "reactivated" sense of tradition in *The Crisis of the European Sciences* (1954). The task of the philosopher, writes Critchley, is the "production of crisis, disturbing the slow accumulation of the deadening sediment of tradition" with "emancipatory intent" (358).

14. Paul J. DiMaggio and Walter W. Powell, "The Iron Cage Revisited: Institutional Isomorphism and Collective Rationality in Organizational Fields," *American Sociological Review* 48, no. 2 (April 1983): 147–160.

15. J. Douglas Toma, "Institutional Strategy: Positioning for Prestige," in *The Organization of Higher Education: Managing Colleges for a New Era*, ed. Michael N. Bastedo (Baltimore: Johns Hopkins University Press, 2012), 118–159.

16. William Clark, *Academic Charisma and the Origins of the Research University* (Chicago: University of Chicago Press, 2006), 11–12, 18. Clark alludes to the "medieval juridico-ecclesiastical" basis of academic life that in the early modern era gives way to the "politico-economic world of ministries and markets" (8).

17. Max Weber, "The Sociology of Charismatic Authority," in *Essays in Sociology*, ed. and trans. H. H. Gerth and C. Wright Mills (Oxford: Oxford University Press, 1946), reprinted in Max Weber, *On Charisma and Institution Building: Selected Papers*, ed. S. N. Eisenstadt (Chicago: University of Chicago Press, 1968), 18–19.

18. S. N. Eisenstadt, introduction to Weber, *On Charisma and Institution Building*, ix–xv.

19. Clark identifies the veneration of the academic or scientific genius as representative both of the "Romantic cult of personality at the modern university" and in terms of a "Weberian charismatic transfiguration of reason." *Academic Charisma*, 16.

20. Clark, *Academic Charisma*, 14–17.

21. Martin Jay, "Name-Dropping or Dropping Names? Modes of Legitimation in the Humanities," in *Force Fields: Between Intellectual History and Cultural Critique* (New York: Routledge, 1993), 167–169.

22. Harold Bloom, *The Anxiety of Influence: A Theory of Poetry* (New York: Oxford University Press, 1973).

23. Thomas S. Kuhn, *The Structure of Scientific Revolutions*, 3rd ed. (1962; Chicago: University of Chicago Press, 1996), 6.

24. Harold Bloom, *The Breaking of the Vessels* (Chicago: University of Chicago Press, 1982).

25. Joseph A. Schumpeter, *The Theory of Economic Development* (Cambridge, MA: Harvard University Press, 1934).

26. Clark, *Academic Charisma*, 15.

27. For an explication of the fallacies associated with such methodologies, see the famous letter from Gerhard Casper, then president of Stanford University, to James Fallows, then editor of *U.S. News and World Report* (September 23, 1996), http://www .stanford.edu/dept/pres-provost/president/speeches/961206gcfallow.html.

28. DiMaggio and Powell, "Iron Cage Revisited," 147–149.

29. DiMaggio and Powell, "Iron Cage Revisited," 150–152.

30. Toma, "Institutional Strategy," 118–119, 152.

31. Anthony P. Carnevale and Jeff Strohl, "How Increasing College Access Is Increasing Inequality, and What to Do about It," in *Rewarding Strivers: Helping Low-Income Students Succeed in College*, ed. Richard D. Kahlenberg (New York: Century Foundation, 2010), 95–96.

32. Toma, "Institutional Strategy," 118, 120–121, 123.

33. Toma, "Institutional Strategy," 120, 123–124, 126–128, 136, 141, 145, 154.

34. Max Weber, *The Protestant Ethic and the Spirit of Capitalism*, trans. Talcott Parsons (New York: Charles Scribner's Sons, 1952), quoted in DiMaggio and Powell, "Iron Cage Revisited," 147.

35. Anthony Downs, *Inside Bureaucracy* (Boston: Little Brown, 1967), 8.

36. Michael T. Hannan and John Freeman, "Structural Inertia and Organizational Change," *American Sociological Review* 49 (April 1984): 149–164.

37. Downs, *Inside Bureaucracy*, 18–19.

38. Clayton M. Christensen, *The Innovator's Dilemma* (Cambridge, MA: Harvard Business School Press, 1997).

39. Richard A. DeMillo, *Abelard to Apple: The Fate of American Colleges and Universities* (Cambridge, MA: MIT Press, 2011), 28–29.

40. Toma, "Institutional Strategy," 150.

41. John V. Lombardi, *How Universities Work* (Baltimore: Johns Hopkins University Press, 2013), 30–31.

42. Louis Menand, *Marketplace of Ideas*, 15. Menand quotes Francis Cornford, *Microcosmographia Academica: Being a Guide for the Young Academic Politician*, 4th ed. (1908; Cambridge: Bowes and Bowes, 1949), 15.

43. Jonathan R. Cole, *The Great American University: Its Rise to Preeminence, Its Indispensable National Role, and Why It Must Be Protected* (New York: Public Affairs, 2009), 134, 143.

44. Laurence R. Veysey, *The Emergence of the American University* (Chicago: University of Chicago Press, 1965), 89.

45. Frank H. T. Rhodes, *The Creation of the Future: The Role of the American University* (Ithaca, NY: Cornell University Press, 2001), 85–86; 250, nn. 3, 4.

46. See the chapter "The Problems of General Education," in Menand, *Marketplace of Ideas*, 23–57.

47. George M. Marsden, *The Soul of the American University: From Protestant Establishment to Established Nonbelief* (New York: Oxford University Press, 1994), 199.

48. Hugh H. Hawkins, "Charles W. Eliot: University Reform and Religious Faith in America, 1869–1909," *The Journal of American History* 51, no. 2 (September 1964): 196, 198–200; Jerome Karabel, *The Chosen: The Hidden History of Admission and Exclusion at Harvard, Yale, and Princeton* (New York: Houghton Mifflin, 2005), 39.

49. Hanna Holborn Gray, *Searching for Utopia: Universities and Their Histories* (Berkeley: University of California Press, 2012), 14.

50. Robert Hutchins, confidential memo (to the Board of Trustees), July 2, 1942, 9, quoted by Gray, *Searching for Utopia*, 17.

51. Hutchins, Trustee-Faculty Dinner Speech, January 12, 1944 (Robert Hutchins Papers, Box 26, Folder 3, University of Chicago Library), quoted by Gray, *Searching for Utopia*, 17.

52. Louis Menand, *The Metaphysical Club: A Story of Ideas in America* (New York: Farrar, Straus and Giroux, 2001), 239.

53. Clark Kerr, *The Uses of the University*, 5th ed. (1963; Cambridge, MA: Harvard University Press, 2001), 15.

54. James Axtell, *The Making of Princeton University: From Woodrow Wilson to the Present* (Princeton, NJ: Princeton University Press, 2006), 1. Axtell quotes from the diary of Colonel Edward House (December 12, 1913), in *The Papers of Woodrow Wilson*, ed. Arthur S. Link et al. (Princeton, NJ: Princeton University Press, 1966–1994), 29, 33–34.

55. Nannerl Keohane in "Woodrow Wilson as a Leader: Successes and Failures," presented at Princeton Colloquium on Public and International Affairs. 2006. http://wws .princeton.edu/research/special_reports/PCPIA2006_PresidentsPanel.pdf

56. Hardin Craig, *Woodrow Wilson at Princeton* (Norman: University of Oklahoma Press, 1960).

57. Arthur Link, "Woodrow Wilson," in *A Princeton Companion*, compiled by Alexander Leitch (Princeton, NJ: Princeton University Press, 1978).

58. Link, "Woodrow Wilson," in *A Princeton Companion*.

59. Cole, *Great American University*, 41.

60. Axtell, *The Making of Princeton University*, 1.

61. Charles Van Hise, quoted in the annual report of the University of Wisconsin Foundation, *The Wisconsin University Thrives* (Madison, 2007), http://www.supportuw .org/wp-content/uploads/annual_report_07.pdf.

62. Jack Stark, *The Wisconsin Idea: The University's Service to the State* (Madison, WI: Legislative Reference Bureau, 1996).

63. "Year of the Wisconsin Idea, 2011–2012." http://wisconsinidea.wisc.edu/yowi/

64. John Aubrey Douglass, *The California Idea and American Higher Education: 1850 to the 1960 Master Plan* (Stanford: Stanford University Press, 2000), 112–113; 140–141; 238; 339–340.

65. Clark Kerr, *The Gold and the Blue: A Personal Memoir of the University of California (1949–1967)*: Volume 2: *Political Turmoil* (Berkeley: University of California Press, 2003).

66. Douglass, *California Idea and American Higher Education*, 206–213.

67. Cole, *Great American University*, 134–135. For a detailed account of the background and legacy of the Master Plan, see the relevant chapters in Douglass, *California Idea and American Higher Education*.

68. Clark Kerr, *The Gold and the Blue: A Personal Memoir of the University of California (1949–1967)*: Volume 1: *Academic Triumphs* (Berkeley: University of California Press, 2001), 173–174, 178, 180, 182.

69. See especially the introduction to Veysey, *Emergence of the American University*.

70. Robert Zemsky, *Making Reform Work: The Case for Transforming American Higher Education* (New Brunswick, NJ: Rutgers University Press, 2009), 107.

71. William J. Baumol, *The Cost Disease: Why Computers Get Cheaper and Health Care Doesn't* (New Haven, CT: Yale University Press, 2012), 4.

72. William J. Baumol and William G. Bowen, "On the Performing Arts: The Anatomy of Their Economic Problems," *American Economic Review* 55, no. 1/2 (March 1965):

495–502; William J. Baumol and William G. Bowen, *Performing Arts: The Economic Dilemma* (New York: The Twentieth Century Fund, 1966).

73. Baumol and Bowen, "On the Performing Arts," 500.

74. Baumol and Bowen, *Performing Arts*, 64.

75. Baumol and Bowen, *Performing Arts*, 164, cited in James Heilbrun, "Baumol's Cost Disease," in *A Handbook of Cultural Economics*, ed. Ruth Towse (Cheltenham, UK: Edward Elgar, 2003), 91.

76. Baumol and Bowen, "On the Performing Arts," 500.

77. Baumol, *Cost Disease*, xi, 19.

78. Lombardi, *How Universities Work*, 2–10; Paul Duguid, "The Art of Knowing: Social and Tacit Dimensions of Knowledge and the Limits of the Community of Practice," *Information Society* 21 (2005): 112–113, 115, n. 1.

79. Gregory Besharov, "The Outbreak of Cost Disease: Baumol and Bowen's Founding of Cultural Economics," *History of Political Economy* 37, no. 3 (2005): 416.

80. Lombardi, *How Universities Work*, 29.

81. Atul Gawande, "Big Med: Should Hospitals Be More Like Chain Restaurants?" *New Yorker* (August 13, 2012): 52–63.

82. Gawande, "Big Med," 52–63.

83. Miriam Joseph, *The Trivium: The Liberal Arts of Logic, Grammar, and Rhetoric* (Philadelphia: Paul Dry Books, 1982), 1–9.

84. Ernst Robert Curtius, *European Literature and the Latin Middle Ages*, trans. Willard R. Trask (Princeton, NJ: Bollingen, 1953), 36–37. Curtius identifies a *locus classicus* for the conception in Seneca's Epistle 88.

85. Joseph, *Trivium*, 4.

86. William Durden, "Liberal Arts for All, Not Just the Rich," *Chronicle of Higher Education* (October 19, 2001).

87. James J. Duderstadt, *Engineering for a Changing World: A Roadmap to the Future of Engineering Practice, Research, and Education* (Ann Arbor: The Millennium Project, University of Michigan, 2008), iii–v.

88. American Academy of Arts and Sciences, *The Heart of the Matter: The Humanities and Social Sciences For A Vibrant, Competitive, and Secure Nation* (Cambridge, MA: American Academy of Arts and Sciences, 2013), 10.

89. Jon Meacham, "In Defense of the Liberal Arts," *Newsweek* (January 9, 2010).

90. Daniel Mark Fogel, "Challenges to Equilibrium: The Place of the Arts and Humanities in Public Research Universities," in *Precipice or Crossroads: Where America's Great Public Universities Stand and Where They Are Going Midway Through Their Second Century*, ed. Daniel Mark Fogel (Albany: State University of New York Press, 2012), 241.

91. Martha Nussbaum, *Not for Profit: Why Democracy Needs the Humanities* (Princeton, NJ: Princeton University Press, 2010), 2, quoted in Fogel, "Challenges to Equilibrium," 251, 255. Tamar Lewin of the *New York Times* cites federal data that show that the "percentage of humanities majors hovers around 7 percent—half the 14 percent share in 1970." She reports that only 15 percent of Stanford undergraduates currently major

in the humanities and that over the past decade, Harvard witnessed a 20 percent decline in humanities majors. Lewin, "As Interest Fades in the Humanities, Colleges Worry," *New York Times* (October 30, 2013).

92. M. H. Abrams, "What's the Use of Theorizing About the Arts?" in *In Search of Literary Theory*, ed. Morton W. Bloomfield (Ithaca, NY: Cornell University Press, 1972), 52–54, quoted in Fogel, "Challenges to Equilibrium," 253–254.

93. Herbert A. Simon, *Reason in Human Affairs* (Stanford: Stanford University Press, 1983), 97.

94. Rebecca Goldstein, *Plato at the Googleplex: Why Philosophy Won't Go Away* (New York: Pantheon, 2014).

# FOUR

# Discovery, Creativity, and Innovation

An open letter to members of Congress signed by the executives of sixteen leading technology corporations regarding proposed reductions in federal support for academic research in 1995 alluded to thousands of technological breakthroughs that are the product of the partnership between research universities, the federal government, and industrial product development. "Imagine life without polio vaccines and heart pacemakers," the letter begins. "Or digital computers. Or municipal water purification systems. Or space-based weather forecasting. Or advanced cancer therapies. Or jet airliners. Or disease-resistant grains and vegetables. Or cardiopulmonary resuscitation."[1]

More recently, in the wake of the economic collapse of 2008, more than fifty leaders in public higher education convened by the Carnegie Corporation of New York submitted an open letter to then president-elect Obama and his administration regarding the proposed Higher Education Investment Act. In the midst of crisis, the authors reaffirmed the partnership between the federal government and our research universities but even more eloquently underscored their critical societal role:

America's colleges and universities, public and private, have always worked in the service of our nation, contributing to our social, economic, scientific, cultural, and technological preeminence by educating millions of citizens who contribute to every sector of society. Today, with millions of students, thousands of laboratories, and outreach that touches countless communities in rural and urban America, the great institutions of public higher education, along with our sister institutions in the private sector, have the capacity to produce the people, ideas, tools, solutions, and knowledge infrastructure our economy needs to regain its momentum and to set a new trajectory.[2]

While fundamental research has transformed our understanding of the universe, the breakthrough technologies of university-based innovation—from lasers to magnetic resonance imaging to global positioning systems to the algorithm for Google searches—have vastly improved our quality of life and contributed incalculably to economic growth. These innovations figure in the compendium compiled by Jonathan Cole along with thousands of other transformational "discoveries, inventions, devices, concepts, techniques, and tools" that have vastly improved our quality of life and contributed incalculably to economic growth. All originated at our nation's research universities. Inasmuch as Cole offers a remarkable synopsis of fundamental and applied academic research in science and technology that spans more than one hundred pages, it would be superfluous in the present context to attempt an adequate summary of his survey.[3]

Although innovations in the science and technology sector are more likely to come to mind because of their tangible impact on our daily lives, creative and scholarly endeavor in the arts, humanities, and social and behavioral sciences arguably shapes our lives in equal measure. Inasmuch as any attempt to assess the extent to which the ivory tower has informed, suffused, shaped, and articulated the real world and how we experience it would be hopeless, if not impossible, suffice it here to suggest that the scope and breadth of the contribution are beyond measure. "Scholars in these fields make discoveries all the time," Cole explains. "We tend not to classify the results of their work as particularly profound or consequential. This is a mistake." Not to belabor the obvious, but these discoveries "often take the form of basic ideas, concepts, theories, and the results of empirical research" and thus differ from scientific discovery and technological invention: "But when scholars translate great authors whose works have been totally unfamiliar to us previously, these are discoveries. When linguists identify the fundamental structure of language and linguistic forms, or when philosophers propose ideas about causality, . . . these, too, are discoveries." And with the advent of information technologies, the diffusion of knowledge has quickened immeasurably: "Major discoveries in one field quickly diffuse into another—say, from economics to sociology, or from psychology into economics. In short order, powerful concepts move from the initial field to cognate disciplines and from there into the language of everyday life. Thus we have all heard of 'human capital,' the 'self-fulfilling prophecy,' or 'relative deprivation.'"[4]

In a chapter about the impact of academic research on our culture, society, and values appropriately entitled *"Nosce te Ipsum"*—know thyself—Cole organizes his tally of important discoveries in the humanities and social and behavioral sciences into five general categories: "concepts related to our decisions and reasoning; values and opinions; culture, economy, and society; ourselves and our sensibilities; and our 'thinking about thinking'—that is, the discoveries made in philosophy, literary theory, and the like." Impact on decision making and reasoning, for example, comes from concepts and theories such as the self-fulfilling prophecy, originated by the sociologist Robert K. Merton; the theory of cognitive dissonance, developed by the psychologist Leon Festinger; game theory and such corollaries as zero-sum games, which he attributes to the pioneering work of the mathematician John von Neumann and economist Oskar Morgenstern; or the tragedy of the commons, a dilemma first addressed by Aristotle and then more recently by economists in the nineteenth century but brought to the forefront in the 1960s by the ecologist Garrett Hardin. Techniques such as election polling and scrutiny of evidence and eyewitness testimony in jury trials similarly have been transformed through academic research.[5]

Examples of the impact of the academy on our culture, economy, and society include the development and application of such concepts as human capital, which, Cole explains, was suggested by Adam Smith but brought to contemporary relevance by economists Milton Friedman and Gary Becker; unintended consequences, which were first systematically addressed by Robert K. Merton in 1946; and deviant behavior, which, while it borrowed from the work of Emile Durkheim, was developed by Merton in an attempt to understand the causes of crime and delinquency. Sociolinguistics, for example, has brought insight into the linguistic patterns of the socioeconomically disadvantaged, while quantitative models derived from econometrics and statistics have informed policy making through assessments of social mobility and the correlates of inequality, poverty, and wealth. Sociologists and anthropologists have articulated structural determinants of patterns of behavior, while social network analysis has brought insight to human interaction. As one example of the latter, Cole considers the strength of weak ties, the insight by Mark Granovetter that communication and information flow more readily through networks of acquaintances than close friends.[6]

The impacts of contributions from economics, political science, and the behavioral sciences are too pervasive to summarize, and their further survey would be superfluous in the present context. No less so with contributions from these fields to our understanding of "ourselves and our sensibilities." Here again we defer to the synopsis offered by Cole: "Studies in such fields as linguistics, social and cultural anthropology, social psychology, and human sexuality, and from professional schools such as law, have helped to shape our understanding of the human condition; they have given us insight into many areas of human life, sometimes influencing policy debates and decisions."[7] And this is to say nothing of the impact of the arts and humanities, which undergird our intellectual culture and flourish in the American research university.

This chapter focuses on the impact of integrated academic research, development, and education (RD&E) on local, regional, national, and global economic development, the majority of which derives from scientific discovery and technological innovation. Advances in knowledge leading to technological innovation enabled by scientific research have increasingly spurred economic growth, leading to the development of entire new industries. Implicit in claims for the economic development function of the research university is the recognition that the institution is a platform to advance broad societal development. We reiterate that our focus on the economic development potential of academic research stems from the contention that prosperity promotes social advancement and the values and ideals of our pluralistic democracy.

## Assessing the Economic Impact of Knowledge

In what has been termed the Great Divergence, average living standards for a portion of the world's population were transformed by the Industrial Revolution: "Around 1800, in northwestern Europe and North America, man's long sojourn in the Malthusian world ended," explains economist Gregory Clark. "The iron link between population and living

standards, through which any increase in population caused an immediate decline in wages, was decisively broken."[8] The economic historian
Joel Mokyr is representative of scholars who find the proximate cause of
the unprecedented and sustained economic growth of the West during
the past two centuries not primarily in geographical, cultural, social, or
political factors but rather in the "knowledge revolution" triggered by the
Scientific Revolution and the Enlightenment: "The central phenomenon
of the modern age is that as an aggregate we know more." His assessment
of the historical origins of the knowledge economy thus provides useful
perspective on the interrelationships between knowledge and economic
development. The stream of basic scientific knowledge about nature produced since the Enlightenment, Mokyr elaborates, spurred the Industrial
Revolution and enabled the technological innovations and attendant efficiency gains that brought about the economic transformation of the
West beginning with the early modern era.[9]

Efforts to define the knowledge economy focus on the impact of
knowledge production on technological innovation. "The key component
of a knowledge economy is a greater reliance on intellectual capabilities
than on physical inputs or natural resources," Walter Powell and Kaisa
Snellman explain. But the "leading edge of the economy in developed
countries has become driven by technologies based on knowledge and
information production and dissemination."[10] An appreciation of the role
of technological innovation in our knowledge-based society requires less
restrictive definitions of both *technology* and *innovation*. According to
the economist and complexity theorist W. Brian Arthur, technology may
refer simply to any "means to fulfill a human purpose . . . . As a means,
a technology may be a method or process or device: a particular speech
recognition algorithm, or a filtration process in chemical engineering, or
a diesel engine." But more broadly, technology is also an "assemblage of
practices and components" and may refer to the "entire collection of devices and engineering practices available to a culture."[11] Innovation, formerly understood to refer primarily to product development in industry,
has more recently come to designate any "reconfiguration of elements
into a more productive combination," writes economist Henry Etzkowitz. In a sense relevant to the impetus for institutional reconceptualization intrinsic to the New American University, this new model for

innovation may thus refer to the "restructuring and enhancement of the organizational arrangements and incentives that foster innovation," a process he terms the "innovation of innovation."[12]

Mokyr underscores the correlation between scientific discovery and technological innovation: "technology is knowledge" but scientific knowledge is the basis for technological progress as well as its adaptability to market demand: "The wider and deeper the epistemic base on which a technique rests, the more likely it is that a technique can be extended and find new applications, product and service quality improved, the production process streamlined, economized, and adapted to changing external circumstances, and the techniques combined with others to form new ones." Without continued elucidation from scientific investigation, the technologically driven economic development that has characterized the West since the Industrial Revolution—and increasingly the rest of the global economy—is certain to stagnate: "Without widening the epistemic base, the continuous development of techniques will eventually run into diminishing returns simply because the natural phenomena can be understood only partially and arguably only superficially."[13] Indeed, according to economists Partha Dasgupta and Paul A. David, "To say that economic growth in the modern era has been grounded on the exploitation of scientific knowledge is to express a truism."[14]

Mokyr terms knowledge that leads to technological innovation and thus economic growth "useful knowledge," following an earlier usage by the economist Simon Kuznets. Thus, "useful knowledge includes 'scientific' knowledge as a subset," as well as what is termed applied science.[15] Mokyr underscores that economic growth in the modern era has been determined not only by knowledge production but also by its dissemination through social networks, including scholarly publication, scientific societies, and especially universities. Only through access does knowledge become useful, however.[16] As centers of knowledge production and dissemination, research universities constitute its primary nodes of access and fulfill the critical function of transmitting knowledge across generations. An assessment of the imperative for such access is implicit in an observation by the economist Paul Romer: "Each person has only a finite number of years that can be spent acquiring skills. When this person dies, the skills are lost, but any nonrival good that this person produces—a scientific law; a principle of mechanical, electrical, or chemical engineering; a mathematical result; software; a patent; a mechanical drawing; or a blueprint—lives on after the person is gone."[17]

Estimates of the economic impact of technological innovation were first developed in the mid-twentieth century by Robert M. Solow and Moses Abramowitz, who initiated research on the determinants of economic growth, hypothesizing that in addition to labor and capital, productivity depends on such variables as the acquisition and application of knowledge. A report from the National Academies explains that Solow and Abramowitz had calculated that "as much as 85 percent of measured growth in U.S. income per capita during the 1890–1950 period could not be explained by increases in the capital stock or other measurable inputs" and could thus be attributed to technological innovation.[18] David Mowery and Nathan Rosenberg elaborate: "No more than 15 percent of the measured growth in U.S. output in the late nineteenth century and the first half of the twentieth century need be accounted for by the growth in measured inputs of capital and labor: The strikingly large 'residual' of 85 percent suggested that twentieth-century American economic growth was overwhelmingly a matter of extracting more output from each unit of input into economic activity." The obvious variable is technological innovation.[19] With the Solow growth model as the basis, economists have more recently modeled technological progress as total factor productivity (TFP), a variable that accounts for differences in output not attributable to inputs of labor and capital.[20] And while technological innovation remained for Solow an estimated external variable, Paul Romer endogenized technological change as driven by the generation of knowledge. In his model, human capital—the stock of knowledge and creativity embodied in individuals—is the factor of production responsible for economic growth.[21] Needless to add, education is the principal means to foster the development of human capital.

Economists have generally concluded that technological progress, as broadly defined in economics, is key to continued growth in developed economies. Technological progress can account for more than half of economic growth as customarily measured in the United States since 1960, and according to estimates comparing differences across countries, roughly 90 percent of differences in the growth rate of income per worker.[22] More broadly, Charles I. Jones determined that "70 percent of the improvement in productivity in the United States between 1950 and 1993 can be attributed to the direct and indirect effects of new knowledge."[23] Other research supports the hypothesis that higher education exercises its greatest impact on nations close to the "technological frontier."[24] The economic impact of science-based technological innovation derived from commercialized academic research has been well documented in a number of more specialized sectors as well.[25]

## The Economic Impact of University-Based Research and Development

To the extent that artistic creativity, humanistic and social scientific insight, and scientific discoveries and technological innovation contribute to the cultural dynamism, economic prosperity, quality of life, and societal vitality of our pluralistic democracy and the global community, the contributions of the American research university are obvious. Apart from their role in the formation of successive generations of our nation's scholars and scientists and experts in every sphere of human endeavor, the set of research universities, both public and private, has served as the primary source of the discovery, creativity, and innovation that fosters economic growth and social development at all levels of analysis in the global knowledge economy. Although the extent of their influence through undergraduate and graduate education is so pervasive as to defy measure, the demand for students educated to the rigorous standards of the contemporary workforce attests to the impact of this set of institutions. Moreover, as we previously considered, projections suggest soaring demand for graduates with advanced levels of educational attainment, and especially for individuals attuned to the knowledge-intensive academic culture characteristic of research universities.

Because these institutions also produce a significant proportion of the most important fundamental and applied research in the world, their impact on society is transformative. The research and development function of these institutions, conducted in coordination with their undergraduate and graduate programs, has spurred economic and social development even as it has contributed incalculably to the standard of living and quality of life most of us take for granted.[26] The comprehensive breadth of this role is delineated in a report from the National Academies commissioned by the U.S. Congress to assess threats to the competitive stature and continued preeminence of these institutions:

America is driven by innovation—advances in ideas, products, and processes that create new industries and jobs, contribute to our nation's health and security, and support a high standard of living. In the past half-century, innovation itself has been increasingly driven by educated people and the knowledge they produce. Our nation's primary source of both new knowledge and graduates with advanced skills continues to be our research universities.[27]

The intrinsic impetus to advance new knowledge distinguishes the American research university from other institutional platforms in higher education, and the impact of these institutions on economic and social development is increasingly correlated with their role in the advancement of scientific discovery and technological innovation. "The production of scientific knowledge has become an economic as well as an epistemological enterprise," Henry Etzkowitz observes, "even as the economy increasingly operates on a knowledge-resource base."[28] Another committee convened by the National Academies provides further context: "Knowledge acquired and applied by scientists and engineers provides the tools and systems that characterize modern culture and the raw materials for economic growth and well-being." To sustain economic growth in an economy characterized by increasing "knowledge density," the committee assesses, societies must "produce, select, adapt, and commercialize" knowledge.[29] To facilitate the impact of this sector, another report advises that universities must perform "double duty: to educate and train not only those who will have careers in research, but also those who will become entrepreneurs, managers, consultants, investors, or policy makers."[30]

The concept of academic enterprise characterizes the economic and social development mission of the American research university, although the coinage "entrepreneurial university" captures this dimension as well.[31] An entrepreneurial approach to knowledge has long been a defining characteristic of American research universities, as we assessed in chapter 2, apparent even in the nineteenth century in the utilitarian orientation and engagement with industry of the land-grant institutions associated with the Morrill Act.[32] "An embryonic entrepreneurial dynamic originated in the U.S. university during the late nineteenth century when lack of a formal research funding system, apart from agriculture, placed a premium on individual and collective initiatives to obtain resources to support original investigation," Etzkowitz elaborates.[33] The concept of academic enterprise is intrinsically interrelated with science-based technological innovation, especially as formulated in the conception of entrepreneurship advanced by Joseph Schumpeter, who ascribed the innovation intrinsic to the processes of creative destruction to entrepreneurs: "The function of entrepreneurs is to reform or revolutionize the pattern of production by exploiting invention or, more generally, an untried technological possibility for producing new commodities or producing an old one in a new way."[34] Policy scholar David M. Hart observes that Schumpeter conceived of technological innovation as a "particularly important mechanism through which entrepreneurial ventures express their novelty and dynamism. Its importance stems in large part from the contribution that new technologies make to economic growth."[35]

With economic growth increasingly tied to knowledge-intensive innovation, interactions between universities, industry, and government became critically important in the period after 1960. These interrelationships constitute what Etzkowitz terms the "triple helix" of university-industry-government innovation. Although industry is the "key actor as the locus of production" and government serves as the "source of contractual relations that guarantee stable interactions and exchange," the role of the university in this triad is preeminent: "The university is the generative principle of knowledge-based societies just as government and industry were the primary institutions in industrial society." The concept embraces the nexus of relatively autonomous institutional sectors and hybrid organizations associated with innovation such as technology transfer offices and venture capital firms.[36] These nodes in the national innovation system, a concept to which we return in the following, intersect with the industrial commons, which Harvard business economists Gary Pisano and Willy Shih define as the "collective R&D, engineering, and manufacturing capabilities that sustain innovation." In an assessment of American economic competitiveness in this context, Pisano and Shih remark, "We cannot emphasize enough the importance of world-class universities in building the commons."[37]

Buoyed by the development of a knowledge-intensive economy, the growth of academic entrepreneurship has been described by Etzkowitz as the "working out of an inner logic of academic development" consistent with the inherent structure of academic research, which is often conducted by a "series of research groups that have firm-like qualities, especially under conditions in which research funding is awarded on a competitive basis." Etzkowitz observes that the "research university shares homologous qualities with a start-up firm even before it directly engages in entrepreneurial activities."[38]

The integrated research, development, and education functions of research universities contribute to the production and dissemination of new knowledge and through its utilization become catalysts spurring regional, national, and global economic development. Through the development of products, processes, and applications across a range of fields and markets, academic research demonstrates the potential to generate significant economic returns, a process that invigorates the broader economic contributions of universities.[39] Academic research attracts external funding from federal, state, and local government agencies, as well as from business and industry. Research-related spending thus reflects the success of an institution in competing for funding from sponsors and is an important indicator of the overall contribution of an institution both to the knowledge base and its regional economy.

A committee of the National Research Council charged with evaluating technology transfer activities and intellectual property rights stemming from publicly and privately sponsored research within the context of the public interest produced a synopsis that suggests the scope and complexity of the commercialization, or capitalization, of academic research:

> Discovery, learning, and societal engagement are mutually supportive core missions of the research university. Transfer of knowledge to those in society who can make use of it for the general good contributes to each of these missions. These transfers occur through publications, training and education of students, employment of graduates, conferences, consultations, and collaboration as well as by obtaining rights to inventions and discoveries that qualify for patent protection (intellectual property, or IP) and licensing them to private enterprises. All of these means of knowledge sharing have contributed to a long history of mutually beneficial relations among U.S. public and private universities, the private sector, and society at large.[40]

We considered the context of federal investment in our nation's research universities in chapter 2. A closer look at the extent of that

commitment and its apportionment between the various sectors responsible for innovation attests to the importance of the academic
research enterprise. Estimated federal investment in research and development across all sectors in the United States in 2013 totaled $128.8 bil-
lion, with roughly 32 percent, or $41.3 billion, provided to universities.
Academia spends $66.6 billion in research dollars derived from various
sources out of the total $423.7 billion available for research and develop-
ment nationally. Academia thus performs roughly 15 percent of research
and development in the United States by dollar, behind industrial R&D,
which conducts over half.[41] But even though industry and academia
comprise the two largest sectors of the research economy, the two are
far from similar in impact per dollar spent, and a glance at the figures
fails to convey the outsized contributions of research universities. Despite its relatively modest R&D budget when compared to industry, academia performs more than 60 percent of all basic research conducted
in the United States. To reiterate, the sector associated with 15 percent
of the US R&D economy performs more than 60 percent of all basic
research. In addition, academia produces more than two-thirds of the
scientific papers published by the United States, meaning that the academy dominates the published discussion of science. In addition, academia and industry are deemed equally most effective for technology
collaborations, according to a survey conducted by Battelle Institute.[42]
Academia may comprise a smaller amount of total research performance
by dollar, but it is clear that the sector is punching well above its weight
in the R&D economy.

With the passage of the Bayh-Dole Act of 1980, which permitted universities to retain intellectual property rights to the ideas, products, and
processes developed as a result of federally funded research, relations
between academic institutions and business and industry were transformed.[43] The legislation was motivated by the anticipation that growth
in patenting and licensing by universities would promote interaction with
industry for commercial development and as a consequence spur economic growth. Research universities were the immediate beneficiaries,
but the extent to which the legislation facilitated technology transfer between universities and industry varies across institutions.[44] Effective
commercialization of academic research requires the judicious coordination of state and federal policies that encourage the diffusion of inno-

vation. Although the Bayh-Dole Act and related legislation facilitated patenting and licensing by academic institutions, continued government initiatives to spur innovation and competitiveness remain an imperative. If the United States is to leverage its dominant position in science and technology, academic and industrial endeavor will require support from programs and policies conducive to technology-based economic development.[45] Advocates of the laissez-faire approach that has dominated national policy in this context from the outset assume investment from the private sector is sufficient to foster innovation, but historic underinvestment from industry, with its limited incentive to value basic research without immediate commercial application, underscores the need for policies aimed at turning the nation's R&D capability to competitive advantage for the greatest possible public benefit. The much-contested policy environment for American science and technology requires continued evaluation and reconceptualization focused on consolidating its relevance to national economic objectives.[46]

The array of correlates of educational attainment begins with its intrinsic value to the individual, as we assessed in chapter 1, but the extent of collateral returns both to the individual and society is considerable. Apart from the direct monetary benefits associated with increased opportunities for more meaningful employment, higher education influences lifestyle choices that correlate with better health and greater civic participation. We cited the well-known government estimates that individuals who complete bachelor's degrees earn nearly $1 million more over the course of their lifetimes than those who have only completed high school, and the marked increase for those with advanced and professional degrees.[47] We observed that citizens able to make more informed choices benefit not only themselves and their families but also their communities and state as well. And we cited data that show that a more educated workforce generates greater tax revenues and influences quality-of-place decision making.[48]

But the discussion of collateral returns to the individual and society sometimes overlooks the extent of the impacts of research universities on their local communities and regions. This begins with the production of educated citizens and a competitive workforce, whose cumulative impacts are manifold. Economic impacts to communities include external funding to institutions from federal, state, and local government agencies as well as from business and industry. These provide an economic return on investment to the communities that support these institutions. Research-related spending reflects the competitive success of an institution in this context and is an important indicator of the extent of its overall contribution both to the knowledge base and the regional economy. Academic research expenditures exert significant impact on private-sector research activities, influencing both the level of industrial research and development and industrial patents.

The returns on investment in a major research university are geographically localized. Local economic impact studies use various methodological approaches, beginning with calculations of the impacts of universities on employment, incomes, and the consumer spending of faculty, staff, and students. In many communities, for example, the university is one of the largest employers, and the institution itself is generally a major consumer of products and services produced by the local economy, including spending on construction projects. The multiplier effect of such spending within local economies generates upstream demands on other producers, which in turn produce additional tax revenues. Calculations of such economic interdependencies are complex, and analysis by one team of economists listed such inputs as "direct employment and payroll, less federal taxes; expenditures for equipment, supplies, and services; construction costs; spending in the local community by faculty members, administrative staff, and students; public and private support of research grants and contracts; tuition and fees paid by students; . . . and expenditures by visitors, including alumni." Additional factors cited include "enhancements in the quality of the local workforce, improvements in the quality of life, public service, . . . and contributions to local culture." Moreover, the report points out, "Multipliers are applied to these sums to account for indirect and induced impacts."[49] But such local economic impact studies tend to minimize the more overarching cumulative impacts of the diffusion of innovation associated with the entrepreneurial ethos of a major research university.

Apart from the role of major research universities in the formation of human capital and their contributions to economic development associated with the commercialization of knowledge, these institutions contribute to the diffusion of innovation through the formation of regional innovation clusters and knowledge spillovers. Assessments of the economic impact of research universities underscore the significance of the clustering or agglomeration of institutions, organizations, and firms within a particular sector. Knowledge spillovers from academic research correlate with the diffusion of innovation, which is spatially distributed or "geographically mediated." Although economic globalization might have led observers to expect the geographic dispersion of industries, economists instead perceive the paradoxical persistence of agglomeration or clustering of economic activity based on new scientific and technological knowledge—for example, the start-ups and spin-offs of university research. Thus, despite economic globalization, flows of knowledge to some extent remain localized.[50]

The formation of regional innovation clusters may appear counterintuitive in an era of globalization, but knowledge has been shown to circulate through related firms, institutions, and organizations, and professional and social networks bound by proximity. In an assessment of the role of innovation clusters in building economic competitiveness, the business economist Michael E. Porter describes the diversity of actors in such agglomerations, including manufacturers, suppliers, universities aligned with industry-specific R&D and education, and government agencies promoting specialized training and infrastructure. Potential synergies may sometimes remain unrealized for lack of coordination between public and private sectors, and between the federal government, regional enterprises, and academic institutions, but the most effective clusters promote cooperation as well as lateral competition.[51]

Regional innovation clusters leverage the tacit dimension of scientific and technical knowledge, referring in this context to practical understanding of a given technology based on direct experience inherent in individuals embedded in organizational processes.[52] In contradistinction to explicit knowledge—that is, the codified principles of science and technology—tacit knowledge represents the practical understanding of "how things are done," which is to say, the "know-how" underpinning the development of a given technology. The significance of the tacit dimension varies by sector and over time, wherein innovation proceeds in accord with respective technological paradigms. Each sector is thus defined by a technological paradigm, which coevolves through its component technologies, industrial infrastructure, and supporting institutions, especially universities.[53]

The correlation of intellectual capital with competitive advantage for metropolitan areas has been assessed by regional economic development experts who underscore the extent of the impacts of academic research and development. Consistent with other estimates, Joel Kotkin and Ross DeVol emphasize that 60 to 75 percent of economic growth during the 1990s was driven by technological advances enabled by fundamental scientific discovery. And although the economic impact of academic research is generally calculated and reported as an aggregate contribution to national prosperity, benefits actually accrue disproportionately to regions that are home to major research universities. Knowledge spillovers from university research occur, not surprisingly, most frequently in communities adjacent to research universities. Because a postindustrial economy does not require industries to settle in strategic locations—near waterways or natural resources, for example—companies and knowledge workers increasingly locate "not where they must, but where they will," Kotkin and DeVol explain. As a consequence, "wherever intelligence clusters, be it small town [or] big city, wealth will accumulate." The presence of research universities is key both to quality-of-place considerations for knowledge workers and the potential for economic prosperity in a given region: "Cities that tap the knowledge assets in their midst, such as universities and research centers, will benefit from the talent that they attract to fuel local economic growth." Despite a globalized economy, "enduring competitive advantages still lie in location-specific competencies—knowledge, workforce skills, . . . entrepreneurial infrastructure, and quality-of-place attributes."[54] A focus on knowledge workers is consistent with the concept of the "creative class" propounded by Richard Florida. He argues that economic development is promoted by the presence of a creative class, which he defines as the sector, representing by his estimate more than 30 percent of the national workforce, comprised of artists, musicians, writers, designers, architects, engineers, scientists, and others for whom creativity is an essential dimension of livelihood. In his usage, creativity is a driving force in the growth of the economy, and almost without exception, higher education is a key determinant to inclusion in the occupations that comprise this sector.[55]

The role of academic institutions as hubs of regional innovation clusters is most famously epitomized in the relationship between Stanford University and Silicon Valley, and Harvard University and MIT with

Route 128, in Boston.[56] Ecologies of innovation similarly radiate from the institutions in North Carolina constituting the Research Triangle (Duke University, University of North Carolina, Chapel Hill, and North Carolina State University), and the University of California, San Diego, and University of Rochester and Rochester Institute of Technology and their respective metropolitan regions. The identity of Silicon Valley as a regional incubator conducive to innovation has been assessed by economists, who describe the interrelationships between what may be perceived as two economies, the first comprising established institutions such as universities and corporate research labs and existing firms, and the second the "institutional infrastructure" of new firm formation, constituted by start-ups led by entrepreneurs and supported by venture capitalists.[57]

Although our colleges and universities perform the dominant majority of the basic research conducted in the United States, industry remains the principal source of the nation's applied research and development.[58] But in addition to their critical role in discovery and innovation, universities mediate the relationship between fundamental research and industrial application, spawning entire industries and anchoring innovation clusters. According to some estimates, 80 percent of new industries may be derived from academic research.[59] Inasmuch as the majority of the scientists and engineers working in private industry in the United States were trained in American research universities, these institutions constitute what Jonathan Cole terms the "main pipeline to our nation's industrial research laboratories." Cole offers the following breakdown: "As of 2003, over 70 percent of all science and engineering graduates were working in private industry. Forty-four percent of all the science and engineering students who had earned PhDs were working in industry."[60]

The interrelationships between American research universities and private sector innovation in industrial laboratories and firms are multidimensional and complex, differing among industries and according to economists even now still poorly understood.[61] Quantification of the impact of academic research on regional, national, and global economic development requires explication of empirical findings through various analytic frameworks and theoretical models, an adequate synopsis of which lies outside the scope of this discussion. Models of economic development that attempt to quantify the contribution of new knowledge to gross domestic product growth, to cite but one approach, may weigh the impact of inputs from human capital, the quality of which is determined by the interrelationships among universities, industries, and governments.[62]

Although the impact of academic research on industrial innovation has long been taken for granted, efforts at rigorous quantification of the relationship came as recently as 1990 when the economist Edwin Mansfield sought to estimate the time lag between and the rate of return on investment in a particular research project and its subsequent industrial operationalization or commercialization. Mansfield termed his objective the attempt to "estimate the social rate of return from academic research." He undertook a random sampling of major American firms in seven manufacturing sectors—information processing, electrical equipment, chemicals, instruments, drugs, metals, and oils—and estimated the overall rate of return for these industries at 23 percent. Moreover, he estimates that "fully one-tenth of the new products and processes commercialized between 1975–1985 could not have been developed (without substantial delay) without recent academic research."[63]

In an assessment of the impact of "public science"—academic research performed at universities and research institutes funded by the government—on industrial technology and economic development, researchers found a striking correlation between citations in scientific research papers and U.S. patents. More than 73 percent of papers cited in industry patents were found to derive from research conducted at publicly funded academic and research institutions. The authors conclude, "The great majority of the science base of U.S. industry comes from the public sector." Moreover, "public science appears to be crucial to the advance of U.S. industrial technology."[64] The exact figures vary, but their estimate is confirmed by the National Science Board, which offers the following assessment: "Over 60 percent of the U.S.-authored articles cited on U.S. patents have academic scientists and engineers as authors, indicating the link between academic research and valuable inventions."[65]

As the central nodes of an integrative discovery and commercialization network, research universities are key institutional actors in national systems of innovation, a concept that encompasses theoretical and analytical frameworks for the interrelationships between entities that determine the rate and direction of innovation.[66] Cole explains that the concept essentially denotes a "social system for producing and applying new knowledge . . . a complex network of affiliations, collaborations, associations, and formal relationships that includes our universities, government agencies and laboratories, and the private sector, including the nonprofit research sector."[67] Broadly construed, the concept embraces the economic, political, and social institutions relevant to learning and discovery, including the patent system, the financial system, monetary policies, and even structure and practices of firms.[68] Interrelationships among these components may be "technical, commercial, legal, social, and financial, inasmuch as the goal of the interaction is the development, protection, financing, or regulation of new science and technology."[69] Although, with the exception of universities, most entities in national systems are firms and corporations, the state often remains dominant because it finances or even executes some portion of research and development.[70] Because innovation is to some extent determined by social and political institutions and economic factors external to the firm, David M. Hart emphasizes that entrepreneurship policy, referring to policy and regulation of entrepreneurial ventures intended to promote economic growth, is essential to "foster a socially optimal level of such venturing."[71] Economic development is further advanced through open innovation systems, which encourage collaboration and coordination of effort through the formation of partnerships and consortiums.[72]

The differentiation of knowledge enterprises further advances the potential for universities to participate in coordinated and synergistic networks. This sort of collaboration expands the potential of academia to offer multiple solutions and exert greater impact across broader swathes of knowledge. The imperative for transdisciplinary organization of teaching and research is obvious, but transinstitutional collaboration coordinating the efforts of academia, industry, and government both aggregates knowledge and prevents unnecessary replication. The amalgamation of transdisciplinary and transinstitutional frameworks maximizes the potential of knowledge production to advance broader social and economic outcomes. Multiplying university-industry-government partnerships is our best hope to foster the innovation that will be required to sustain our planet. As the United States engages competition from across the globe, the path forward will require both strategic collaboration and perpetual innovation.[73]

## Notes

1. "A Moment of Truth for America," an open letter to the U.S. Congress signed by W. Wayne Allen, Norman R. Augustine, John L. Clendenin et al., *Washington Post* (May 2, 1995). Chapter 4 contains revised and expanded sections from our coauthored book chapter, Michael M. Crow and William B. Dabars, "University-Based Research and Economic Development: The Morrill Act and the Emergence of the American Research University," in *Precipice or Crossroads: Where America's Great Public Universities Stand and Where They Are Going Midway through Their Second Century*, ed. Daniel Mark Fogel (Albany: State University of New York Press, 2012), 119–158, and also Michael M. Crow, "The Research University as Comprehensive Knowledge Enterprise: A Prototype for a New American University," in *University Research for Innovation*, ed. Luc E. Weber and James J. Duderstadt (London: Economica, 2010), 211–225.

2. "Higher Education Investment Act: An Open Letter to President-Elect Obama and His Administration," A Statement by Public Higher Education Leaders Convened by the Carnegie Corporation of New York, *New York Times* (December 16, 2008).

3. Jonathan R. Cole, *The Great American University: Its Rise to Preeminence, Its Indispensable National Role, and Why It Must Be Protected* (New York: Public Affairs, 2009), 4. The overview of academic research that comprises section 2 of the book, "Discoveries That Alter Our Lives," 191–342, suggests its parameters, but to document the full range of discoveries from the past seventy-five years, Cole launched a website: http://university-discoveries.com.

4. Cole, *Great American University*, 299–300. Cole explains that his compendium does not purport to be comprehensive or systematic (301). Apart from the quantitative metrics of citation indices, he observes, remarkably little effort has been undertaken to systematically assess the most important discoveries in these fields. One such tally he deems "highly subjective." See Karl W. Deutsch, John Platt, and Dieter Senghaas, "Conditions Favoring Major Advances in the Social Sciences," *Science* 171 (February 5, 1971): 450–459.

5. Cole, *Great American University*, 301–312.

6. Cole, *Great American University*, 314–329.

7. Cole, *Great American University*, 329–342.

8. Gregory Clark, *A Farewell to Alms: A Brief Economic History of the World* (Princeton, NJ: Princeton University Press, 2007), 193.

9. Joel Mokyr, *The Gifts of Athena: Historical Origins of the Knowledge Economy* (Princeton, NJ: Princeton University Press, 2002), 1–8. For additional historical perspective, see Mokyr, *The Lever of Riches: Technological Creativity and Economic Progress* (New York: Oxford University Press, 1992); and Nathan Rosenberg and L. E. Birdzell, *How the West Grew Rich: The Economic Transformation of the Industrial World* (New York: Basic Books, 1986).

10. Walter W. Powell and Kaisa Snellman, "The Knowledge Economy," *Annual Review of Sociology* 30 (2004): 199.

11. W. Brian Arthur, *The Nature of Technology: What It Is and How It Evolves* (New York: Free Press, 2009), 28.

12. Henry Etzkowitz, *The Triple Helix: University-Industry-Government Innovation in Action* (New York: Routledge, 2008), 4.

13. Mokyr, *Gifts of Athena*, 1–8, 34–35. See also Nathan Rosenberg, *Inside the Black Box: Technology and Economics* (Cambridge: Cambridge University Press, 1982), especially the chapter "How Exogenous Is Science?," 141–159.

14. Partha Dasgupta and Paul A. David, "Toward a New Economics of Science," *Research Policy* 23 (1994): 487.

15. Mokyr, *Gifts of Athena*, 1–5. Mokyr paraphrases Kuznets: "Simply put, technology is knowledge, even if not all knowledge is technological." Simon Kuznets, *Economic Growth and Structure* (New York: W. W. Norton, 1965); *Economic Growth of Nations* (Cambridge, MA: Belknap Press, 1971), cited by Mokyr, 3, n. 1. Technology has been defined as "applied knowledge embedded in tools, equipment, and facilities, in work methods, practices and processes, and in the design of products and services." Further, "It is 'know-how' in contrast to the 'know-why' that characterizes science . . . . In terms of traditional stages of innovation, science is most closely related to pure, fundamental, or basic research, while technology is most closely associated with applied development and engineering." Suleiman K. Kassicieh and H. Raymond Radosevich, *From Lab to Market: Commercialization of Public Sector Technology* (New York: Plenum Press, 1994), 127. The historian Ronald Kline offers further conceptualization of the relationships between scientific advance and technological innovation, parsing the generalized assumption that "technology is simply applied science." Ronald Kline, "Construing 'Technology' as 'Applied Science': Public Rhetoric of Scientists and Engineers in the United States, 1880–1945," *Isis* 86 (1995): 194–195. In this context Kline cites Otto Mayr, "The Science-Technology Relationship as an Historiographic Problem," *Technology and Culture* 17, no. 4 (1976): 663–672.

16. Mokyr, *Gifts of Athena*, 1–8.

17. Paul M. Romer, "Endogenous Technological Change," *Journal of Political Economy* 98, no. 5, pt. 2 (1990): S75. The definition of knowledge as a public good by Joseph Stiglitz clarifies the concept of nonrivalry: "A public good has two critical properties: non-rivalrous consumption—the consumption of one individual does not detract from that of another—and non-excludability—it is difficult if not impossible to exclude an individual from enjoying the good." See "Knowledge as a Global Public Good," in *Global Public Goods: International Cooperation in the Twenty-First Century*, ed. Inge Kaul, Isabelle Grunberg, and Marc Stern (Oxford: Oxford University Press, 1999).

18. National Academies. Committee on Prospering in the Global Economy of the Twenty-First Century, *Rising Above the Gathering Storm: Energizing and Employing American for a Brighter Economic Future* (Washington, DC: National Academies Press, 2007), 1, nn. 1, 43–45. The report cites Robert M. Solow, "Technical Change and the Aggregate Production Function," *Review of Economics and Statistics* 39 (1957): 312–320.

19. David C. Mowery and Nathan Rosenberg, *Paths of Innovation: Technological Change in Twentieth-Century America* (Cambridge: Cambridge University Press, 1998), 4.

20. Diego Comin, "Total Factor Productivity," in *The New Palgrave Dictionary of Economics*, ed. Steven N. Durlauf and Lawrence E. Blume (London: Palgrave Macmillan, 2008). Comin defines total factor productivity as the "portion of output not explained by the amount of inputs used in production."

21. Romer, "Endogenous Technological Change," S72–S74.

22. Arthur Blakemore and Berthold Herrendorf, "Economic Growth: The Importance of Education and Technological Development" (Tempe: W. P. Carey School of Business, Arizona State University, January 2009). In this context, Blakemore and Herrendorf cite Peter J. Klenow and Andrès Rodríguez-Clare, "The Neoclassical Revival in Growth Economics: Has It Gone Too Far?" *NBER Macroeconomics Annual* 12 (1997): 73–103; Robert E. Hall and Charles I. Jones, "Why Do Some Countries Produce So Much More Output Per Worker Than Others?" *Quarterly Journal of Economics* 114, no. 1: 83–116; Philippe Aghion and Peter Howitt, "Appropriate Growth Policy: A Unifying Framework," *Journal of the European Economic Association* 4, no. 2/3 (2006): 269–314. We are indebted to Arthur Blakemore and José Lobo for their assessment of the relevant literature.

23. Charles I. Jones, "Sources of U.S. Economic Growth in a World of Ideas," *American Economic Review* 92, no. 1 (2002): 220–239, cited by Blakemore and Herrendorf, 23.

24. Jérôme Vandenbussche, Philippe Aghion, and Costas Meghir, "Growth Distance to Frontier and Composition of Human Capital," *Journal of Economic Growth* 11, no. 2 (2006): 97–127.

25. A recent report on the commercialization of academic research in the biotechnology sector, for example, documents a "flourishing global landscape of spin-offs, start-ups, and collaborations between biotechnology firms, financiers, and academia." See Ross DeVol and Armen Bedroussian, *Mind to Market: A Global Analysis of University Biotechnology Transfer and Commercialization* (Santa Monica, CA: Milken Institute, 2006), 5. To cite but a few further representative examples, see Walter Powell et al., "The Spatial Clustering of Science and Capital: Accounting for Biotech Firm and Venture Capital Relationships," *Regional Studies* 36, no. 3 (2002): 291–316; E. Mansfield and J. Y. Lee, "The Modern University: Contributor to Industrial Innovation and Recipient of Industrial R&D Support," *Research Policy* 25 (1996): 1047–1058; Henry Etzkowitz and Loet Leydesdorff, *Universities in the Global Economy: A Triple Helix of Academic-Industry-Government Relations* (London: Croom Helm, 1997).

26. See especially Roger L. Geiger, *Research and Relevant Knowledge: American Research Universities since World War II* (Oxford: Oxford University Press, 1993); Geiger, *Knowledge and Money: Research Universities and the Paradox of the Marketplace* (Stanford: Stanford University Press, 2004); Nathan Rosenberg and Richard R. Nelson, "American Universities and Technical Advance in Industry," *Research Policy* 23, no. 3 (1994): 323–348; and Richard C. Atkinson and William A. Blanpied, "Research Universities: Core of the U.S. Science and Technology System," *Technology in Society* 30 (2008): 30–38.

27. National Research Council. Committee on Research Universities, *Research Universities and the Future of America: Ten Breakthrough Actions Vital to Our Nation's Prosperity and Security* (Washington, DC: National Academies Press, 2013), 1.

28. Etzkowitz, *Triple Helix*, 28.

29. National Academies, *Rising Above the Gathering Storm,* 43–45. According to the Organisation for Economic Co-operation and Development (OECD), "Underlying long-term growth rates in OECD economies depend on maintaining and expanding the knowledge base." OECD, "Technology, Productivity, and Job Creation: Best Policy Practices (Paris: OECD, 1998): 4, cited in the National Academies report (43–45).

30. National Academies. Committee on Prospering in the Global Economy of the Twenty-First Century, *Capitalizing on Investments in Science and Technology* (Washington, DC: National Academies Press, 1999), 56.

31. Henry Etzkowitz, "Entrepreneurial Scientists and Entrepreneurial Universities in American Academic Science," *Minerva* 21 (1983): 1–21.

32. Rosenberg and Nelson, "American Universities and Technical Advance in Industry," 324–333.

33. Henry Etzkowitz, "Research Groups as Quasi-Firms: The Invention of the Entrepreneurial University," *Research Policy* 32 (2003): 109.

34. Joseph A. Schumpeter, *The Theory of Economic Development* (Cambridge, MA: Harvard University Press, 1934), 8.

35. David M. Hart, "Entrepreneurship Policy: What It Is and Where It Came From," in *The Emergence of Entrepreneurship Policy: Governance, Start-Ups, and Growth in the U.S. Knowledge Economy*, ed. David M. Hart (Cambridge: Cambridge University Press, 2003), 6. Hart quotes Schumpeter to emphasize the extent to which he "conceived of the entrepreneurial venture as the 'fundamental engine that sets and keeps the capitalist engine in motion' by creating new goods, devising new business models, and opening new markets." Schumpeter, *Capitalism, Socialism, and Democracy* (New York: Harper, 1942).

36. Etzkowitz, *Triple Helix*, 1.

37. Gary P. Pisano and Willy C. Shih, "Restoring American Competitiveness," *Harvard Business Review* 87, no. 7–8 (July–August 2009): 121. Pisano and Shih provide perspective on the complex interrelationships between academia, business, industry, and government in spurring innovation and argue that both outsourcing and lack of sufficient investment in research have sapped American competitiveness.

38. Etzkowitz, "Research Groups as Quasi-Firms," 109.

39. Geiger, *Knowledge and Money;* see also Geiger, "Milking the Sacred Cow: Research and the Quest for Useful Knowledge in the American University since 1920," *Science, Technology, and Human Values* 13, no. 3 and 4 (Summer and Autumn, 1988): 332–348.

40. National Research Council. Committee on Management of University Intellectual Property, *Managing University Intellectual Property in the Public Interest* (Washington, DC: National Academy Press, 2011), 1.

41. Battelle Institute and *R&D* magazine, "2013 Global R&D Funding Forecast" (December 2012): 6. The "Source-Performer Matrix" breaks down R&D execution by sector, which includes the federal government, industry, academia, federally funded research and development centers (FFRDCs), referring to national laboratories, and nonprofit organizations (research institutions).

42. "2013 Global R&D Funding Forecast," 12.

43. Officially known as the Patent and Trademark Law Amendments Act (P.L. 96-517), enacted into law in 1980, together with amendments included in P.L. 98-620, enacted into law in 1984. Council on Governmental Relations, *The Bayh-Dole Act: A Guide to the Law and Implementing Regulations* (Washington, DC: Council on Governmental Relations, October 1999): 1.

44. David C. Mowery et al., *University-Industry Technology Transfer Before and After the Bayh-Dole Act* (Stanford: Stanford University Press, 2004), 2; David C. Mowery et al., "The Growth of Patenting and Licensing by U.S. Universities: An Assessment of the Effects of the Bayh-Dole Act of 1980," *Research Policy* 30 (2000): 99–101.

45. Robert D. Atkinson provides a useful survey of legislation consistent with the objectives of the Bayh-Dole Act, including the Omnibus Trade and Competitiveness Act of 1988 and National Technology Transfer and Advancement Act (NTTAA), signed into law in 1996; related programs and initiatives such as the Small Business Innovation Research program; and measures such as cooperative research and development agreements (CRDA), R&D tax credits, and adjustments to capital gains and corporate tax rates. See Atkinson, "Deep Competitiveness," *Issues in Science and Technology* 23, no. 2 (2007): 69–75.

46. Michael M. Crow, "Science and Technology Policy in the United States: Trading In the 1950 Model," *Science and Public Policy* 21, no. 4 (August 1994): 202–212.

47. "The Big Payoff: Educational Attainment and Synthetic Estimates of Work-Life Earnings" (Current Population Survey P23-210) (U.S. Census Bureau, July 2002), 4. The estimates are derived from calculations based on 1999 dollars over a hypothetical working life of forty years (8).

48. Thomas G. Mortenson et al., "Why College? Private Correlates of Educational Attainment," *Postsecondary Education Opportunity: The Mortenson Research Seminar on Public Policy Analysis of Opportunity for Postsecondary Education* 81 (March 1999).

49. John J. Siegfried, Allen R. Sanderson, and Peter McHenry, "The Economic Impact of Colleges and Universities," Department of Economics, Vanderbilt University, Working Paper No. 06-W12 (Nashville: Vanderbilt University, May 2006): 2–3.

50. Assessments of clustering include David B. Audretsch and Maryann P. Feldman, "R&D Spillovers and the Geography of Innovation and Production," *American Economic Review* 86, no. 3 (June 1996): 630–640; Maryann P. Feldman, "The New Economics of Innovation, Spillovers, and Agglomeration: Review of Empirical Studies," *Economics of Innovation and New Technologies* 8 (1999): 5–25.

51. Michael E. Porter, "Clusters and the New Economics of Competition," *Harvard Business Review* 76, no. 6 (November/December 1998): 77–90.

52. The concept of tacit knowledge derives from the scientist and philosopher Michael Polanyi. See *The Tacit Dimension* (Garden City, NY: Doubleday, 1966). For the economic context of this discussion, see especially Richard R. Nelson and Sidney G. Winter, *An Evolutionary Theory of Economic Change* (Cambridge, MA: Harvard University Press, 1982). Feldman offers the following synopsis of the concept by Eric von Hippel: "Knowledge with a low degree of tacitness may be easily standardized, codified, and

transmitted via journal articles, project reports, prototypes, and other tangible mediums. In contrast, tacit knowledge has a higher degree of uncertainty and the precise meaning is more interpretative . . . . As a consequence, when knowledge is more tacit in nature, face to face interaction and communication are important and geographic proximity may promote commercial activity." Eric von Hippel, "Sticky Information and the Locus of Problem Solving: Implications for Innovation," *Management Science* 40: 429–439, cited in Feldman, "New Economics," 17.

53. Richard R. Nelson, "The Simple Economics of Basic Scientific Research," *Journal of Political Economy* 67, no. 3 (June 1959): 297–306.

54. Joel Kotkin and Ross DeVol, *Knowledge-Value Cities in the Digital Age* (Santa Monica, CA: Milken Institute, 2001), vi–3.

55. Richard Florida, *The Rise of the Creative Class: And How It Is Transforming Work, Leisure, Community, and Everyday Life* (New York: Basic Books, 2002).

56. Anna Lee Saxenian, *Regional Advantage: Culture and Competition in Silicon Valley and Route 128* (Cambridge, MA: Harvard University Press, 1994).

57. Martin Kenney and Urs von Burg, "Technology, Entrepreneurship, and Path Dependence: Industrial Clustering in Silicon Valley and Route 128," *Industrial and Corporate Change* 8, no. 1 (1999): 69–74.

58. National Science Board, "Key Science and Engineering Indicators: 2010 Digest" (January 2010): 6.

59. Richard C. Atkinson and Patricia A. Pelfrey, "Science and the Entrepreneurial University," *Issues in Science and Technology* 26, no. 4 (Summer 2010): 39.

60. Cole, *Great American University*, 195.

61. David C. Mowery and Scott Shane, "Introduction to the Special Issue on University Entrepreneurship and Technology Transfer," *Management Science* 48, no. 1 (January 2002): v.

62. A useful overview of these interrelationships is to be found in the collection of articles edited by Shahid Yusuf and Kaoru Nabeshima, *How Universities Promote Economic Growth* (Washington, DC: International Bank for Reconstruction and Development, 2007). Yusuf cites as particularly germane to this discussion the article by Robert E. Lucas, "On the Mechanics of Economic Development," *Journal of Monetary Economics* 22 (1988): 3–42.

63. Edwin Mansfield, "Academic Research and Industrial Innovation," *Research Policy* 20 (1991): 1–12.

64. Francis Narin, Kimberly Hamilton, and Dominic Olivastro, "The Increasing Linkage Between U.S. Technology and Public Science," *Research Policy* 26 (1997): 317, 328.

65. National Science Board, "Key Science and Engineering Indicators: 2010 Digest" (January 2010): 12.

66. The concept of national innovation systems was coined by the Swedish economist Bengt-Åke Lundvall and explored in "Innovation as an Interactive Process: From User-Producer Interaction to National Systems of Innovation," in *Technical Change and Economic Theory*, ed. Giovanni Dosi et al. (London: Pinter, 1988).

67. Cole, *Great American University*, 195.

68. Christopher Tucker and Bhaven Sampat, "Laboratory-Based Innovation in the American National Innovation System," chapter 2 in Michael M. Crow and Barry Bozeman, *Limited By Design: R&D Laboratories in the U.S. National Innovation System* (New York: Columbia University Press, 1998), 42.

69. Jorge Niosi et al., "National Systems of Innovation: In Search of a Workable Concept," *Technology in Society* 15 (1993): 207–208.

70. Richard Nelson, "Institutions Supporting Technical Change in the United States," in Giovanni Dosi et al., *Technical Change and Economic Theory* (London: Pinter, 1988), cited in Niosi et al., "National Systems of Innovation," 208–212.

71. Hart, "Entrepreneurship Policy: What It Is and Where It Came From," 5. In this context, see also Michael M. Crow and Christopher Tucker, "The American Research University System as America's *de facto* Technology Policy," *Science and Public Policy* 28, no. 1 (2001): 2–10.

72. Henry Chesbrough, *Open Innovation: The New Imperative for Creating and Profiting from Technology* (Boston: Harvard Business Review Press, 2003), cited in Shahid Yusuf, "University-Industry Links: Policy Dimensions," in Yusuf and Nabeshima, eds., *How Universities Promote Economic Growth*, 5.

73. Don E. Kash, *Perpetual Innovation: The New World of Competition* (New York: Basic Books, 1989).

# FIVE

# Designing Knowledge Enterprises

The concept of design may call to mind associations of blueprints or the specifications for a next-generation technological device. A less obvious correlation is to the structure or organization of an institution, which, when the context is knowledge production, introduces the imperative to consider the reflexive relationship between knowledge and its institutional context. Many would dismiss a critique of academic organization as mere quibbling over some obvious and self-evident bureaucratic substratum. But the design of knowledge enterprises is neither arbitrary nor adventitious to the advancement of knowledge. We reiterate the assessment of John Seely Brown and Paul Duguid: "In a society that attaches particular value to 'abstract knowledge,' the details of practice have come to be seen as nonessential, unimportant, and easily developed once the relevant abstractions have been grasped."[1] Brown, Duguid, and another colleague make the important point that "knowledge is situated, being in part a product of the activity, context, and culture in which it is developed and used." In other words, the context of knowledge production is not "merely ancillary."[2] Thus, although knowledge is generally regarded as untethered from its organizational context, following the sociologist Anthony Giddens, we contend that to an extent insufficiently appreciated, knowledge, organizational structure, and social relations are intrinsically interrelated.[3] In the context of institutional design as elsewhere, we take it as axiomatic that form follows function, but conversely function follows form.[4]

Denizens of academe are inclined to assume that our institutions have as a matter of course already been long ago optimally structured. We recur to the formulation of Louis Menand, who makes this point so eloquently: "One thing about systems, especially systems as old as American higher education, is that people grow unconscious of them. The system gets internalized. It becomes a mind-set. It is just 'the way things are,' and it can be hard to recover the reasons *why* it is the way things are." After all, academics are "socialized to operate in certain ways, and when they are called upon to alter their practices, they sometimes find that they lack a compass to guide them." And when Menand points out that "underlying systemic elements" are often to blame for problems that appear intractable,[5] we take this to mean institutional design.

Design is a central concept for the New American University, and it is precisely the "details of practice" of institutional design that we address in this chapter, especially with regard to the organization of research and the implementation of interdisciplinarity. Concern with institutional design criteria and optimal organization for research may well be framed in more epistemologically grounded discussion. Indeed, the question "How should inquiry be organized so as to fulfill its proper function?" has been crucial to modern science, we are reminded by the philosopher Philip Kitcher, beginning with the quests of Bacon and Descartes for suitable methods of discovery and justification. The search for a "community well-designed for the attainment of epistemic goals" elucidated by Kitcher—balancing consideration of social institutions with abstract knowledge—requires no further justification.[6] With reference to the development of science in the early American republic, the historian A. Hunter Dupree captures the essence of this correlation: "For science is not often the sudden blossoming of the flower of genius, even in the soil of freedom. It is a group activity carried on by limited and fallible men, and much of their effectiveness stems from their organization and the continuity and flexibility of their institutional arrangements."[7]

### Replicate or Innovate?

To the present day, the academic organization and practices of the American research university are based on the historical model realized during the consolidation of the fifteen "gold standard" institutions in the late nineteenth century.[8] Although the intrinsic impetus to advance new knowledge distinguishes the research university from other institutional platforms, inherent design limitations inevitably diminish the potential of this set of institutions. We assume that our institutions have been optimally structured and inherently calibrated not only to facilitate the production and diffusion of knowledge but also to seek knowledge with purpose and link useful knowledge with action for the common good. Leaving aside important considerations of equity and accessibility, this filiopietistic entrenchment in the status quo of academic culture sometimes represents a major impediment to the further evolution of this set of institutions. If an institution does not achieve its purposes and functions, its design criteria must be reevaluated. A critique of institutional design thus represents no mere quibbling over the arbitrary disposition of bureaucratic underpinnings.

Of all that has been said about the reflexive relationship between knowledge and its organizational context, insufficient focus has been devoted to an appreciation of the concept of design and the role of institutional design in the advancement of discovery, creativity, and innovation. Institutional design, in our usage, refers broadly both to the process of design and its product, the organization of a knowledge enterprise and the social formations and knowledge networks its configuration engenders. The dynamics of this relationship in the American research university may appear at first glance to be a perfunctory administrative consideration. "All arts and sciences faculties contain more or less the same list of departments," observes the sociologist Andrew Abbott, remarking on the traditional correlation between academic disciplines and departments. But any institutional platform constructed to support the growth of knowledge is only the product of a sequence of decisions that determine its structure and functions, which may over time require calibration or reconfiguration.

The concept of design is itself often taken for granted or only perfunctorily considered. In his collection of essays on the design process, the computer scientist Frederick P. Brooks paraphrases the definition of the verb *design* found in the *Oxford English Dictionary*: "To form a plan or scheme of, to arrange or conceive in the mind for subsequent execution."[9] His point is to emphasize the imperative for planning prior to execution, but he overlooks another sense of the noun, which in this context seems especially pertinent: "That which is aimed at; an end in view; an ultimate goal or purpose."[10] Brooks reminds us that the design process both expresses a vision and facilitates its accomplishment. Plato, he informs us, articulated this correlation when in a dialogue he spoke of "corresponding ideas and forms"—in this case, the idea of a bed or table facilitating its construction "for our use, in accordance with the idea."[11] The value of the design concept behind implementation has been obvious since antiquity—Brooks in this context cites the writings of the Roman architect Vitruvius, whose treatise *De Architectura* would inspire generations of designers since its rediscovery during the early Renaissance.[12] The allusion to Vitruvius is germane to the present discussion inasmuch as one may appropriately term the designer of knowledge enterprises a "knowledge architect."

We begin to conceptualize the basis for an appreciation of the concept of design and an approach to the optimal design of knowledge enterprises using the fundamental distinction between the natural and the artificial explored by the polymath Herbert A. Simon in his 1969 book *The Sciences of the Artificial.* In his usage of these concepts, "artificial" simply refers to objects and phenomena—artifacts—that are man-made as opposed to natural. He terms knowledge of such products and processes "artificial science" or the "science of design" and observes that the most obvious designers of artifacts are engineers. But he broadly extends the sphere of the artificial even to our use of symbols—the "artifacts" of written and spoken language. In his expansive usage, everyone is a designer who "devises courses of action aimed at changing existing situations into preferred ones." The natural sciences are concerned with how things are, as he puts it, while the artificial sciences address how things "ought to be in order to *attain goals,* and to *function.*" Artificial science— or design science—determines the form of that which we build—tools, farms, or urban agglomerations alike—but also our institutional structures. Implicit within Simon's conceptualization is an affirmation of the potential for evolution and differentiation in the structure and organization of knowledge enterprises. There is thus no reason why the reconceptualization of an institution or organization cannot represent a process as focused and deliberate and precise as scientific research or technological innovation.[13]

At the same time, any effort to understand institutional innovation may be subsumed by the model of organizational adaptation propounded by Daniel Katz and Robert L. Kahn in their classic account of the process. In this model, open systems theory and the biological metaphor of interaction between an organism and its environment serves as the basis for an assessment of survival and growth in organizations. Open systems theory conceptualizes the interdependence of a social structure and its external environment, and its advancement through processes of input, throughput, and output.[14] Structure determines the dynamics of the operations of a system, and increasing complexity is a function of adaptation. In knowledge formations such as universities, information is the principal input, which with the operations of throughput yields outcomes useful to society. Restructuring is thus key to adaptation and determines the quality of output—that is, the production of educated citizens and the dissemination of useful knowledge.

The process of organizational adaptation assumes an evolutionary model. Technological innovation has been modeled as an evolutionary process,[15] and, by extrapolation, institutional innovation may be similarly understood. As Frederick Brooks puts it, with reference to this usage of "evolutionary" in a design context: "*Evolution* is used loosely here. The model is evolutionary in that both the understanding of the problem and the development of the solution are incrementally generated and incrementally evaluated."[16] The process of design thus modeled has been described by industrial designers Kees Dorst and Nigel Cross as a sort of coevolution between problem and solution:

> It is widely accepted that creative design is not a matter of first fixing the problem and then searching for a satisfactory solution concept; instead it seems more to be a matter of developing and refining together both the formulation of the problem and ideas for its solution, with constant iteration of analysis, synthesis, and evaluation processes between the two "spaces"— problem and solution.[17]

With these conceptualizations and models in mind, we may begin to assess the design limitations inherent in contemporary knowledge formations to posit complementary new models more ideally suited to the complex challenges that confront society in the twenty-first century.

The New American University represents a differentiated model for the contemporary research university defined by its conduciveness to innovation, individuation, and adaptation. Innovation generally refers to the ideas, products, and processes that academic research generates, but in our usage the concept is reflexive and also specifies institutional design itself. Lack of innovation merely perpetuates long-standing design limitations and mires institutions in bureaucratic patterns and disciplinary social constructs that serve primarily to perpetuate the status quo. Filiopietism leads institutions to remain entrenched in tradition, inwardly focused, and internally adaptive. Consistent with our discussion of isomorphism in chapter 3, insufficient differentiation produces stultifying homogeneity among institutions, leading to generic colleges and universities that resemble one another so closely as to be indistinguishable. Individuation specifies a trajectory of change leading to institutional differentiation. Adaptation encompasses the imperative for universities to conduct teaching and research that facilitate societal adaptability.

Key to the reconceptualization of a university as a knowledge enterprise is institutional restructuring that advances a unique set of objectives appropriate to a given institution. Each such initiative is necessarily *sui generis* because at bottom there should be nothing generic about institutional design. The imperative for adaptability, rigor, and quick but astute decision making is obvious. Because academic wristwatches mark time in increments of quarters or semesters, clock speed may need to be recalibrated. Faculty committees tend to deliberate while shifts in policy, culture, and technology flash by at warp speed. As transinstitutional collaboration with business, industry, and government becomes the norm, ambitious universities seeking collaborative engagement will set their clocks to the pace of real time. Knowledge enterprises represent a new stage in the evolution of universities that with their adaptability and scalability will accelerate the production and dissemination of knowledge—new ideas, theories, concepts, objects, algorithms, processes, and forms of artistic expression. Teaching, research, and public service will be enhanced when construed in the framework of innovation, differentiation, and adaptation.

The reconceptualization of an institution undertaken to remediate its design limitations may in some cases require "massive change," a concept we adapt from the design theorist Bruce Mau, who conceives of change in terms of "designing systems, designing organizations, designing organisms" to "meet human needs the world over." Change at this scale requires the exploration of "design economies" wherein the "patterns that emerge reveal complexity, integrated thinking across disciplines, and unprecedented interconnectivity."[18] But change at any scale does not require repudiation of the millennium-long trajectory that constitutes our institutional heritage. The genetic code our universities have inherited from antecedent institutional forms—beginning with the academies of ancient Greece and the earliest universities in medieval Europe—remains vital. Inasmuch as the goals or purposes of academic inquiry in a world of encroaching complexity might justifiably be characterized as critical to our survival as a species, we contend that deliberation regarding the design of our knowledge enterprises should become integral to the discourse of our academic culture, if not an aspect of a larger public debate. In the following we consider models for institutional design that promote interdisciplinary knowledge production and use-inspired research.

## Transcending the "Gulf of Mutual Incomprehension"

On the occasion of his now famous 1959 Rede Lecture, the annual public address delivered by a designated honoree of Cambridge University, C. P. Snow recounted an anecdote about an Oxford don whose attempts at polite conversation with dinner companions during a visit to Cambridge were met with indifference and incomprehension. In exasperation and by way of apology, his host explained, "Oh, those are mathematicians! We never talk to *them*." In "The Two Cultures and the Scientific Revolution," Snow reduced contemporary intellectual culture to broad categories he designated the sciences on the one hand, which in his usage refer to the natural sciences and mathematics and sometimes engineering, and, on the other hand, the humanities. These expansive categories, purported respectively to comprise the domains of "natural scientists" and "literary intellectuals," were given resonant formulation in the popular imagination by Snow, whose framing of the bifurcation informed it with the gravitas of a cultural schism. Snow perceived a "gulf of mutual incomprehension" between the two polarized camps, which had "almost ceased to communicate at all." He contended that those whom he termed literary intellectuals engage in "about as much communication with MIT as though the scientists spoke nothing but Tibetan." His intent that evening was to warn that the "degree of incomprehension on both sides is the kind of joke that has gone sour."[19]

Although Snow conceded a lack of general cultural awareness on the part of many natural scientists, he particularly censured literary intellectuals, representing them as lacking even the most rudimentary scientific literacy:

> A good many times I have been present at gatherings of people who, by the standards of the traditional culture, are thought highly educated and who have with considerable gusto been expressing their incredulity at the illiteracy of scientists. Once or twice I have been provoked and have asked the company how many of them could describe the Second Law of Thermodynamics, the law of entropy. The response was cold: it was also negative. Yet, I was asking something that is about the scientific equivalent of "Have you read a work of Shakespeare's?"[20]

Snow laments that the majority of "non-scientists have no conception of that edifice at all . . . . It is rather as though, over an immense range of intellectual experience, a whole group was tone-deaf. Except that this tone-deafness doesn't come by nature, but by training, or rather the absence of training."[21]

In his useful explication of the essay, the historian Stefan Collini ponders the implications of Snow's strenuous bifurcation: "For in effect Snow was doing more than asking what the relation should be between the two cultures he believed he had identified, and doing more even than asking how the curricula of schools and universities should be arranged to give people an adequate education in both branches of knowledge." Collini argues that by "thrusting into the spotlight of public discussion" this notion of two cultures, Snow had in mind both the imperative to address the challenges that confront humanity and the inadequacy of academic culture, balkanized into disciplinary fiefdoms, to mount an adequate response to those challenges.[22]

In the following we focus on the implications of Snow's summary formulation for academic organization and especially the implementation of interdisciplinary teaching and research, here taken broadly to convey the various subtypes, including transdisciplinarity, multidisciplinarity, pluridisciplinarity, postdisciplinarity, and intellectual fusion. Where distinctions appear superfluous, we conflate discussion of the categories, consistent with the justification provided by philosophers Robert Frodeman and Carl Mitcham: "Both science and society now recognize that disciplinarity and interdisciplinarity are not mutually exclusive but complementary."[23] The precondition for the implementation of interdisciplinarity, we argue, is mutual intelligibility between disciplines and disciplinary and interdisciplinary areas, just as the precondition for mounting responses to the challenges that confront society is interdisciplinary teaching and research itself.[24]

Insufficient focus has been devoted to an appreciation of the role of institutional design in the implementation of interdisciplinarity. This reflexive relationship is nowhere more critically instantiated than in the institutionalization of the disciplines and interdisciplinary configurations in the American research university. Although the various strains of interdisciplinarity have been subject to sophisticated explication from any number of perspectives, the concept of design in the present context—the advancement of interdisciplinary collaboration in knowledge enterprises, and especially the American research university—is itself often taken for granted. Whether one focuses on disciplinary genealogies or interdisciplinary confluence, an understanding of the dynamics that determine their institutionalization and dissemination requires an appreciation of their institutional determination.[25] The prerequisite for the implementation of interdisciplinarity, we argue, is an appropriate institutional platform, as well as mutual intelligibility between and among academic disciplines and interdisciplinary fields. Within the context of advancing interdisciplinary inquiry, the outcome of optimal institutional design aligned with the various purposes of the university is aptly characterized by Jonathan Cole: "Almost all truly distinguished universities create a seamless web of cognitive influence among the individual disciplines that affects the quality of the whole."[26]

The persistence of the traditional correlation between academic disciplines and departments is perhaps the chief design limitation in the American research university. Despite broad consensus regarding the imperative for inter- or transdisciplinary approaches to inquiry and scholarship, the traditional correlation between academic disciplines and departments remains the basis for academic organization and administration. We recur to the observation by Andrew Abbott previously cited: "All arts and sciences faculties contain more or less the same list of departments." Although disciplines are now increasingly interrelated or conjoined with rapidly speciating interdisciplinary fields, their locus in disciplinary departments, or, as the case may be, units such as centers, institutes, schools, or colleges, remains the norm. Because of their "extraordinary ability to organize individual careers, faculty hiring, and undergraduate education," Abbott observes, disciplinary departments appear to be the "essential and irreplaceable building blocks" of American academia. Similarly, "Americans seem unable to conceive of an undergraduate curriculum without majors. And of course, there are no majors without disciplines." Once consolidated into their present configuration during the final decades of the nineteenth century, the department-based "American system of disciplines" would remain "uniquely powerful and powerfully unique."[27] The political scientist Mattei Dogan offers a corresponding synopsis of the administrative correlate to disciplinary knowledge: "In all universities, teaching, recruitment, promotion, peer review, and administration are organized along disciplinary lines."[28] And from his perspective as president emeritus of the University of Michigan, James Duderstadt similarly perceives the "deification of the disciplines," which through departmental structures "continue to dominate the modern university, developing curriculum, marshaling resources, administering programs, and doling out rewards."[29]

Academic disciplines are "three things simultaneously," the sociologist Immanuel Wallerstein points out: "The so-called disciplines . . . are, of course, intellectual categories—modes of asserting that there exists a defined field of study with some kind of boundaries, however disputed or fuzzy, and some agreed-upon modes of legitimate research . . . . The disciplines are in addition institutional structures that since the late nineteenth century have taken on ever more elaborate forms . . . . Finally, the disciplines are cultures."[30] Although the disciplines and interdisciplinary fields that constitute our academic culture thus first and foremost represent epistemological categories—referring here in the most general sense to the stock of knowledge in any given area—they may be construed secondarily in their administrative contexts. The important sociocultural context of disciplinarity undergirds the epistemological and administrative dimensions. Often termed social constructs, these formations represent the outcome of "disciplinary socialization." Assessments of the epistemological "flux" of disciplines must be counterbalanced by an appreciation of what Abbott terms the "extraordinary stasis of disciplinary social structure."[31]

Rather than exploring new paradigms for inquiry, academia too often restricts its focus to existing organizational models. The well-known call to action issued by the National Academies regarding the imperative for interdisciplinary collaboration and problem-driven research, *Facilitating Interdisciplinary Research,* offers an approach that represents a fundamental model for institutional efforts in this context. The report envisions "scientists, engineers, social scientists, and humanists . . . addressing complex problems that must be attacked simultaneously with deep knowledge from different perspectives," and serves here broadly as proxy for our general recommendations. The committee called for new structural models to "stimulate new modes of inquiry and break down the conceptual and institutional barriers to interdisciplinary research that could yield significant benefits to science and society" and experimentation with "substantial alteration of the traditional academic structures or even replacement with new structures and models to reduce barriers" to interdisciplinary research.[32]

Recommendations for new institutional structures that support the implementation of interdisciplinarity are based on the "matrix model." In contrast to existing configurations of disciplinary-based "silos," the committees recommend structures long evident in industry and government laboratories: "a matrix, in which people move freely among disciplinary departments that are bridged and linked by interdisciplinary centers, offices, programs, courses, and curricula. There are many possible forms of coupling between departments and centers, including appointments, salary lines, distribution of indirect-cost returns, teaching assignments, . . . curricula, and degree-granting." The report similarly stresses the imperative for "institutional policies that govern faculty appointments and salary lines, faculty recruitment, responsibility for tenure and promotion decisions, allocations of indirect-cost returns on grants, development of new course and curricular materials, and so on."[33]

With economic growth increasingly tied to knowledge-intensive innovation, interactions among universities, industry, and government have been critically important during the past half-century. These interrelationships constitute the triple helix of university-industry-government innovation described by Henry Etzkowitz.[34] The National Academies report stresses that interdisciplinary research in industrial and government laboratories should serve as a model for academia: "Industrial and national laboratories have long experience in supporting IDR. Unlike universities, industry and national laboratories organize by the problems they wish their research enterprise to address. As problems come and go, so does the design of the organization." Moreover, "collaborative interdisciplinary research partnerships among universities, industry, and government have increased and diversified rapidly. Although such partnerships still face significant barriers, well-documented studies provide strong evidence of both their research benefits and their effectiveness in bringing together diverse cultures."[35]

New structural models are also required because "prevailing academic cultures and structures tend to replicate existing areas of expertise, reward individual effort rather than collaborative work, limit hiring input to a single department in a single school or college, and limit incentives and rewards for interdisciplinary and collaborative work."[36] The implementation of institutional policies conducive to interdisciplinarity are critical for two reasons: academic careers have historically been forged within strictly demarcated disciplinary delimitations, and disciplinary affiliation defines the social organization of American higher education to such an extent that recipients of interdisciplinary training or practitioners of interdisciplinary scholarship often find recognition among peers and advancement difficult. Such policies must moreover advance recognition of interdisciplinary research by professional associations, business and industry, and, most important, within federal agencies, which in the estimation of this report remain resistant to interdisciplinary categorization.[37]

Communication is intrinsic to the vision for interdisciplinary collaboration of the National Academies committees that produced the report: "At the heart of interdisciplinarity is communication—the conversations, connections, and combinations that bring new insights to virtually every kind of scientist and engineer." Although it focuses on science and engineering, the report recapitulates the imperative for interdisciplinarity relevant across the spectrum of disciplines. Consistent with its call for new structural models, the report underscores the importance of concordant and supportive institutional policies: "Whatever their structure, interdisciplinary projects flourish in an environment that allows researchers to communicate, share ideas, and collaborate across disciplines."[38]

Consistent with recent discussions of knowledge networks, we contend that conceptualization of the flow of knowledge—as opposed to its accumulation or maintenance within stocks of knowledge—represents a fundamental metaphor for enhanced interdisciplinary collaboration facilitated through interpersonal and group dynamics. The inverse correlation between the proverbial silo mentality of disciplinary knowledge and the synergies unleashed during interdisciplinary exchange becomes apparent. The value of stocks of knowledge is diminishing, according to organizational theorists John Hagel, John Seely Brown, and Lang Davison. Instead we must "continually refresh our stocks of knowledge by participating in relevant 'flows' of knowledge—interactions that create knowledge or transfer it across individuals." They envisage institutional change driven not by an administrative elite but rather by "passionate individuals distributed throughout and even outside the institution, supported by institutional leaders who . . . realize that this wave of change cannot be imposed from the top down." But access to knowledge depends on optimal organizational structure, especially in large corporations or institutions. An oft-cited remark by former Hewlett-Packard CEO Lew Platt reinforces this point: "If HP knew what HP knows, we would be three times as profitable."[39]

Although institutional design is fraught with the potential for unforeseen misalignments between disciplinary factions and may require individuals and groups to transcend entrenched sociocultural barriers, reorganization to enhance interdisciplinary collaboration offers new ways of shaping and examining problems and advancing questions through interaction between heterogeneous groups, programs, and initiatives. Novel interdisciplinary configurations—what are in a sense institutional experiments—possess the potential to alter the course of inquiry and the application of research, and even to reveal new paradigms for knowledge production, organization, and application. In other words, if academic units commensurate to the resolution of a given challenge or problem do not already exist, appropriate new units must be purpose-built. In its inception, the new aggregation may simply represent a best-guess strategic amalgamation combining researchers from different disciplines and interdisciplines or particular specializations. The amalgamation may even begin or remain resolutely multidisciplinary. But such novel organizational configurations may lead to unexpected discovery through serendipity, the role of which in scientific research has been assessed by Robert K. Merton and Elinor Barber.[40] Any such arrangement offers at the very least new potential to address critical challenges or resolve intractable problems—or even evolve into differentiated new interdisciplines. An overarching objective in institutional design is thus to engender an ecosystem of innovation.

### Models for Interdisciplinary Collaboration

A number of knowledge formations that might appear extraneous to orthodox theorists of interdisciplinarity constitute relevant models of interdisciplinary collaboration for the New American University, including invisible colleges, communities of practice, epistemic communities, and knowledge-based theories of the firm. An important historical model is to be found in the knowledge networks termed "invisible colleges," a concept that derives from the early modern period and refers to any informal collaborative engagement of scholars and scientists focused on similar or related problems. Robert Merton attributes the metaphor to the pioneering seventeenth-century chemist and "natural philosopher" Robert Boyle, who coined the term with reference to his peers in the Royal Society of London. The historian of science Derek J. de Solla Price explains that these early scientists "communicated by letter to gain an appreciative audience for their work, to secure priority, and to keep informed of work being done elsewhere by others."[41] With reference to the knowledge revolution of this period, Joel Mokyr explains the relevance of the concept thus: "The blossoming of open science and the emergence of invisible colleges—that is, informal scholarly communities spanning different countries, within which seventeenth-century scholars and scientists kept close and detailed correspondences with each other—compounded these advances."[42] His analysis underscores that the growth of knowledge in the early modern period was determined not only by the differentiation and codification of disciplinary knowledge within scientific institutes and later in universities but also by its dissemination through social networks and scientific associations constituted by the scientists and scholars comprising invisible colleges. Peter Weingart corroborates this point: "The exchange among scholars in the academy began to suffer from the increasing distance between the disciplines. Actual investigations, and reports and discussions about new developments, were taken to the new specialized scientific associations that . . . assumed the function of publishing specialized journals, which accelerated the speed of communication."[43] Only through such access to the epistemic base does knowledge become "useful" in the present and for future generations, Mokyr explains: "Much of the likelihood that knowledge will be transmitted depends on the social organization of knowledge . . . and who controls access to it."[44]

Much like their historic counterparts, Price explains, contemporary invisible colleges comprise the "in-group" in any given research frontier and thus serve to advance collaboration.[45] He estimated that a hypothetical contemporary invisible college would "correspond with the work of something like the order of one hundred scientists who probably constitute the peer group . . . at that particular segment of the research front." Such an assemblage represents the vanguard of scientific research in a given arena, for "whenever we see invisible colleges we have research-front science." Price underscored the significance of informal communication in advancing knowledge in such groups: "In fields that are cumulating strongly," he explained, "the news of research flows by personal contact and verbal report through the invisible college and the surrounding peer group." The process has become "blatantly obvious" only recently, but Price deemed it to have been operative since the convention of scientific publication became standard practice in the mid-seventeenth century.[46]

An invisible college has been characterized by Diana Crane as a "network of influence and communication" constituted by scientists, sometimes geographically dispersed, whose "productivity is sufficient to make them visible to most of those who enter the field." Formal collaboration is facilitated through informal communication, which may be intermittent or "relatively unstructured." She underscored the extent to which the growth of knowledge and innovation is a process of diffusion at once both cognitive and social. Through sociometric data she demonstrated that social interaction with colleagues despite geographic dispersion—what she termed "relatedness and connectivity"—produces cumulative and even exponential growth in scientific knowledge through a "contagion process in which early adopters influence later adopters."[47] A recent case study of an interdisciplinary research group corroborates her socio-metric analysis and finds that in the collaborative milieu certain individuals inevitably emerge as "interdisciplinary linchpins."[48] Karim Lakhani and colleagues present a compelling argument for collaboration in such knowledge networks, drawing the following conclusion: "Lack of openness and transparency means that scientific problem solving is constrained to a few scientists who work in secret and who typically fail to leverage the entire accumulation of scientific knowledge available."[49] Creative collaboration in scientific discovery could thus in some sense be likened to crowdsourcing and the application of "cognitive surplus" described by Clay Shirky.[50]

The concept of "communities of practice" elucidated by Etienne Wenger, which is predicated on the assumption that learning is a process of social participation, represents a model especially relevant to interdisciplinary collaboration. Wenger argues that whether one is a mechanic, a poet, or a scientist, competence is established not merely through knowledge but also meaningful engagement. Whether on the playground or in the office or laboratory, he contends, "participation shapes not only what we do, but also who we are and how we interpret what we do." Communication is fundamental to the four interrelated components of his social theory of learning: meaning, practice, community, and identity, each of which he characterizes as discursive. Thus, community itself is defined as "a way of talking about the social configurations in which our enterprises are defined."[51]

From playground to classroom to workplace to cyberspace, Wenger explains, communities of practice are ubiquitous and sometimes "so informal and so pervasive that they rarely come into explicit focus." His examples range from garage bands to the academic research environment: "In laboratories, scientists correspond with colleagues, near and far, in order to advance their inquiries." In this context, and relevant to our assessment of the collaborative research environment, Wenger considers the analytical framework of his concept as derivative from theories of both social structure and "situated experience." Theories of social structure underscore the primacy of institutions, norms, and rules, but theories of situated experience accord primacy to the "dynamics of everyday existence," which include "improvisation, coordination, and interactional choreography."[52] Paul Duguid points out the interdependence of such communities, noting that the concept is frequently applied to the sort of ad hoc teams sometimes formed in academic research. His insight regarding apprenticeship as a method shared equally by the manual trades and academic disciplines is here relevant. When dispersed globally, Duguid recommends conceptualization of the pattern as networks of practice.[53]

Participation in communities of practice emphasizes learning by doing, and Wenger identifies three conceptual dimensions by which practice contributes to the cohesion of a community: mutual engagement, joint enterprise, and shared repertoire. Through mutual engagement, a community of practitioners negotiates a joint enterprise, which engenders a "communal regime of mutual accountability" that sometimes transcends explicit rules, policies, and standards. Such accountability develops sensitivities that Wenger characterizes in aesthetic terms, which may become integral to collaboration. Wenger identifies the shared repertoire of a community of practice as comprising all facets of the participative dimension of the enterprise, including routines, gestures, symbols, narratives, and discourse that in their totality secure the meaning and identity of the enterprise.[54] His conceptualization of marginality and peripherality in learning communities is of particular relevance to interdisciplinary collaboration, which by some accounts advances on the margins of disciplines.[55] On the margins of "regimes of competence," one may find the "wisdom of peripherality," which includes "paths not taken, connections overlooked, choices taken for granted" by core participants. Wenger explains that such peripheral participation correlates with the practice of apprenticeship, as disclosed in a number of ethnographic studies.

"Learning happens, design or no design," Wenger observes. Yet, he underscores the importance of appropriate institutional accommodation because there are "few more urgent tasks than to design social infrastructures that foster learning." According to Wenger, "A learning community must be given opportunities to become involved in the institutional arrangements in the context of which it defines its enterprise." Consistent with the oft-quoted maxim attributed variously to computer scientist Alan Kay and management consultant Peter Drucker that "the best way to predict the future is to invent it," Wenger writes, "Those who understand the informal yet structured, experiential yet social, character of learning—and can translate their insight into designs in the service of learning—will be the architects of our tomorrow."[56]

Another model relevant to interdisciplinary collaboration is the "epistemic community," which has been defined simply as a "group of inquirers who have knowledge problems to solve." Any such community shares norms of inquiry determined by tradition, Hugh Miller and Charles Fox observe, which socialize apprentices and shape "institutions and attitudes, scholarly practices, and standards of evidence."[57] Although broadly analogous to communities of practice and other knowledge-based social formations, the concept underscores the dynamics of knowledge creation, which Burkart Holzner equated with cognitive socialization.[58] Epistemic communities are often associated with scientific research, Peter M. Haas explains, but disciplinary affiliation is irrelevant. Because participants in respective domains share norms regarding expertise and competence, the concept is roughly correlate with the Kuhnian paradigm ("an entire constellation of beliefs, values, techniques, and so on shared by members of a given community"). The community may be interdisciplinary, because in this sense the paradigm "governs not a subject matter but a group of practitioners."[59] Epistemic communities tend to be interdisciplinary as well as problem-focused, according to other theorists: "Epistemic communities engage in transdisciplinary and/or transfunctional activities, at the interstices between the various disciplines. In contrast with communities of practice, they are not organized around a common discipline but around a common topic or problem."[60] Consistent with knowledge-based theories of the firm, epistemic communities may be "premised on a contextual conceptualization of knowledge" to "denote groups of people mastering the theories, codes, and tools of a common practice regardless of their geographical location."[61]

An appreciation of the organizational correlates to interdisciplinary collaboration may be derived from an emerging literature on knowledge-based theories of the firm. Business economist David J. Teece has characterized the firm, referring to a business enterprise either small or large, as a "repository for knowledge" that is "embedded in routines and processes." Competitive advantage derives from the communication of knowledge ("intellectual capital"): "The essence of the firm is its ability to create, transfer, assemble, integrate, and exploit knowledge assets."[62]

In a knowledge-based conceptualization of the firm, the enterprise has moreover been construed as a communication network, albeit concerned primarily with variables of specialization and the exploitation of efficiencies: "The internal organization of firms is seen as a communication network that is designed to minimize both the costs of processing new information and the costs of communicating this information among its agents."[63] Another assessment proposes that because "firms offer superior governance structures primarily for knowledge processes, which involve exchanges of tacit, poorly articulated knowledge across epistemic boundaries," they can "meaningfully be seen as epistemic communities in their own right."[64]

The recognition that firms may be understood as knowledge-centric is confirmed by their correlation with academic, and especially scientific, research groups by Etzkowitz, whose work both delineates the dynamic interrelationships among academia, industry, and government, and elucidates the broader parallel between academic research and economic development. Indeed, Etzkowitz terms the entrepreneurial academic model of the contemporary research university a "teaching, research, and economic development enterprise." He observes that academic research groups have "firm-like qualities, especially under conditions in which research funding is awarded on a competitive basis." Moreover, the "research university shares homologous qualities with a start-up firm even before it directly engages in entrepreneurial activities."[65] Indeed, along with firms and corporations, universities are key institutional actors in national systems of innovation because of their crucial role in discovery as well as the commercialization of university-based research.[66]

Institutional design that engenders interdisciplinary collaboration promotes both basic and applied research, but further leverage is attained when research engages transinstitutionally. The triple helix of university-industry-government innovation described by Etzkowitz comprises a plurality of knowledge networks that intersect to leverage input from diverse and, given the multiplicity of actors, inherently multidisciplinary perspectives. In this context, Etzkowitz comments on the "radical epistemological transformation" ongoing in science: "From research based on questions that arise within separate disciplines (mode 1) to an alternative format with researchers from different disciplines collaborating on projects that are sourced in practical issues (mode 2)." Etzkowitz makes the important point that "paradoxically, the so-called mode 2 interdisciplinary research, with both theoretical and practical applications, is the original format of science from its institutionalization in the seventeenth century."[67] The triple helix conception is representative of the literature on economic development derived from technological innovation, which offers concepts and models relevant to our understanding of interdisciplinary collaboration within the research environment.[68]

Another conceptualization relevant to interdisciplinary collaboration proposes that a firm be understood as a "social community specializing in speed and efficiency in the creation and transfer of knowledge."[69] Bruce Kogut and Udo Zander invoke Michael Polanyi to underscore the extent to which both explicit and tacit forms of knowledge inform this process: although the "central competitive dimension of what firms know how to do is to create and transfer knowledge efficiently within an organizational context," the capacity to do so derives from the "combinative capability to synthesize and apply current and acquired knowledge."[70] Other scholars, following sociologist Pierre Bourdieu, construe "organizational advantage" as derivative of social capital, which is said to engender the creation of intellectual capital. Social capital has been variously interpreted but in general usage refers to the significance of networks of relationships that define individuals or groups, while intellectual capital refers broadly to possession by an individual or collective of various types of knowledge. In one such analysis, social capital produces intellectual capital within a "framework of combination and exchange."[71]

In some cases the models here delineated correspond to the structures and purposes of the ad hoc interdisciplinary research cohorts that fortuitously crop up on campuses. Observers have noted that such cohorts, especially when convened for a particular task at hand, sometimes lack the perspective to more fully assess the implications and application of their collaboration. The formation of more or less permanent interdisciplinary research groups and centers and institutes is thus often held to be essential. However, the potential of interdisciplinary research is not contingent on its affiliation with formally recognized units but emerges whenever two or more faculty members collaborate on a research problem.[72]

Models are heuristic devices and the knowledge networks and knowledge-centric social formations here considered—invisible colleges, communities of practice, epistemic communities, and firms construed as knowledge-centric—represent efforts to discern more optimal forms of organization for teaching and research. Interdisciplinary collaboration may not be strictly required for their operation, but it is generally implicit to their success even if sometimes perceived as adventitious. Theoretical discussions of interdisciplinarity tend to overlook such formations, which may be deemed extraneous to the repertoire of favored models. Yet, each is relevant to knowledge production because any research enterprise is dependent on its social context and organizational or institutional structure. Recognition of the potential of these various models to enhance interdisciplinary collaboration along the epistemological, administrative, and sociocultural dimensions of knowledge described by Immanuel Wallerstein may be especially relevant for research universities because these institutions operate on the frontiers of discovery.[73]

## Some Historical Perspective on the Implementation of Interdisciplinarity

The proceedings of the first international conference on interdisciplinarity, convened at the University of Nice, September 7–12, 1970, explicitly established the contemporary context for the discussion of interdisciplinary teaching and research. Organized by the Centre for Educational Research and Innovation (CERI) in collaboration with the Organisation for Economic Co-operation and Development (OECD) and the French Ministry of Higher Education (Ministère de l'Enseignement Supérieur et de la Recherche), the "Seminar on Interdisciplinarity in Universities" put the subject on the agenda of academic institutions, especially in England. The conference proceedings were published in an influential report—Robert Frodeman terms this the "Ur-text of interdisciplinarity"[74]—edited by an international committee of scholars, from Belgium, France, and England.[75] To a remarkable extent, this report consolidated the taxonomy and codified the lexicon of interdisciplinarity, as well as provided a point of departure for our contemporary discourse on the topic.[76] In an introductory overview, for example, the German psychologist Heinz Heckhausen delineated "criterion levels" for disciplinarity to elucidate the epistemological concerns at issue. And in an effort to delineate the relevant taxonomy, Guy Michaud, director of the Centre d'Études des Civilisations of the University of Paris, Nanterre, and one of the editors of the report, distinguished among disciplinarity, interdisciplinarity, multidisciplinarity, pluridisciplinarity, and transdisciplinarity—categories the parsing of which preoccupies theorists to the present day.[77]

But the conference in Nice and publication of the proceedings by the OECD by no means mark the onset of the interdisciplinary imperative. Research in scientific and technological fields constitutes the overarching model for interdisciplinary collaboration. One need only adduce the multidisciplinarity of the Manhattan Project to glimpse the extent to which scientific discovery and technological innovation have served as sources of inspiration in this context. Leaving aside discussion of their institutional accommodation as outside the scope of the present chapter, it is possible to construct a short list of important prototypes in this context in the humanities and social sciences. The survey begins as recently as the decade of the 1920s, when, according to Andrew Abbott, the Social Science Research Council (SSRC) focused conceptually on the objective of "eliminating barriers between the social sciences." He quotes the following passage from their 1934 ten-year retrospective report:

> The Council has felt a primary concern with the inter-discipline or interstitial project for the reason that new insights into social phenomena, new problems, new methods leading to advances in the scientific quality of social investigation, cross-fertilization of the social disciplines, were thought more likely to emerge here than from work in the center of established fields where points of view and problems and methodology have become relatively fixed.[78]

And in 1935, to cite a contemporaneous exemplar of this impetus, the president and fellows of Harvard University established the University Professorships, chairs intended for "individuals of distinction . . . working on the frontiers of knowledge, and in such a way as to cross the conventional boundaries of the specialties."[79]

But frustration with disciplinary limitations had led to a more comprehensive organizational reconfiguration at another institution a decade earlier. Syracuse University established the Maxwell School of Citizenship and Public Affairs in 1924 to offer graduate professional education in public administration and international relations and graduate degrees in the social sciences, including political science, economics, and history.[80] Another leading example of interdisciplinary configuration in the social sciences and humanities is the celebrated Committee on Social Thought at the University of Chicago, instituted in 1941 by then president Robert M. Hutchins. With themes including literature, philosophy, history, religion, art, politics, and society, "the Committee differs from the normal department in that it has no specific subject matter and is organized neither in terms of a single intellectual discipline nor around any specific interdisciplinary focus."[81] A more recent aggregation of the social sciences, the short-lived Department of Social Relations at Harvard University, merging social anthropology, social psychology, and sociology, dissolved with the retirement of its founder, sociologist Talcott Parsons.[82]

A number of institutions spearheaded some notable organizational configurations in the humanities during this period as well, including the formation of an avowedly interdisciplinary program for undergraduates at Princeton University in 1936 termed the "Special Program in the Humanities." In 1937, Columbia University initiated its interdisciplinary freshman "sequence in the humanities" ("a reading list of literary, philosophical, and religious texts from Homer to Goethe").[83] But several more decades passed before the University of California would attempt a more comprehensive conceptualization in the humanities. From its inception in 1966, the Program in the History of Consciousness at the University of California, Santa Cruz, is said to have fostered interrelations between the humanities and the social sciences, natural sciences, and the arts, and advanced a "focus on problems rather than disciplines" with a curriculum predicated on methodological and theoretical issues and the integration of disciplines.[84] During the same academic year, the Humanities Center at Johns Hopkins University began offering graduate degrees in both comparative literature and intellectual history. Program literature specifies "because of the interdisciplinary interests of some of its most distinguished faculty, Hopkins has fostered to a remarkable degree the free exchange between scholars and students across departmental boundaries."[85] In 1969, Stanford University established the doctoral program in Modern Thought and Literature (MTL). Deriving its methodological approach from the emerging field of cultural studies, the program sought to position itself "firmly and decisively within a rigorous inter-disciplinary framework with fields such as science and technology, media and film studies, legal studies, race and ethnic studies, gender and sexuality studies, medicine, education, anthropology, and history and philosophy."[86]

The decade that witnessed the establishment of the programs at UC Santa Cruz, Stanford, and Johns Hopkins thus appears to have been particularly propitious to the formation of interdisciplinary academic configurations. In Europe, for example, the establishment of Universität Bielefeld in 1969 as an interdisciplinarily structured new "reform" university reflects a vanguard approach to institutional design that contrasts sharply with the entrenchment of most American colleges and universities in conventional disciplinary academic organization. The Zentrum für interdisziplinäre Forschung (ZiF), or Center for Interdisciplinary Research—modeled on the Institute for Advanced Study, in Princeton, New Jersey, and comprising the nucleus of the university—has deservedly been termed the "premier example" of an interdisciplinary "think tank."[87] Its centrality within the institutional matrix underscores the incisiveness and foresight of sociologist Helmut Schelsky, founding rector of Bielefeld, and his colleagues who perceived the transformative potential of an inherently interdisciplinary organizational structure for knowledge enterprises. The prescience of their conception is further underscored by its precedence in relation to the groundswell of interest in the various forms of interdisciplinary inquiry and collaboration that would follow in succeeding decades. As we have assessed, it is an impetus that too often would meet with inertia and resistance from an academic culture attuned to disciplinary processes and practices.[88]

The innovative character of the conception for institutional organization at Universität Bielefeld is attested by its emergence in near contemporaneity with the international conference on interdisciplinarity at Nice in September 1970. The Institute for Advanced Study, Princeton, may be the most appropriate prototype, but Björn Wittrock, director of the Swedish Collegium for Advanced Study in the Social Sciences (SCASSS), suggests others, including All Souls College, Oxford University, and the Collège de France.[89] Its lineage may be traced to other organizational and institutional sources conceived interdisciplinarily as well; one need only think of the networks of scholars that Robert Boyle termed invisible colleges to appreciate the extent to which historical models for collaboration across disciplines abound. Leaving aside the many historical exemplars of such knowledge networks, organizations, and institutions that brought scientists and scholars from diverse disciplines together, the formation of the Zentrum für interdisziplinäre Forschung represents an important organizational development because it sought from its inception to advance the comprehensive institutional implementation of interdisciplinarity. At many institutions to this day, this implementation remains piecemeal and restricted to mere recombinations of individual academic units. The comprehensive conception of Universität Bielefeld with ZiF constituting its core thus represents a prototype for interdisciplinary collaboration that deserves recognition and emulation. Although institutional reconceptualization of this order is clearly essential for major research universities, the broad consensus or collective sense of urgency that would transform analysis into action is little in evidence.

### Use-Inspired Research and the Paradigm of the Solitary Investigator

Entrenchment in discipline-based departments corresponds to an academic culture that prizes individualism over teamwork and the discovery of specialized knowledge over problem-based collaboration. A corollary to the assumption that the organizational configuration of the research university has once and for all been suitably disposed is that research or scholarship is necessarily an individual endeavor and that optimal outcomes will inevitably emerge from the amalgamation of the results of individual efforts. Our competitive nature values the individual over the group, and while we valorize the discovery of the unknown by individual scientists, less prestige attaches to collaborative endeavors that target real-world problems and team participation in projects that accomplish assessment, assimilation, synthesis, implementation, and application. Without sufficient coordination and strategic collaboration, however, the ad hoc aggregation of individual endeavors does not necessarily transcend the inevitable limitations of an isolated investigator.[90] As Scott Cook and John Seely Brown frame the dilemma, "Not every action by a human collective can be meaningfully or usefully reduced to an account of actions taken by the individuals in them."[91]

"In recent decades, the growth of scientific and technical knowledge has prompted scientists, engineers, social scientists, and humanists to join in addressing complex problems that must be attacked simultaneously with deep knowledge from different perspectives," the National Academies committee on interdisciplinarity observes, underscoring the imperative for problem-driven collaborative research that is "use-inspired."[92] In an effort to reveal the limitations of the standard binary opposition between basic and applied research, the policy scholar Donald Stokes constructed a table to represent types of research ("Quadrant Model of Scientific Research"), which may variously be inspired by the quest for fundamental understanding or considerations of use. In this conceptualization, "Bohr's quadrant" (so-called, he explains, for the quest of a model atomic structure by Niels Bohr) represents pure basic research. "Pasteur's quadrant," however, represents "basic research that seeks to extend the frontiers of understanding but is also inspired by considerations of use." The designation memorializes the research of the eminent chemist and microbiologist, whose late career was devoted to the development of vaccines that have protected millions from disease: "Pasteur's drive toward understanding and use illustrates this combination of goals."[93]

Use-inspired research demands transdisciplinary collaboration, especially the coordination of scientific discovery with technological innovation. The distinction Joel Mokyr observes between "propositional" and "prescriptive" knowledge is relevant to our understanding of the transdisciplinary research environment because the categories correlate with the movement of fundamental knowledge (basic research) toward application. Unlike standard distinctions between science and technology, Mokyr explains, propositional knowledge refers to knowledge "what," or beliefs about natural phenomena, while prescriptive knowledge corresponds to knowledge "how," or techniques. This is the distinction between *episteme* and *techne*.[94]

Application is moreover operationalized through what is commonly characterized as "know-how." The economist Richard R. Nelson has defined "know-how" as the "wide range of techniques and understandings human societies have acquired over the years that enable them to meet their wants." Know-how is "multifaceted and variegated, and stored in different places and forms," he explains. Although some of it is "relatively well articulated 'how it is done' knowledge," much is "embodied in particular human skills, as contrasted with 'blueprint-like' know-how." Here Nelson aligns his analysis with the distinction between the tacit and explicit dimensions of knowledge elucidated by Michael Polanyi. Moreover, he continues, "it is important to recognize the variety of particular skills involved, and that effective performance is a group achievement."[95] Progress in medical know-how, for example, is produced through the interaction of three "distinct but interdependent" pathways, according to Nelson and colleagues. Basic biomedical research must be complemented by technological advances and "learning by doing in clinical practice."[96] Such conclusions are consistent with findings from other realms of innovation, as considered by the economist Nathan Rosenberg, who argued that basic research is not an autonomous "beginning" of innovation but merely one component in a complex evolutionary process, with mutual interdependencies among system components.[97]

In many instances, the application of existing knowledge is sufficient to advance innovation or produce solutions to problems. Mokyr defines technological progress as "any change in the application of information to the production process in such a way as to increase efficiency, resulting either in the production of a given output with fewer resources (i.e., lower costs), or the production of better or new products." He underscores the significance of the application of existing knowledge because progress is often "derived from the deployment of previously available information rather than the generation of altogether new knowledge."[98] The synthesis of existing knowledge in this context has been termed "recombinant innovation," referring to the combination or recombination of existing ideas, products, and processes to create new innovations. Economist Brian Arthur explains that "novel technologies arise by combination of existing technologies and . . . existing technologies beget further technologies." In other words, "to invent something is to find it in what previously exists."[99] Recent analysis of nearly 18 million scientific papers confirms the extent to which new knowledge derives from novel insights into existing knowledge. According to economist Brian Uzzi and colleagues, "The highest-impact science is primarily grounded in exceptionally conventional combinations of prior work yet simultaneously features an intrusion of unusual combinations." Their assessment suggests that the interdisciplinary collaboration found in team science is especially conducive to innovation and impact: "Teams are 37.7 percent more likely than solo

authors to insert novel combinations into familiar knowledge domains."[100] The trend toward team science has led to the precipitous decline in single-author research papers, which across all scientific fields
have declined from 30 percent in 1981 to 11 percent in 2012, according to
analysis by Thomson Reuters. In some fields, scientific papers now average five authors.[101]

Insufficiently robust interdisciplinary collaboration restricts negotiation of emergent, nonlinear, and unpredictable new complexities and
thus impedes progress in efforts to mount responses to intractable global
problems. This lack of adaptive capacity is nowhere more evident than
in the institutional posture of our research universities when confronted
by the need to address the "grand challenges" of our epoch; one need only
think in terms of global climate change, air and water pollution, overpopulation, hunger and poverty, extinction of species, exhaustion of natural resources, and destruction of ecosystems. As the report of the National Academies on interdisciplinarity explains, such challenges require
interdisciplinary collaboration, which facilitates applied research initiatives that often engage large-scale team efforts to address complex and
intractable problems.[102] Such collaboration may perhaps more accurately
be designated transdisciplinary.

Although we have used the terms *interdisciplinarity* and *transdisciplinarity* more or less interchangeably, the research enterprise of the New
American University model may perhaps more appropriately be designated *transdisciplinary*, following the usage suggested by Robert Frodeman, because the effort advances to the extent possible collaboration
among universities and business and industry and government. Frodeman observes, "More accurate usage would have 'interdisciplinarity' denote changes needed within the academy, 'transdisciplinarity' to efforts
to move beyond university walls and toward the co-production of knowledge between academic and non-academic actors."[103] When knowledge
is coproduced and coordinated transinstitutionally, it becomes the "combined creation of producer and user." Such knowledge will be coevalu-
ated as well as coproduced, Frodeman points out, and thus its evaluation
will no longer invariably be controlled exclusively by the process of peer
review.[104] Peter Weingart makes the corollary point that because the university has "lost its monopoly as the institution of knowledge production,
since many other organizations are also performing that function," the

criteria for the evaluation of quality in transdisciplinary research thus become social, political, and economic, as well as disciplinary.[105]

Such transinstitutional coordination of knowledge production moreover generally implies a context of application and thus concern with outcomes. The coordination of research effort beyond the academy is implicit in the concept of convergence, which in one context a report from the National Research Council defines as an "approach to problem solving that integrates expertise from life sciences with physical, mathematical, and computational sciences, medicine, and engineering to form comprehensive synthetic frameworks that merge areas of knowledge from multiple fields to address specific challenges." Implicit in this conception is not only the "convergence of the subsets of expertise necessary to address a set of research problems" but also the "formation of the web of partnerships involved in supporting such scientific investigations and enabling the resulting advances to be translated into new forms of innovation and new products."[106] An amalgamation of transdisciplinary, transinstitutional, and transnational frameworks has the potential to advance knowledge and innovation on the requisite scale in real time toward desired social and economic outcomes.

## Toward Mutual Intelligibility within the Academy

"There is only one way out of all this," C. P. Snow observed with reference to the schism of the two cultures he had diagnosed in his Cambridge lecture, which we have taken as emblematic of the interdisciplinary imperative. "It is, of course, by rethinking our education." But the academy remains a Tower of Babel where, as Snow put it, "persons educated with the greatest intensity we know can no longer communicate with each other on the plane of their major intellectual concern."[107] The maintenance of strict disciplinary boundaries undermines our impetus to initiate a conversation with those outside our own focus of disciplinary expertise. We cannot expect biologists alone to solve the loss of biodiversity, nor chemists in isolation to negotiate the transition to renewable energy. Because each academic discipline has over time developed its own vernacular, the impetus may be lacking to cultivate "interlanguages" intelligible to other disciplines: the pidgins or creoles, which in the metaphor enlisted by Peter Galison are the mutually comprehensible languages of different subcultures found in trading zones. The exchanges of knowledge between "theoretical subcultures" thus represent the "movement of ideas, objects, and practices as . . . local coordination through the establishment of pidgins and creoles."[108] But chemists have not sufficiently developed a *lingua franca* to communicate with either philosophers or engineers. Collini aptly frames this objective as the "growth of the intellectual equivalent of bilingualism," which he defines as a "capacity not only to exercise the language of our respective specialisms, but also to attend to, learn from, and eventually contribute to, wider cultural conversations."[109] The debate must engage a broad community of disciplines and advance not only on the basis of the understanding found within the academy but also the wisdom and expertise developed in commerce, industry, and government.

Our academic culture not only perpetuates traditional disciplinary thinking but also assigns inordinate significance to distinctions in an implicit hierarchy. Avowals of parity between the various disciplinary cultures notwithstanding, the prestige and preeminence accorded science in the academy remains undiminished just as disciplines trump other disciplines based on their quantitative capacities. Each disciplinary culture must overcome its ambivalence toward different orientations and approaches to solving problems that may have arisen through more than a millennium of institutional evolution. We must organize for collaboration across disciplines to establish the preconditions essential to effective teaching and research as well as constructive social and economic outcomes. Mutual intelligibility between academic disciplines and robust interdisciplinary collaboration are foundational to all aspects of the academic enterprise. But the persistence of disciplinary entrenchment interrelates with other shortcomings and so must be understood in the broader context of critical societal goals. This, then, is to reiterate the contention that the academy must seek knowledge with purpose and link useful knowledge with action for the common good.[110]

"Throughout the eighteenth century, books, articles, and even experiments were still addressed to the general public," Peter Weingart explains. But the focus in science and scholarship became self-referential as specialization necessarily progressed. "The increasingly esoteric nature of knowledge production led to a growing distance from practical concerns and increased resistance to commercial and technical applications that had previously legitimized the utility of the sciences."[111] But even before the advent of organized science and the formation of the modern research university, our intellectual progenitors intuitively understood the imperative to think at scale and across disciplines. Four centuries of scientific focus on the ever smaller and more fundamental secrets of nature have seemingly impaired our ability to frame standpoints of inquiry commensurate to the challenges that confront us. Through our increasingly sophisticated manipulation of limited knowledge coupled with brute force and an astonishing measure of hubris, we have shaped a world that in all likelihood cannot sustain our collective standard of living. Although disciplinary specialization has been key to scientific success, such specialization will inevitably diminish holistic understanding. It has also diminished our ability to construe teaching and research between and among the disciplines. Our academic culture, and science in particular, uses disciplinary organization to recognize and focus on questions that *can* be answered, while there is absolutely no a priori reason to assume that what we *can* know is what we most *need* to know.[112]

## Notes

1. John Seely Brown and Paul Duguid, "Organizational Learning and Communities-of-Practice: Toward a Unified View of Working, Learning, and Innovation," *Organization Science* 2, no. 1 (February 1991): 40. Our discussion of interdisciplinarity and institutional design in chapter 5 includes revised portions from our coauthored book chapter, Michael M. Crow and William B. Dabars, "Interdisciplinarity as a Design Problem: Toward Mutual Intelligibility among Academic Disciplines in the American Research University," in *Enhancing Communication and Collaboration in Interdisciplinary Research*, ed. Michael O'Rourke et al. (Los Angeles: Sage, 2013), and our chapter "Toward Interdisciplinarity by Design in the American Research University," in *University Experiments in Interdisciplinarity: Obstacles and Opportunities*, ed. Peter Weingart and Britta Padberg (Bielefeld: Transcript, 2014). The chapter also includes revised portions of the dissertation by William Dabars, "Disciplinarity and Interdisciplinarity: Rhetoric and Context in the American Research University" (University of California, Los Angeles, 2008).

2. John Seely Brown, Allan Collins, and Paul Duguid, "Situated Cognition and the Culture of Learning," *Educational Researcher* 18, no. 1 (January–February 1989): 33.

3. The theory of "structuration" proposed by Giddens assesses the "situated activities of human agents." See Giddens, *The Constitution of Society: Outline of the Theory of Structuration* (Berkeley: University of California Press, 1984), 25. As Scott Cook and Brown explain, structuration treats "praxis as constitutive of social structure, while

social structure informs praxis." Scott D. N. Cook and John Seely Brown, "Bridging Epistemologies: The Generative Dance between Organizational Knowledge and Organizational Knowing," *Organization Science* 10, no. 4 (July–August 1999): 399, n. 8.

4. An appreciation of the implications of the organizational context for knowledge may derive from reference to more than a half-century of empirical study and theoretical analysis, beginning with pioneering work by Thomas S. Kuhn, especially his seminal *Structure of Scientific Revolutions* (Chicago: University of Chicago Press, 1970). For an account that traces the lineage of the "awareness that science is a social formation amenable to sociological investigation" to Kuhn, as well as such figures as Ludwig Wittgenstein, Jean-François Lyotard, and Richard Rorty, see Hugh T. Miller and Charles J. Fox, "The Epistemic Community," *Administration and Society* 32, no. 6 (2001): 668–669. Approaches including the sociology of science, organizational theory, and social network analysis model interrelationships in scientific and scholarly collaboration. Analysis of such patterns of collaboration underscores the reflexive relationship between knowledge and its organizational context. Robert K. Merton similarly provides a conceptualization of "socio-cognitive networks" that points to the importance of milieu for discovery. See especially Merton, *The Sociology of Science: Theoretical and Empirical Investigations* (Chicago: University of Chicago Press, 1973). Derek J. de Solla Price brought both historical perspective to assessments of knowledge networks and quantitative approaches to the proliferation of scientific publications. See, for example, *Little Science, Big Science, and Beyond,* 2nd ed. (New York: Columbia University Press, 1986), 103–134; and "Networks of Scientific Papers," *Science* 149 (1965): 510–515. An appreciation of the organizational context of knowledge may also be derived from the emerging literature on knowledge-based theories of the firm.

5. Louis Menand, *The Marketplace of Ideas: Reform and Resistance in the American University* (New York: W. W. Norton, 2010), 17.

6. Philip Kitcher, *Science, Truth, and Democracy* (Oxford: Oxford University Press, 2001), 109, 113.

7. A. Hunter Dupree, *Science in the Federal Government: A History of Policies and Activities* (Baltimore: Johns Hopkins University Press, 1986), 9.

8. Roger L. Geiger, *To Advance Knowledge: The Growth of American Research Universities, 1900–1940* (Oxford: Oxford University Press, 1986), 2–3.

9. Frederick P. Brooks, *The Design of Design: Essays from a Computer Scientist* (Boston: Addison-Wesley, 2010), 4.

10. *Oxford English Dictionary,* 3rd ed. (Oxford: Oxford University Press, 2012), online version March 2012.

11. Plato, *The Republic,* Book X, quoted by Brooks, *Design of Design,* 6.

12. Brooks, *Design of Design,* 8–9.

13. Herbert A. Simon, *The Sciences of the Artificial,* 3rd ed. (Cambridge, MA: MIT Press, 1996), 1–24. Italics in the original. Regarding symbols, Simon writes: "Symbol systems are almost the quintessential artifacts, for adaptivity to an environment is their *raison d'être.* They are goal-seeking information-processing systems, usually enlisted in the service of the larger systems in which incorporated" (22). Our usage of the term

*knowledge formation* derives from the invaluable overview of knowledge production found in Peter Weingart, "A Short History of Knowledge Formations," in *The Oxford Handbook of Interdisciplinarity*, ed. Robert Frodeman, Julie Thompson Klein, and Carl Mitcham (Oxford: Oxford University Press, 2010), 3–14.

14. Daniel Katz and Robert L. Kahn, *The Social Psychology of Organizations* (New York: Wiley, 1966).

15. John Ziman, ed., *Technological Innovation as an Evolutionary Process* (Cambridge: Cambridge University Press, 2000), cited by Brooks, *Design of Design*, 54.

16. Brooks, *Design of Design*, 53.

17. Nigel Cross and Kees Dorst, "Co-Evolution of Problem and Solution Spaces in Creative Design," in *Computational Models of Creative Design*, vol. 4, ed. J. S. Gero and M. L. Maher (Sydney: University of Sydney, 1999), 243–262, cited in Brooks, *Design of Design*, 51. A variant formulation is to be found in Kees Dorst and Nigel Cross, "Creativity in the Design Process: Co-Evolution of Problem-Solution," *Design Studies* 22 (2001): 425–437.

18. Bruce Mau and Jennifer Leonard, *Massive Change* (London: Phaidon Press, 2004), 16–17.

19. C. P. Snow, *The Two Cultures and the Scientific Revolution* (Cambridge: Cambridge University Press, 1960), 2–4, 12.

20. Snow, *Two Cultures,* 15–16.

21. Snow, *Two Cultures*, 15.

22. Stefan Collini, introduction to C. P. Snow, *The Two Cultures* (Cambridge: Cambridge University Press, 1998), viii. In a revised assessment published four years after the lecture as "A Second Look," Collini explains, Snow attempted to remedy the oversimplification of his initial dichotomization with the introduction of a third category. According to Collini, the "feeble attempt" to remedy the initial omission of the social sciences marked the growing influence of these disciplines in British universities (liv).

23. Robert Frodeman and Carl Mitcham, "New Directions in Interdisciplinarity: Broad, Deep, and Critical," *Bulletin of Science, Technology, and Society* 27, no. 6 (2007): 506–507.

24. Our usage of the linguistic concept of mutual intelligibility was suggested by a phrase in the introduction to the new edition of the Snow essay by Collini. The inevitable limitations imposed by our fragmented knowledge, Collini posits, "threaten to make it impossible to sustain the kind of debate or mutually intelligible exchange of views upon which the effective conduct of a society's affairs depends" (lvii).

25. For further elaboration regarding the trajectory of the institutionalization of interdisciplinarity, see William B. Dabars, "Disciplinarity and Interdisciplinarity: Rhetoric and Context in the American Research University," PhD diss., University of California, Los Angeles, 2008.

26. Jonathan R. Cole, *The Great American University: Its Rise to Preeminence, Its Indispensable National Role, and Why It Must Be Protected* (New York: Public Affairs, 2009), 5.

27. Andrew Abbott, *Chaos of Disciplines* (Chicago: University of Chicago Press, 2001), 126–128.

28. Mattei Dogan, "The New Social Sciences: Cracks in the Disciplinary Walls," *International Social Sciences Journal* 153 (September 1997): 429.

29. James J. Duderstadt, *A University for the Twenty-First Century* (Ann Arbor: University of Michigan Press, 2000), 120–121.

30. Immanuel Wallerstein, "Anthropology, Sociology, and Other Dubious Disciplines," *Current Anthropology* 44, no. 4 (August–October 2003): 453–465.

31. Abbott, *Chaos of Disciplines*, 122–125.

32. National Academies, Committee on Facilitating Interdisciplinary Research (CFIR) and Committee on Science, Engineering, and Public Policy (COSEPUP), *Facilitating Interdisciplinary Research* (Washington, DC: National Academies Press, 2005), ix, xi, 17.

33. *Facilitating Interdisciplinary Research*, ix, 172.

34. Henry Etzkowitz, *The Triple Helix: University-Industry-Government Innovation in Action* (New York: Routledge, 2008), 1.

35. *Facilitating Interdisciplinary Research*, 3.

36. *Facilitating Interdisciplinary Research*, 100. With reference to the implementation of interdisciplinarity in European systems of higher education, which are typically subject to the authority of centralized administration, Burton Clark observes the unintended consequence that government councils sometimes exercise their authority to veto innovations that favor emerging disciplines when these threaten established authority and resources. See "Places of Inquiry," in *The Academic Profession: National, Disciplinary, and Institutional Settings*, ed. Burton Clark (Berkeley: University of California Press, 1987), 375.

37. *Facilitating Interdisciplinary Research*, x, 6.

38. *Facilitating Interdisciplinary Research*, ix, 172.

39. John Hagel, John Seely Brown, and Lang Davison, *The Power of Pull: How Small Moves, Smartly Made, Can Set Big Things in Motion* (New York: Basic Books, 2010), 7, 11, 73. The quote from Lew Platt comes from Charles G. Sieloff, "If Only HP Knew What HP Knows: The Roots of Knowledge Management at Hewlett-Packard," *Journal of Knowledge Management* 3, no. 1 (1999): 47–53.

40. Robert K. Merton and Elinor Barber, *The Travels and Adventures of Serendipity: A Study in Sociological Semantics and the Sociology of Science* (Princeton, NJ: Princeton University Press, 2004).

41. Derek J. de Solla Price, *Little Science, Big Science, and Beyond* (New York: Columbia University Press, 1986), viii–ix, 119.

42. Joel Mokyr, *The Gifts of Athena: Historical Origins of the Knowledge Economy* (Princeton, NJ: Princeton University Press, 2002), 56.

43. Weingart, "Short History of Knowledge Formations," 7.

44. Mokyr, *Gifts of Athena*, 1–8; 34–35. The invention of the printing press and, more recently, proliferation of ubiquitous information technologies provide unparalleled examples of increased access at reduced costs.

45. Price, *Little Science, Big Science, and Beyond*, 119.

46. Derek J. de Solla Price, "Is Technology Historically Independent of Science? A Study in Statistical Historiography," *Technology and Culture* 6, no. 4 (Autumn 1965): 557, 562, 567.

47. Diana Crane, *Invisible Colleges: Diffusion of Knowledge in Scientific Communities* (Chicago: University of Chicago Press, 1972), 3–5, 22–23, 41–42, 52; and Diana Crane, "Social Structure in a Group of Scientists: A Test of the 'Invisible College' Hypothesis," *American Sociological Review* 34, no. 3 (June 1969): 349.

48. Howard D. White, Barry Wellman, and Nancy Nazer, "Does Citation Reflect Social Structure? Longitudinal Evidence from the Globenet Interdisciplinary Research Group," *Journal of the American Society for Information Science and Technology* 55, no 2 (2004): 111–126

49. Karim R. Lakhani et al., "The Value of Openness in Scientific Problem Solving," Harvard Business School working paper 07-050 (October 2006), 2.

50. Clay Shirky, *Cognitive Surplus: Creativity and Generosity in a Connected Age* (New York: Penguin, 2010). We wish to express our appreciation to Gregory Britton for pointing out this correlation.

51. Etienne Wenger, *Communities of Practice: Learning, Meaning, and Identity* (Cambridge: Cambridge University Press, 1998), 3–5.

52. Wenger, *Communities of Practice*, 6–7, 12–13.

53. Paul Duguid, "The Art of Knowing: Social and Tacit Dimensions of Knowledge and the Limits of the Community of Practice," *Information Society* 21 (2005): 112–113, 115, n. 1.

54. Wenger, *Communities of Practice*, 72–83.

55. For discussion of a model of interdisciplinary formation that focuses on the fragmentation of disciplines into subfields followed by their strategic recombination or hybridization, see Mattei Dogan and Robert Pahre, *Creative Marginality: Innovation at the Intersections of Social Sciences* (Boulder, CO: Westview Press, 1990).

56. Wenger, *Communities of Practice*, 11, 100–101, 216–217, 225, 274.

57. Miller and Fox, "Epistemic Community," 669, 681, 683.

58. Burkart Holzner, *Reality Construction in Society* (Cambridge, MA: Schenkman, 1968), 28.

59. Peter M. Haas, "Epistemic Communities and International Policy Coordination," *International Organization* 46, no. 1 (1992): 3, n. 4; Kuhn, *Structure of Scientific Revolutions*, 175.

60. Irma Bogenrieder and Bart Nooteboom, "The Emergence of Learning Communities: A Theoretical Analysis," in *Organizations as Knowledge Systems: Knowledge, Learning, and Dynamic Capabilities*, ed. H. T. Tsoukas and N. Mylonopoulos (Hampshire: Palgrave MacMillan, 2004), 49.

61. Lars Håkanson, "The Firm as an Epistemic Community: The Knowledge-Based View Revisited," *Industrial and Corporate Change* 19, no. 6 (2010): 1804, 1809.

62. David J. Teece, "Knowledge and Competence as Strategic Assets," in *Handbook on Knowledge Management*, vol. 1, ed. C. W. Holsapple (Berlin: Springer Verlag, 2003), 149.

63. Patrick Bolton and Mathias Dewatripont, "The Firm as a Communication Network," *Quarterly Journal of Economics* 109, no. 4 (1994): 809.

64. Håkanson, "The Firm as an Epistemic Community," 1806

65. Henry Etzkowitz, "Research Groups as Quasi-Firms: The Invention of the Entrepreneurial University," *Research Policy* 32 (2003): 109–110.

66. Jorge Niosi et al., "National Systems of Innovation: In Search of a Workable Concept," *Technology in Society* 15 (1993): 207–208.

67. Etzkowitz, *Triple Helix*, 141–142.

68. Michael M. Crow and William B. Dabars, "University-Based Research and Economic Development: The Morrill Act and the Emergence of the American Research University," in *Precipice or Crossroads?: Where America's Great Public Universities Stand and Where They Are Going Midway through Their Second Century*, ed. Daniel Mark Fogel (Albany: State University of New York Press, 2012).

69. Bruce Kogut and Udo Zander, "What Firms Do: Coordination, Identity, and Learning," *Organization Science* 7, no. 5 (September–October 1996): 503.

70. Bruce Kogut and Udo Zander, "Knowledge of the Firm, Combinative Capabilities, and the Replication of Knowledge," *Organization Science* 3, no. 3 (August 1992): 384.

71. Janine Nahapiet and Sumantra Ghoshal, "Social Capital, Intellectual Capital, and Organizational Advantage," *Academy of Management Review* 23, no. 2 (April 1998): 251.

72. Association of American Universities, "Interdisciplinarity Task Force Report" (Washington, DC, October 2005); Roger L. Geiger, "Organized Research Units: Their Role in the Development of the Research University," *Journal of Higher Education* 61, no. 1 (January/February 1990): 1–19; Gerald J. Stahler and William R. Tash, "Centers and Institutes in the Research University: Issues, Problems, and Prospects," *Journal of Higher Education* 65, no. 5 (September/October 1994): 540–554.

73. Immanuel Wallerstein, "Anthropology, Sociology, and Other Dubious Disciplines," *Current Anthropology* 44, no. 4 (August–October 2003): 453–465.

74. Robert Frodeman, *Sustainable Knowledge: A Theory of Interdisciplinarity* (Basingstoke: Palgrave Macmillan, 2014), 16.

75. Léo Apostel, Guy Berger, Asa Briggs et al., eds., *Interdisciplinarity: Problems of Teaching and Research in Universities* (Paris: Organisation for Economic Co-operation and Development/Center for Educational Research and Innovation, 1972); Geoffrey Squires, "Interdisciplinarity in Higher Education in the United Kingdom," *European Journal of Education* 27, no. 3 (1992): 205–210.

76. Julie Thompson Klein, "A Taxonomy of Interdisciplinarity," in *Oxford Handbook of Interdisciplinarity*, 15.

77. Heinz Heckhausen, "Discipline and Interdisciplinarity" (86–89) and Guy Michaud, introduction (25–26) in *Interdisciplinarity: Problems of Teaching and Research in Universities*, ed. Apostel, Berger, Briggs, et al. Heckhausen termed interdisciplinarity a "new and highly valued fad," institutionalization of which may be "premature."

78. Social Science Research Council (1934), cited by Abbott (2001), 131–132.

79. According to the *Harvard University General Catalogue*: "By vote of the President and Fellows on June 19, 1935, a plan was adopted for the establishment of new pro-

fessorships for individuals of distinction not definitely attached to any particular department, and these were to be known as University Professorships. It was proposed to reserve these new chairs for individuals working on the frontiers of knowledge, and in such a way as to cross the conventional boundaries of the specialties." *Official Register of Harvard University* 14, no. 9 (August 29, 1991).

80. http://www.maxwell.syr.edu/deans/

81. http://socialthought.uchicago.edu/Introduction.htm

82. Abbott, *Chaos of Disciplines*, 126.

83. Steven Marcus, "Humanities from Classics to Cultural Studies: Notes Toward the History of an Idea," *Daedalus* 135, no. 2 (Spring 2006): 15–21.

84. http://humwww.ucsc.edu/HistCon/

85. http://www.jhu.edu/admis/catalog/artsci/humanities.pdf

86. http://www.stanford.edu/dept/MTL/index.html

87. Julie Thompson Klein, *Interdisciplinarity: History, Theory, and Practice* (Detroit, MI: Wayne State University Press, 1990), 48.

88. See, for example, the discussion by Peter Weingart, "Interdisciplinarity and the New Governance of Universities," in *University Experiments in Interdisciplinarity: Obstacles and Opportunities*, ed. Peter Weingart and Britta Padberg (Bielefeld: Transcript, 2014), 151–174.

89. Björn Wittrock, "Institutes for Advanced Study: Ideas, Histories, Rationales," keynote address on the occasion of the inauguration of the Helsinki Collegium for Advanced Studies, University of Helsinki (December 2, 2002).

90. Michael M. Crow, "None Dare Call it Hubris: The Limits of Knowledge," *Issues in Science and Technology* 23, no. 2 (Winter 2007): 29–32.

91. Scott D. N. Cook and John Seely Brown, "Bridging Epistemologies: The Generative Dance Between Organizational Knowledge and Organizational Knowing," *Organization Science* 10, no. 4 (July–August 1999): 399.

92. *Facilitating Interdisciplinary Research*, 17.

93. Donald E. Stokes, *Pasteur's Quadrant: Basic Science and Technological Innovation* (Washington, DC: Brookings Institution Press, 1997), 72–75.

94. Mokyr, *Gifts of Athena*, 4.

95. Richard R. Nelson, "On the Uneven Evolution of Human Know-How," *Research Policy* 32 (2003): 909–910.

96. Richard R. Nelson et al., "How Medical Know-How Progresses," *Research Policy* 40 (2011): 1339–1344.

97. Nathan Rosenberg, *Inside the Black Box: Technology and Economics* (Cambridge: Cambridge University Press, 1982).

98. Joel Mokyr, *The Lever of Riches: Technological Creativity and Economic Progress* (Oxford: Oxford University Press, 1990), 6.

99. W. Brian Arthur, *The Nature of Technology: What It Is and How It Evolves* (New York: Free Press, 2009), 21, 122, the latter cited in Erik Brynjolfsson and Andrew McAfee, *The Second Machine Age: Work, Progress, and Prosperity in a Time of Brilliant Technologies* (New York: W. W. Norton, 2014), 79.

100. Brian Uzzi et al., "Atypical Combinations and Scientific Impact," *Science* 342 (October 25, 2013): 468.

101. Paul Voosen, "Microbiology Leaves the Solo Author Behind," *Chronicle of Higher Education* (November 11, 2013).

102. *Facilitating Interdisciplinary Research*, xi, 3, 16–17, 52.

103. Frodeman, *Sustainable Knowledge*, 61.

104. Robert Frodeman, "Interdisciplinarity, Communication, and the Limits of Knowledge," in *Enhancing Communication and Collaboration in Interdisciplinary Research*, ed. Michael O'Rourke et al. (Los Angeles: Sage, 2013), 106, 108, 110.

105. Weingart, "A Short History of Knowledge Formations," 12.

106. National Research Council, *Convergence: Facilitating Transdisciplinary Integration of Life Sciences, Physical Sciences, Engineering, and Beyond* (Washington, DC: National Academies Press, 2014), 17.

107. Snow, *Two Cultures*, 19; Snow, *The Two Cultures: A Second Look* (1963), 60.

108. Peter Galison, *Image and Logic: A Material Culture of Physics* (Chicago: University of Chicago Press, 1997), 48.

109. Collini, introduction to Snow, *Two Cultures*, lvii.

110. Articulation of the objective of "useful knowledge" in the academic culture of the early American republic is attributed to Benjamin Franklin, Jonathan Cole explains. The intent to promote useful knowledge informed Franklin's intentions for the American Philosophical Society and his plans for the University of Pennsylvania. Cole, *Great American University*, 1, 14, 526n68.

111. Weingart, "Short History of Knowledge Formations," 6.

112. Crow, "None Dare Call It Hubris," 29–32.

# SIX

# A Pragmatic Approach
# to Innovation and Sustainability

Although the ideals of the Enlightenment informed the conception of the American republic and its fledgling institutions, the values of
the nation came to be equally imbued with the utilitarian ethos of the
frontier. This practical orientation shaped the land-grant institutions and
the emerging American research university during the later nineteenth
century. A philosophical tradition coalesced in New England during this
period that expressed these values and concurrent cultural strands, including the new impetus toward scientific inquiry and political progressivism.[1] Pragmatism has been termed our nation's most significant contribution to philosophy, and we briefly sketch its outlines to suggest its
influence on the American research university. Pragmatists contend that
thought and action are indivisible and that ideas should lead to practical action. Pragmatism is thus characterized by its emphasis on the practical application of knowledge understood within the context of social
practice.[2] The claims for the impacts of pragmatism are various, but we
contend, principally, that the pragmatist stance interrelating knowledge
with action implicitly informs the defining tenets of the New American
University, especially its concern that knowledge should lead to action
with the objective of real-world impact.

Pragmatism traces its origins to a circle of Harvard academics and
Cambridge intellectuals that convened informally in a discussion group
during the 1870s—and thus contemporaneously with the founding of
Johns Hopkins University. The so-called Metaphysical Club, masterfully
elucidated by Louis Menand in his intellectual history of the era, included
two of the three chief proponents of the initial phase of pragmatism: the
logician, mathematician, and scientist Charles Sanders Peirce and the

philosopher and psychologist William James. Its most eloquent and influential proponent in the twentieth century would be the philosopher and educational theorist John Dewey.[3] More recently, neopragmatist stances have been assumed by such philosophers as John Rawls, Jürgen Habermas, and Richard Rorty.[4] And although pragmatism has been taken in general usage to refer to conduct in accord with common sense, its relevance in the present context requires primarily that we appreciate its "insistence that ideas and beliefs are always in the service of interests," as Menand paraphrases the contention of Dewey.[5]

A concern with the practical consequences of knowledge situated within a particular social context guided pragmatism from its inception. Peirce set forth what became known as the "principle of Peirce" or "pragmatist maxim" in a paper published in 1878. The objective is to establish the validity of a hypothesis or concept through a determination of its practical consequences. William James expounded the work of Peirce and brought it to the attention of the wider academic community. In a lecture delivered to the Philosophical Union of the University of California, Berkeley in August 1898, James presented pragmatism as a "perfectly familiar attitude" consistent with the empiricism of the natural sciences. He explained that for pragmatists, theories, concepts, and hypotheses become "instruments," deliberation with which advances their practical consequences. Thus, James asserted that a scientific theory is to be construed as "an instrument: it is designed to achieve a purpose—to facilitate action or increase understanding."[6] According to James, the pragmatic principle contends that "any part of a thought that made no difference in the thought's practical consequences" be discarded as inessential.[7] We reiterate that this concern for the practical consequences of knowledge marks the pragmatist method as undergirding the New American University advocacy of use-inspired research.

Dewey took up the pragmatist argument and devoted decades to its elaboration, especially with regard to its relevance to education. He propounded the pragmatist contention that thought and action must be indivisible. And he concurred with James that knowledge must be an "instrument or organ of successful action."[8] "All the pragmatists, but most of all Dewey, challenge the sharp dichotomy . . . between theoretical beliefs and practical deliberations," the philosopher Christopher Hookway explains. For pragmatists, "all inquiry is practical, concerned with transforming and evaluating the features of the situations in which we find ourselves." Moreover, "the content of a theory or concept is determined by what we should do with it."[9] Dewey thus conceives of knowledge as neither more nor less than the "results of particular inquiries," explains the philosopher John Stuhr. He paraphrases Dewey: "These inquiries always arise within particular contexts, particular times and places . . . . There is no other knowledge, no knowledge unmediated by inquiry." Stuhr observes that for Dewey, pragmatic inquiry must never "part company substantially with real investigations that aim at real amelioration of real problems." Thus, pragmatic inquiry "on its own terms, can establish its effectiveness only case by case . . . and only in practice through its consequences."[10]

Pragmatism is concerned with the resolution of problems. As befits a pragmatist, writes Martin Jay, truth for Dewey was "not based on an accurate correspondence with an external world of objects or eternal ideas, but was a result of a successful resolution of a problem."[11] With this approach to knowledge, its abstract truth-criterion becomes less important than its effectiveness in solving problems. As the philosopher Michael Bacon puts it, "In place of the attempt to identify a fixed framework for inquiry, the pragmatists see inquiry as open-ended, seeking to provide tools which will enable us, as participants, to cope with the world."[12] For the pragmatist, the truth-content of a hypothesis is always subject to revision, and ideas are to be conceived, discussed, accepted, or dismissed based upon what contemporary parlance would term their actionable potential. Inquiry for Dewey thus represented the "power to reconstruct or exercise control of transformation," Stuhr elaborates. He quotes Dewey: "There is no inquiry that does not involve the making of some change in environing conditions."[13] In its concern with the resolution of problems and intent that inquiry be transformational, pragmatism thus anticipated key tenets of the New American University.

"Pragmatism, in the most basic sense, is about how we think, not what we think," Menand observes.[14] Dewey identified the pragmatist method of using evidence to test hypotheses as none other than scientific method, Bacon explains.[15] Thus, James spoke of the "radical empiricism" inherent in the pragmatist approach to knowledge.[16] But more broadly, Stuhr finds in pragmatism "openness, hope, and an insistence on embodiment, enactment, and putting theory into practice." Its tenets express a "tolerant and pluralistic concern for individuals, their growth, and their differences" as well as an "urgent commitment to communities and democracy as a way of life." And because such an approach animates the potential of philosophy to offer critique and guide inquiry, pragmatism is "always concerned with values and creation." Indeed, Stuhr contends that the pragmatic tradition enjoins one and all to "think and live differently," which he frames in terms of the Emersonian injunction that, as against the"retrospective," we "must enjoy an original relation to the universe." He thus perceives within pragmatism a melioristic commitment: "In its largest sense, this is an educational task, and pragmatism offers crucial, liberating tools for this task," especially its "understanding of education and democracy as intrinsically and reciprocally linked."[17] In its overarching focus on the individual and concern with the advancement of communities, the New American University is similarly optimistic, pluralistic, and melioristic.

Parallels between the educational tenets of pragmatism, especially as propounded by John Dewey, and the objectives of the New American University are readily apparent. The pragmatist contention that thought and action are indivisible and realized in social practice corresponds to the assumptions undergirding the New American University, which advocates use-inspired research with societal impact. This objective resonates with the pragmatist concern, propounded by Dewey, for actionable knowledge exercised in a particular context, time, and place in response to real-world problems. "Knowing and doing are indivisible aspects of the same process," Louis Menand paraphrases Dewey, "which is the business of adaptation."[18] With this formulation, Menand articulates a critical objective both of use-inspired research, which is the advancement of societal adaptability, and, more generally, the contention that the New American University may be understood as a complex and adaptive knowledge enterprise. Because the design aspirations are interrelated and interdependent as well as mutually reinforcing, these pragmatist objectives for knowledge correspond as well to the design aspirations that advocate societal transformation and social embeddedness.

A period of flagging interest in pragmatism coincided roughly with the Cold War, but a resurgence of its arguments has been evident beginning in the 1980s and 1990s. The approaches of the German philosopher and social theorist Jürgen Habermas and the American philosopher Richard Rorty toward the significance of community and the role of deliberation and discourse in social practice are especially emblematic. Whether disciplinary, transdisciplinary, virtual, or international, participation in communities guided by the normative standards of academic freedom represents an imperative value within the pluralistic and cosmopolitan milieu of the American research university. The relevance of neopragmatism for the New American University thus comes especially with its explicit advocacy of social embeddedness and recognition of its role in societal transformation. We considered the significance of epistemic communities and communities of inquiry in our discussion of paradigms for interdisciplinary research. But for our purposes here, the most general everyday sense of the concept of community interrelates the fundamental tenets of the New American University.

Jürgen Habermas is among the most influential proponents of the pragmatist revival, and like the classical pragmatists, Michael Bacon points out, he "presents an account of knowledge as generated and legitimated through social interaction." Habermas terms this process "communicative action" or "communicative rationality."[19] In this context Habermas cites his adaptation of Peirce's theory of knowledge and truth. Knowledge, in Peirce's view, is a consensus position generated through discourse between many observers. This idea of the consensus position functions as a core proposition in communicative rationality. For Habermas, social agents deliberate what, in their view, is true; social truth is the product of negotiation and accommodation that eventually produces consensus.[20] Bacon thus speaks of "discursive mediation," and Martin Jay terms the process "intersubjective consensus and linguistic transparency through symmetrical rational dialogue."[21] The philosopher Seyla Benhabib follows Habermas in her call for a community of inquirers guided by a "discursive communicative concept of rationality." In this community, the "illusions of a self-transparent and self-grounding reason, the illusion of a disembedded and disembodied subject, and the illusion of having found an Archimedean standpoint, situated beyond historical and cultural contingency" are abandoned for consensus "sufficient to ensure intersubjective agreement among like-thinking rational minds."[22]

Habermas follows Peirce in his contention that society at large contains myriad groups discussing and negotiating different experienced realities, which he terms "lifeworlds" (*Lebenswelt*), a concept he adapted
from Edmund Husserl. Whereas Peirce believed that the discursive process might lead to objective facts or even truth, Habermas contends that
communicative rationality should strive merely to reconcile and mediate social or political truths. As opposed to a preoccupation with abstract
principles such as truth and moral goodness, communicative reason seeks
merely the "rational resolution of problems."[23] For strict pragmatists, even
the vaunted commitment of the academy to the abstract principle of
truth—epitomized in the Harvard motto *Veritas* and implicit in the *Fiat
Lux* of the University of California—might require legitimation by the
evidence of real-world application. For Habermas, this rationality governs everything from casual interactions in our daily lives to historical
conflicts between the practitioners of political ideologies. Habermas concedes that his approach coincides precisely with pragmatist advocacy of
sustained public debate in the service of democracy.[24]

Richard Rorty similarly sees pragmatism as a way to steer philosophical inquiry toward questions that matter in our daily lives and practices.
He concurs with the pragmatist intent to resolve social problems through
deliberation and discourse rather than appeals to abstract principles or
concepts such as order, democracy, or due process: "Pragmatists think
that the history of attempts to isolate the True and the Good, or to define the 'true' or 'good,' supports their suspicion that there is no interest-
ing work to be done in this area," Rorty observes.[25] He suggests that when
grounded in actual experience and not arcane or abstract moral schemes,
deliberation can provide a "workable" truth for society.[26] As was the case
with the early pragmatists, even truth for Rorty is an outcome of consensus within our communities and institutions. And even the authority of
empiricism is thus trumped by the normative standards of communicative reason. To this extent, Rorty contends that pragmatism appropriately rejects any "source of normativity other than the practices of the
people around us."[27]

"Pragmatism shares Emerson's distrust of institutions and systems,"
notes Louis Menand, and not surprisingly, Rorty underscores what he
terms the "anti-authoritarianism" inherent to pragmatism. "The core of
Rorty's pragmatism is a rejection of any authority over and above that of

human agreement," Bacon observes and cites his demand that inquiry "respect only freely secured human agreement."[28] The New American University similarly takes up the pragmatist refusal to acquiesce to tradition or cede authority beyond an appeal to relevant communities of inquiry. As one outcome, it seeks to redefine its terms of engagement rather than blindly emulate the arrangements and practices of the gold standard institutions.

The pragmatist contention that knowledge implies action has been taken up by various organizational theorists. John Seely Brown, together with philosopher S. D. Noam Cook, explicitly invokes the pragmatist tradition in an analysis of the role of organizational knowledge in innovation. In knowledge-based organizations, Cook and Brown correlate organizational knowledge with what they term the "epistemology of possession," referring to what is known and "typically treated as something people possess." In contrast, the "epistemology of practice" designates *knowing*, which is "dynamic, concrete, and relational." Knowing refers to the "coordinated activities of individuals and groups in doing their 'real work' as informed by a particular organizational or group context." Because knowledge and knowing are complementary, their interplay has the potential to engender productive outcomes: "Understanding the generative dance (how to recognize, support, and harness it) is essential, we believe, to understanding the types of learning, innovation, and effectiveness that are prime concerns for all epistemologically oriented organizational theories."[29]

Cook and Brown align their distinction between knowledge and knowing with pragmatism: "The pragmatist perspective takes a primary concern not with 'knowledge,' which is seen as abstract and static, but with 'knowing,' which is understood as part of concrete, dynamic human action." And in bridging the epistemologies of possession and practice, Cook and Brown call for what Dewey termed "productive inquiry." The concept is framed thus: "It is *inquiry* because what motivates us to action is in some sense a query: a problem, a question, a provocative insight, or a troublesome situation. It is *productive* because it aims to produce (to make) an answer, solution, or resolution."[30]

Dewey's pragmatism has proven its resilience as well through its relevance to policy scholars such as Barry Bozeman. In his assessment of public values and the public interest in an era defined by economic individualism, Bozeman explicitly draws on a number of pragmatist premises. He contends that pragmatism offers the potential resolution of many perceived shortcomings of public interest theories as well as measures to advance deliberation in public policy: "If we follow the lead set decades ago by pragmatist John Dewey, we can conceive of a pragmatic approach to public value in which the pursuit of the public interest is a matter of using open minds and sound, fair procedures to move ever closer to an ideal that is revealed during the process and, in part, by the process." Terming his own approach "pragmatic idealism," Bozeman recommends "keeping in mind an ideal of the public interest, but without specific content, and then moving toward that ideal, making the ideal more concrete as one moves toward it."[31] Here Bozeman enlists the pragmatist approach to specifying the content of broad and vague concepts such as public value—or abstract principles such as equity or justice—through measured steps and incremental units.

For Dewey, Bozeman explains, the public interest "cannot be known in any important sense in the absence of social inquiry and public discussion and debate." Bozeman thus takes the pragmatist position that public values and public interest cannot be known apart from their determination through deliberation. "The public interest is an ideal that is given shape, on a case-by-case basis, by a public motivated to secure its common interests as a public." The approach toward normative consensus through discursive contexts is consistent with the pragmatist emphasis on civic discourse and commitment to a pluralistic and communitarian ethic: "The public interest, in Dewey's view, is thus not an absolute, universal, or ahistorical good. It is constructed in each policy and problem context as conjoint activity produces indirect social consequences that the democratic public wishes to direct into collectively identified and validated channels." In another key passage, Bozeman reiterates and enlarges on this pragmatist argument and moreover identifies social inquiry with experimentation, which is the signature pragmatist method for the resolution of complex problems:

> The public interest in the pragmatic view is a contextual and pluralistic good, one constructed in each policy and problem context by a democratic public committed to the cooperative and deliberative process of experimental social inquiry . . . . In the Deweyan account the designated "public interest"

on any given policy question cannot be known prior to social inquiry and public discussion and debate. The public interest is therefore always created by a public motivated to secure its common interests as a political community, a commitment that ensures not only the identification and maintenance of such interests but also the development of individuals as fully self-realized and enriched citizens.[32]

Taking these conceptualizations into account, a true public university would be an institution defined by its alignment with public values as well as service to the public interest. Bozeman and colleague Torben Beck Jørgensen offer an inventory of seventy-two public values elicited from the political science and public administration literature.[33] If the intent were to construct a university based on these values, it would be sustainable, forward thinking, and concerned with the common good. It would balance the interests of constituencies, while protecting minorities and individual rights. It would be user-friendly, exhibit some level of user democracy, and remain responsive to the will of the people. It would engage citizen involvement as well as support local governance. The academic organization would be characterized by robust adaptability, innovation, efficacy, and productivity, and would also contribute to employee self-development. And finally, the administration would engage the public reasonably, fairly, with dialogue and responsiveness, in a timely manner. Above all, the institution would be committed to the public interest, evincing neutrality, openness, and justice. Of course, many of these values delineated by Jørgensen and Bozeman are essentially contested concepts in philosophy, and their mere enumeration does not provide sufficiently meaningful direction for building an institution. But this is where the pragmatic idealism that Bozeman derives from Dewey comes into play, as these values are fleshed out by discourse and deliberation within the public—or some publics—to which the institution is committed.

The transformational thrust of the pragmatist lineage for the New American University that we have delineated is eloquently captured in an assessment of the pragmatist attitude toward knowledge formulated by Louis Menand:

> [Pragmatists] all believed that ideas are not "out there" waiting to be discovered, but are tools . . . that people devise to cope with the world in which they

find themselves. They believed that ideas are produced not by individuals—
that ideas are social. They believed that ideas do not develop according to
some inner logic of their own, but are entirely dependent, like germs, on
human careers and environment. And they believed that since ideas are
provisional responses to particular situations, their survival depends not
on their immutability but on their adaptability.[34]

What is remarkable is that this approach to knowledge, which anticipated
by a full century some of the central arguments of postmodernism,
emerged in the decades that witnessed the emergence of the American
research university.[35] Although the pragmatist tradition broadly informs
our academic culture, we see it as especially relevant to central tenets of
the New American University.

## Toward Academic Leadership in Sustainable Development

In the summer of 1787, two watershed processes that would shape the
course of the modern era were unfolding on opposite sides of the Atlantic. The Industrial Revolution was gathering momentum in Britain and
beginning to exert its impact on the burgeoning American economy.
Meanwhile the new American republic was just completing its earliest
aspirational blueprint: the Constitution of the United States. These revolutionary processes—one economic and the other political—would define the lives of subsequent generations but both represent merely incremental progress in the evolution of human consciousness because neither
was undertaken with any evident cognizance of their context within the
natural world.[36] The American Constitution represents an extraordinary
articulation of the design of a state that at once established democratic
governance, liberty, and justice, and fostered core personal and social aspirations intended to be realized through political institutions. The Industrial Revolution unleashed technological progress to leverage the fundamental mechanisms of capitalism, which would reorganize society
around new kinds of economic institutions. But neither the Constitution
nor the principles of capitalism, formulated contemporaneously by Adam
Smith in the *Wealth of Nations*, provide evidence of meaningful awareness of the natural systems of the earth or the realization that our constructs and designs might advance in sustainable ways.

The well-known definition of sustainability that comes to mind for many derives from the report of the World Commission on Environment and Development, more commonly known as the Brundtland Commission, presented to the United Nations General Assembly in 1987: "development that meets the needs of the present without compromising the ability of future generations to meet their own needs."[37] The commission is credited with reorienting the discussion from scientific research on the environment to the interdependence of nature and emergent social goals, underscoring the possibility of reconciling environmental concerns with the objectives of development. According to climate change expert David G. Victor, the report introduced the concept of sustainable development: "The report argued that boosting the economy, protecting natural resources, and ensuring social justice are not conflicting but interwoven and complementary goals."[38]

The emergence of the concept of sustainable development during the decade of the eighties begins with the scientific and comes to be informed by the political. Whereas in 1980 the vanguard thinking on the environment couched the discussion in terms of conservation and focused primarily on scientific resolutions, over the course of the decade the privileging of the scientific gave way to greater focus on the political dimensions of the challenge. The National Research Council committee drafting the landmark report *Our Common Journey* in the late nineties defined sustainability as the effort to "meet human needs while conserving the earth's life support systems and reducing hunger and poverty." From the perspective of the committee, the seminal *World Conservation Strategy* published at the outset of the previous decade remained "firmly grounded in a scientific understanding of the workings and limits of resources and environmental systems." By contrast, important, more recent, developments were perceived to have ensued in the domains of policy and institutional innovation.[39]

Although science remains informed by the political in issues of sustainability as elsewhere, an effort to develop the science of sustainability, or sustainability science, has emerged as a dominant concern in the twenty-first-century academy. Environmental policy and sustainability science scholars William C. Clark and Nancy Dickson consider the challenge of sustainable development to be the "reconciliation of society's development goals with the planet's environmental limits over the long term." Clark and Dickson underscore the imperative to understand the "dynamic interactions between nature and society, with equal attention to how social change shapes the environment and how environmental change shapes society," and emphasize the need for knowledge collaboratively produced between scientists and practitioners to inform policy that advances sustainable development.[40] Clark explains that, like health science, sustainability science is "defined by the problems it addresses rather than the disciplines it employs."[41]

An appreciation of the interrelationship between natural processes and human design is a prerequisite for any conception of sustainable development. This hybrid concept can be summarily defined as the stewardship of natural capital for future generations, but its implications are far broader, embracing not only the environment and economic development, but also health care, urbanization, energy, materials, agriculture, business practices, social services, and government. Sustainable development means balancing wealth generation with continuously enhanced environmental quality and social well-being, and it is a concept of a complexity and richness comparable to other guiding principles of modern societies, such as human rights, justice, liberty, capital, property, governance, and equality.

This list of the implications of sustainability may appear incomplete on its face, but any such tally is the product of twenty-first-century hindsight. Any notion of a collective responsibility to maintain natural capital for future generations or to advance economic and technological progress with a sense of stewardship was not operative in the eighteenth-century designs that still inform so much of our economic thinking. Although we may parse the deliberations of the era for evidence of some incipient appreciation of our predicament, we only know with certainty that societies were trapped by the Malthusian paradigm. The understanding we derive from such figures as John Muir, Aldo Leopold, and Rachel Carson had yet to be formulated, much less realized. Two hundred twenty-five years plus into this new political and economic order, the quality of life for many is vastly improved. The subsistence agrarian economies that predominated prior to the Industrial Revolution have given way to agricultural production methods that have reduced widespread starvation. The preindustrial social order dominated by grinding poverty endured by all but a privileged elite has largely ameliorated: "The richest modern economies are now ten to twenty times wealthier than the 1800 average," economist Gregory Clark points out.[42] The masses, formerly voiceless and lacking political representation, now speak loudly and often. Yet, at the same time, we find ourselves on the brink of colossal disorder. Neither our economic nor our political model has factored in the natural limits of the earth, and the Constitution outlines neither aspirations nor outcomes relative to our relationship with the natural world. We thus find ourselves mediating the dictates of economic individualism on the one hand and the limitations of the natural systems of the earth on the other, to the potential ruinous long-term detriment of all.

Our economic and political designs fail to engage such interrelated and interdependent dimensions of sustainable development as intergenerational equity, biodesign, adaptive management, industrial ecology, and natural capital conservation. Each such interrelationship demands new principles for organizing knowledge production and application. Our apparent limitations in the face of these challenges are a consequence not only of the relative immaturity of our conceptual tools but also the implicit economic individualism that the Constitution endorses. We all operate more or less out of self-interest, which is entirely rational, but to some extent the parameters that our foundational national document establishes constitute a justification for us to indulge in nakedly self-interested pursuits. As a consequence of our economic and political expectations, the perspective of the individual outweighs the collective to the extent that adequate protection for the common good is compromised. In part due to the inevitable limitations of a document drafted in the eighteenth century—however brilliant and visionary—efforts to advance the long-term interests of the whole by controlling the short-term behavior of the individual appear doomed to failure.[43]

Many of us have come to terms with an increasing realization that there may be a limit to what we as a species can plan or accomplish. The U.S. failure to protect against and respond to Hurricane Katrina in the summer of 2005 and the apparent futility of plans to democratize and modernize the Middle East provide particularly salient evidence that we seem to be operating beyond our ability to plan and implement effectively, or even to identify conditions where action is needed and can succeed. Our disappointing performances in these episodes might be less disheartening if these were the most daunting problems on the horizon, but they are nominal compared to the looming challenges of global terrorism, climate change, or possible ecosystem collapse—problems that are not only maddeningly complex but also potentially inconceivably destructive.

Our current approach to framing problems can be traced back to the publication of the 1972 report *The Limits to Growth*.[44] Commissioned by the Club of Rome, the report posed the still unanswered question "How much population growth and development, how much modification of natural systems, how much resource extraction and consumption, and how much waste generation can the earth sustain without provoking regional or even global catastrophe?" Since that time, how we think about human activity and the environment and then translate this thinking into our science policy and subsequent R&D, public debate, and political action has been framed by the idea of external limits—defining them, measuring them, seeking to overcome them, denying their existence, or insisting that they have already been exceeded.

For technological optimists these limits are ever-receding, perhaps even nonexistent, as science-based technologies allow progressive increases in productivity and efficiency that allow the 1.5 billion people living in industrialized and industrializing nations today to achieve a standard of living that was unimaginable at the beginning of the twentieth century. For the pessimists there are global climate change, the ozone hole, air and water pollution, overpopulation, natural and human-caused environmental disasters, widespread hunger and poverty, rampant extinction of species, exhaustion of natural resources, and destruction of ecosystems. In the face of these conflicting perceptions, it makes no sense to try to use external limits as a foundation for inquiry and action on the future of humans and the planet.

All sides in the limits-to-growth debate would probably agree on two observations. First, the dynamic, interactive system of complex biogeochemical cycles that constitutes the earth's surface environment is falling increasingly under the influence of a single, dominant life-form: us. Second, this life form, notable for its ability to learn, reason, innovate, communicate, plan, predict, and organize its activities, nonetheless exhibits serious limitations in all these same areas. Although scientific and technological innovation—most of it the product of our research universities—has in many respects immeasurably improved our standard of living and quality of life over the past one hundred and fifty years, the prima facie evidence that the present model is not working is abundant. At the same time that the average life span of those living in the industrialized nations has doubled, agricultural productivity increased by a factor of five, the size of the U.S. economy increased more than several hundredfold, and the volume of globally retrievable information stored in analog and digital form expanded by incalculable orders of magnitude. Twenty percent of the planet's bird species have been driven into extinction, 50 percent of all freshwater runoff has been consumed, 70,000 synthetic chemicals have been introduced into the environment, the sediment load of rivers has increased fivefold, and more than two-thirds of the major marine fisheries on the planet have been fully exploited or depleted.

There are many possible futures available to us, as Joel Cohen has brilliantly argued.[45] The only certainty is that present trajectories of growth cannot be maintained indefinitely. (Thomas Malthus got this point right over two hundred years ago. He simply failed to appreciate the productivity gains that science and technology could deliver.) The central question that faces us is whether we will be able to position ourselves to choose wisely among alternative future trajectories or if we will simply blunder onward. The markets will indeed adjust to the eventual depletion of fossil fuel reserves, for example, but will likely be too shortsighted to prevent global economic disruption on an unprecedented scale, a situation that could even lead to global war.

### Negotiating Human Limitation

If we continue to define our problem as external to ourselves—as limitations imposed by nature and the environment—then we consign ourselves to a future of blundering. The limitations that matter are internal. They are the inevitable limitations on our collective ability to acquire, integrate, and apply knowledge. Although it is difficult to clearly distinguish these limitations, it is helpful to assign them to six categories: limitations of the individual, of sociobiology, of socioeconomics, of technology, of knowledge, and of philosophy. Although these limitations might at first seem to be insurmountable shortcomings, we submit that our best hope for finding our place in nature and on the planet resides in embracing our limitations and recognizing them as explicit design criteria for moving forward with our knowledge production and organization. The potential for progress in each is obvious, especially through the insight and understanding our academic culture lends to all aspects of society.

Rational self-interest, perhaps tempered by community spirit and bursts of altruism, is our modus operandi. Given that we cannot know the effects of our individual actions on the larger systems in which we are enmeshed, the only reasonable alternative is for each of us to pursue our conception, however imperfect, of our own interests. Yet, as social systems grow more and more complex and as they impinge more and more on natural systems, our individual vision inevitably captures less and less of the big picture. Our only option is to accept the inevitability and the limitations of individual rationality and to take it into account in formulating public policy and collective action.

Over the course of human development, our special capabilities in areas such as toolmaking, language, self-awareness, and abstract thought have rendered us extraordinarily fit to engage in the competitive business of individual and species survival. We compete among ourselves at every organizational level and with other species at virtually every ecological niche. Cooperation, therefore, most often occurs at one level (a tribe or a nation, for example) to be able to compete at a higher level (a war between tribes or nations). But at the highest levels—the behavior of an entire species competing with or, as the case may be, dominating billions of other species—we have run out of reasons to cooperate or structures to foster effective cooperation. We need to consciously search for ways to transcend our sociobiological impetus toward competition.

We have done our best to make a virtue out of our individual and sociobiological limitations through market economics and democratic politics. Yet, we are unable to integrate the long-term consequences of our competition-based society into our planning processes. Our competitive nature values the individual over the group, but the aggregation of individual actions constantly surprises us. Despite our best intentions, our actions are consistent with a global economy predicated on the expectation of continued growth and development derived from ever-increasing resource exploitation. Thus, for example, we all climb into our cars in the morning thinking only that this is the most convenient way to get to work. We are not deliberately choosing to waste time in traffic jams, exacerbate the trade deficit, and pump greenhouse gases into the atmosphere.

We find it extraordinarily difficult to anticipate or accurately account for the costs and risks incurred over the long term by such group behavior. Indeed, those costs and risks vary wildly from individual to individual and from group to group. An example of this is the cost-benefit calculation that must have been made regarding the probability of catastrophic flooding in New Orleans. At every level of the political system, the individual perspective outweighed the collective, with the result that adequate protection for the whole community lost out. Because of these complexities, efforts to advance the long-term interests of the whole by controlling the short-term behavior of the individual are doomed to failure, which is one of the lessons of the global collapse of communism.

To evade the behavioral limitations of biology and economics, we have turned to technology. Indeed, technology, harnessed to the marketplace, has allowed industrialized societies to achieve remarkably high standards of living. In doing so, however, we have put our future into the hands of the lowest bidder. Cheap oil and coal, for example, ensure our continued dependence on the internal combustion engine and the coal-burning power plant. The problem we face is not a shortage of polluting hydrocarbon fuels but an excess. History shows that we will develop increasingly efficient energy technologies but that gains in efficiency will be more than offset by the increased consumption that accompanies economic growth. The increased efficiency and cleanliness of today's cars when compared with those built in 1980 is an example. Technology has allowed us to pollute less per mile of driving, but pollution has declined little because we drive so many more miles. Too often we choose technologies that save us from today's predicament but add to the problems of tomorrow.

There is absolutely no a priori reason to expect that what we can know is what we most *need* to know. Science uses disciplinary organization to recognize and focus on questions that *can* be answered. Disciplines, in turn, are separated by methodology, terminology, sociology, and disparate bodies of fact that resist synthesis. Although disciplinary specialization has been the key to scientific success, such specialization simultaneously takes us away from any knowledge of the whole. Our science remains culturally biased and isolated. Western science is derivative of a philosophical model of domination and the manipulation of nature, as opposed to the acceptance of natural systems and dynamics.

Today the whole encompasses more than 7 billion people with the collective capability of altering the biogeochemical cycles on which we depend for our survival. Can science generate the knowledge necessary to govern the world that science has made? Do we even know what such knowledge might be? Producing 70,000 synthetic chemicals is easy compared to the challenge of understanding and dealing with their effects. Despite the billions we have spent studying our interference with the planet's biogeochemical cycles, we really do not have a clue about the long-term consequences. And we have even less knowledge about how to organize and govern ourselves to confront this challenge. The intrinsic difficulties of creating a transdisciplinary synthesis are compounded dramatically by a dangerous scientific and technological illiteracy among senior policy makers and elected officials. An ironic effect of technology-created wealth is the growth of an affluent class that prizes individualism over civic engagement and that feels insulated from the need to understand and confront complex technology-related social issues.

The scientific and philosophical intellectuals of the academy remain focused on the relatively simple question of understanding nature. The much more complicated and challenging—and meaningful—quest is to understand nature with a purpose, with an objective, with an end. What is the purpose of our effort to understand nature? Is it to learn how to live in harmony with nature or to exploit it more efficiently? For thousands of years, philosophical inquiry has been guided by fundamental questions like why we are here and how we should behave. Such questions were difficult enough to confront meaningfully when our communities were small, our mobility limited, and our impact restricted. In our hyperkinetic society, how can we possibly hope to find meaning? The literal answers provided by science amount to mockery: We are here because an expanding cloud of gas some 15 billion years ago eventually led to the accretion of planets, the formation of primordial nucleotides and amino acids, the evolution of complex organisms, the growth of complex social structures in primates, and the dramatic expansion of cognitive and analytical capabilities made possible by the rapid evolution of neocortical brain structures. Such explanation is entirely insufficient to promote the commonality of purpose necessary for planetary stewardship. A unified or unifiable metaphysical basis for action is not a requisite, as we have learned from pragmatism, but surely we must proceed as if the mandate to address the grand challenges that confront us is plainly manifest.

These limits are the boundary conditions that we face in learning how to manage our accelerating impact on the earth. How can we create knowledge and foster institutions that are sensitive to these boundary conditions? This is a sensitivity that we have hardly begun to develop and that will not be found in any of the compartmentalized traditional disciplines that we so earnestly nurture. We maintain the illusion of understanding and refuse even to consider the possibility that we do not understand. We need new ways to conceive the pursuit of knowledge and innovation; to understand and build our economic, political, and social institutions; and to endow philosophy with meaning for people other than philosophers.

Through a remarkable manipulation of limited knowledge, brute force, and an overwhelming arrogance, humans have shaped a world that in all likelihood cannot sustain the standard of living and quality of life we have come to take for granted. Our approach to energy, to look at only one sector, epitomizes our limitations. We remain fixated on short-term goals and a simplistic model governed by what one might term Stone Age logic: We continue to dig deep holes in the ground, extract dark substances that are the remains of prehistoric plants and animals, and deliver this treasure to primitive machines for combustion to maintain the energy system on which we base our entire civilization. We invest immense scientific and technological effort to procure it more efficiently, burn it more cleanly, and bury it somewhere we will never have to see it again within a time horizon that might concern us. Find it, burn it, bury it. Our dependency on fossils fuels would be worthy of cavemen.

Hubris, exemplified in the demands we make on science, is a major obstacle to coming to grips with our situation. We are obsessed with trying to predict, manage, and control nature, and consequently we pour immense intellectual and fiscal resources into huge research programs—from the Human Genome Project to the U.S. Global Change Research Program—aimed at this unattainable goal. On the other hand, we devote little effort to the apparently modest yet absolutely essential question of how, given our unavoidable limitations, we can manage to live in harmony with the world that we have inherited and are continually remaking.

As is obvious from our failure to embrace the concept in our national deliberations, sustainability is clearly not yet a core value in our society or any other. Although the general public and especially younger generations have begun to think in terms of sustainability, the task remains to improve our capacity to implement advances in knowledge through sound policy decisions. We have yet to coordinate transnational responses commensurate with the scale of looming problems such as global terrorism, climate change, or possible ecosystem disruption. Our approach to the maddening complexity of the challenges that confront us must be transformative rather than incremental and will demand major investment from concerned stakeholders. Sustainability will require the reconceptualization and reorganization of our ossified knowledge enterprises. Our universities remain disproportionately focused on perpetuating disciplinary boundaries and developing increasingly specialized new knowledge at the expense of collaborative endeavors targeting real-world problems. We recur to the previously cited skepticism of Robert Frodeman, who questions the efficacy of the contemporary "epistemological regime . . . of infinite, largely laissez-faire knowledge production."[46]

Anthony Cortese, cofounder of Second Nature, offers five useful recommendations for achieving transformative change in academic institutions in this context:

> The content of learning will reflect interdisciplinary systems thinking, dynamics, and analysis for all majors and disciplines . . . . The context of learning will change to make human and environmental interdependence, values, and ethics a seamless core of teaching in all disciplines . . . . The process of education will emphasize active, experiential, inquiry-based learning and real-world problem solving . . . . Higher education will practice and model sustainability . . . . Finally, institutions will implement new forms of partnership with their local and regional communities to help make them socially vibrant, economically secure, and environmentally sustainable."[47]

He aptly specifies that a campus must practice what it preaches, which requires it to "model economically and environmentally sustainable practices in its operations, planning, facility design, purchasing, and investments," as well as the charge to relate these efforts to the formal curriculum. And with regard to the curriculum, he cites the observation by Frank Rhodes that the concept of sustainability offers a "new foundation for the liberal arts and sciences."[48]

If the academic sector hopes to spearhead the operationalization of knowledge for the public good, colleges and universities will need to drive innovation while forging much closer ties to the private sector and government alike. The growing involvement of corporate visionaries and government leaders from both sides of the aisle in the sustainability initiatives of major research universities is evidence of an expanded franchise not only of individuals but of institutional capabilities for response. But more flexibility, resilience, and responsiveness will be required of institutions and organizations in the public and private sectors alike. Society will never be able to control the large-scale consequences of its actions, but the realization of the imperative for sustainability positions us at a critical juncture in our evolutionary history. Progress will occur when advances in our understanding converge with our evolving social, cultural, economic, and historical circumstances and practices to allow us to glimpse and pursue new opportunities. Realizing the potential of this moment will require both a focused collective commitment and the realization that sustainability, like democracy, is not a problem to be solved but rather a challenge that requires constant vigilance.

Let us acknowledge and evaluate the design limitations of our social and political order, derived from the founders of the republic in the eighteenth century. However belatedly, we might add one more value to the conception of the self expressed in or implied by the Constitution. To provide for the common good, we cannot consider justice only for those of us present; we must conceptualize and enact into law provisions for justice for future generations. To ensure the equitable pursuit of happiness, we cannot look only at the four or five decades ahead of or behind us; individually we must come to terms with the realization that decisions made during the past 250 years have put humanity at potential risk over the next several thousand years. In the twenty-first century our universities and colleges must take the lead in bringing sustainability to the status of a core aspirational value of the American people, on the same level as liberty and justice and equality. Such awareness would bring transformation to our economic and political systems and at last begin to fulfill the expectations of the framers of the Constitution.

## Notes

1. Louis Menand, "An Introduction to Pragmatism," in *Pragmatism: A Reader*, ed. Menand (New York: Vintage, 1997), xxvi. He likens pragmatism to a "kind of knot in the tapestry, a pulling together of threads that reach into many other areas of thought, with many other consequences." The confluence of influences Menand cites include the "emergence of theories of cultural pluralism and political progressivism; the fascination with pure science and the logic of scientific inquiry; the development of probability theory as a means for coping with randomness and uncertainty; the spread of historicist approaches to the study of culture; the rapid assimilation of the Darwinian theory of evolution; and the Emersonian suspicion of institutional authority." Menand clarifies: "None of these developments is 'pragmatist,' but pragmatism was one of the places where they came into focus."

2. Useful introductions to pragmatism are to be found in Michael Bacon, *Pragmatism: An Introduction* (Cambridge: Polity, 2012) and Richard J. Bernstein, *The Pragmatic Turn* (Cambridge: Polity, 2010).

3. See especially chapter 9 of Louis Menand, *The Metaphysical Club: A Story of Ideas in America* (New York: Farrar, Straus, and Giroux, 2001). While we underscore the utilitarian correlates of pragmatism, Menand points out another dimension: "Pragmatism belongs to a disestablishmentarian impulse in American culture—an impulse that drew strength from the writings of Emerson, who attacked institutions and conformity, and from the ascendancy, after the Civil War, of evolutionary theories, which drew attention to the contingency of all social forms" (89).

4. See, for example, Richard Rorty, *Philosophy and the Mirror of Nature*, Thirtieth-Anniversary Edition (Princeton, NJ: Princeton University Press, 2009); Rorty, *Consequences of Pragmatism* (Minneapolis: University of Minnesota Press, 1982).

5. Menand, *Metaphysical Club*, 362.

6. C. S. Peirce, "How to Make Our Ideas Clear," *The Essential Peirce* (Bloomington: Indiana University Press, 1992–1999), vol. 1, 132; William James, *Pragmatism: A New Name for Some Old Ways of Thinking* (1907; Cambridge, MA: Harvard University Press, 1975), 33; both quoted in Christopher Hookway, "Pragmatism," *The Stanford Encyclopedia of Philosophy*, Spring 2010 edition, ed. Edward N. Zalta, http://plato.stanford.edu /archives/spr2010/entries/pragmatism.

7. William James, quoted in Menand, *Metaphysical Club*, 354.

8. John Dewey, "The Bearing of Pragmatism on Education," *The Middle Works*, 1899–1924, ed. Jo Ann Boydston (Carbondale: Illinois University Press, 1976–83), vol. 4, 180, quoted in Menand, *Metaphysical Club*, 361.

9. Hookway, "Pragmatism," 22, 25.

10. John J. Stuhr, *Pragmatism, Postmodernism, and the Future of Philosophy* (New York: Routledge, 2002), 129, 154–155. Stuhr explains that what Dewey termed "pragmatic inquiry" equates logic with inquiry and inquiry with knowledge. He takes this up in *John Dewey: The Late Works, 1925–1953*, ed. Jo Ann Boydston (Carbondale: Southern Illinois University Press, 1981–1990), vol. 12: 14.

11. Martin Jay, *Songs of Experience: Modern American and European Variations on a Universal Theme* (Berkeley: University of California Press, 2005), 291. For elaboration on Dewey's conception of the truth, Jay refers the reader to "A Short Catechism Concerning Truth" (1909) and "The Problem of Truth" (1911), in *Middle Works*, vol. 6.

12. Bacon, *Pragmatism: An Introduction*, 4.

13. As Dewey elaborated, "Inquiry is the controlled or directed transformation of an indeterminate situation into one that is so determinate in its constituent distinctions and relations as to convert the elements of the original situation into a unified whole." *Late Works*, vol. 12: 41, 108, cited in Stuhr, *Pragmatism*, 156. A situation is indeterminate for Dewey, Michael Bacon explains, when it presents an issue or problem that demands resolution. Bacon, *Pragmatism: An Introduction*, 53.

14. Menand, "Introduction to Pragmatism," xxvi.

15. Bacon, *Pragmatism: An Introduction*, 54.

16. William James, *The Meaning of Truth* (1909; Cambridge, MA: Harvard University Press, 1975), 6, quoted in Hookway, "Pragmatism," 23.

17. Stuhr, *Pragmatism*, 1–2. Dewey considered the communication of "aims, beliefs, aspirations, and knowledge" to be the basis for both education and democracy. Communication "insures participation in a common understanding," wrote Dewey. Moreover, "consensus demands communication. Not only is social life identical with communication, but all communication, and hence all genuine social life is educative." *Middle Works*, vol. 9, 7–8, quoted in Stuhr, *Pragmatism*, 13. The quote from Emerson, which we cited in chapter 3, comes from his essay *Nature* (1836).

18. Menand, "Introduction to Pragmatism," xxiii.

19. Bacon, *Pragmatism: An Introduction*, 124–125.

20. Jürgen Habermas, *The Theory of Communicative Action*, vol. 2: *Reason and the Rationalization of Society*, trans. Thomas McCarthy (Cambridge, MA: MIT Press, 1987), 86; Habermas, "Postscript," in *Habermas and Pragmatism*, eds. Mitchell Adoulafia, Myra Bookman, and Catherine Kemp (London: Routledge, 2002), 227.

21. Bacon, *Pragmatism: An Introduction*, 124; Jay, *Songs of Experience*, 379.

22. Seyla Benhabib, *Situating the Self: Gender, Community, and Postmodernism in Contemporary Ethics* (New York: Routledge, 1992), 4–5.

23. Andrew Edgar, *Habermas: Key Concepts* (New York: Routledge, 2006), 23–24.

24. Habermas, "Postscript," 223–233.

25. Richard Rorty, *Consequences of Pragmatism* (Minneapolis: University of Minnesota Press, 1982), xiv.

26. Richard Rorty, "Postmodernist Bourgeois Liberalism," in *Pragmatism: A Reader*, ed. Louis Menand (New York: Random House, 1997): 330, 334–335.

27. Richard Rorty, *Philosophy as Cultural Politics: Philosophical Papers, Volume 4* (Cambridge: Cambridge University Press, 2007), 107, quoted by Bacon, *Pragmatism*, 100. See also Rorty, "Postmodernist Bourgeois Liberalism," 330, 334–335.

28. Menand, *Metaphysical Club*, 370; Michael Bacon, "Rorty and Pragmatic Social Criticism," *Philosophy and Social Criticism* 32, no. 7 (2006): 865. See also Rorty, "Pragmatism as Anti-Authoritarianism," *Revue Internationale de Philosophie* 1 (1999): 7–20.

29. Scott D. N. Cook and John Seely Brown, "Bridging Epistemologies: The Generative Dance between Organizational Knowledge and Organizational Knowing," *Organization Science* 10, no. 4 (July–August 1999): 383, 386–387. The "epistemology of possession" corresponds to what Joel Mokyr terms "propositional knowledge," while the "epistemology of practice" corresponds to "prescriptive knowledge." Mokyr thus makes the distinction between knowledge "what," referring to beliefs about natural phenomena, and knowledge "how," referring to techniques. It is the distinction between *episteme* and *techne*. Joel Mokyr, *The Gifts of Athena: Historical Origins of the Knowledge Economy* (Princeton, NJ: Princeton University Press, 2002), 4.

30. Cook and Brown, "Bridging Epistemologies," 386–388. Italics in the original.

31. Barry Bozeman, *Public Values and Public Interest: Counterbalancing Economic Individualism* (Washington, DC: Georgetown University Press, 2007), 13, 20, 101. In this context, he cites Dewey, *The Public and Its Problems* (New York: Holt, 1927).

32. Bozeman, *Public Values and Public Interest*, 13, 108, 110.

33. Torben Beck Jørgensen and Barry Bozeman, "Public Values: An Inventory," *Administration and Society* 39, no. 3 (May 2007): 354–381.

34. Menand, *Metaphysical Club*, xi–xii, quoted by Bernstein, *Pragmatic Turn*, 10.

35. Richard Bernstein points out that postmodernist assaults on foundationalism, metaphysics, and grand narratives and systems were similarly targets of pragmatist skepticism. See Bernstein, *Pragmatic Turn*, 29. See also Perry Anderson, *The Origins of Postmodernity* (London: Verso, 1998).

36. The discussion of sustainability in this chapter includes revised portions from the book chapter by Michael M. Crow, "Sustainability as a Founding Principle of the United States," in *Moral Ground: Ethical Action for a Planet in Peril*, ed. Kathleen Dean Moore and Michael P. Nelson (San Antonio, TX: Trinity University Press, 2010), 301–305, and his articles, "Overcoming Stone Age Logic," *Issues in Science and Technology* 24, no. 2 (2008): 25–26, and "None Dare Call It Hubris: The Limits of Knowledge," *Issues in Science and Technology* 23, no. 2 (2007): 29–32. The discussion of human limitation that concludes the chapter is substantially derived from the latter article.

37. World Commission on Environment and Development, *Our Common Future* (Oxford: Oxford University Press, 1987). Convened by the United Nations in 1983, the WCED is more commonly known as the Brundtland Commission, after its chairman, Gro Harlem Brundtland, then prime minister of Norway. In her foreword to the report, Brundtland explains that the special independent commission was charged with formulating a "global agenda for change" with the objective of "safeguarding the interests of coming generations" (ix–x).

38. David G. Victor, "Recovering Sustainable Development," *Foreign Affairs* 85, no. 1 (January/February 2006): 91–103.

39. National Research Council, *Our Common Journey: A Transition toward Sustainability* (Washington, DC: National Academies Press, 1999); International Union for the Conservation of Nature and Natural Resources (IUCN), *World Conservation Strategy: Living Resource Conservation for Sustainable Development* (Gland, Switzerland: IUCN, 1980).

40. William C. Clark and Nancy M. Dickson, "Sustainability Science: The Emerging Research Program," in *Proceedings of the National Academy of Sciences* 100, no. 14 (July 8, 2003): 8059.

41. William C. Clark, "Sustainability Science: A Room of Its Own," in *Proceedings of the National Academy of Sciences* 104, no. 6 (February 6, 2007): 1737.

42. Gregory Clark, *A Farewell to Alms: A Brief Economic History of the World* (Princeton, NJ: Princeton University Press, 2007), 2.

43. A nuanced analysis of the issues associated with governing what is invariably termed the "tragedy of the commons" is to be found in Elinor Ostrom, *Governing the Commons: The Evolution of Institutions for Collective Action* (Cambridge: Cambridge University Press, 1990).

44. Donella H. Meadows et al., *The Limits to Growth: A Report for the Club of Rome's Project on the Predicament of Mankind* (New York: Universe, 1972). The Club of Rome, characterized in the foreword to the report as an "invisible college," first convened in 1968 to "foster understanding of the varied but interdependent components—economic, political, natural, and social—that make up the global system in which we all live" (9).

45. Joel E. Cohen, *How Many People Can the Earth Support?* (New York: W. W. Norton, 1995).

46. Robert Frodeman, *Sustainable Knowledge: A Theory of Interdisciplinarity* (Basingstoke: Palgrave Macmillan, 2014), 62.

47. Anthony D. Cortese, "Promises Made and Promises Lost: A Candid Assessment of Higher Education Leadership and the Sustainability Agenda," in *The Sustainable University: Green Goals and New Challenges for Higher Education Leaders*, ed. James Martin and James E. Samels (Baltimore: Johns Hopkins University Press, 2012), 22–23.

48. Cortese quotes Frank H. T. Rhodes, "Sustainability: The Ultimate Liberal Art," *Chronicle of Higher Education* (October 20, 2006).

# SEVEN

# Designing a New American University at the Frontier

In the course of a decade, Arizona State University has reconstituted itself through a deliberate design process as a foundational prototype for a New American University—an institutional model predicated on the pursuit of discovery and knowledge production, inclusiveness to a broad demographic representative of the socioeconomic diversity of the region and nation, and, through its breadth of functionality, maximization of societal impact. The reconceptualization has represented an effort to accelerate a process of institutional evolution that might otherwise have proceeded only incrementally over a far more protracted duration. More broadly, its implementation represents a reconceptualization of the American research university as a complex and adaptive comprehensive knowledge enterprise committed to discovery, creativity, and innovation, an institution accessible to the broadest possible demographic, both socioeconomically and intellectually.[1] Initiated to reconceptualize the curriculum, organization, and operations of the institution, the design process constitutes an institutional experiment at scale and in real time; the proposition that it be regarded as a case study in American higher education derives in part from its scope and rigor, as well as its reflexive implementation. To the extent that the objectives of the design process are realized, the institution recurs to the intentions and aspirations of the historical public research university model, which sought to provide broad accessibility to academic platforms characterized by discovery and knowledge production as well as engagement with society. For reasons delineated in the previous chapters—lack of scalability, fiscal constraint, filiopietism, isomorphism, the pursuit of prestige—many institutions have abandoned this commitment. The contemporary reconstitution of the historical model should be construed as the basis for an alternative model of the American research university, which some institutions may wish to adapt and that is intended to complement the set of existing research universities, both public and private.

Any number of indicators might attest to the advancement of an institution, but those cited in this chapter must be evaluated in terms of their complexity and simultaneity of accomplishment by an institution committed to offering broad accessibility to an environment underpinned by discovery and a pedagogical foundation of knowledge production. Measures such as increases in degree production, socioeconomic diversity, minority enrollment, and freshman persistence; improvements in academic achievement and faculty accomplishment and diversity; and the expansion of the research enterprise must be evaluated within the context of their accomplishment by a university committed to offering admission to all academically qualified Arizona residents[2] regardless of financial need, and that strives to maintain a student body representative of the spectrum of socioeconomic diversity of American society. The improvement of graduation rates or freshman persistence to hypothetical target levels could readily be taken for granted in institutions that handpick freshman classes or limit admissions to applicants from the upper 5 percent of graduating high school seniors.[3] Nearly all leading colleges and universities offer opportunities to a number of students of exceptional academic ability from socioeconomically disadvantaged or historically underrepresented backgrounds in the interest of diversity, as we observed in chapter 1. But ASU offers admission to a range of academically qualified students from throughout the spectrum of varied and diverse backgrounds, giving them the opportunity to attend a world-class research university to which they would otherwise be denied access if admissions policies were less inclusive. ASU has thus succeeded in assembling a student body that is roughly representative of the socioeconomic diversity of the state. The unprecedented upswing in the academic achievement of students as well as the trajectory of the research enterprise during a period of robust enrollment growth and historic public disinvestment defy the conventional wisdom that correlates excellence with exclusivity, which sometimes means exclusion of the majority of qualified applicants. We contend that the increased accessibility to a research-grade academic platform for the broad demographic that these numbers reflect is an outcome of a new model for the American research university.

As set forth in the foundational white paper delineating the parameters of the design process, the objective of the reconceptualization was to build a comprehensive metropolitan research university that is an "unparalleled combination of academic excellence and commitment to its social, economic, cultural, and environmental setting." The report called for an institution that "measures its academic quality by the education that its graduates have received rather than the academic credentials of its incoming freshman class; one at which researchers, while pursuing their scholarly interests, also consider the public good; one that does not just engage in community service, but rather takes on major responsibility for the economic, social, and cultural vitality of its community."[4] The institutional vision statement subsequently formulated specifies the basic tenets of the process, which was initiated in July 2002. These tenets are at once egalitarian in terms of their intent to expand accessibility yet competitive with regard to their aspiration toward world-class academic excellence intended to produce outcomes commensurate with the needs of society: "to establish ASU as the model for a New American University, measured not by those whom we exclude, but rather by those whom we include and how they succeed; pursuing research and discovery that benefits the public good; assuming major responsibility for the economic, social, and cultural vitality and health and well-being of the community."[5]

The foundational white paper introduced the set of eight interrelated and mutually interdependent design aspirations, which represent ideals for institutional culture as well as strategic approaches to the accomplishment of goals and objectives. To be understood as general guidelines intended to inspire creativity, spark innovation, and foster institutional individuation, these call for the academic community to (1) respond to its cultural, socioeconomic, and physical setting; (2) become a force for societal transformation; (3) pursue a culture of academic enterprise and knowledge entrepreneurship; (4) conduct use-inspired research; (5) focus on the individual in a milieu of intellectual and cultural diversity; (6) transcend disciplinary limitations in pursuit of intellectual fusion (transdisciplinarity); (7) embed the university socially, thereby advancing social enterprise development through direct engagement; and (8) advance global engagement. A number of variant formulations of the design aspirations have appeared, including the following more succinct delineation:

1. Leverage Our Place: ASU embraces its cultural, socioeconomic, and physical setting.
2. Transform Society: ASU catalyzes social change by being connected to social needs.
3. Value Entrepreneurship: ASU uses its knowledge and encourages innovation.
4. Conduct Use-Inspired Research: ASU research has purpose and impact.
5. Enable Student Success: ASU is committed to the success of each unique student.
6. Fuse Intellectual Disciplines: ASU creates knowledge by transcending academic disciplines.
7. Be Socially Embedded: ASU connects with communities through mutually beneficial partnerships.
8. Engage Globally: ASU engages with people and issues locally, nationally, and internationally.

The design aspirations were not drawn from whole cloth. Correlations with the characteristics for a new American university deemed essential by Frank Rhodes, to take but one source of inspiration, are evident. His discussion of these characteristics underscores their interrelatedness because, as he explains, "the new American university will prosper to the extent that it can maintain a dynamic equilibrium between several inherent tensions." For example, "the successful university will maintain institutional autonomy, lively faculty independence, and vigorous academic freedom, but will enjoy strong, impartial, public governance and decisive, engaged, presidential leadership." Or "the successful university will be increasingly privately supported but increasingly publicly accountable and socially committed." Correlates to the design aspirations are obvious. His dictum that the "successful university will be campus rooted but internationally oriented," for example, recalls the design aspirations recommending that an institution leverage its cultural, socioeconomic, and physical setting as well as the aspiration enjoining global engagement. His call for the successful university to be "academically independent but constructively partnered" parallels dimensions of academic enterprise as well as social embeddedness, categories also relevant to his recommendation for universities to be "technologically sophisticated but community dependent." His call for universities to be "professionally attuned but humanely informed" engages dimensions of transdisciplinarity. And certainly no research university could dispute his recommendation that the "successful university will be knowledge based but student centered, research driven but learning focused."[6] These characteristics engage dimensions of use-inspired research as well as the New American University emphasis on individual outcomes and commitment to diversity.

A focus on the social embeddedness of the university as well as its transformational potential engaged the Spanish philosopher José Ortega y Gasset, whose examination of the various missions of the university in a series of lectures delivered at the University of Madrid in 1930 served to inspire some of the principal tenets of the New American University model. Although some of his arguments regarding university reform are restricted to the political upheaval and social ferment of his historical period and national context, his recommendations remain remarkably universal and broadly applicable, beginning with his willingness to question the university model and academic culture of his era. Ortega did not hesitate to pose fundamental questions regarding the status of the academy: "What is a university for, and what must it consequently be?" He correlated purpose with function in a thoroughgoing and analytical manner: "An institution is a machine in that its whole structure and functioning must be devised in view of the service it is expected to perform. In other words, the root of university reform is a complete formulation of its purpose." Ortega identifies as fundamental to reform the "creation of new usages." But an institution cannot implement such optimal functionalities "until its precise mission has been determined." The determination of a new model, however, will not be achieved through the imitation of historical models or extrapolation from the structure and practices of existing institutions, he cautions. He called for a university attuned to the needs of its nation. The English or German model is "not transferable," he remarks. "Imitation is fatal." Nor, he contends, should the university be accessible only to the "children of the well-to-do classes."[7]

As against an excessive focus on training for the "learned professions" and what he perceived to be the valorization of scientific research to the exclusion of the humanities and social sciences, Ortega called for universities to impart what he termed "general culture," which may be interpreted as equivalent to the sort of general education requirements associated with a liberal education. Until only recently, he contends, the "learner was no factor in pedagogy" and curricula were determined by the research interests of the faculty. Apart from training students for the professions and scientific research, he called for universities to proffer a student-centric curriculum dedicated to the "transmission of culture," a task to be undertaken by a professoriate with a "genius for integration" and not only the "pulverization of research." He inveighed against what he termed the "barbarism of specialization": "The engineer possesses engineering; but that is just one piece, one dimension . . . . The whole man is not to be found in this fragment called 'engineer.'" In this context he propounds a formulation that correlates with the New American University conviction that universities are obligated to provide broad accessibility to a pedagogical milieu that produces individual success and contributes to the formation of an educated citizenry: "What we must achieve is that every individual, or (not to be Utopian) many individuals, should each succeed in constituting the type of the whole man in its entirety." Nor was Ortega to be satisfied with incremental change: "very gradual preparation" leading to "gradual evolution" would not be sufficient. As against an institution that Ortega contends had in Spain become a "sad, inert, spiritless thing," he envisioned a university that would be an "uplifting force." Ortega thus posed a question at the crux of the argument for the imperative for a New American University: "What force can bring this about, if it is not the university?"[8]

Rather than extrapolate from existing academic structure and operations or recur to historical models, the design process sought to articulate a unique and self-determined institutional identity, which is especially critical for public universities if institutional identity is not to be generic or imposed by legislative fiat. Self-determination is the crux of the distinction between the bureaucratic mindset of an agency and the boundary spanning dynamism of an academic enterprise. Absent the formulation of a unique institutional identity, the forces of isomorphic replication described in chapter 3 would likely lead to reversion to the norm—the Generic Public University.[9] The design process sought to create a distinctive institutional profile by building on existing strengths to produce a federation of unique transdisciplinary departments, centers, institutes, schools, and colleges—henceforth generally referred to "colleges and schools," with colleges being a particular amalgamation of schools—and a deliberate and complementary clustering of programs arrayed across four differentiated campuses. The university is conceived as a single and unified academic and administrative operation without campus-level governance. In this decentralized model, deans and directors of colleges and schools provide academic leadership. A nonhierarchical relationship obtains between the four campuses. The formation of satellite campuses of large public universities inevitably imposes implicit hierarchization, which is counterproductive to student success. Because the "school-centric" model devolves intellectual and entrepreneurial responsibility to the level of the college and school, academic units are empowered to exercise a measure of autonomy and compete for renown and resources not intramurally but to the extent of market limits with peer entities globally. In this sense the federation of semi-autonomous constituent academic units loosely corresponds to the prototype of the University of London, which was formed in 1836 primarily for administrative purposes to join University College London with King's College London, established respectively in 1826 and 1829. Nineteen autonomous and self-governing institutions presently constitute the University of London federation, which apart from the two founding universities includes such heterogeneous and differentiated institutions as the London School of Economics, London Business School, London School of Hygiene and Tropical Medicine, School of Oriental and African Studies, and Royal Academy of Music.[10]

Concurrent with the reconfiguration of academic units across four campuses, ASU has sought to advance the production of new transdisciplinary knowledge through the consolidation of a number of traditional academic departments, which henceforth no longer serve as the sole institutional locus of a given discipline, including, for example, anthropology, geology, sociology, and several areas of biology. Transdisciplinarity thus augments and enhances traditional academic organization and encourages team participation in projects that accomplish implementation and application. But the reconfiguration of academic departments and disciplinary fields undertaken to advance interdisciplinary teaching and research must be understood within the broader and interrelated context of the overall reconfiguration of the various academic platforms. More than two dozen new transdisciplinary schools were conceptualized and operationalized, and some of them have been subsequently further reconfigured or merged.[11]

Although institutional initiatives such as the design process are often fraught with interminable phases of planning presided over by committees and consultants, assigning conceptualization and implementation to respective academic units undergirded by a pragmatic approach grounded in shared governance expedited planning and minimized contention. Each stage of the process has in practice been negotiated largely through exhaustive trial and error—often construed in terms of a "design-build" metaphor. Design-build is a paradigm we borrow from the architectural profession and construction industry, which refers to the integration of conception and execution by a single team. The concept has been defined as the reintegration of the roles of designer and constructor. And although institutional reference to the design process generally connotes the totality of the reconceptualization, in practice the process unfolded episodically and represented the aggregate efforts of many individuals, teams, and ad hoc committees. The sequence of interactions might thus be likened to a series of charettes, another term derived from the architectural community, which is defined as a "period of intense (group) work, typically undertaken in order to meet a deadline. Also: a collaborative workshop focusing on a particular problem or project."[12] In some cases the relative autonomy of design teams arguably assumed the tenor of a "skunkworks," an industry term that in broad usage specifies a "small, frequently informal group within an engineering, computing, or other company, working, often in isolation from the rest of the company, on a radical and innovative project."[13]

Reconceptualization of the institution has proceeded in part through restructuring in academic organization and processes initiated in response to designated objectives, functions, or outcomes. In a broad sense, for example, the intent may be to facilitate teaching and research in a given field or, more narrowly, to address a specific research challenge. The process of identifying an objective may suggest the need to establish a particular academic unit—a multidisciplinary research institute, for example, or a new transdisciplinary school. Or the objective may be strategic or tactical or methodological, as in the case of the intent to advance the implementation of interdisciplinarity. In any event, identifying the objective discloses the parameters of a novel design challenge. The process may be tumultuous and argumentative, but it is the only path to radical differentiation, which demands reversion to a zero-point of preconception. This is the proverbial going back to the drawing board. Incremental change is generally insufficient to accomplish transformative reconceptualization. And as opposed to futile attempts to anticipate every possible nuance of a given design problem by committee and ahead of the fact, the reversion to a "blank slate" standpoint impels productive thought experiments. Such exercises suggest a possible course of action and what teams might be assembled to undertake its realization. In other words, identifying an objective initiates a new segment or phase of the design-build process.

We reiterate that the architectonic metaphors enlisted in this context suggest the imperative for structural change as well as continuous adaptation and recalibration through repeated course corrections. No less significant are the best efforts of participants to abide by the dictates of common sense. The extent to which the design process achieved consensus through deliberation and discourse is a signal trait of the institutional culture of American research universities. More broadly, such communitarian approaches are characteristic of American academic culture, which values shared governance as well as academic freedom. These ideals are implicitly undergirded by the tenets of American pragmatism, which was conceived at the time of the emergence of the American research university. As we observed in the preceding chapter, the New American University shares the pragmatist concern with the practical consequences of knowledge situated within a particular social context and seeks to actualize the intent that knowledge should lead to action with the objective of "real-world" impact.

The University Design Team, guided by the support of the Arizona Board of Regents, collaborated to transform the institution and, at the same time, rethink the research university model. The design team was comprised of the provost and a cohort of vice presidents, deans, department chairs, and senior faculty members. Ongoing strategic planning advanced the process with participation from all sectors of the university as well as input from policy makers and the public. The challenge was considerable, because in 2002, ASU was still an emerging research university just beginning to gain a reputation but not yet committed to any particular trajectory. An organization as large and complex as a major research university operating in one of the most rapidly growing metropolitan regions in the nation would face daunting challenges during the implementation of any large-scale planning adjustment, but the conceptualization and successful operationalization of comprehensive institutional change on this scale is arguably without precedent.

"In the literature of complaint and reform, and in the endless reports from distinguished groups identifying a crisis in some element or all of higher education in America, a key defect is often the absence of practical solutions," observes John Lombardi.[14] The operationalization of the New American University model has demonstrated that it is possible both to negotiate challenges and achieve practical solutions, some examples of which we consider in this chapter. Individually none of the design strategies undertaken is especially remarkable. What is distinctive is the symbiotic outcome of their interrelated, interdependent, and mutually reinforcing deployment. The purposes of this chapter therefore do not include the prescription of a set of design strategies applicable in all contexts. Rather, through an examination of one particular exemplar, we hope to call attention to the focus and deliberation requisite to successful innovation in the American research university.

## The Imperative for a New American University in Arizona

The impetus for the reconceptualization began with the imperative for an institutional response to the unprecedented shift in the regional demographic profile in one of the fastest-growing states in the nation. ASU has committed to the state of Arizona to admit any Arizona resident prepared for university-level work. Because the population of Arizona is projected to reach 7.5 million by 2020, an increase of more than 45.8 percent in just twenty years, the commitment is no trivial promise. The college-age population is expected to increase even more dramatically, with a projected 48.6 percent growth by 2020. Students from historically underrepresented and socioeconomically disadvantaged backgrounds, many of whom will be the first in their families to attend college, will contribute the majority of this growth. Half of all children and two-thirds of Latino children in Arizona come from low-income families.[15] College participation rates for Arizona students from lower-income families lag well behind the national average.[16] More than half of Arizona high school graduates are ineligible for admission into one of the three state public universities.[17] These student characteristics are predictive of lower average SAT scores and high school grade point averages than those associated with students who account for the majority share at other leading research universities.

A first priority was to diversify the student body and improve outcomes while matching academic excellence with broad access and meeting the special needs of underserved populations. As the sole comprehensive research university in a metropolitan area projected to double in population by midcentury, ASU confronted burgeoning enrollment demand as well as issues associated with its setting in the heart of the so-called Sun Corridor. As one of two dozen megapolitan agglomerations emerging in coming decades, the Sun Corridor comprises a rapidly urbanizing patchwork of municipalities confronted with unprecedented cultural, demographic, economic, and social transformation.[18] Associated challenges that motivated the establishment of a new institutional platform included lagging educational attainment in an underperforming prekindergarten through grade 12 educational system; limited public and private support for the university, including declining state government investment when measured on a per-student basis; and the need for research-driven, knowledge-based economic development in an economy insufficiently diversified to accommodate population expansion. Further issues included inadequate personal income growth and increasing income inequality; explosive urbanization in a fragile Sonoran Desert ecosystem; and reluctant public investment in social services and civic infrastructure. The increasing competitiveness among research universities for limited funding and resources brought with it the imperative for more robust intellectual capital.[19]

Most colleges and universities in the United States define themselves in relation to the set of elite institutions that comprise the putative gold standard in higher education: the Ivies, the land-grant universities, and those constructed on the foundations of private fortunes.[20] In twenty-first-century Arizona, institutional models appropriate to colonial New England or the agrarian Midwest following the Civil War, although not entirely irrelevant, warrant a degree of skepticism. Despite the egalitarian conception of higher education that has from the outset of our republic been integral to our collective identity as a nation, and despite such egalitarian initiatives as the Morrill Act that in 1862 established the system of land-grant colleges and universities, the gold standard institutions represent an elitist model that remains to a remarkable extent impervious to change, aloof from society, and inaccessible to the majority of Americans. While leading universities, both public and private, have become increasingly exclusive, the approach adopted during the implementation of the new model has been to expand the capacity of the institution to meet enrollment demand. The objective is to provide unmatched educational opportunities to the many gifted and creative students who do not conform to a standard academic profile, as well as to offer access to students who demonstrate every potential to succeed but lack the financial means to pursue a four-year baccalaureate education.

Public higher education in the United States during the twentieth century produced a level of educational attainment unmatched anywhere in the world. Our nation's colleges and universities have served as a springboard to intergenerational economic mobility and as catalysts to innovation and thus national economic competitiveness.[21] To revive the social compact implicit in American public higher education, ASU resolved to expand enrollment capacity, promote diversity, and provide accessibility to world-class research and scholarship to a diverse and heterogeneous student body that includes a significant proportion of students from socioeconomically differentiated and underrepresented backgrounds, including a preponderant share of first-generation college applicants. ASU thus implemented admissions policies similar to those adopted by the University of California, Berkeley in the 1950s and 1960s, when graduating California high school seniors who had completed a set of ten required courses with a 3.0 grade point average qualified for admission to the state's leading public university.[22]

Constraints in admissions to University of California system campuses attributable to the economic downturn have made headlines during the past several years, but the progressive exclusion of more and more applicants from UC Berkeley and UCLA has been ongoing for decades. The ratio of California resident freshman applicants to students admitted at UC Berkeley from 1975 to 1995 declined from 77 percent to 39 percent.[23] Between fall semester 1989 and 2013, admissions declined from 40 percent to 16.35 percent. The comparable figures for UCLA show decline from 46.5 percent to 17.6 percent. The actual numbers present the scenario even more starkly. Of 43,255 resident applicants to Berkeley in fall semester 2013, only 7,073 were admitted, which means that 36,182 were turned away. At UCLA, 55,079 applied, but only 9,741 were admitted, which means that 44,338 were excluded. And although the UC system as a whole accepted 76.6 percent of resident freshmen in fall semester 1989, by 2013 the acceptance rate had declined to 63 percent. This pattern of exclusion is consistent with the trend among leading public universities, which continue to raise standards even while enrollment demand increases. Although the minimum grade point average for resident applicants to the UC system is specified as 3.0, the average unweighted GPA for admitted freshmen at Berkeley is 3.90, the average weighted GPA is 4.37, and the average SAT score is 2077.[24]

ASU's attempt to realize an institutional platform that combines world-class teaching and research with broad accessibility may arguably be likened to coupling in a single academic platform the research-intensive milieu of the University of California system with the accessibility offered by the Cal State system. Although the California Master Plan for Higher Education, which in 1960 established the tripartite hierarchical differentiation of roles for the systems of the University of California, California State University (CSU), and California Community Colleges, represents a historically successful prototype for promoting both excellence and accessibility, the top-tier research-grade UC campuses, especially Berkeley and UCLA, have become notoriously inaccessible to the majority of qualified applicants. While opportunities for students to transfer from the community colleges and Cal State campuses to one of the UC schools undeniably exist, ASU's institutional model encourages immersion in a residential research-intensive environment for academically qualified Arizona students beginning with their freshman year. Of course, ASU is also committed to establishing and sustaining partnerships with community colleges and local school districts that provide opportunities to qualified transfer students and encourage baccalaureate degree completion. The intent is to advance ASU as an exemplar of a public institution defined by academic excellence but committed to accessibility based on ability without regard for socioeconomic status.

## Recalibrating Missions and Goals

"Universities are prime examples of organizations that survive long after their initial goals have vanished, transforming them almost beyond recognition," James March and Herbert Simon observed in their classic study of organizational theory.[25] Articulation of institutional mission and goals is a critical step toward self-determination and in response to change, both internal and external, must periodically be revised. The mission and goals specified for Arizona State University for the time frame 2014 and beyond are a product of achievements between 2002 and 2013 as well as a response to the dynamics of social change. The objectives specified correspond to the outputs of the most highly selective public universities and must be evaluated within the context of their accomplishment by a large public university committed to drawing from the broader talent pool of socioeconomic diversity. Their attainment assumes an institutional culture committed to academic enterprise and improved cost effectiveness through productivity gains and constant innovation. These goals are moreover representative of the intent of the nation's youngest major research university to redefine its terms of engagement rather than entering into head-to-head competition with institutions that have matured over the course of centuries.

*Demonstrate leadership in academic excellence and accessibility*
Maintain the fundamental principle of accessibility to all students
    qualified to study at a research university;
Maintain university accessibility to match Arizona's socioeconomic
    diversity;
Improve freshman persistence to 90 percent;
Enhance university graduation rate to 75 to 80 percent and 25,000
    graduates annually;
Enhance quality, while reducing the cost of a degree;
Enroll 100,000 online and distance education degree-seeking students;
Enhance linkages with community colleges so as to expand baccalau-
    reate degree production to national leadership levels;

Enhance measured student development and individual student learning to national leadership levels.

*Establish national standing in academic quality and impact of colleges and schools in every field*

Attain national standing in academic quality for each college and school (top 5 to 10 percent for each college);

Attain national standing in the learning value added to our graduates in each college and school;

Become the leading university academically, in terms of faculty, discovery, research, and creativity, in at least one department or school within each school/college.

*Establish ASU as a global center for interdisciplinary research, discovery, and development by 2020*

Become a leading global center for interdisciplinary scholarship, discovery, and development;

Become a leading American center for discovery and scholarship in the social sciences, arts, and humanities;

Enhance research competitiveness to more than $700 million in annual research expenditures;[26]

Augment regional economic competitiveness through research and discovery and value-added programs.

*Enhance local impact and social embeddedness*

Provide Arizona with an interactive network of teaching, learning, and discovery resources that reflects the scope of ASU's comprehensive knowledge enterprise;

Develop solutions to real-life challenges (e.g., reducing the urban heat island index and improving long-term air quality in metropolitan Phoenix);

Increase the number of qualified K–12 teachers by 25 percent, and develop a tool for teachers and administrators to evaluate educational performance and outcomes;

Establish, with Mayo Clinic, innovative health solutions pathways capable of educating 200 million people about health care; engaging 20 million people in online health care delivery; and enhancing treatment for 2 million patients.

In operationalizing a reconceptualized institution, recalibrations are inevitable, and strategic thinking must become inherent to institutional culture. An institution undergoing transformation must identify new partners, press its case to investors, seize unexpected opportunities, remain responsive to changing conditions, deploy its resources in ways that empower its many component parts, and prepare to advance in novel and unexpected ways.

We recur to the charter statement for the reconceptualized institution, which articulates its self-determined institutional identity: *Arizona State University is a comprehensive public research university, measured not by whom it excludes, but by whom it includes and how they succeed; advancing research and discovery of public value; and assuming fundamental responsibility for the economic, social, cultural, and overall health of the communities it serves.* The formulation sought to encapsulate the commitment of the academic community to serve the state and the nation as a prototype for a New American University. Such an institution provides accessibility to an academic platform underpinned by discovery and a pedagogical foundation of knowledge production to a student body representative of the socioeconomic and intellectual diversity of our society; a research enterprise committed to discovery, creativity, and innovation commensurate with the scale, pace, and complexity of the challenges that confront society; public service to advance the common good, including the quality of life and standard of living of the diverse communities of the metropolitan region and state, as well as nationally and internationally; and collaborative engagement construed globally to spur innovation across academia, business and industry, and government. The university seeks the success of each student regardless of socioeconomic background and assumes responsibility for contributing to and being held accountable for the economic, social, and cultural health and well-being of the community.

## Academic Accomplishment and Scale of Impact

Over the course of a decade, enrollment growth has correlated with unprecedented increases in degree production, freshman persistence, and minority enrollment. Record numbers of students have been honored with national scholarships and awards, and the academic profile of successive freshman classes surpasses each previous. The emerging impact of the university is underscored by the growing number of recipients of prestigious national and international honors, including three Nobel laureates and more members of the National Academies than have served on the faculty during the entire history of the institution. And as a consequence of an ambitious expansion of the research enterprise, research expenditures over the period FY 2002 to FY 2014 have grown by a factor of 3.5, which represents an increase of over 250 percent, without significant growth in the size of the faculty, surpassing the $400 million level for the first time in FY 2013, up from $123 million in FY 2002. We look more closely at these accomplishments in the following and reiterate that although any number of such indicators attest to institutional advancement, those cited in this chapter must be evaluated in terms of their comparative scale and the complexity and simultaneity of their accomplishment by a university committed to offering admission to all academically qualified Arizona residents regardless of financial need, and an institution that strives to maintain a student body representative of the full socioeconomic diversity of American society.

During the time frame of the reconceptualization, degree production increased more than 68 percent, while enrollment increased 38.3 percent, from 55,491 in fall semester 2002 to 76,771 undergraduate, graduate, and professional students in fall 2013. Preliminary figures for fall 2014 indicate enrollment of approximately 83,145 students—roughly an 8.3 percent increase from the previous year and a 49.8 percent increase over fall 2002. Enrollment of graduate students has increased over the past decade by 39.4 percent, from 10,912 to 15,214. ASU awarded 18,916 degrees in academic year 2012–2013, including 5,003 graduate and professional degrees, up from 11,278 during AY 2001–2002.[27] The university has conferred more than 100,000 degrees during the past six academic years. The fall 2013 freshman class numbered 10,232, with a mean high school grade point average of 3.39 and median SAT score of 1100. Preliminary figures for fall 2014 indicate freshman enrollment of 11,124, which represents an 8.7 percent year-over-year increase and a 63 percent increase over fall 2002. Of those who reported class rank in fall 2013, 27.6 percent graduated in the top 10 percent of their class, up 7 percent from 25.8 percent in fall 2002. A cohort with these academic qualifications comprises more freshmen from the top decile than the total number of students in the freshman class of Harvard University.[28] The six-year graduation rate for the freshman cohort entering 2007 was 58.6 percent, up 19.1 percent from the 49.2 percent rate for the cohort that entered in fall 1995 and almost 13 percent higher than the average for all public universities in the nation. In an increasingly diverse student body, freshman persistence in fall 2012 increased to 83.8 percent, 9.3 percent higher than in fall 2002.[29] ASU ranks ninth among public universities in its enrollment of National Merit Scholars, with 440 enrolled in fall 2012, a 28 percent increase over fall 2001. More than 4,800 academically robust undergraduates enroll in Barrett, the residential honors college, which has been named best in the nation.[30] Barrett recruits academically gifted undergraduates from across the nation and now enrolls more National Merit Scholars than Stanford, MIT, Duke, Brown, or the University of California, Berkeley, as well as more National Hispanic scholars than any other institution. National Hispanic Scholars numbered 245 in fall 2013, up 227 percent over the 75 students so designated in fall 2002. ASU is also among the top three producers of Fulbright Scholars in the nation, tied with Princeton and Rutgers and coming in behind only Harvard and the University of Michigan.[31]

Within the context of a research-intensive milieu, ASU is committed to fostering a diverse and collegial academic community, with a distinctive focus on the individual. The university champions intellectual and cultural diversity and welcomes students from all fifty states and more than 167 nations across the globe. Minority enrollment from fall 2002 through fall 2013 soared 124 percent, from 11,487 to 25,732, the latter constituting 33.5 percent of total enrollment. While the first-time full-time freshman class has increased in size by 50 percent since 2002, enrollment of students of color has significantly outpaced this growth. Students from typically underrepresented ethnic backgrounds made up 39.5 percent of the fall 2013 first-time freshman class, which represents a 165 percent increase in minority enrollment in the entering freshman class since 2002. Overall, total minority undergraduate enrollment has increased 137 percent during this period. The number of African American students grew 107.2 percent, from 1,768 to 3,663; the number of Asian students grew from 2,535 to 4,261, a 68.1 percent increase; and the number of Hispanic students grew from 6,018 to 13,892, a 130.8 percent increase. The number of graduate degrees awarded to underrepresented ethnic minorities continues to increase. For example, ASU ranks first in the nation for doctorates awarded to Native Americans in all disciplines. And in the field of mathematics, ASU ranks sixth for doctorates awarded to all minority groups combined, as well as first in the nation for PhD degrees in mathematics awarded to Hispanic students.[32]

Academic talent coming out of high schools is not limited to students from privileged backgrounds. ASU reports continued success in efforts to ensure that qualified Arizona undergraduates from diverse and previously underrepresented socioeconomic backgrounds have access to a research-grade milieu. For example, during academic year 2013, 39 percent of undergraduates were first-generation college students. Since FY 2002, ASU has made major progress in delivering on its promise that no qualified Arizona student be denied access to a baccalaureate degree for lack of financial means. During this period the university has moved from a model of low-tuition/low-access to a moderate-tuition/high-access approach. As a result, the number of first-time, full-time Arizona freshmen whose families meet federal poverty guidelines increased from 300 in FY 2002, which represented 6.9 percent of the freshman class, to 952 in FY 2014, which according to preliminary figures represents 16.6 percent of the freshman class.[33] ASU increased the enrollment of freshmen coming from families with incomes below $20,000 per year from 219 in fall 2002 to 919 in fall 2012, an increase of 319 percent. The keystone initiative in this context is the President Barack Obama Scholars Program, which, since May 2009, ensures that in-state freshmen from families with moderate annual incomes are able to earn baccalaureate degrees with little or no debt. The Obama Scholars program has more than tripled the number of students from families with the greatest financial need who are eligible for financial aid that covers the direct cost of college attendance.

In FY 2013, ASU awarded a record $1 billion in all forms of financial aid to 66,551 students. Of that total, $414 million was awarded in the form of scholarships and grants to 51,920 students. Total financial aid for undergraduate students grew from $195 million in FY 2002 to $773 million in FY 2013, an increase of 296 percent. The number of undergraduate students receiving financial aid grew from 25,594 in FY 2002 to 54,608 in FY 2012, a 113 percent increase. The number of Pell Grant recipients has increased from 10,344 during the 2002–2003 academic year to 26,074 in 2011–2012. These awards provide need-based grants to low-income undergraduate and certain postbaccalaureate students to promote access to postsecondary education. First-time freshman Pell Grant recipients increased 205 percent from FY 2003 to FY 2011, from 1,209 to 3,688 students (figure 14). In FY 2013, 78 percent of undergraduate students received financial aid. The average student financial aid package for full-time Arizona resident undergraduate students with need was $11,849. According to the College Board, average indebtedness of ASU undergraduates continues to be below the national average for public universities, which for the academic year 2011–2012 was estimated to be $25,000. ASU baccalaureate degree recipients who were Arizona residents had an average loan debt of $20,827. ASU's success in offering access to resident undergraduates regardless of their financial means is easily one of the most significant achievements in the history of the institution. By contrast, the much-touted investment of selective private universities in financial aid for socioeconomically disadvantaged students, while commendable, must be considered within the context of its scale of impact.

The transformation of the academic community following the reconceptualization is epitomized by the presence on the faculty roster of two Nobel laureates, three fellows of the Royal Society, and more members of the National Academies than have served during the entire history of the institution. Of the twelve members of the National Academy of Sciences currently on the faculty, eleven have either been elected or joined the university since FY 2002, as well as seven of the nine members of the National Academy of Engineering and all three members of the Institute of Medicine. Of sixty-six fellows of the American Association for the Advancement of Science, forty-six have been recruited since FY 2002, during which time membership in the American Academy of Arts and Sciences has grown from a single member to ten. Of twenty-seven Guggenheim Fellows, twenty have either become recipients or joined the university since FY 2002, as well as three of four Pulitzer Prize winners. The majority of awardees honored by the American Council of Learned Societies, Ford Foundation, Fulbright Program, Guggenheim Foundation, National Academy of Education, National Academy of Public Administration, and National Institutes of Health have likewise either been recognized or joined the university during this time frame. The same obtains for the sixty-two members of the faculty who have been recipients of the National Science Foundation Early Career Development Award. ASU faculty and researchers also contributed to the Intergovernmental

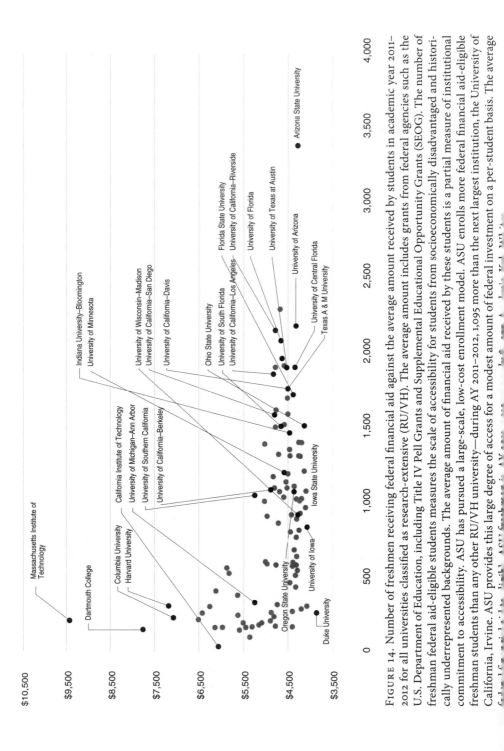

FIGURE 14. Number of freshmen receiving federal financial aid against the average amount received by students in academic year 2011–2012 for all universities classified as research-extensive (RU/VH). The average amount includes grants from federal agencies such as the U.S. Department of Education, including Title IV Pell Grants and Supplemental Educational Opportunity Grants (SEOG). The number of freshman federal aid-eligible students measures the scale of accessibility for students from socioeconomically disadvantaged and historically underrepresented backgrounds. The average amount of financial aid received by these students is a partial measure of institutional commitment to accessibility. ASU has pursued a large-scale, low-cost enrollment model. ASU enrolls more federal financial aid-eligible freshman students than any other RU/VH university—during AY 2011–2012, 1,095 more than the next largest institution, the University of California, Irvine. ASU provides this large degree of access for a modest amount of federal investment on a per-student basis. The average

Panel on Climate Change (IPCC), whose members shared the 2007 Nobel Peace Prize. Excellence is a correlate of increasing diversity: between fall 2002 and 2013, minority tenured and tenure-track faculty as a percentage of the total for this category increased from 18.5 percent to 25.8 percent, a 39.4 percent increase. In this time frame total tenured and tenure-track faculty grew from 1,671 to 1,827, a 9.3 percent increase, while minority tenured and tenure-track faculty grew from 309 to 471, a 52.4 percent increase.

## A Research Enterprise at the Frontiers of Knowledge

"Quality is an end in itself," John Lombardi observes. "Quality is the main event because universities are quality engines acquiring the highest-quality students, faculty, and educational and research programs." Competition is intense, however, because quality is scarce: "The institution's success as an enterprise comes from its ability to compete in the marketplace for a substantial share of quality." An emphasis on indicators of quality is fundamental to assessments of academic institutions, and for a major research institution, quality is unmistakably manifest in its research enterprise: "Even when research institutions teach thousands of undergraduate students, the quality of their faculty and the breadth and depth of their programs—graduate or undergraduate—depends on the research enterprise."[34] The breadth of the research enterprise correlates with quality in undergraduate and graduate education, driven in a research-intensive milieu by the interaction of students with scientists and scholars working at the cutting edge of discovery.

Research productivity reflects the success of an institution in competing for funding from sponsors, including federal, state, and private sources, and is an important indicator of the overall contribution of an institution both to the knowledge base and the regional economy. Because world-class research has the potential both to attract external funding and provide an economic return on investment to the community, ASU has sought to be especially strategic in its investment in science and technology research projects. Growth in research expenditures in the social sciences and humanities has been significant as well. The operationalization of the New American University model has mobilized the institution for the ambitious expansion of its research enterprise. Between FY 2002 and FY 2014, research expenditures have grown by a factor of 3.5, which represents an increase of over 250 percent, without significant growth in the size of the faculty.[35] Research-related expenditures surpassed the $300 million level for the first time in FY 2009 and during FY 2014 reached a record $425 million, up from $123 million in FY 2002. Among U.S. universities with research portfolios exceeding $100 million in expenditures, ASU has conducted one of the fastest-growing research enterprises over the period FY 2007 to FY 2012, according to data from the National Science Foundation. ASU has outperformed peer institutions in this context, with total research expenditures growing 62 percent from FY 2007 to FY 2012, more than 2.5 times the average growth rate of its peer institutions during the same period.[36]

Along with Caltech, Princeton, Carnegie Mellon, University of Texas, Austin, University of California, Santa Barbara, Florida State University, and Georgia Tech, ASU is one of only eight institutions without both land-grant status and a medical school to have surpassed the $200 million level in research expenditures. In terms of total research expenditures, ASU now ranks among the top twenty universities in the nation without a medical school, according to data from the National Science Foundation. Since nearly half of federal investment in university-based research and development goes directly to medical schools, the significance of appropriate comparison among these institutional peers must be underscored.[37] Among the top 100 universities ranked by federally funded research expenditures, over the period between FY 2002 and FY 2012, ASU had the second largest increase in ranking—a twenty-seven position increase. In FY 2012, ASU ranked fifteenth out of 763 U.S. universities without a medical school for research expenditures; thirteenth out of 907 universities for research expenditures in the humanities; eighth out of 907 for expenditures in the social sciences; twentieth out of 907 for expenditures in engineering; and twelfth out of 907 universities for NASA-funded research expenditures.[38]

A determination to advance the frontiers of knowledge corresponds to the maturation of the research enterprise of an institution. To provide some perspective on the momentum of the trajectory of the research enterprise, as well as the university's claim to be one of the nation's youngest major research institutions, ASU attained university status only in 1958 and conducted no significant funded research prior to 1980. The institution was granted "Research I" status by the Carnegie Foundation in

1994, conferring on it recognition as one of only a handful of major research universities without both an agricultural and medical school to be thus designated. ASU has crossed a threshold during the past decade positioning it among the leading knowledge enterprises on the planet with the capacity to advance on any challenge with entrepreneurial creativity. Growth in research expenditures across all disciplines and investment from an increasing number of funding agencies indicates that the research enterprise is on track to reach $700 million in annual research expenditures by 2020, consistent with the intent to establish ASU as a global center for interdisciplinary research, discovery, and development (figure 15). Perspective regarding the projected attainment of $700 million in research expenditures comes from consideration of current figures. During FY 2012, only two institutions without medical schools reported total research expenditures exceeding $700 million: Massachusetts Institute of Technology ($824.1 million) and University of California, Berkeley ($730.3 million). Only twenty other institutions with medical schools reported $700 million in research expenditures. In descending order, these are Johns Hopkins University, University of Michigan, University of Wisconsin, University of Washington, University of California, San Diego, University of California, San Francisco, Duke University, University of California, Los Angeles, Stanford University, Columbia University, University of North Carolina, University of Pittsburgh, University of Pennsylvania, University of Minnesota, Cornell University, Harvard University, Pennsylvania State University, Ohio State University, University of California, Davis, and Washington University in St. Louis.[39]

ASU maintains one of the most productive technology transfer operations as well when compared with the performance metrics of peer research institutions per $10 million in expenditures. ASU ranks thirty-third among universities worldwide for patents issued to its researchers and fourth among U.S. universities without a medical school, behind only MIT, Caltech, and Georgia Tech.[40] Management of patents for campus-based discoveries is provided by Arizona Technology Enterprises (AzTE), which was formed in 2003 as the exclusive intellectual property management and technology transfer operation for the university. AzTE works with faculty, investors, and industry partners to speed the flow of innovation from the laboratory to the marketplace. In FY 2013, ASU researchers

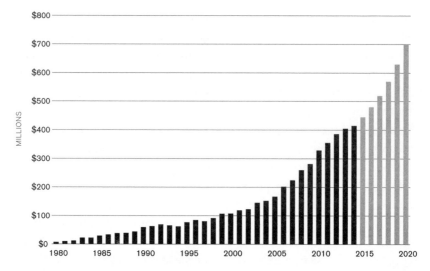

FIGURE 15. Arizona State University actual and projected research expenditures, 1980–2020. Source: National Science Foundation; ASU Office of Knowledge Enterprise Development.

submitted a record 250 invention disclosures and spun out eleven new start-up companies. In the same fiscal year, start-up companies that have licensed intellectual property from ASU received more than $68 million in venture capital and other funding. For fiscal years 2011 through 2013, ASU ranked among the top ten of all institutions with more than $300 million in research inputs (invention disclosures) and outputs (licensing agreements and start-ups) per $10 million in research expenditures, according to annual surveys by the Association of University Technology Managers (AUTM).

### Further Indicators of the Viability of the Model

A decade ago, ASU was regarded primarily as an emerging regional public research university with an uneven academic reputation, but its ascent in comparative evaluations of academic institutions signals that ASU has attained international recognition as a major research university even while advancing an institutional commitment to accessibility and diversity—factors that would be regarded as extraneous to evaluations of output or performance. Because of its commitment to educate all Arizona students qualified for research-grade academic success, ASU has assembled a student body with a more diverse and heterogeneous demographic profile than found in most leading research universities.

Among authoritative assessments of comparative institutional rankings, the Academic Ranking of World Universities, compiled by the Institute of Higher Education, Shanghai Jiao Tong University, is highly regarded. ARWU ranked ASU 79th among the top 100 universities in the world in 2013 and 88th in 2014. In 2002, ASU did not appear even among the top 200 institutions and first achieved top 100 status only in 2006. The 2014 ranking corresponds to the 48th position among all universities in the United States and 26th among public universities. The assessment compares 1,200 institutions worldwide and is considered one of the most rigorous such evaluations.[41] *The Economist* called ARWU the "most widely used annual ranking of the world's research universities," and the *Chronicle of Higher Education* termed it the "most influential international ranking." We cite the Shanghai rankings as credible proxy for a trajectory of academic achievement, which correlates with literally thousands of indicators of accomplishment. Similarly, the enrollment growth and increasing diversity to which we allude are by no means the only metrics relevant to equity and accessibility.

Other estimates corroborate the global impact of the institution. The Center for World University Rankings, which purports to improve on the Shanghai methodology, ranked ASU 73rd in the world and 46th in the United States in 2013, taking into account quality of faculty, published research, influence, citations, patents, alumni employment, and quality of education. CWUR compiles the only global performance tables that measure the quality of education as well as the prestige of the faculty and quality of their research without relying on surveys and institutional data submissions. The *Times Higher Education* World University Rankings 2013–2014, for example, ranked ASU 146th in the world, using measures of excellence in research, teaching, and knowledge transfer. And the Leiden Rankings, produced by the Center for Science and Technology Studies, Universiteit Leiden, in the Netherlands, ranked ASU 95th in terms of global impact for 2011–2012, which corresponds to the 63rd position among institutions in the United States. The Leiden methodology is based on publication output in the sciences, social sciences, and humanities.[42] Evaluations of specific indicators and rankings of disciplinary fields at both the undergraduate and graduate levels similarly point to a trajectory of increasing excellence. At the graduate level, for example, the National Research Council report released in September 2010 ranks more than half of ASU's doctoral programs in the top 25 percent in the nation.[43] Representative of more specialized metrics is the 2011 *Times Higher Education* ranking of ASU as 21st in the world in mathematics, above Columbia, Cornell, Oxford, MIT, and Cambridge. And certainly any number of less methodologically rigorous rankings abound that reflect well on the reconceptualization of the past decade.

Because ASU has assembled a student body with a more diverse and heterogeneous demographic profile than found in most leading research universities, methodologies for rankings such as those produced by *U.S. News & World Report* impact the university negatively. Although skepticism of their methodology remains warranted,[44] *USN&WR* has nevertheless assigned ASU to the top tier of national universities since 2008, and since 2009 as one of the top "Up and Coming Schools," ranking second in the 2014 edition of "America's Best Colleges"—the assessment highlighting innovative change in measures of academics, faculty, students, campus life, and diversity. In 2012, the magazine ranked ASU the top institution in the nation for online student services and technology. And to cite but one further example of recognition, a survey of corporate recruiters conducted by the *Wall Street Journal* in September 2010 that aimed to identify "the majors and schools that best prepare students to land jobs that are satisfying, well-paid, and have growth potential" ranked ASU fifth in the nation. According to *WSJ*, "Recruiters say graduates of top public universities are often among the most prepared and well-rounded academically, and companies have found they fit well into their corporate cultures and over time have the best track record in their firms."[45]

Inasmuch as the *USN&WR* methodology favors highly selective schools that accept only a scant fraction of applicants, ASU's success has permitted the university to demonstrate that it is possible to combine academic excellence with inclusiveness to a broad demographic representative of the socioeconomic diversity of the region and nation. Quality undergraduate teaching does not correlate positively with traditional performance indicators. Standard calculations do not control for the impact of teaching on faculty productivity ratios. Yet, a disproportionate number of ASU faculty members assume higher teaching loads to meet the mandate of educating one of the largest student bodies in the nation. As a result, the relatively high percentage of faculty actively engaged in teaching skews faculty productivity ratios downward, even while absolute values and growth indicators become more and more competitive. Recognition of the growth of the research enterprise underscores not only faculty creativity and productivity but also their commitment to the institutional objective to focus on each individual student. ASU is a large institution in its aggregate but not in its implementation modality.

## Interrelated and Interdependent Design Aspirations

The successful application of the set of eight interrelated and mutually interdependent design aspirations is best appreciated in its sustained operationalization. Because the New American University assumes major responsibility for the economic, social, and cultural vitality of its community, the aspiration to leverage place, for example, encourages research with application for the region in which an institution is situated. Leveraging place does not necessarily imply preference for the cultivation of local knowledge, however, because even when regionally focused, research should strive for global relevance. And although ASU is committed to teaching and research that improve the quality of life in Arizona, innovative approaches to local and regional problems are certain to find application globally. Scholarship, scientific research, technological innovation, and creative endeavor all implicitly address a global audience, advancing a modality of transdisciplinary and transinstitutional global engagement. Because place refers to the intersection of the natural, built, social, and cultural environments, the intent to leverage place is interdependent with the aspirations to transform society, for example, or to advance social embeddedness. An initiative termed Community Connect offers the academic community opportunities to engage in collaborative endeavors to promote social and economic development and community capacity building, which seeks to maximize the impact of community-based organizations. ASU currently operates 498 community outreach programs in 180 locations offered by more than 120 different units. It may appear counterintuitive for a major research institution to focus on place in an era marked by technological advances that seem to diminish its significance. Yet, although globalization has become a dominant cultural, economic, and social force, the persistent significance of place reasserts its hold on our identities even as economists underscore the extent of the regional economic impact of major research universities.

The design aspiration enjoining academic enterprise advances an entrepreneurial academic culture that generates the intellectual capital that is the most valuable asset of every college and university. An entrepreneurial approach to knowledge encourages experimentation and risk taking in all fields and sets the pattern for scientific discovery, technological innovation, humanistic insight, social scientific rigor, and creative expression. The ideas, products, and processes of academic culture are thus brought to scale to promote the advancement of our society and the economic competitiveness of our nation. The commercialization of intellectual property through the formation of spin-off and start-up companies comes to mind in this context, but the movement of knowledge from the laboratory to the marketplace is just one manifestation of this process. Although critics allege that collaboration between the academy and business and industry commoditizes knowledge and compromises disinterested inquiry, such engagement across sectors is essential if universities are to leverage their knowledge production to catalyze innovation that benefits the public good.[46] Business and industry have become increasingly dependent on the research and development conducted by the nation's leading research universities, as we assessed in chapter 4, and universities are the key actors in the triple helix of university-industry-government innovation.[47] Academic enterprise is thus not just about the money, but, this said, money is a dimension of academic enterprise. As John Lombardi put it, "While most university conversations focus on issues of academic substance—program content, research results, and curriculum issues, for example—almost every conversation carries a subtext about money."[48]

Major research universities are often compared to Fortune 500 corporations in terms of their scale and complexity. But while corporations are perceived to navigate in the turbulent currents of the marketplace, universities are commonly thought to conduct their affairs in monastic seclusion. Nothing could be further from the truth, especially if one conceives of colleges and universities as transformative societal catalysts critical to our survival as a species, charged with the responsibility of spurring national competitiveness in a globalized knowledge economy. Because academic institutions operate in the real world, they need be no less entrepreneurial than corporations, and those at their helms must imbue respective institutional cultures with appropriate competitive spirit. To a degree rarely appreciated, major research universities, whether public or private, function in a fiercely competitive marketplace, and in such a context each must operate in real time and at scale. But academic enterprise is not about replacing an archaic academic culture with an efficient corporate variant.

Generally associated with the private sector, enterprise is a concept often overlooked in discussions about higher education. Universities generally err on the side of being too deliberative, which means they often miss out on opportunities. Academe might well take a cue from the private sector and recognize the imperative for adaptability and quick but intelligent decision making. The objective at ASU has been to move institutional culture away from the agency model characteristic of bureaucratic entrenchment toward a boundary spanning enterprise model, which is to say, ASU seeks to be energetic, resilient, and adaptive, and to leverage engagement with business, industry, and government. The speed with which ASU is prepared to deploy the full complement of its resources in competitive engagement may be unprecedented for a university, but it is crucial to the success of a knowledge enterprise.

Academic enterprise informs the institutional culture of the entire university and is by no means confined to the W. P. Carey School of Business or Ira A. Fulton Schools of Engineering. Despite the obvious correlation between entrepreneurship and business and the tech sector, the university promotes the conviction that students in all disciplines possess the potential to approach knowledge entrepreneurially. Although entrepreneurship is embedded throughout the curriculum, for students seeking focused instruction to launch a start-up or pursue social enterprise development, the university offers classes and discrete certificate and degree programs. For example, the W. P. Carey School offers a bachelor of science degree in business entrepreneurship; the Fulton Schools of Engineering offer a bachelor of science degree in technological entrepreneurship and management; and the Herberger Institute for Design and the Arts offers a bachelor of arts degree in digital culture with a concentration in technological entrepreneurship. A university-wide undergraduate certificate in entrepreneurship is available, as well as eight graduate degree programs that feature entrepreneurship as intrinsic to their curricula. In recognition of its entrepreneurial ecosystem and success in bolstering student entrepreneurship, the Ewing Marion Kauffman Foundation designated ASU a Kauffman Campus. The award places ASU among the elite in entrepreneurial education, along with such institutions as Brown, Carnegie Mellon, New York University, and the University of Wisconsin, Madison.

An institutional culture committed to academic enterprise correlates the undergraduate experience with student success following graduation. A focus on promoting excellence in STEM fields—science, technology, engineering, and mathematics—is emblematic of this concern. In response to the critical national need for more graduates with quantitative and scientific literacy, ASU has set a goal to double the number of STEM majors as quickly as possible and, more broadly, to produce students with a new spirit of engagement in the scientific and technological futures of global society. At a time when both the economic competitiveness of the nation and its continued scientific and technological dominance are compromised by poor student performance in these fields, ASU has redoubled its commitment to revive flagging interest in science- and technology-based careers through pedagogical innovation in K–20 STEM education.

To accomplish these objectives for science and technology education, faculty members were encouraged to conceptualize new teaching, learning, and discovery platforms. Reconfigured academic units arising from merged and restructured departments in these fields, such as the School of Earth and Space Exploration (SESE), now complement large-scale research initiatives such as the Biodesign Institute and Global Institute of Sustainability. The effort to transcend conventional pedagogical approaches has produced promising outcomes. Traditional core disciplines like physics and chemistry have seen robust expansion in the number and diversity of students, and general quantitative literacy throughout the university has witnessed remarkable improvement. In the life sciences alone, enrollment recently exceeded 4,600, up from 1,675 in 2001. Enrollment in engineering and technology fields has doubled during the past decade and now exceeds 10,000 students. Undergraduate enrollment in all STEM areas has increased to approximately 16,000, doubling the number over the past decade. The enrollment of women in STEM majors has nearly doubled, and the enrollment of minority students has increased by 141 percent.

The Entrepreneurship and Innovation Group, a joint initiative of the Office of Knowledge Enterprise Development and Arizona Technology Enterprises, serves as the hub of operations for entrepreneurial activity at the university. Ranking among the top twenty university-based business incubators globally and tenth in the United States, the group directs a suite of programs that includes the Edson Student Entrepreneur Initiative. Each year this start-up accelerator offers teams of student entrepreneurs from all disciplines mentorship from industry experts and opportunities to transform innovative ideas into viable businesses. The 2012 cohort of student companies secured $1.1 million in equity investment and grant awards. Of twenty companies, three have been angel funded, and seven currently generate revenue. The potential for social return on investment from student entrepreneurs is epitomized by the fledgling start-up Pollen-Tech, which has developed a process to eliminate dependence on bee pollination to produce agricultural yield. Representative of initiatives spearheaded by the E&I group is the Arizona Furnace Technology Transfer Accelerator, a public-private partnership that seeks to launch new companies from intellectual property licensed from Arizona research institutions. Furnace takes unencumbered intellectual property held by university technology transfer offices and develops it through a proprietary process. Because technology transfer has become an increasingly important strategic objective for federal government laboratories, the success of the ASU approach led the U.S. Department of Defense to award ASU a $1 million grant to create a new "Pracademic Center of Excellence in Technology Transfer" (PACE/T2).

Although we define enterprise as the spirit of competitive risk taking that characterizes vanguard intellectual endeavor, entrepreneurial initiatives at ASU also produce solid returns on investment. ASU research has led to the formation of sixty-seven start-up companies, including Fluidic Energy, which has developed such auxiliary power solutions as a rechargeable zinc-air battery, and Heliae, which develops algae production technologies. Spinout companies based on technologies developed by ASU researchers raised $68 million in external funding during FY 2013. By 2020, Arizona has the potential to become one of America's leading centers for knowledge-based technological innovation with global leadership in such industries as solar energy, aerospace, defense, and biotechnology. Toward this end, ASU operates as the central node of an integrative knowledge discovery and commercialization network and through translation between university-based discovery and market application aligns its public mission with strategies to spur regional economic development.

ASU operations dedicated to entrepreneurship, economic development, and corporate engagement are based at SkySong, the ASU Scottsdale Innovation Center. SkySong is a global business and innovation center that links research and education with technology and entrepreneurship to position ASU and the metropolitan region in the knowledge economy. Organized around a central plaza with a signature shade structure, SkySong is a 1.2 million–square–foot mixed-use complex located on a forty-two-acre campus in Scottsdale. SkySong is home to more than seventy affiliated companies, which have generated more than 800 jobs and $460 million in economic impact for the metropolitan region. Estimates project total economic output related to SkySong to exceed $9 billion over the next three decades.

The design aspirations enjoining focus on the individual and societal transformation are representative of the dynamic interrelatedness of consonant themes underpinning an institutional culture. In evolving a new model for inclusive higher education, ASU takes to heart its essential responsibilities to educate young adults and to support their character development as part of the learning process. Advancing the pursuit of knowledge while nurturing integrity within our diverse academic community is a complex challenge that calls to mind the ideal of *Bildung*, referring broadly to education or culture but more precisely to the formation of the individual, which we considered in our historical overview of the university envisioned by Humboldt. The New American University is wholly and unwaveringly committed to this challenge. Universities bear an intrinsic responsibility to advance the intellectual growth of their students through learning that results not only in a diploma but also the maturation of their character. As Dr. Martin Luther King Jr. wrote in the Morehouse College campus newspaper in 1947: "We must remember that intelligence is not enough. Intelligence plus character—that is the goal of true education."

The conventional wisdom that represents large public universities as impersonal is expressed in a report from the National Institute of Education: "The greater the size of institutions, the more complex and bureaucratic they tend to become, the fewer the opportunities for each student to become intensely involved with intellectual life, and the less personal the contact between faculty and students." In his assessment of normative assumptions implicit in a number of authoritative reports on undergraduate education, higher education scholar Gary Rhoades finds correlate juxtapositions that inevitably favor elite and selective private institutions.[49] Because no two students follow the same path to success, however, ASU has sought to cultivate unique and differentiated research and learning environments that address the needs of students with differing levels of academic preparation and professional intent. Differentiated learning platforms in engineering education, for example, focus either on research and the theoretical aspects of technology or practical application. The Ira A. Fulton Schools of Engineering comprise five distinct research-intensive transdisciplinary schools, including the School of Biological and Health Systems Engineering; School of Computing, Informatics, and Decision Systems Engineering; and School of Sustainable Engineering and the Built Environment, as well as the Polytechnic School, which focuses on use-inspired translational research and offers students interested in direct entry into the workforce an experiential learning environment.

A focus on the individual comes as well through the creative adaptation of digital technologies. The digital revolution that has been termed the "second machine age" has brought artificial intelligence and "thinking machines" that enhance our cognitive potential, MIT researchers Erik Brynjolfsson and Andrew McAfee explain. "Machines that can complete cognitive tasks are even more important than machines that can accomplish physical ones." The relevance to higher education is obvious: "Our digital machines have escaped their narrow confines and started to demonstrate broad abilities in pattern recognition, complex communication, and other domains that used to be exclusively human."[50] Despite his misgivings about the implications of the Internet for cognitive function, technology analyst Nicholas Carr describes the potential inherent in the application of artificial intelligence techniques to online learning, which promise to "bring higher education out of the industrial era." If the objective is to "translate pedagogical theories into software code," Carr explains, insight will come from the vast amounts of information amassed during the classroom experience: "The bigger the data sets, the more

adept the systems become at providing each student with the right information in the right form at the right moment." Adaptive learning ac-
commodates individual approaches: "Software for, say, teaching algebra can be written to reflect alternative theories of learning, and then,
as many students proceed through the program, the theories can be tested
and refined and the software improved."[51] We are witnessing the transition from teaching and learning based on the fifteenth-century technology of the printed book to twenty-first-century digital technologies that
offer the potential for adaptive, interactive personalized learning at an infinite scale.[52]

New information technologies promise not only pedagogical innovation but also performance enhancement and cost containment. ASU
has become "ground zero for data-driven teaching in higher education,"
according to one assessment. "The university has rolled out an ambitious
effort to turn its classrooms into laboratories for technology-abetted
'adaptive learning'—a method that purports to give instructors real-time
intelligence on how well each of their students is getting each concept."[53]
Elizabeth Capaldi Phillips, former ASU provost and now University Professor and professor of psychology, developed a comprehensive student
advising system based on data analytics known as eAdvisor: "This
method . . . helps students find majors in which they are likely to succeed;
keeps them progressing toward a degree; and makes advisors more informed, efficient, and effective. It also allows the university to manage enrollments effectively, thereby saving money while improving student success." Moreover, "the analytical framework not only allows advisors to
chart a path for each student, but it enables the university to offer courses
(with the necessary seats) that students must have in order to complete a
major on time." Because data that track patterns of success for large student populations are available, the method "allows for the development
of criteria predictive of student success in each major." She describes
eAdvisor as a "general-purpose design adaptable to almost any large
comprehensive and diverse academic institution."[54]

Through a combination of traditional classroom instruction and online technologies that deliver interactive content, monitor individual
progress, and accommodate multiple learning styles, universities can deliver coursework customized to students that accelerates learning while
lowering costs. In pilot tests of what is termed "blended learning," uni-

versities offering blended courses in the humanities and the sciences report that in some cases students demonstrated mastery of material at a faster rate than by traditional methods. But ASU currently enrolls 9,869 undergraduates fully online, and the objective is to increase that number to 27,500 by 2020. Fully online graduate student enrollment is currently 3,549. ASU Online is committed to delivering academic content through interactive modes of online learning for improving educational effectiveness at reduced costs. Students earning degrees through ASU Online can choose from forty-one undergraduate degree programs and thirty-seven graduate degree programs that have been designed by the same faculty members teaching on our campuses. The typical student takes two or three classes per semester, and most courses cover material from the traditional semester in seven and one-half weeks. Planning has focused on increasing accessibility and affordability without sacrificing the quality of course content.

ASU aggressively enters into partnerships to expand and improve the online learning experience, utilizing over one hundred third-party tools and services. This enables the university to use the best technologies available, while students benefit from an increasingly personalized experience both inside and outside the classroom. Additionally, our instructional designers work with faculty members to reconceptualize their lectures for online students with an emphasis on engagement and interaction, which is highly individualized and interactive. The quality of the student experience builds community and increases retention. The recent announcement of the partnership between ASU and Starbucks, in which the corporation provides tuition reimbursement toward baccalaureate completion for qualified associates through ASU's online component,[55] is just one example of the potential for innovation spurred by academic enterprise to promote economic and social development.

The design aspiration enjoining global engagement encourages transcultural teaching and research and fosters transinstitutional collaboration with academia, business and industry, and government agencies worldwide. Even service to local communities has global implication; by scaling local solutions for global impact, ASU develops prototypes for programs and practices with application throughout the world. Like any major research institution, ASU strives to facilitate scholarly and scientific exchange under the assumption that it advances knowledge as well as the global agenda of the nation. But through collaborative engagement that promotes mutual or reciprocal learning opportunities, ASU advances knowledge production that benefits all participating institutional partners. Unlike universities that establish outreach programs in such areas as agriculture or even launch medical schools or business schools or entire campuses abroad—for example, Cornell set up a medical school in Qatar, and New York University has opened a research university campus in Abu Dhabi—global engagement at ASU is focused on reciprocity in the resolution of global challenges.

In Mexico, for example, ASU launched sustainability initiatives with the Instituto Tecnológico de Monterrey, or Tec de Monterrey. In China, ASU has brought the prototype of the Decision Theater, an immersive screening room developed for the visualization of three-dimensional complex multivariate relationships, to a number of universities, where scientists and policy makers can use it to analyze environmental data and modeling simulations. In collaboration with the government of Vietnam, the Higher Engineering Education Alliance Program, or HEEAP, brings the Fulton Schools of Engineering together with Intel and Siemens and other industry partners to improve the quality of the Vietnamese curriculum, which in turn supports the country's growing high-tech industry. And through an initiative called Global Resolve, ASU is collaborating with a range of partners to develop programs and sustainable technologies in the areas of energy, clean water, and local economic development for rural communities in the developing world.

To expand its global footprint, ASU has engaged the Institute of International Education to participate in academic partnership programs with India, Brazil, and Myanmar. A growing relationship with Brazil has led to increased enrollment of Brazilian students whose objective is to maximize scientific mobility. Engagement with Myanmar has been initiated through a cooperative program in the digitization of libraries with Rutgers, the University of Washington, and Northern Illinois University. Another set of initiatives brought ASU into association with Sichuan University, which has served as an institutional partner for the Confucius Institute. Along with a range of scholarly exchanges and study abroad, cooperative programs include a jointly administered Center for American Culture. Advanced projects include a program in disaster management and the development of the first school of global studies in Western China.

The ASU-Sichuan University collaboration was held as an exemplar of bilateral cooperation by the U.S. Department of State during the "people-to-people diplomacy" component of the U.S.-China Strategic and Economic Dialogue initiated in April 2009. The Sichuan relationship is but one aspect of overall linkages with China. In Chengdu, for example, ASU has launched an effort to establish a new research and development platform that will focus on critical sustainability issues. This initiative is only one of several to focus explicitly on scientific and technological collaboration to advance shared intellectual capital with Chinese partners. Through a significant grant from the Walton Family Foundation, for example, ASU is developing practical solutions to local sustainability challenges from platforms around the globe, including Amsterdam and Hong Kong.

### Advancing a Transdisciplinary Research Enterprise Committed to Societal Outcomes

Arizona State University pursues teaching, research, and creative excellence focused on the major challenges and questions of our time, as well as those central to the quality of life, sustainable development, and economic competitiveness of Arizona and the nation. In an effort to bolster the contributions of the research enterprise to national economic competitiveness and global well-being, ASU conducts critical national research in such areas as earth and space science, renewable energy, advanced materials, microelectronics, health care, national security, and urban systems design. ASU seeks to advance knowledge through teaching and research conducted within flexible organizational frameworks that maximize collaboration and communication between the core disciplines and interdisciplinary fields. Some disciplines remain departmentally based, whereas others are construed across departments, centers, institutes, schools, and colleges and new explicitly interdisciplinary configurations. These new academic entities ("new schools") have been established to advance teaching and engender research, both fundamental and applied, that possesses the interdisciplinary breadth to address the large-scale "grand challenges."[56] Although the correlation between discipline and department represents the conventional norm, in practice the interrelationships are sometimes complex and not always self-evident. A comprehensive unit-level assessment sought to articulate the identities of disciplines and interdisciplinary fields and clarify their interrelationships and anticipated trajectories. Alignments between fundamental and irreducible disciplines and interdisciplinary configurations were calibrated, inasmuch as these may be synergistic, symbiotic, or even antagonistic.

The impetus to reorganize and recombine discipline-based academic departments had already gained a foothold at ASU before the full operationalization of the design process. An ambitious reorganization of the life sciences faculties to overcome disciplinary entrenchment epitomized the momentum. In July 2003, the biology, microbiology, and plant biology departments and the program in molecular and cellular biology merged to form the new ASU School of Life Sciences (SOLS). Although administrative efficiency was cited as an objective, the motivation for the creation of SOLS was largely to advance interdisciplinarity: "to facilitate collaboration across the range of disciplines covered by the school; . . . and to exploit the fact that the key research challenges in the life sciences lie at the interface of sub-disciplines, often involving integration of knowledge from different levels of biological organization and across different kinds of organisms." Its mission statement specifies that the school was conceived "without internal disciplinary barriers, allowing it to plan strategically at the seams of intersecting disciplines." The school is currently organized into seven faculty groups: biomedicine and biotechnology; cellular and molecular biosciences; genomics, evolution, and bioinformatics; ecology, evolution, and environmental science; human dimensions of biology; organismal, integrative, and systems biology; and basic medical sciences.[57] The arrangement allows more than one hundred life scientists, engineers, philosophers, social scientists, and ethicists to self-organize around the socially and environmentally relevant questions of the day.

Among the new transdisciplinary schools conceptualized and operationalized during the past decade within the College of Liberal Arts and Sciences are the School of Human Evolution and Social Change; School of Earth and Space Exploration; School of Politics and Global Studies; School of Social and Family Dynamics; School of Social Transformation; and School of Historical, Philosophical, and Religious Studies. These schools complement initiatives such as the Global Institute of Sustainability (GIOS), which incorporates the School of Sustainability, the first of its kind, and the Biodesign Institute, the premier multidisciplinary research center dedicated exclusively to advancing biologically inspired design to address global challenges in health care, sustainability, and national security. The research of this large-scale array of labs and centers is aimed at improving human health and the environment through interdisciplinary efforts in such areas as personalized diagnostics and treatment, infectious diseases and pandemics, and renewable sources of energy. The Biodesign Institute houses ten research centers that are leveraged in a highly collaborative, team-oriented, and synergistic manner to address complex problems. Working in the broad domains of biological, nanoscale, cognitive, and sustainable systems, the transdisciplinary research centers are advancing our understanding in such areas as biosignatures, biosensors, bionics, and biofactories, ubiquitous sensing, optimized human performance, environmental sustainability, and personalized medicine.

Other transdisciplinary configurations include the Complex Adaptive Systems Initiative (CASI), a collaborative effort to address global challenges in health, sustainability, and national security through the creation of new technologies and novel solutions; Security and Defense Systems Initiative, which addresses national and global security and defense challenges through an integrative systems approach that examines technological solutions; legal and policy issues; and social, cultural, and economic factors that contribute to potential conflicts as well as their alleviation and resolution; Flexible Display Center, a cooperative agreement with the U.S. Army to advance the emerging flexible electronics industry; LightWorks, a multidisciplinary endeavor in renewable energy fields, including artificial photosynthesis, biofuels, and next-generation photovoltaics; and initiatives in the humanities and social sciences, including the Institute for Humanities Research, Center for the Study of Religion and Conflict, Institute for Social Science Research, and Consortium for Science, Policy, and Outcomes (CSPO). The Herberger Institute for Design and the Arts comprises the School of Art; School of Film, Dance, and Theater; the Design School, which offers degrees in architecture, environmental design, industrial design, interior design, landscape architecture, urban design, and visual communication; School of Music; and in collaboration with the Fulton Schools of Engineering, the School of Arts, Media, and Engineering, which conducts research and education on experiential media that integrate computation and digital media with the physical human experience.

The School of Earth and Space Exploration (SESE) combines the fields of astronomy and astrophysics, cosmology, Earth systems sciences, planetary sciences, and systems engineering to deepen our understanding of our planet and the universe. Within an inherently transdisciplinary framework, the school is advancing strategic research initiatives in a number of areas, including the origin and evolution of the universe; the emergence and function of planetary bodies; the origin, evolution, and distribution of life; the coevolution of Earth's surface environment and human societies; and science and engineering education. The school aspires to methodological fluidity in a conceptual framework that recombines modes of inquiry to address some of the most profound challenges of the epoch. The broad theme of exploration represents a transdisciplinary conceptualization of the quest to discover the origins of the universe and expand our understanding of space, matter, and time. Although the conventional disciplines of the earth and space sciences are predominantly historical, the transdisciplinary conceptualization of SESE makes it possible to construe both as predictive to address such questions as the ultimate fate of the universe.[58]

Established in July 2006 through an amalgamation of the former Department of Geological Sciences and the astronomy, astrophysics, and cosmology faculties of the former Department of Physics and Astronomy—thereafter the Department of Physics—SESE offers a faculty roster that includes theoretical physicists, systems biologists, biogeochemists, and electrical engineers. Affiliated engineers bring technological expertise that advances the development and deployment of critical scientific instrumentation on Earth and in space. The transdisciplinary fluidity of the school facilitates collaboration and communication between scientists and engineers, engaging researchers from other schools and institutes, including the Biodesign Institute and Ira A. Fulton Schools of Engineering. The wealth of subfields within given disciplinary areas suggests the breadth their recombination enables. Within astrophysics and cosmology, for example, subfields include computational astrophysics; physics of the early universe and the formation of large-scale structure;

and the formation and evolution of galaxies, stars, and planetary systems. Subfields within Earth system sciences include biogeoscience; continental tectonics and structural geology; geochemistry; geophysics (including geodynamics and seismology); petrology, mineralogy, mineral physics, and mineral resources; surface processes (including geomorphology and hydrology); and volcanology and volcanic hazards.[59]

In 2005, ASU launched the School of Human Evolution and Social Change (SHESC), combining the major areas of anthropological enquiry, including archaeology, bioarchaeology, physical anthropology, cultural anthropology, linguistics, and museum anthropology, with such areas as mathematics and computer science, geography, political science, museum studies, epidemiology, economics, and sociology. The new school boasts such transdisciplinary research centers as the Archaeological Research Institute, Center for Global Health, Center for Digital Antiquity, and Institute of Human Origins. The allied Consortium for Biosocial Complex Systems engages the Complex Adaptive Systems Initiative. Transdisciplinary collaboration allows SHESC scientists and scholars to address complex problems from comparative and holistic perspectives, whether the challenge is epidemics of infectious disease, sustainable management of natural resources, or adaptation to climate change. The quest to understand human origins, evolution, and diversity engages research in such areas as societies and their natural environments; biocultural dimensions of global health; culture, heritage, and identity; global dynamics and cultural interactions; and the sustainability of the built environment. The school thus provides students with an integrated curriculum in the social, behavioral, and natural sciences focused on the evolution of our species and trajectories of human societies.[60]

With the establishment of the Julie Ann Wrigley Global Institute of Sustainability in 2004 and the School of Sustainability three years later, ASU has positioned itself in the vanguard of interdisciplinary research on environmental, economic, and social sustainability. The institute brings together scientists and engineers with government policy makers and industry leaders to share knowledge and expertise and develop solutions to the challenges of sustainability. With research in areas as diverse as agriculture, air quality, marine ecology, materials design, nanotechnology, policy and governance, renewable energy, risk assessment, transportation, and urban infrastructure, the faculty members affiliated with GIOS are addressing some of the most critical challenges of our time, as well as training future generations of scholars, scientists, and practitioners.

To prepare students capable of integrating a broad range of disciplines in a rapidly changing knowledge economy, the School of Sustainability offers both undergraduate and graduate degree programs. The school is educating a new generation of leaders through collaborative, transdisciplinary, and problem-oriented training that addresses environmental, economic, and social challenges. Teaching and research seek adaptive solutions to such issues as rapid urbanization, water quality, habitat transformation, the loss of biodiversity, and the development of sustainable energy, materials, and technologies. In addition, to engender an institutional culture of sustainability, ASU offers sustainability-themed courses in fields as diverse as anthropology, architecture, biology, economics, engineering, industrial design, law, philosophy, nonprofit leadership, and urban planning. Along with such guiding principles of modern societies as human rights, sustainability is an epochal question that must be addressed by the citizens of a planet with a population that already exceeds 7 billion and is projected to approach 10 billion. Entrenchment in disciplinary silos undermines the capacity of our institutions to advance research that can provide us with the means to balance wealth generation with continuously enhanced environmental quality and social well-being. Interdisciplinary research and teaching associated with sustainability is representative of the ASU effort to design a new model for the American research university.[61]

Transdisciplinary initiatives in the social sciences and humanities are common enough in the contemporary research university, but ASU is intent on bringing new societal engagement and impact to such efforts. The Center for the Study of Religion and Conflict, for example, promotes transdisciplinary research and teaching on the dynamics of religion and conflict with the objectives of advancing knowledge but also seeking solutions and informing policy. By serving as a research hub that fosters exchange and collaboration across the university, as well as nationally and globally, the center fosters discourse and dialogue about some of the most pressing issues facing society today. Committed to a model of scholarship that is collaborative and problem-focused, the center stimulates new research by bringing together faculty and students from anthropology, history, languages and literature, political science, religious studies, and sociology. CSRC creates links between academia and professionals, policy makers, practitioners, and religious leaders, and fosters cross-cultural exchange through partnerships with scholars, students, and institutions internationally.

Along with Princeton and MIT, ASU was one of seven institutions in 2009 selected from more than 200 to receive a Minerva award from the Department of Defense. The project proposed by the Center for the Study of Religion and Conflict is titled "Finding Allies for the War of Words: Mapping the Diffusion and Influence of Counter-Radical Muslim Discourse." The Minerva Research Initiative focuses on areas of strategic importance to U.S. national security policy and supports university-based basic research to expand the intellectual capital of the Department of Defense in the social sciences and humanities. Earning one of the first Minerva awards is a testament to the potential for scholars in the humanities and social sciences to influence foreign policy. Investigators in the project come from disciplines as varied as religious studies, political science, mathematics, sociology, and computer science. Especially representative of the potential for the social science and humanities to exert broad societal impact is the Consortium for Science, Policy, and Outcomes.

"What types of scientific knowledge should society choose to pursue?" asks Daniel Sarewitz, a science and technology policy scholar and codirector of the Consortium for Science, Policy, and Outcomes (CSPO) at Arizona State University. "How should such choices be made and by whom? How should society apply this knowledge, once gained? How can 'progress' in science and technology be defined and measured in the context of broader social and political goals?" With these questions Sarewitz formulates the organizing questions behind one of the world's leading centers for social and policy studies in this sector. CSPO is dedicated to these concerns, and an examination of what Sarewitz terms the "inescapable cultural context" within which science is conducted.[62] The most recent formulation of the CSPO mission statement specifies that the consortium "forge an intellectual community that can help enhance the contribution of science and technology to society's pursuit of equality, justice, freedom, and overall quality of life."[63]

Science and technology are among the most important drivers of social, cultural, economic, environmental, and political change in the world today. Science policy—the process of making decisions about what science will do, who will do it, where it will be done, and who will use the results—crucially influences the types of benefits that science confers, the distribution of benefits, and the emergence of new problems. One would expect science policy therefore to occupy a central position in the global debate on how to build a better world. That it remains a marginal part of public discourse and policy action is the principal motivation for the consortium.

Science and technology have transformed our lives but are implicated in a range of troubling correlations—the footprint of industrialization, to take the single most obvious example, brought with it rampant environmental degradation that has yet to be adequately restored or managed to promote sustainability. And although our postindustrial knowledge economy has produced unprecedented prosperity for certain segments of society, its rewards have not been equally distributed, and social, cultural, and political disruption persist; the conspicuous inequity of access to the benefits of science and technology remains a vexing correlate of modernity. Despite our growing scientific and technological sophistication, our current science policy lacks even a rudimentary capacity to confront the complex implications of our own advancing ingenuity.

Universities are crucibles of scientific and technological advance, of economic growth, and of societal transformation. But they assume these roles tacitly, failing to embrace not only their responsibility for the outcomes they help create but also their capacity to influence the evolutions of those outcomes by the choices and priorities they embrace. As conduits in the transnational exchange of knowledge, our universities are uniquely positioned to ensure that in coming decades the cresting waves of scientific discovery and technological innovation lead to equitable societal benefit and contribute to global economic, environment, and civic security.

Initially conceived in 1997 by Crow and Sarewitz as the Center for Science, Policy, and Outcomes as a project of Columbia University, CSPO was augmented by strategic alliances with other institutions and foundations. Located in Washington, D.C., the center connected science policy scholarship with policy discourse aimed at enhancing the contributions of science and technology to an improved quality of life, with particular attention to distributional impacts—to questions of who is likely to benefit from public investments in knowledge creation and innovation. This focus, in turn, gave rise to the imperative to determine how science agendas, programs, and institutions may be designed so a concern for equity is built in from their inception. Yet, even posing this challenge went against the grain of the mainstream thinking behind science and technology policy, which was grounded in the presupposition that science is unpredictable and efforts to guide it, and to demand accountability for societal outcomes, are impossible and counterproductive. Science must be left to govern itself; technological outcomes are a reflection on society, not on the technologies themselves or the knowledge that helped make them possible. To question this dogma was to subject oneself to accusations of being hostile to science or neo-luddite.

CSPO thus had to pursue an agenda that was at once intellectual and political: how to develop theories, methods, tools, and even language that provide a robust and defensible foundation for a more socially valuable knowledge production and innovation enterprise. The first fifteen years of CSPO can be best understood as an increasingly comprehensive effort to pursue this agenda. A crucial contribution to these efforts was early support from the V. Kann Rasmussen Foundation, which enabled CSPO to launch high-risk intellectual and publicly oriented projects and to attract additional support from other philanthropic sources and government agencies. A major conference held at Columbia University in 2002—Living with the Genie: Governing the Scientific and Technological Transformation of Society in the Twenty-First Century—brought together leading thinkers from diverse fields, institutions, and cultures to help legitimate the urgency of a serious, society-wide discourse about science, technology, and society.[64] A grant from the Rockefeller Foundation allowed Barry Bozeman to lead a project to develop the new theory and method of public values mapping that could lend intellectual guidance for the assessment of the potential social value of investments in science. Through an NSF-funded project on decision making under uncertainty for climate change, CSPO, collaborating with colleagues at the University of Colorado, developed a conceptual and practical framework for improving the societal value of information through reconciling the supply of and demand for information. These endeavors began to contribute to a new intellectual infrastructure for an outcomes-oriented science policy.

Yet, if the Washington setting for CSPO bespoke its commitment to relevance and influence at the national level, what was still lacking was an academic milieu committed to the goals of outcome-oriented science that could serve as both home for the necessary sorts of inquiry and a test-bed for experiments linking research, policy design, and social outcomes. The center reconstituted as the consortium at ASU in July 2004 with Sarewitz as director. Sarewitz and codirector David Guston observe that three concepts remain operative from the formative period of concep-tualization: desired outcomes can drive science; the societal value of new knowledge is determined by how it is used and by whom; and the defi-nition of the problem helps determine the relevance of the research. Building on the activities of the previous several years, their first effort at ASU was a major proposal for a national Center for Nanotechnology in Society, to be funded by the National Science Foundation. The pro-posal was successful, and the nanotech center became the prototype of the CSPO integrated approach, with transdisciplinary research and train-ing characterized by close collaboration between social and physical scientists, and a strong commitment to public and policy outreach, integrated across the center's activities. The idea was to build into the nanotechnology research process a commitment to reflexiveness about how and why science was being advanced along particular lines as it was being conducted. In short, the nanotech center was an institutional test-bed for a new type of science policy, aimed at creating a capacity for the anticipatory governance of powerful emerging technologies. What tra-ditional science policy proclaimed to be impossible—the prediction of the future of science and technology—was redefined as irrelevant. Prediction was unnecessary for good governance; instead, methods of real-time technology assessment were applied to help steer trajectories of inquiry toward socially desirable outcomes.

Continuing to build on these foundations, additional faculty hires and grant support expanded the CSPO portfolio of work across an increas-ingly diverse set of problems and opportunities, such as greater public participation in technological decision making; understanding the role of social media in democratic movements; enhancing decisions about en-ergy technology; and improving future-scenario visualization techniques as a tool for science and technology governance. In 2008, Sarewitz returned to Washington to open a CSPO office responsible for diffusion of its ideas and tools to the policy world and for building a community of like-minded, outcomes-oriented science and technology policy practitioners and scholars inside the Beltway. As part of its efforts to improve societal capacity to understand and manage its ever-growing scientific and technological power, CSPO also developed a novel and comprehensive approach to making its ideas accessible to multiple audiences, through programs aimed at narrative writing, direct collaboration with museums and science centers, and involvement of high schools and citizens groups in structured deliberations about complex scientific dilemmas. Most recently CSPO has moved aggressively into the editorial and production end of conventional and online publishing, including entering into a partnership with the National Academy of Sciences to publish the magazine *Issues in Science and Technology*; launching a new electronic books series, *The Rightful Place of Science*; and developing a new scholarly print journal, the *Journal of Responsible Innovation*. The goal here is to reach diverse audiences—from scholars to policy makers to the interested public—for high-risk, innovative ideas, clearly and engagingly communicated, that are emerging from a growing international community of scholars and practitioners working at the interfaces of science, policy, and outcomes.

Equally significant are CSPO's continued efforts to promote a university-wide focus on science, policy, and outcomes. The ideal would be for the CSPO approach to be used across science and technology endeavors so the pursuit of new scientific knowledge and innovation is always in the everyday course of academic life integrated with research and deliberation on their social contexts. This integration would become seamless in planning and conduct, in the development and delivery of curriculum, and in the way that ideas are explained and discussed outside of the academic context. But communication across administrative domains remains challenging, reinforced by relict disciplinary norms of intellectual merit and peer approval. Although these obstacles have proven to be surmountable through the crucial process of building social relations across intellectual domains, the traditional funders of scientific research remain unprepared to provide the resources necessary for this broader, integrative model of science. Yet, recent CSPO events in

Washington, D.C., on responsible innovation and outcomes-oriented science management have drawn considerable audiences, mostly from government science agencies. So perhaps what was once unmentionable in science policy discussions is gradually becoming the ruling paradigm.

## Managing Change during a Period of Historic Public Disinvestment

As the nation negotiated its recovery from the near meltdown of global economic markets that precipitated the Great Recession, most institutions of higher education engaged in some form of damage control and reassessment. Confronted by fallout from the repercussions of the fiscal crisis, many colleges and universities retrenched as if under siege, while others focused on restoring equilibrium. Still others determined to seize the moment as an opportunity to restructure their academic organization or administrative mechanisms, generally with the intent of becoming more efficient. Much of the discussion surrounding the implications of the downturn for the academy were couched in terms of a desire to attain some degree of new normalcy in higher education. For ASU, the period was particularly challenging. We recur to the evidence of the report from the Center on Budget and Policy Priorities that shows that between fiscal years 2008 and 2013, Arizona led the nation in its disinvestment in higher education: "Eleven states have cut funding by more than one-third per student, and two states—Arizona and New Hampshire—have cut their higher education spending per student in half."[65] State disinvestment in ASU during the Great Recession represented the largest sum both in absolute dollars and as a percentage of general funds from legislative appropriations for any public university in the nation, and to our knowledge in the history of American higher education (figure 16). The economic stresses occurred within the context of continuing record enrollment demand, with ASU absorbing roughly 85 percent of enrollment growth in the Arizona University System.

It is difficult for the general public to envision the scope, scale of operation, and complexity of the contemporary research university, with its multiple objectives, including undergraduate, graduate, and professional education; basic and applied research; and leadership role in community service and regional economic development. It is similarly difficult to ap-

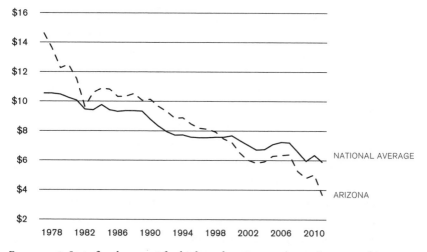

FIGURE 16. State fiscal support for higher education per $1,000 in personal income, FY 1978–2012. Source: Postsecondary Education Opportunity.

preciate the costs associated with fulfilling the educational aspirations of more than 76,000 students enrolled in undergraduate, graduate, and professional programs; the construction costs of research infrastructure; and the operating expenses associated with libraries, laboratories, and athletic facilities. In such an environment, rigorous budgetary efficiency is an imperative, and ASU has sought to operate both more efficiently and more effectively than peer institutions. The comprehensive institutional reconceptualization undertaken during a period of unprecedented reductions in state investment demonstrates both the adaptiveness and resilience of the New American University model.

During the Great Recession, ASU acknowledged and responded to the challenging financial situation of the state of Arizona, while continuing to advance the implementation of its strategic goals. ASU restructured and cut costs, which in combination with accelerated growth in tuition and research revenue provided a base for continued expansion in its research enterprise and enrollment growth. Moreover, ASU has consistently pursued strategies to increase revenue source diversification and to decrease reliance on state appropriations. Continued progress during a period of historic disinvestment in public higher education is a consequence of a set of measures calibrated to introduce economy, efficiency, productivity, and performance that surpasses the efforts of institutional peers even as ASU delivers on its promise to provide all qualified Arizona students with unrivaled educations without financial barriers.

Through strategic organizational streamlining designed to cut costs while preserving the quality of the academic core, ASU has become one of the nation's most efficient producers of both college graduates and cutting-edge research, which contributes hundreds of millions of dollars annually to the Arizona economy. Although peer institutions are typically funded by state appropriations and tuition at levels exceeding $20,000 per FTE student, and the FY 2012 median level of all sixty-eight public universities with a research-extensive (RU/VH) categorization was $18,816, state support per FTE student at ASU has declined from $7,976 in FY 2008 to $4,134 in FY 2012, bringing the level of funding from tuition, fees, and state appropriations to $16,082, which is 15 percent below that of the peer group. Perhaps a better measurement of cost effectiveness is to examine the resources available and the outcomes produced. In FY 2012, tuition, fees, and state appropriations per degree/certificate produced at ASU was $55,604, which placed it 24 percent below the median of $68,168 among the sixty-eight public research-extensive institutions in the peer group.[66] ASU has focused on cost control, application of technology in educational design and delivery, innovation in advising and course scheduling to speed time to degree, and aggressive improvements in retention and graduation rates to drive down the resources needed per degree produced. Cost effectiveness is a key metric for ASU. Whether the indicator is total spending per degree produced or the output of its research enterprise, the advancement of the university is demonstrable when measured against all other public research universities (figure 17).

## Further Perspective on the Scale of Operation

As evidence that large-scale enrollment need not be incompatible with academic excellence, we cited the example of the University of Toronto. The largest major research university in Canada and a public member institution of the Association of American Universities (AAU), the University of Toronto enrolls 67,128 undergraduates and 15,884 graduate students at three campuses and reports research expenditures exceeding $1.2 billion annually. Among the most acclaimed of Canadian universities, the institution ranks twenty-eighth globally in the Academic Ranking of World Universities, and twentieth globally according to the *Times*

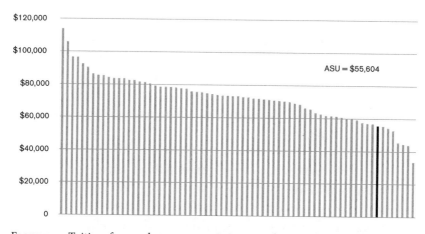

FIGURE 17. Tuition, fees, and state appropriations per degree awarded comparing all public research-extensive (RU/VH) institutions, FY 2012. Source: IPEDS data.

*Higher Education* World University Report. We reiterate the contention that size is the function of the breadth of an institution. In a recent assessment of the significance of institutional scale in this context, Goldie Blumenstyk, senior writer for the *Chronicle of Higher Education*, considers its relevance for the reconceptualization of ASU:

> By itself, Arizona State University's transformation over the past decade into the nation's biggest public university wouldn't be all that significant. Yet, by the measures on which it prides itself—its 9-percentage-point increase in freshman-to-sophomore retention rates, its 48 percent increase in bachelor's graduates in STEM fields, its tripling of spending on research, its top-5 rank as a producer of Fulbright students, its above-average increase in the proportion of Pell Grant recipients enrolled, and even its increasing efficiency in spending per degree awarded—it's clear that the size of this university has been key. ASU's size helped make those achievements possible, and it makes them all the more significant.[67]

In subsequent paragraphs, Blumenstyk provides a further synopsis of the various dimensions of the transformation and hints at the tenor of its reception by academic filiopietists:

> The grand (or, as some deride it, grandiose) experiment that ASU calls its New American University model, set here amid the sprawl of one of the

nation's fastest-growing metro areas, aims to be one answer to that challenge: a capacious institution with what Mr. Crow calls "the research intensity of the best of them," an unusual academic structure with "fused intellectual disciplines" meant to reflect the way knowledge is developed and applied today, and a culture deliberately focused on admitting and graduating a student body that is ethnically and economically representative of the community.[68]

Large-scale universities—we might term them "super-publics"—can offer a comprehensive spectrum of degree programs as well as micro-learning environments that match the broadest ambitions of the students they serve. Their size also allows them to provide hundreds of distinctive learning environments dedicated to diverse disciplines and subfields ranging from nanoscience to classical piano to supply chain management. Varied opportunities support the development of students in special and invaluable ways, not to speak of the matchless excitement for undergraduates studying under the direction of scholars, scientists, professionals, and artists working at the frontiers of knowledge. Although "big" has undeniably produced countless schools lacking rigorous academic standards, ASU and its peer institutions are driven by the objectives of discovery and knowledge production and the education of world-class graduates. Graduates from major public research universities reflect the broadest cross section of national talent and as a group are powerful drivers for economic competitiveness and progress on all fronts. In 2012–2013, ASU was the top producer of degrees among public research universities, awarding 18,916 undergraduate, graduate, and professional degrees, ahead of the University of Florida and Ohio State University, which awarded 14,977 and 13,721 degrees, respectively. Other major public research universities each of which produced at least ten thousand graduates include the University of Texas at Austin, Penn State, University of Michigan, University of Minnesota, Texas A&M, University of Washington, University of Illinois, UCLA, and UC Berkeley. Moreover, when one considers the aggregate number of students enrolled in some systems of higher education—the ten campuses of the University of California, for example, boast more than 234,000 students—enrollment numbers for ASU appear in perspective.

Because ASU offers broad accessibility to qualified students from Arizona families at scale, the opportunity to attend a world-class research university is available to socioeconomically disadvantaged but academically gifted students. Such accessibility resolves the issue of "undermatching" that we introduced in chapter 1. Recent studies have shown that socioeconomically disadvantaged but academically gifted high school seniors are disproportionately "undermatched" in their choices of universities and colleges. As William Bowen and colleagues frame the problem, "Surprisingly large numbers of high school seniors who were presumptively qualified to attend strong four-year colleges but did not do so, instead attending less selective four-year colleges, two-year colleges, or no college at all." The researchers blame some combination of inertia or lack of information, planning, and encouragement and contend that had these students attended more selective institutions, they would more likely graduate in normative time and benefit from superior institutional resources.[69]

The recent analysis by economists Caroline Hoxby and Christopher Avery has brought the ostensible problem of undermatching to national attention: "We show that a large number—probably the vast majority—of very high-achieving students from low-income families do not apply to a selective college or university." Hoxby and Avery argue that the failure to attend one of the 236 colleges and universities identified in the top categories of Barron's Profiles of American Colleges ("Very Competitive Plus," "Highly Competitive," "Highly Competitive Plus," and "Most Competitive") represents lack of success for these low-income high achievers. While roughly 4 percent of American high school students are high achievers, Hoxby and Avery are concerned with a smaller subset: high achievers from families with incomes in the bottom two quartiles. "We estimate that there are at least 25,000 and probably something like 35,000 low-income high achievers in the U.S."[70] With 3 million high school graduates annually, this represents roughly 1 percent of high school graduates.[71]

Research on undermatching relies solely on test scores, but we contend that other factors explain much of the undermatching trend, including self-selection based on subjective personal considerations that cannot be readily measured. Increased familial obligations and a higher relative burden of travel, for example, may make more distant schools less attractive options to lower-income students. Predictably, the regression developed by Hoxby and Avery shows that geographic proximity is the strongest predictor of a low-income student applying to a specific college. The tendency for low-income students to apply to local schools necessarily removes many highly selective schools from the set of possible institutions. Additional self-selection effects may have bearing as well. The predilection of admissions officers for "well-rounded" candidates with volunteer experience and leadership in extracurricular activities, for example, is common knowledge. As a consequence, many socioeconomically disadvantaged students may not apply to selective schools simply because they realize that they are not competitive relative to students who have the financial resources and social capital to accrue a distinguished portfolio of extracurricular experiences. The undermatching trend identified by Hoxby and Avery is surely the result of many factors, and any single explanation would be insufficient. Because of subjective considerations, many lower-income students may simply elect to self-select themselves out of the applicant pools of highly selective institutions.[72]

On a broader level, the research on undermatching highlights the long-held and unfortunate notion that American higher education is better served by greater access to highly selective institutions. The authors clearly confirm this assumption by considering only a small fraction of high school graduates who choose not to apply to a small subset of colleges and universities. We contend that the public debate needs to be reframed: meaningful progress on advancing accessibility to higher education will require focus on the other 96 percent of high school students and the thousands of colleges and universities deemed less "competitive" and thus overlooked in Hoxby and Avery's analysis. Research should consider the implications of the enrollment of all students in both high- and low-performing schools, rather than simply focusing on the allocation of students between "elite" and less competitive schools.

Among public and private universities across the nation, the median SAT/ACT scores of incoming freshmen are used to predict undergraduate graduation rates. At the same time, however, there is variation: some schools have higher or lower graduation rates than expected, given their standardized test score profiles. Similarly, schools under- and over-

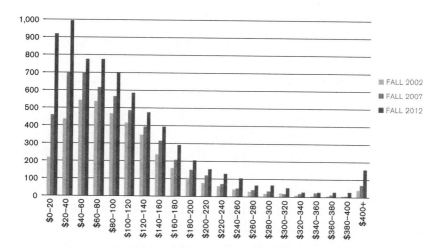

FIGURE 18. Arizona State University first-time, full-time freshman enrollment by annual family income, fall 2002, 2007, and 2012. All figures in 2012 dollars.

perform in a variety of ways with respect to other input measures. The imperative for methods to measure the "adjusted performances" of institutions and to operationalize the information through the administration of Title IV aid programs is obvious. The observation that low-income students tend to seek out local institutions only emphasizes the need for federal policy to support and advance diverse college and university models that are geographically, financially, culturally, and intellectually accessible to diverse student groups.

To the extent that undermatching does occur, Arizona State University's performance over the past decade demonstrates that institutions not deemed "elite" in conventional assessments can provide accessibility as well as quality educational outcomes for low-income students. ASU has taken an "all the above" strategy to addressing income inequality in higher education by pairing increased financial aid programs with technological solutions, such as the innovative degree-tracking system eAdvisor, and sociocultural interventions, such as the President Barack Obama Scholars Program. The result of these efforts has been a dramatic increase in accessibility for lower-income students: from fall 2002 through fall 2012, ASU more than tripled the enrollment of traditional resident freshmen students coming from families with incomes less than $40,000 per year in 2012 dollars (figure 18).

As ASU has dramatically expanded accessibility to low-income students, it has also increased its ability to keep students enrolled and making progress toward a degree. The retention rate for first-time, full-time freshmen has steadily increased. The *Wall Street Journal* poll of corporate recruiters in September 2010, which ranked ASU fifth in the nation for producing the best-qualified graduates, provides further evidence. The New American University model now operational demonstrates that universities can combine broad accessibility with world-class academic excellence. Clearly, notions that non-"elite" schools are not able to enroll and provide high-quality educational experiences and outcomes to low-income students are false, and the model helps to resolve the ostensible crisis of undermatching. We contend that the recent focus on the issue only serves to deflect attention from more productive discussions of higher-education reform.

## Replicating the Model of a New American University

When the Thirteenth Territorial Legislature established a normal school in Tempe in 1885, Arizona Territory epitomized the frontier in our national consciousness. More than a quarter century would pass before Arizona became the last of the forty-eight continental states to join the union. When President Theodore Roosevelt spoke from the steps of the normal school in March 1911, a few days after the dedication of the dam on the Salt River that would bear his name, he predicted that with adequate irrigation the population of the Valley of the Sun could someday soar to 75,000—or maybe even 100,000. At the time Phoenix boasted little more than 10,000 citizens, and no one could have foreseen the demographic trends that within a century would lead to the transformation of a region dominated by ranching and mining into one of the fastest-growing megapolitan agglomerations in the nation. Similarly, no one could have foreseen the evolution of a territorial normal school into one of the nation's largest public universities and a major research institution operating at the frontiers of knowledge.

The predication of a New American University model comes with the caveat that institutions seeking reconceptualization must not succumb to a new form of isomorphism in attempting to embrace the foundational prototype. Although it is possible to extrapolate and generalize from this particular account of institutional innovation, we must emphasize that individually none of the basic tenets or design strategies delineated is especially remarkable. What is essential in other institutional contexts is the sustained deployment of design strategies uniquely correlated to address the objectives of respective institutions. It would be counterproductive to profess the prescription of a set of design strategies applicable in all contexts because no such algorithm or protocol exists. Rather, through an examination of one particular reconceptualization, our intent has been to call attention to the potential for institutional innovation— or even massive change—in colleges and universities throughout the nation and even abroad. But any such reconceptualization must proceed according to its own intrinsic logic.

The public research university is a highly successful model, but this does not diminish the imperative for new and differentiated models that more squarely address the needs of the nation in the twenty-first century. The success of Arizona State University in bringing world-class academic excellence to a broad demographic representative of the socioeconomic diversity of the region should in itself be sufficient to initiate public dialogue regarding the need for a new charter for American public universities. But a pioneering effort by a coalition of large public research universities represents the potential inherent in collective effort to promote institutional innovation in the interest of desired societal outcomes. The formation of the University Innovation Alliance is a collaboration between eleven major research universities that collectively enroll nearly half a million students undertaken to increase educational attainment among low-income students. Apart from ASU, member institutions include Georgia State University, Michigan State University, Ohio State University, Oregon State University, Purdue University, and the University of Texas, Austin. According to the vision and prospectus working paper: "Our vision is that by piloting new interventions, sharing insights about their relative costs and effectiveness, and scaling those interventions that are successful, we will significantly increase the number of low-income Americans graduating with quality college degrees and that, over time, our collaborative work will catalyze systemic changes in the entire higher education sector."[73]

## Notes

1. Michael M. Crow articulated the vision for a New American University when he became the sixteenth president of Arizona State University in July 2002. For a prior discussion of the model, see, for example, Michael M. Crow, "The Research University as Comprehensive Knowledge Enterprise: A Prototype for the New American University," in *University Research for Innovation*, ed. Luc Weber and James J. Duderstadt (London: Economica, 2010), 211–225. We reiterate that complexity and adaptivity in knowledge enterprises refers to the evolution of "fitness" in both individuals and institutions to respond to the scale and complexity of emergent challenges. Maximization of the capacity to adapt is a core outcome of education. Adaptation refers also to institutional evolution, which is the aggregate product of interactions between "fit" agents. See John Holland, "Complex Adaptive Systems," *Daedalus* 121, no. 1 (1992): 17–30.

2. Requirements for assured admission for Arizona residents conform to Arizona Board of Regents (ABOR) policy 2-121, which specifies criteria for general aptitude and competence. General aptitude requires graduation from a regionally accredited high school in the upper quartile of the graduating class. Competence is evaluated through the completion of appropriate course work with a 3.0 grade point average in the following areas: English (four years), math (four years), laboratory science (three years), social science (two years), foreign language (two years), and fine arts (one year). In some cases, admission may be granted despite deficiencies, except in both math and laboratory science. However, consistent with ABOR policy, the university may exercise discretion in admissions for applicants who do not meet these requirements. Admissions criteria vary for transfer students, nonresidents, and international students. ABOR academic policy 2-121B creates two additional categories of admission: delegated and special. Delegated admission may be used for students earning at least a 2.5 GPA who demonstrate completion of a minimum of fourteen of the sixteen core competencies, while special admission allows universities to admit students not meeting either assured or delegated requirements up to a maximum of 10 percent of incoming classes. https://students.asu.edu/freshman/requirements

3. We recur to the observation of William Bowen and colleagues: "More selective universities, by definition, enroll students with stronger entering credentials who are more likely to graduate regardless of where they go to college." William G. Bowen, Matthew M. Chingos, and Michael S. McPherson, *Crossing the Finish Line: Completing College at America's Public Universities* (Princeton, NJ: Princeton University Press, 2009), 192.

4. "One University in Many Places: Transitional Design to Twenty-First-Century Excellence" (Tempe: Arizona State University, 2004). Throughout this chapter, some of the exposition of the argument and rationale behind the reconceptualization and design process parallels or extrapolates from this and other institutional white papers, which in some instances are not cited.

5. The interrelated formulation "academic excellence, inclusiveness to a broad demographic, and maximum societal impact" subsequently inspired the tagline "Excellence, Access, Impact."

6. Frank H. T. Rhodes, *The Creation of the Future: The Role of the American University* (Ithaca, NY: Cornell University Press, 2001), 234–242.

7. José Ortega y Gasset, *The Mission of the University*, ed. and trans. Howard Lee Nostrand (1944; New Brunswick: Transaction, 1992), 17–18, 20, 23.

8. Ortega y Gasset, *Mission of the University*, 32–33, 36.

9. Paul J. DiMaggio and Walter W. Powell, "The Iron Cage Revisited: Institutional Isomorphism and Collective Rationality in Organizational Fields," *American Sociological Review* 48, no. 2 (1983): 147–160.

10. For an overview of academic federation, see Sheldon Rothblatt, "Historical and Comparative Remarks on the Federal Principle in Higher Education," *History of Education* 16, no. 3 (1987): 151–180. For a sense of the challenges associated with continued federation, see Malcolm Grant, "The Future of the University of London: A Discussion Paper from the Provost of University College London" (March 2005).

11. Elizabeth Capaldi, "Intellectual Transformation and Budgetary Savings through Academic Reorganization," *Change* (July/August 2009): 19–27.

12. *Oxford English Dictionary*, 2nd ed. (Oxford: Oxford University Press, 1989), online version June 2013.

13. *Oxford English Dictionary*, 3rd ed. (Oxford: Oxford University Press, 2003), online version December 2013. The dictionary informs us that the term derives from the name of an outdoor still in the comic strip *L'il Abner*, where moonshine was produced from "old shoes and dead skunk."

14. John Lombardi, *How Universities Work* (Baltimore: Johns Hopkins University Press, 2013), 31.

15. National Center for Childhood Poverty, http://nccp.org/profiles/AZ_profile_6 .html (January 2014). "Low-income" is defined as 200 percent of the federal poverty level.

16. College Participation Rates for Students from Low-Income Families by State, FY 1993 to FY 2012, available at www.postsecondary.org.

17. A report from the Arizona Board of Regents estimates that 53 percent of Arizona high school graduates are not qualified to enroll in one of the state's three public universities: "Arizona High School Eligibility Study" (2009).

18. Arthur C. Nelson and Robert E. Lang, *Megapolitan America: A New Vision for Understanding America's Metropolitan Geography* (Chicago: American Planning Association, 2011), 143–153.

19. "One University in Many Places," 2–9.

20. Roger L. Geiger, *To Advance Knowledge: The Growth of American Research Universities, 1900–1940* (Oxford: Oxford University Press, 1986), 2–3.

21. Claudia Goldin and Lawrence F. Katz, *The Race between Education and Technology* (Cambridge: Belknap Press of Harvard University Press, 2008), 11–43.

22. John Aubrey Douglass, *The Conditions for Admission: Access, Equity, and the Social Contract of Public Universities* (Stanford: Stanford University Press, 2007), 42, 80. To reiterate, in the late 1950s, the subject area requirement for resident freshman applicants from accredited high schools specified a B average in the last three years in an array of ten high school academic subjects. The implementation of the Master Plan in 1960

reduced the percentage of eligible students from its historical figure of approximately 15 percent to the top 12.5 percent of California high school graduates.

23. Douglass, *Conditions for Admission*, 127.

24. University of California Office of the President, "Application, Admissions, and Enrollment of California Resident Freshmen for Fall 1989 through 2013."

25. James G. March and Herbert A. Simon, *Organizations*, 2d ed. (Cambridge, MA: Blackwell, 1993), 14.

26. For perspective on the projected attainment of $700 million in research expenditures, see the subsequent discussion of the research enterprise. During FY 2012, only two institutions without medical schools reported total research expenditures exceeding $700 million: MIT ($824.1 million) and University of California, Berkeley ($730.3 million). Twenty institutions with medical schools reported research expenditures surpassing $700 million. NSF HERD Survey FY 2012.

27. We reiterate that by contrast the number of bachelor's degrees awarded by the eight institutions of the Ivy League during academic year 2012–2013 totaled 15,541, while the top fifty liberal arts colleges awarded 23,672. Data is the most recent available from IPEDS (Integrated Postsecondary Education Data System). Assessment of top fifty liberal arts colleges derived from the 2015 *U.S. News & World Report* ranking excluding military academies. Analysis for University Innovation Alliance by Archer Analytics LLC.

28. Roughly 66 percent of freshmen in this cohort reported class rank. Of these, 1,865 graduated in the top 10 percent of their class—more students than Harvard's entire freshman class of 1,659.

29. All figures for enrollment trends, degree production, and student characteristics have been provided by Melinda Gebel and her staff in the Office of Institutional Analysis. We wish to express our appreciation to Kyle Whitman and George Raudenbush for data and policy analysis. For assistance with research, we thank Robert M. Brecht, Levi J. Wolf, and Daniel Ober-Reynolds.

30. *Reader's Digest*, "Best Honors College: Barrett Honors College" (May 2005): "A selective small undergraduate college responsible for recruiting academically outstanding undergraduates to ASU and organizing the resources of that major research university for their benefit."

31. The twenty top-producing institutions in the Fulbright U.S. Student Program, 2013–2014: Harvard University; University of Michigan, Ann Arbor; Arizona State University; Princeton University; Rutgers; Northwestern University; University of Texas, Austin; Columbia University; Yale University; Cornell University; University of Chicago; Boston College; University of California, Berkeley; Duke University; Ohio State University; Stanford University; University of Pennsylvania; University of Maryland, College Park; University of Rochester; College of William and Mary. http://us.fulbright online.org/top-producing-institutions

32. According to 2012 data from the National Center for Education Statistics published in the journal *Diverse: Issues in Higher Education*, ASU ranks highly in minority graduates in architecture, business, computer and information sciences, education, engineering, law, mathematics, psychology, and public administration.

33. Respective cohorts comprise fall census enrolled first-time, full-time resident dependent freshmen with a valid FAFSA on file.

34. Lombardi, *How Universities Work*, 55, 116.

35. Between fall 2001 and fall 2013, tenured and tenure-track faculty increased from 1,657 to 1,827, or 10.3 percent. ASU Office of Institutional Analysis.

36. ASU Office of Knowledge Enterprise Development analysis of 2012 National Science Foundation data.

37. Donna Fossum et al., "Vital Assets: Federal Investment in Research and Development at the Nation's Universities and Colleges" (Santa Monica, CA: RAND, 2004), 12. The RAND study showed that 45 percent of all federal R&D funds went directly to medical schools in FY 2002.

38. NSF 2012 HERD Survey. The most recent available data is from FY 2012.

39. NSF 2012 HERD Survey.

40. National Academy of Inventors and International Property Owners Association, based on data from the U.S. Patent and Trademark Office (PTO). The report ranked ASU 48th worldwide but undercounts the number of patents issued to ASU inventors in 2012 due to language variation in assignments of patents.

41. Shanghai Rankings Consultancy, "Academic Ranking of World Universities" (2013). The criteria and weight assigned to each indicator in the Shanghai methodology are as follows: quality of education, assessing the scientific and scholarly contributions of alumni (10 percent); quality of faculty, assessing the scientific and scholarly contributions of faculty (20 percent); highly cited researchers in twenty-one broad subject categories (20 percent); research output, measured by the number of articles published in leading journals such as *Nature* and *Science* (20 percent); research output, measured by articles in Science Citation Index Expanded and Social Science Citation Index (20 percent); size of institution, assessing academic performance with respect to the size of an institution (10 percent).

42. The Leiden methodology is based on publications that appeared in the Thomson Reuter Web of Science database between 2008 and 2011. http://www.leidenranking.com/ranking.aspx

43. The National Research Council "Data-Based Assessment for Research-Doctorate Programs in the United States (2010)" identified the characteristics that best represent doctoral graduate quality across universities and PhD programs nationally. ASU submitted data for twenty-six PhD programs in broad fields defined by NRC (life sciences, physical sciences, mathematics, engineering, social and behavioral sciences, arts and humanities). The majority of data were statistically calculated to reflect two rankings. S-rankings (performance) were based on twenty direct measures of doctoral program quality: (1) faculty research/scholarship (e.g., publications, citations, grants, honors/awards); (2) PhD student outcomes (e.g., completion rates, time to degree, percent students with full funding); and (3) diversity (percent minority faculty/students, percent international). R-rankings (reputation) were based on reputational ratings provided by a select number of faculty members within disciplines across the country. Ranked sets of universities on doctoral program quality were based on the twenty variables.

44. We refer the reader once again to the explication of the fallacies associated with such methodologies in the letter from Gerhard Casper, then president of Stanford University, to James Fallows, then editor of *U.S. News and World Report* (September 23, 1996). http://www.stanford.edu/dept/pres-provost/president/speeches/961206gcfallow.html

45. Teri Evans, "Penn State Tops Recruiter Rankings," *Wall Street Journal* (September 10, 2010).

46. See, for example, Eyal Press and Jennifer Washburn, "The Kept University," *Atlantic Monthly* 285, no. 3 (March 2000): 39–54. More balanced discussion is to be found in Sheila Slaughter and Larry L. Leslie, *Academic Capitalism: Politics, Policies, and the Entrepreneurial University* (Baltimore: Johns Hopkins University Press, 1997); and Sheila Slaughter and Gary Rhoades, *Academic Capitalism and the New Economy: Markets, State, and Higher Education* (Baltimore: Johns Hopkins University Press, 2004).

47. Henry Etzkowitz, *The Triple Helix: University-Industry-Government Innovation in Action* (New York: Routledge, 2008); Gary P. Pisano and W. C. Shih, "Restoring American Competitiveness," *Harvard Business Review* 87, no. 7–8 (July–August 2009): 114–125. See also Luc E. Weber and James Duderstadt, eds., *Universities and Business: Partnering for the Knowledge Society* (London: Economica, 2006); Roger L. Geiger, *Knowledge and Money: Research Universities and the Paradox of the Marketplace* (Stanford: Stanford University Press, 2004).

48. Lombardi, *How Universities Work,* 69: "Universities use special words to describe money questions," Lombardi elaborates. "They talk about 'resources' or 'program support' when what they actually mean is 'money.'"

49. Gary Rhoades, "Calling on the Past: The Quest for the Collegiate Ideal," *Journal of Higher Education* 61, no. 5 (September–October 1990): 512, 517. Rhoades quotes from the report "Involvement in Learning: Realizing the Potential of American Higher Education" (Washington, DC: National Institute of Education, 1984).

50. Erik Brynjolfsson and Andrew McAfee, *The Second Machine Age: Work, Progress, and Prosperity in a Time of Brilliant Technologies* (New York: W. W. Norton, 2014), 7, 91.

51. Nicholas Carr, "The Crisis in Higher Education," *MIT Technology Review* 116, no. 6 (September 27, 2012).

52. Nicole Howard, *The Book: The Life Story of a Technology* (Baltimore: Johns Hopkins University Press, 2009).

53. Steve Kolowich, "Arizona State and Knewton's Grand Experiment with Adaptive Learning," *Inside Higher Ed* (January 25, 2013).

54. Elizabeth D. Phillips, "Improving Advising Using Technology and Data Analytics," *Change: The Magazine of Higher Learning* (January–February 2013).

55. Richard Pérez-Peña, "Starbucks to Provide Free College Education to Thousands of Workers," *New York Times* (June 15, 2014); Joe Nocera, "A New College Model," *New York Times* (June 16, 2014).

56. The formulation of the concept of "grand challenge" is various. See, for example, National Academy of Engineering, *Grand Challenges for Engineering* (Washington, DC: National Academy of Sciences, 2008). Those specified include solar energy, renewable energy, carbon sequestration, clean water, urban infrastructure, health informatics,

cybersecurity, and personalized learning. University College London has organized its research enterprise according to grand challenge themes, which initially were those of global health, sustainable cities, intercultural interaction, and human well-being, but they have since undergone considerable elaboration. See the report from the vice provost for research.

57. Arizona State University School of Life Sciences, Strategic Plan (April 15, 2010): 1–4. http://www.sols.asu.edu/publications/pdf/strategic_plan_april_2010.pdf

58. Ronald Greeley et al., Academic Program Review for the School of Earth and Space Exploration (SESE), Arizona State University (November, 2010): 1–7.

59. Greeley et al., 3–4.

60. Arizona State University School of Human Evolution and Social Change, Seven-Year Program Review (2005–2011). http://shesc.asu.edu/; http://casi.asu.edu/

61. Michael M. Crow, "Organizing Teaching and Research to Address the Grand Challenges of Sustainable Development," *Bioscience* 60, no. 7 (August 2010): 488–489.

62. Daniel Sarewitz, *Frontiers of Illusion: Science, Technology, and the Politics of Progress* (Philadelphia: Temple University Press, 1996), ix.

63. David Guston, Daniel Sarewitz, and Lori Hidinger, "Consortium for Science, Policy, and Outcomes at Arizona State University," Arizona Board of Regents Program Review (October 2009), 3

64. See the collection of essays that explore issues and themes discussed at the conference, *Living with the Genie: Essays on Technology and the Quest for Human Mastery*, ed. Alan Lightman, Daniel Sarewitz, and Christina Desser (Washington DC: Island Press, 2003).

65. Phillip Oliff et al., "Recent Deep State Higher Education Cuts May Harm Students and the Economy for Years to Come" (Washington, DC: Center on Budget and Policy Priorities, March 2013).

66. Analysis of IPEDS data by the Office of the University Planner.

67. Goldie Blumenstyk, "Change Takes Root in the Desert: Embracing Inclusiveness, Arizona State University Pursues Transformation on a Grand Scale," *Chronicle of Higher Education* (November 19, 2012).

68. Blumenstyk, "Change Takes Root in the Desert."

69. Bowen, Chingos, and McPherson, *Crossing the Finish Line*, 88, 104, 109–110.

70. Caroline M. Hoxby and Christopher Avery, "The Missing 'One-Offs': The Hidden Supply of High-Achieving, Low-Income Students," NBER Working Paper 18586 (Cambridge, MA: National Bureau of Economic Research, 2012), 11.

71. IPEDS gives the figure of 3.039 million high school graduates in 2008–2009. Thomas D. Snyder and Sally A. Dillow, Digest of Education Statistics 2011 (NCES 2012-001) (Washington, DC: National Center for Education Statistics, U.S. Department of Education, 2012), 70, table 35.

72. We wish to express our appreciation to Kyle Whitman for his analysis of the implications of undermatching in this chapter.

73. University Innovation Alliance, "University Innovation Alliance: Vision and Prospectus" (2014).

CONCLUSION

# Toward More
# New American Universities

For our nation to achieve the ambitious objectives for educational attainment specified by President Obama in his first address to a joint session of Congress in February 2009—the president envisioned an America that by the end of the present decade would once again boast the highest proportion of college graduates in the world[1]—we must begin in earnest to educate to competitive levels of achievement not only the top 5 percent but also the most capable 25 percent of academically qualified students representative of the socioeconomic and intellectual diversity of our society, and to build a higher education infrastructure commensurate to the task. But the admissions policies of our leading institutions favor a mere fraction of qualified applicants, and the demographic trends shaping our nation militate against the success of students from the middle classes and especially those from socioeconomically disadvantaged and historically underrepresented backgrounds, whose prospects for advanced educational attainment and economic prosperity remain bleak. Despite the projected shortfall in highly educated citizens that threatens our nation's prosperity and economic competitiveness, our leading colleges and major research universities, both public and private, choose not to embrace more expansive admissions policies to draw students from the broader talent pool of socioeconomic and intellectual diversity. The disequilibrium between burgeoning enrollment demand and the limited number of available seats at our leading research institutions is generally exacerbated by public disinvestment in higher education—without sufficient resources, our schools cannot hope to produce the graduation rates called for by the president. But we must not attribute shortfalls in accessibility solely to insufficient resources. What in some cases may be lacking is the inspiration or impetus within academic communities to advance innovation in the structures and practices of our colleges and universities. As we have argued, what is required is a new model for the American research university that offers accessibility to academic platforms of world-class knowledge production to a broad demographic range of students, socioeconomically as well as intellectually. This is a pivotal moment to develop new and scalable models for research-grade institutions committed to accessibility to complement the existing set of major research universities.

Relative to the scale of our nation, the entire complement of institutions with highly selective admissions standards, both public and private, operates on a limited bandwidth of engagement. Unable to accommodate burgeoning enrollment demand at scale, many of these institutions appear content to maintain the status quo and predicate their identities on the exclusion of the majority of applicants. And although our leading universities, both public and private, retain their dominance in global rankings, our success in maintaining excellence in a relative handful of elite institutions does little to ensure our continued national competitiveness, especially if we stop to consider the disproportionately slender margin of students fortunate enough to be admitted to these top schools. To this extent, as we have contended, American higher education is dominated by a model in which status is attained through the maintenance of scarcity, and academic elitism has become a defensive posture and abdication of implicit responsibility. The issue of broad accessibility to research-grade academic platforms is far more urgent than most realize, even those on the national stage charged with advancing higher education policy. Our national discussion on higher education must not be limited merely to arbitrary goals for the production of more college graduates. Mere access for greater numbers to rudimentary forms of instruction will in itself be insufficient to ensure desired societal outcomes and national economic competitiveness. Policy deliberations should accord priority to the imperative for broader accessibility to research grade academic platforms in response to projections that forecast the imminent shortfall of college-educated individuals with advanced skills commensurate with the demands of the knowledge economy.[2]

Higher education in the United States is decentralized and largely the responsibility of states,[3] a consequence of the defeat of proposals to establish a national university that began with the Constitutional Convention. But in a sense our leading public research universities collectively comprise a de facto national university. It is these institutions that educate the majority of our students in a milieu that advances knowledge production while contributing to the development of a highly skilled workforce. With elite universities content to maintain modest levels of enrollment, the broad accessibility to quality higher education that could once be taken for granted is no longer available to the majority of academically qualified applicants. Although some may argue on behalf of this sort of meritocracy, we reiterate that the extent of this exclusion frequently deprives individuals from achieving their potential and generally impoverishes our society. Restoring sufficient levels of public investment in higher education and finding ways to increase the enrollment capacities of our great public universities are challenges that policy makers and citizens alike must address. As John Aubrey Douglass argues, "Broad and equitable access to a quality education, and the role of government to make that happen, is an integral part of our nation's political culture."[4]

The perception that the contemporary research university is imperiled and scientific and humanistic investigation threatened must be qualified. The demand for advanced teaching and research and for the production of new ideas, products, and processes that are its outputs is at fever pitch and exceeds the currently available supply. The foremost challenge is to increase the capacity of research universities by an order of magnitude. Appropriate historical models from which to derive a course of action commensurate to the challenges that confront us do not exist. Inherent design limitations in our universities hamper rapid change in response to real-time demand, impeding our potential to develop appropriate organizational structures and transdisciplinary curricula. Entrenched assumptions and rigid social constructs hinder adaptability. To accelerate the evolution of our universities, we must develop new models focused not merely on discovery but also accessibility to a broad demographic, both socioeconomically and intellectually. The imperative to implement new and differentiated institutional models is fully consistent with the most fundamental values of the academy. While the success of American higher education may be attributable to competition at all levels, cooperation and collaboration among institutions will be required if we are to move beyond current patterns that exclude a majority of academically qualified students.

We have remarked that the routine, standardization, and inertia of bureaucracies are inimical to discovery, creativity, and innovation. We have observed that conformity to rules does not produce great art. And that there is no efficient way to discover the origins of the universe. The purposes of the research university, which distinguish this category of institution from those concerned primarily with the dissemination of existing knowledge, must be self-determined but need not be narrowly circumscribed. Self-determination is the crux of the distinction between the bureaucratic mindset of an agency and the boundary spanning dynamism of an academic enterprise. Even while academic culture sustains its commitment to the ideals institutionalized by Wilhelm von Humboldt in his conception for the University of Berlin, including *Wissenschaft*, or the pursuit of knowledge wherever it may lead, there is no reason why new models might not embrace a broader set of objectives. Nicholas Lemann has characterized the necessary premises for vanguard knowledge production in the standard model: "Research universities . . . grant extraordinary freedom and empowerment to a small, elaborately trained and selected group of people whose mission to pursue knowledge and understanding without the constraints of immediate practical applicability under which most of the rest of the world has to operate."[5] A significant portion of the investment in research yields outcomes in the education of both undergraduates and graduate students, of course, but how much more powerful this model would become if it operated at a scale commensurate with the needs of society and prioritized research intended to produce outcomes of "immediate practical applicability" equally with the discovery of new knowledge.

The well-known observation by Clark Kerr that universities dominate the list of institutions established before 1500 that still exist "in recognizable forms, with similar functions, and with unbroken histories" expresses the intergenerational sweep of great teaching and research.[6] Against the present backdrop of uncertainty, ambiguity, and complexity, it is obvious that we need new ways to conceive the pursuit of discovery, creativity, and innovation; to understand and build our knowledge enterprises; and to endow academia with meaning for people other than academicians. As institutions dedicated to the realization of human potential, universities must endeavor toward societal transformation as well as the discovery of new knowledge. Throughout the past millennium, complex social forces no less than the intellectual currents and aspirations of a given era compelled the formation and subsequent development of organizations and institutions committed to knowledge production and dissemination. Established in response to social needs, the earliest universities were no exception: "What is notable about these early institutions is the direct social stimulus that led to their formation," writes historian Wolfram Swoboda. "They were not institutions of abstract learning but rather were intended to serve the direct needs of society."[7] The enlargement of the curriculum beyond the trivium and quadrivium came as a consequence of the social, political, and economic requirements of society.[8] From the outset, moreover, in the eleventh and twelfth centuries, these institutions coalesced first and foremost as academic communities. As Ernst Robert Curtius explains, "The word 'university' does not, as is generally believed, mean 'the sum total of disciplines' ('universitas litterarum') but the corporation of students and teachers."[9] The New American University model seeks to build on this legacy to expand the scope and impact of academic communities committed to knowledge production and dissemination in service to the needs of society.

    In 1818, Thomas Jefferson observed that the objects of education are "To give to every citizen the information he needs for the transaction of his own business; To enable him to calculate for himself, and to express and preserve his ideas, his contracts and accounts, in writing; To improve by reading, his morals and faculties; To understand his duties to his neighbors and country, and to discharge with competence the functions confided to him by either; To know his rights .... And, in general, to observe with intelligence and faithfulness all the social relations under which he shall be placed."[10] In some measure, little has changed since Jefferson summarized these purposes for his report to the commissioners for the University of Virginia, known as the Rockfish Gap report after the site of the tavern in the Blue Ridge Mountains where dignitaries and citizens had assembled in August of that year to form a board that would designate Charlottesville as the setting for the newly formed institution. But in another sense everything has changed, and our collective survival as a species may depend on the evolution of our knowledge enterprises. Our colleges and universities, and especially the set of major research universities, must be prepared to lend direction and purpose to the artistic creativity and humanistic and social scientific insight and the scientific discoveries and technological innovations that are the products of an academic culture that arguably represents the best hope of our pluralistic democracy as we negotiate the currents of encroaching complexity. We could do worse than to draw inspiration from the likes of Thomas Jefferson and his contemporaries, whose vision for the republic was animated by the civic ideals of an earlier experiment in democracy. This, then, is a call for renewal in the American research university and the recovery of the aspirations of the founders of our republic for the educational attainment of its citizens.

## Notes

1. Barack Obama, Remarks of President Barack Obama to Joint Session of Congress (February 24, 2009).

2. Anthony P. Carnevale, Nicole Smith, and Jeff Strohl, "Help Wanted: Projections of Jobs and Education Requirements through 2018" (Washington, DC: Georgetown University Center on Education and the Workforce, June 2010); Anthony P. Carnevale and Stephen J. Rose, "The Undereducated American" (Washington, DC: Georgetown University Center on Education and the Workforce, June 2011).

3. Michael Mumper et al., "The Federal Government and Higher Education," in *American Higher Education in the Twenty-First Century: Social, Political, and Economic Challenges*, 3rd ed., ed. Philip G. Altbach et al. (Baltimore: Johns Hopkins University Press, 2011), 113–138.

4. John Aubrey Douglass, *The Conditions for Admission: Access, Equity, and the Social Contract of Public Universities* (Stanford: Stanford University Press, 2007), 8.

5. Nicholas Lemann, "The Soul of the Research University," *Chronicle of Higher Education* (April 28, 2014).

6. "About eighty-five institutions in the Western World established by 1500 still exist in recognizable forms, with similar functions and with unbroken histories, including the Catholic Church, the parliaments of the Isle of Man, of Iceland, and of Great Britain, several Swiss cantons, and seventy universities." Clark Kerr, *"The Uses of the University* Two Decades Later: Postscript 1982," *Change* 14 (October 1982): 23–31.

7. Wolfram W. Swoboda, "Disciplines and Interdisciplinarity: A Historical Perspective," in Joseph J. Kockelmans, ed., *Interdisciplinarity and Higher Education* (University Park: Pennsylvania State University Press, 1979), 50.

8. Fritz Machlup, *Knowledge: Its Creation, Distribution, and Economic Significance*, vol. 2: *The Branches of Learning* (Princeton, NJ: Princeton University Press, 1982), 122–123.

9. Ernst Robert Curtius, *European Literature and the Latin Middle Ages*, trans. Willard R. Trask (1952; Princeton, NJ: Princeton University Press, 2013), 54.

10. Thomas Jefferson, "Report of the Commissioners for the University of Virginia" (August 4, 1818), quoted in American Academy of Arts and Sciences, "The Heart of the Matter: The Humanities and Social Sciences for a Vibrant, Competitive, and Secure Nation" (Cambridge, MA: American Academy of Arts and Sciences, 2013).

# BIBLIOGRAPHY

Abbott, Andrew. *Chaos of Disciplines*. Chicago: University of Chicago Press, 2001.

Adams, James D. "Is the United States Losing Its Preeminence in Higher Education?" In *American Universities in a Global Market*. Edited by Charles T. Clotfelter, 33–68. Chicago: University of Chicago Press for the National Bureau of Economic Research, 2010.

Aldrich, Howard E., and Jeffrey Pfeffer. "Environments of Organizations." *Annual Review of Sociology* 2, no. 1 (1976): 79–105.

Allen, Douglas W. *The Institutional Revolution: Measurement and the Economic Emergence of the Modern World*. Chicago: University of Chicago Press, 2012.

Altbach, Philip G., Patricia J. Gumport, and Robert O. Berdahl, eds. *Higher Education in the Twenty-First Century: Social, Political, and Economic Challenges*, 3rd ed. Baltimore: Johns Hopkins University Press, 2011.

American Academy of Arts and Sciences. *The Heart of the Matter: The Humanities and Social Sciences for a Vibrant, Competitive, and Secure Nation*. Cambridge, MA: American Academy of Arts and Sciences, 2013.

Anderson, Perry. *The Origins of Postmodernity*. London: Verso, 1998.

Anderson, R. D. "Before and After Humboldt: European Universities between the Eighteenth and Nineteenth Centuries." *History of Higher Education Annual* 20 (2000): 5–14.

———. *Universities and Elites in Britain since 1800*. Cambridge: Cambridge University Press, 1995.

Arrow, Kenneth J. "Economic Welfare and the Allocation of Resources for Invention." In *The Rate and Direction of Inventive Activity: Economic and Social Factors*. Edited by Richard R. Nelson, 618, 623. Cambridge, MA: National Bureau of Economic Research, 1962.

Arthur, W. Brian. *The Nature of Technology: What It Is and How It Evolves*. New York: Free Press, 2009.

Arum, Richard, and Josipa Roksa. *Academically Adrift: Limited Learning on College Campuses*. Chicago: University of Chicago Press, 2010.

Ash, Mitchell G. "Bachelor of What, Master of Whom? The Humboldt Myth and Historical Transformations of Higher Education in German-Speaking Europe and the United States." *European Journal of Education* 41, no. 2 (2006): 245–267.

Atkinson, Richard C., and William A. Blanpied. "Research Universities: Core of the U.S. Science and Technology System." *Technology in Society* 30 (2008): 30–38.

Atkinson, Richard C., and Patricia A. Pelfrey. "Science and the Entrepreneurial University." *Issues in Science and Technology* 26, no. 4 (Summer 2010): 39–48.

Atkinson, Robert D. "Deep Competitiveness." *Issues in Science and Technology* 23, no. 2 (2007): 69–75.

Audretsch, David B., and Maryann P. Feldman. "R&D Spillovers and the Geography of Innovation and Production." *American Economic Review* 86, no. 3 (June 1996): 630–640.

Autor, David H. "The Polarization of Job Opportunities in the U.S. Labor Market: Implications for Employment and Earnings." Washington, DC: Center for American Progress, April 2010.

———. "Skills, Education, and the Rise of Earnings Inequality Among the 'Other 99 Percent.'" *Science* 344, no. 6186 (May 23, 2014): 843–850.

Autor, David H., Lawrence F. Katz, and Melissa S. Kearney. "The Polarization of the Labor Market." *American Economic Review* 96, no. 2 (May 2006): 189–194.

Axtell, James. *The Making of Princeton University: From Woodrow Wilson to the Present.* Princeton, NJ: Princeton University Press, 2006.

Bacon, Michael. *Pragmatism: An Introduction.* Cambridge: Polity, 2012.

———. "Rorty and Pragmatic Social Criticism." *Philosophy and Social Criticism* 32, no. 7 (2006): 863–880.

Bailey, Martha J., and Susan M. Dynarski. "Gains and Gaps: Changing Inequality in U.S. College Entry and Completion." NBER Working Paper 17633. Cambridge, MA: National Bureau of Economic Research, December 2011.

Bastedo, Michael N., ed. *The Organization of Higher Education: Managing Colleges for a New Era.* Baltimore: Johns Hopkins University Press, 2012.

Baumol, William J. *The Cost Disease: Why Computers Get Cheaper and Health Care Doesn't.* New Haven, CT: Yale University Press, 2012.

Baumol, William J., and William G. Bowen. "On the Performing Arts: The Anatomy of Their Economic Problems." *American Economic Review* 55, no. 1/2 (March 1965): 495–502.

———. *Performing Arts: The Economic Dilemma.* New York: The Twentieth Century Fund, 1966.

Benhabib, Seyla. *Situating the Self: Gender, Community, and Postmodernism in Contemporary Ethics.* New York: Routledge, 1992.

Bernstein, Richard J. *The Pragmatic Turn.* Cambridge: Polity, 2010.

Besharov, Gregory. "The Outbreak of Cost Disease: Baumol and Bowen's Founding of Cultural Economics." *History of Political Economy* 37, no. 3 (2005): 413–430.

Blakemore, Arthur, and Berthold Herrendorf. "Economic Growth: The Importance of Education and Technological Development." Tempe: W. P. Carey School of Business, Arizona State University, 2009.

Bleicher, Josef. "Bildung." *Theory, Culture, and Society* 23 (2006): 364–365.

Bloom, Allan. *The Closing of the American Mind.* New York: Simon and Schuster, 2012.

Bloom, Harold. *The Anxiety of Influence: A Theory of Poetry.* New York: Oxford University Press, 1973.

———. *The Breaking of the Vessels.* Chicago: University of Chicago Press, 1982.

Blumenstyk, Goldie. "Change Takes Root in the Desert: Embracing Inclusiveness, Arizona State University Pursues Transformation on a Grand Scale." *Chronicle of Higher Education* (November 19, 2012).

Bok, Derek. *Beyond the Ivory Tower: Social Responsibilities of the Modern University.* Cambridge, MA: Harvard University Press, 1982.

———. *Universities in the Marketplace: The Commercialization of Higher Education.* Princeton, NJ: Princeton University Press, 2003.

Bound, John, Michael F. Lovenheim, and Sarah Turner. "Why Have College Completion Rates Declined? An Analysis of Changing Student Preparation and Collegiate Resources." *American Economic Journal: Applied Economics* 2, no. 3 (2010): 129–157.

Bourdieu, Pierre. "The Forms of Capital." In *Handbook for Theory and Research in the Sociology of Education.* Edited by John G. Richardson, 241–258. Westport, CT: Greenwood Press, 1986.

Bowen, William G., Matthew M. Chingos, and Michael S. McPherson. *Crossing the Finish Line: Completing College at America's Public Universities.* Princeton, NJ: Princeton University Press, 2009.

Bowen, William G., Martin A. Kurzweil, and Eugene M. Tobin. *Equity and Excellence in American Higher Education.* Charlottesville: University of Virginia Press, 2006.

Bozeman, Barry. *Public Values and Public Interest: Counterbalancing Economic Individualism.* Washington, DC: Georgetown University Press, 2007.

Brooks, Frederick P. *The Design of Design: Essays from a Computer Scientist.* Boston: Addison-Wesley, 2010.

Brown, John Seely, Allan Collins, and Paul Duguid. "Situated Cognition and the Culture of Learning." *Educational Researcher* 18, no. 1 (January–February 1989): 32–42.

Brown, John Seely, and Paul Duguid. "Knowledge and Organization: A Social-Practice Perspective." *Organization Science* 12, no. 2 (March–April 2001): 198–213.

———. "Organizational Learning and Communities-of-Practice: Toward a Unified View of Working, Learning, and Innovation." *Organization Science* 2, no. 1 (February 1991): 40–57.

Brynjolfsson, Erik, and Andrew McAfee. *The Second Machine Age: Work, Progress, and Prosperity in a Time of Brilliant Technologies.* New York: W. W. Norton and Company, 2014.

Bush, Vannevar. *Science—The Endless Frontier: A Report to the President on a Program for Postwar Scientific Research.* Washington, DC: U.S. Government Printing Office, 1945.

Calinescu, Matei. *Five Faces of Modernity: Modernism, Avant-Garde, Decadence, Kitsch, Postmodernism.* Durham, NC: Duke University Press, 1987.

Capaldi, Elizabeth. "Intellectual Transformation and Budgetary Savings through Academic Reorganization." *Change* (July/August 2009): 19–27.

Carnevale, Anthony P., and Stephen J. Rose. "The Undereducated American." Washington, DC: Georgetown University Center on Education and the Workforce, June 2011.

Carnevale, Anthony P., and Jeff Strohl. "How Increasing College Access Is Increasing Inequality, and What to Do about It." In *Rewarding Strivers: Helping Low-Income Students Succeed in College.* Edited by Richard D. Kahlenberg, 71–190. New York: Century Foundation, 2010.

Carr, Nicholas. "The Crisis in Higher Education." *MIT Technology Review* 116, no. 6 (September 27, 2012).

Castel, Albert. "The Founding Fathers and the Vision of a National University." *History of Education Quarterly* 4, no. 4 (December 1964): 280–302.

*China Daily.* "Chinese Ivy League" (October 21, 2009).

Chomsky, Noam, ed. *The Cold War and the University: Toward an Intellectual History of the Postwar Years.* New York: New Press, 1997.

Christensen, Clayton M. *The Innovator's Dilemma*. Cambridge, MA: Harvard Business School Press, 1997.

Christensen, Clayton M., and Henry J. Eyring. *The Innovative University: Changing the DNA of Higher Education from the Inside Out*. San Francisco: Jossey-Bass, 2011.

Christensen, Clayton M., Michael B. Horn, Louis Caldera, and Louis Soares. "Disrupting College: How Disruptive Innovation Can Deliver Quality and Affordability to Postsecondary Education." Washington, DC: Center for American Progress, February 2011.

Clark, Burton. "Places of Inquiry." In *The Academic Profession: National, Disciplinary, and Institutional Settings*. Edited by Burton Clark. Berkeley: University of California Press, 1987.

Clark, Gregory. *A Farewell to Alms: A Brief Economic History of the World*. Princeton, NJ: Princeton University Press, 2007.

Clark, William. *Academic Charisma and the Origins of the Research University*. Chicago: University of Chicago Press, 2006.

Clark, William C. "Sustainability Science: A Room of Its Own." In *Proceedings of the National Academy of Sciences* 104, no. 6 (February 6, 2007): 1737–1738.

Clark, William C., and Nancy M. Dickson. "Sustainability Science: The Emerging Research Program." In *Proceedings of the National Academy of Sciences* 100, no. 14 (July 8, 2003): 8059–8061.

Cohen, Arthur M. *The Shaping of American Higher Education: Emergence and the Growth of the Contemporary System*, 2nd ed. San Francisco: Jossey-Bass, 2010.

Cohen, Joel E. *How Many People Can the Earth Support?* New York: W. W. Norton and Company, 1995.

Cole, Jonathan R. *The Great American University: Its Rise to Preeminence, Its Indispensable National Role, and Why It Must Be Protected*. New York: Public Affairs, 2009.

Collini, Stefan. Introduction to C. P. Snow, *The Two Cultures*. Cambridge: Cambridge University Press, 1998.

Comin, Diego. "Total Factor Productivity." In *The New Palgrave Dictionary of Economics*. Edited by Steven N. Durlauf and Lawrence E. Blume. London: Palgrave Macmillan, 2008.

Cook, Scott D. N., and John Seely Brown. "Bridging Epistemologies: The Generative Dance between Organizational Knowledge and Organizational Knowing." *Organization Science* 10, no. 4 (July–August 1999): 381–400.

Cornford, Francis. *Microcosmographia Academica: Being a Guide for the Young Academic Politician*, 4th ed. Cambridge: Bowes and Bowes, 1949, 15. First published 1908.

Cortese, Anthony D. "Promises Made and Promises Lost: A Candid Assessment of Higher Education Leadership and the Sustainability Agenda." In *The Sustainable University: Green Goals and New Challenges for Higher Education Leaders*. Edited by James Martin and James E. Samels, 17–31. Baltimore: Johns Hopkins University Press, 2012.

Craig, Hardin. *Woodrow Wilson at Princeton*. Norman: University of Oklahoma Press, 1960.

Critchley, Simon. "What Is Continental Philosophy?" *International Journal of Philosophical Studies* 5, no. 3 (1997): 347–365.

Cross, Nigel, and Kees Dorst. "Co-Evolution of Problem and Solution Spaces in Creative Design." In *Computational Models of Creative Design*. Edited by J. S. Gero and M. L. Maher, 243–262. Sydney: University of Sydney, 1999.

Crow, Michael M. "None Dare Call It Hubris: The Limits of Knowledge." *Issues in Science and Technology* 23, no. 2 (Winter 2007): 29–32.

———. "Organizing Teaching and Research to Address the Grand Challenges of Sustainable Development." *Bioscience* (American Institute of Biological Sciences) 60, no. 7 (July/August 2010): 488–489.

———. "The Research University as Comprehensive Knowledge Enterprise: A Prototype for a New American University." In *University Research for Innovation*. Glion Colloquium, no. 6. Edited by Luc E. Weber and James J. Duderstadt, 211–225. London: Economica, 2010.

———. "Science and Technology Policy in the United States: Trading In the 1950 Model." In *New Technology Policy and Social Innovations in the Firm*. Edited by Jorge Niosi, 38–57 (London: Pinter, 1994).

———. "Sustainability as a Founding Principle of the United States." In *Moral Ground: Ethical Action for a Planet in Peril*. Edited by Kathleen Dean Moore and Michael P. Nelson, 301–305. San Antonio, TX: Trinity University Press, 2010.

Crow, Michael M., and Barry Bozeman. *Limited by Design: R&D Laboratories in the U.S. National Innovation System*. New York: Columbia University Press, 1998.

Crow, Michael M., and William B. Dabars. "Interdisciplinarity as a Design Problem: Toward Mutual Intelligibility among Academic Disciplines in the American Research University." In *Enhancing Communication and Collaboration in Interdisciplinary Research*. Edited by Michael O'Rourke, Stephen Crowley, Sanford D. Eigenbrode, and J. D. Wulfhorst, 294–322. Los Angeles: Sage, 2013.

———. "Knowledge without Borders: American Research Universities in a Global Context." *Cairo Review of Global Affairs* 5 (Spring 2012): 35–45.

———. "University-Based Research and Economic Development: The Morrill Act and the Emergence of the American Research University." In *Precipice or Crossroads?: Where America's Great Public Universities Stand and Where They Are Going Midway through Their Second Century*. Edited by Daniel Mark Fogel and Elizabeth Malson-Huddle, 119–158. Albany: State University of New York Press, 2012.

Curtius, Ernst Robert. *European Literature and the Latin Middle Ages*. Translated by Willard R. Trask. 1952; Princeton, NJ: Princeton University Press, 2013.

Dabars, William B. "Disciplinarity and Interdisciplinarity: Rhetoric and Context in the American Research University." PhD dissertation, University of California, Los Angeles, 2008.

Dasgupta, Partha, and Paul A. David. "Toward a New Economics of Science." *Research Policy* 23 (1994): 487–521.

Delbanco, Andrew. *College: What It Was, Is, and Should Be*. Princeton, NJ: Princeton University Press, 2012.

DeMillo, Richard A. *Abelard to Apple: The Fate of American Colleges and Universities*. Cambridge, MA: MIT Press, 2011.

DiMaggio, Paul J. and Walter W. Powell. "The Iron Cage Revisited: Institutional Isomorphism and Collective Rationality in Organizational Fields." *American Sociological Review* 48, no. 2 (April 1983): 147–160.

Deutsch, Karl W., John Platt, and Dieter Senghaas. "Conditions Favoring Major Advances in the Social Sciences." *Science* 171 (February 5, 1971): 450–459.

Dogan, Mattei. "The New Social Sciences: Cracks in the Disciplinary Walls." *International Social Sciences Journal* 153 (September 1997): 429–443.

Dogan, Mattei, and Robert Pahre, *Creative Marginality: Innovation at the Intersections of Social Sciences*. Boulder, CO: Westview Press, 1990.

Dorst, Kees, and Nigel Cross. "Creativity in the Design Process: Co-Evolution of Problem-Solution." *Design Studies* 22 (2001): 425–437.

Douglass, John Aubrey. *The California Idea and American Higher Education: 1850 to the 1960 Master Plan*. Stanford: Stanford University Press, 2000.

———. *The Conditions for Admission: Access, Equity, and the Social Contract of Public Universities*. Stanford: Stanford University Press, 2007.

———. "The Waning of America's Higher Education Advantage: International Competitors Are No Longer Number Two and Have Big Plans in the Global Economy." Berkeley: Center for Studies in Higher Education, University of California, 2006.

Downs, Anthony. *Inside Bureaucracy*. RAND Corporation Research Study. Boston: Little Brown, 1967.

Dreier, Peter, and Richard D. Kahlenberg. "Making Top Colleges Less Aristocratic and More Meritocratic." *New York Times* (September 12, 2014).

Duderstadt, James J. *Engineering for a Changing World: A Roadmap to the Future of Engineering Practice, Research, and Education*. Ann Arbor: The Millennium Project, University of Michigan, 2008.

———. *A University for the Twenty-First Century*. Ann Arbor: University of Michigan Press, 2000.

Duguid, Paul. "The Art of Knowing: Social and Tacit Dimensions of Knowledge and the Limits of the Community of Practice." *Information Society* 21 (2005): 109–118.

Duncan, Greg J., and Richard J. Murname. "Introduction: The American Dream, Then and Now." In *Whither Opportunity? Rising Inequality, Schools, and Children's Life Chances*. Edited by Greg J. Duncan and Richard J. Murname, 3–23. New York: Russell Sage Foundation, 2011.

Dupree, A. Hunter. *Science in the Federal Government: A History of Policies and Activities to 1940*. Cambridge, MA: Belknap Press of Harvard University, 1957.

Durden, William. "Liberal Arts for All, Not Just the Rich." *Chronicle of Higher Education* 48 (October 19, 2001).

Edsall, Thomas B. "The Reproduction of Privilege." *New York Times* (March 12, 2012).

Ehrenberg, Ronald G. *Tuition Rising: Why College Costs So Much*. Cambridge, MA: Harvard University Press, 2000.

Eisenhower, Dwight D. "Farewell Address to the Nation" (January 17, 1961). Public Papers of the Presidents (1960): 1035–1040.

Etzkowitz, Henry. "Entrepreneurial Scientists and Entrepreneurial Universities in American Academic Science." *Minerva* 21 (1983): 1–21.

———. "Research Groups as Quasi-firms: The Invention of the Entrepreneurial University." *Research Policy* 32 (2003): 109–121.

———. *The Triple Helix: University-Industry-Government Innovation in Action*. New York: Routledge, 2008.

Feldman, Maryann P. "Entrepreneurship and American Research Universities: Evolution in Technology Transfer." In *The Emergence of Entrepreneurship Policy: Gover-*

*nance, Start-ups, and Growth in the U.S. Knowledge Economy.* Edited by David M. Hart, 92–112. Cambridge: Cambridge University Press, 2003.

———. "The New Economics of Innovation, Spillovers, and Agglomeration: Review of Empirical Studies." *Economics of Innovation and New Technologies* 8 (1999): 5–25.

Florida, Richard. *The Rise of the Creative Class: And How It Is Transforming Work, Leisure, Community, and Everyday Life.* New York: Basic Books, 2002.

Fogel, Daniel Mark. "Challenges to Equilibrium: The Place of the Arts and Humanities in Public Research Universities." In *Precipice or Crossroads: Where America's Great Public Universities Stand and Where They Are Going Midway through Their Second Century.* Edited by Daniel Mark Fogel, 241–257. Albany: State University of New York Press, 2012.

Frodeman, Robert. "Interdisciplinarity, Communication, and the Limits of Knowledge." In *Enhancing Communication and Collaboration in Interdisciplinary Research.* Edited by Michael O'Rourke, Stephen Crowley, Sanford D. Eigenbrode, and J. D. Wulfhorst, 103–116. Los Angeles: Sage, 2013.

———. *Sustainable Knowledge: A Theory of Interdisciplinarity.* Basingstoke: Palgrave Macmillan, 2014.

Frodeman, Robert, Julie Thompson Klein, and Carl Mitcham, eds. *The Oxford Handbook of Interdisciplinarity.* Oxford: Oxford University Press, 2010.

Frodeman, Robert, and Carl Mitcham. "New Directions in Interdisciplinarity: Broad, Deep, and Critical." *Bulletin of Science, Technology, and Society* 27, no. 6 (December 2007): 506–514.

Galison, Peter. *Image and Logic: A Material Culture of Physics.* Chicago: University of Chicago Press, 1997.

Gawande, Atul. "Big Med: Should Hospitals Be More Like Chain Restaurants?" *New Yorker* (August 13, 2012): 52–63.

Gee, Gordon. "Colleges Face Reinvention or Extinction." *Chronicle of Higher Education* (February 9, 2009).

Geiger, Roger L. *Knowledge and Money: Research Universities and the Paradox of the Marketplace.* Stanford: Stanford University Press, 2004.

———. "Milking the Sacred Cow: Research and the Quest for Useful Knowledge in the American University since 1920." *Science, Technology, and Human Values* 13, no. 3 and 4 (Summer and Autumn 1988): 332–348.

———. "Organized Research Units: Their Role in the Development of the Research University." *Journal of Higher Education* 61: no. 1 (January/February 1990): 1–19.

———. *Research and Relevant Knowledge: American Research Universities since World War II.* Oxford: Oxford University Press, 1993.

———. "Science, Universities, and National Defense, 1945–1970." *Osiris* 2nd series, 1992, no. 7: 26–48.

———. "The Ten Generations of American Higher Education." In *Higher Education in the Twenty-First Century: Social, Political, and Economic Challenges,* 3rd ed. Edited by Philip G. Altbach, Patricia J. Gumport, and Robert O. Berdahl, 37–68. Baltimore: Johns Hopkins University Press, 2011.

———. *To Advance Knowledge: The Growth of American Research Universities, 1900–1940.* Oxford: Oxford University Press, 1986.

Gersick, C. J. G. "Revolutionary Change Theories: A Multilevel Exploration of the Punctuated Equilibrium Paradigm." *Academy of Management Review* 16, no. 1: 10–36.

Giddens, Anthony. *The Constitution of Society: Outline of the Theory of Structuration.* Berkeley: University of California Press, 1984.

Golden, Daniel. *The Price of Admission: How America's Ruling Class Buys Its Way into Elite Colleges—And Who Gets Left Outside the Gates.* New York: Crown, 2006.

Goldin, Claudia, and Lawrence F. Katz. *The Race between Education and Technology.* Cambridge, MA: Belknap Press of Harvard University Press, 2008.

Goldstein, Rebecca. *Plato at the Googleplex: Why Philosophy Won't Go Away.* New York: Pantheon, 2014.

Gordon, Robert J. "The Demise of U.S. Economic Growth: Restatement, Rebuttal, and Reflections." NBER Working Paper 19895. Cambridge, MA: National Bureau of Economic Research, February 2014.

Grafton, Anthony. "Can the Colleges Be Saved?" Review of Andrew Delbanco, *College: What It Was, Is, and Should Be* (Princeton, NJ: Princeton University Press, 2012). *New York Review of Books* (May 24, 2012).

Graham, Hugh Davis, and Nancy Diamond. *The Rise of American Research Universities: Elites and Challengers in the Postwar Era.* Baltimore: Johns Hopkins University Press, 1997.

Gray, Hanna Holborn. *Searching for Utopia: Universities and Their Histories.* Berkeley: University of California Press, 2012.

Gross, David. *The Past in Ruins: Tradition and the Critique of Modernity.* Amherst: University of Massachusetts Press, 2009.

Guston, David H., and Kenneth Keniston. "The Social Contract for Science." In *The Fragile Contract: University Science and the Federal Government.* Edited by Guston and Keniston. Cambridge, MA: MIT Press, 1994.

Haas, Peter M. "Epistemic Communities and International Policy Coordination." *International Organization* 46, no. 1 (1992): 1–35.

Habermas, Jürgen. "Postscript." In *Habermas and Pragmatism.* Edited by Mitchell Adoulafia, Myra Bookman, and Catherine Kemp. London: Routledge, 2002.

———. *The Theory of Communicative Action,* Volume 2: *Reason and the Rationalization of Society.* Translated by Thomas McCarthy. Cambridge, MA: MIT Press, 1987.

Hacker, Andrew. "Is Algebra Necessary?" *New York Times* (July 28, 2012)

Hacker, Andrew, and Claudia Dreifus. *Higher Education? How Colleges Are Wasting Our Money and Failing Our Kids—And What We Can Do about It.* New York: Henry Holt and Company, 2010.

Hacking, Ian. *Historical Ontology.* Cambridge, MA: Harvard University Press, 2002.

Hagel, John, John Seely Brown, and Lang Davison. *The Power of Pull: How Small Moves, Smartly Made, Can Set Big Things in Motion.* New York: Basic Books, 2010.

Hannan, Michael T., and John Freeman. "Structural Inertia and Organizational Change." *American Sociological Review* 49 (April 1984): 149–164.

Hart, David M. "Entrepreneurship Policy: What It Is and Where It Came From." In *The Emergence of Entrepreneurship Policy: Governance, Start-ups, and Growth in the U.S. Knowledge Economy.* Edited by David M. Hart. Cambridge: Cambridge University Press, 2003.

———, ed. *The Emergence of Entrepreneurship Policy: Governance, Start-ups, and Growth in the U.S. Knowledge Economy.* Cambridge: Cambridge University Press, 2003.

Hawkins, Hugh H. "Charles W. Eliot: University Reform and Religious Faith in America, 1869–1909." *The Journal of American History* 51, no. 2 (September 1964): 191–213.

Heller, Donald E. "State Support of Higher Education: Past, Present, and Future." In *Privatization and Public Universities*, 11–37. Edited by Douglas M. Priest and Edward P. St. John. Bloomington: Indiana University Press, 2006.

Hoachlander, Gary, Anna C. Sikora, and Laura Horn. "Community College Students." *Education Statistics Quarterly* 5, no. 2 (2003): 121–128.

Hofstadter, Richard, and C. DeWitt Hardy. *The Development and Scope of Higher Education in the United States*. New York: Columbia University Press for the Commission on Financing Higher Education, 1952.

Holland, John. "Complex Adaptive Systems." *Daedalus* 121, no. 1 (1992): 17–30.

Holzner, Burkart. *Reality Construction in Society*. Cambridge, MA: Schenkman, 1968.

Hossler, Donald et al. "State Funding for Higher Education: The Sisyphean Task." *Journal of Higher Education* 68, no. 2 (March/April 1997): 160–190.

Howard, Nicole. *The Book: The Life Story of a Technology*. Baltimore: Johns Hopkins University Press, 2009.

Institute of Higher Education, Shanghai Jiao Tong University. Academic Ranking of World Universities, http://www.shanghairanking.com/ARWU2011.html.

Jaimovich, Nir, and Henry E. Siu. "The Trend Is the Cycle: Job Polarization and Jobless Recoveries." Working Paper 18334. Cambridge, MA: National Bureau of Economic Research, August 2012.

Jay, Martin. *Force Fields: Between Intellectual History and Cultural Critique*. New York: Routledge, 1993.

———. *Songs of Experience: Modern American and European Variations on a Universal Theme*. Berkeley: University of California Press, 2005.

Jones, Charles I. "Sources of U.S. Economic Growth in a World of Ideas." *American Economic Review* 92, no. 1 (2002): 220–239.

Jørgensen, Torben Beck, and Barry Bozeman. "Public Values: An Inventory." *Administration and Society* 39, no. 3 (May 2007): 354–381.

Joseph, Miriam. *The Trivium: The Liberal Arts of Logic, Grammar, and Rhetoric* (Philadelphia: Paul Dry Books, 1982), 1–9.

Karabel, Jerome. *The Chosen: The Hidden History of Admission and Exclusion at Harvard, Yale, and Princeton*. New York: Houghton Mifflin, 2005.

Kash, Don E. *Perpetual Innovation: The New World of Competition*. New York: Basic Books, 1989.

Katz, Daniel, and Robert L. Kahn. *The Social Psychology of Organizations*. New York: Wiley, 1966.

Kenney, Martin, and Urs von Burg. "Technology, Entrepreneurship, and Path Dependence: Industrial Clustering in Silicon Valley and Route 128." *Industrial and Corporate Change* 8, no. 1 (1999): 67–103.

Keohane, Nannerl O. "The American Campus: From Colonial Seminary to Global Multiversity." Wolfson College Lecture Series. "The Idea of a University." Oxford University (February 3, 1998).

Kerr, Clark. *The Gold and the Blue: A Personal Memoir of the University of California (1949–1967)*: Volume 1: *Academic Triumphs*; Volume 2: *Political Turmoil*. Berkeley: University of California Press, 2001–2003.

———. *Higher Education Cannot Escape History: Issues for the Twenty-First Century*. Albany: SUNY Press, 1994.

———. *The Uses of the University*, 5th ed. Cambridge, MA: Harvard University Press, 2001. First published 1963.

———. "*The Uses of the University* Two Decades Later: Postscript 1982." *Change* 14 (October 1982): 23–31.

Kevles, Daniel J. "The National Science Foundation and the Debate over Postwar Research Policy, 1942–1945: A Political Interpretation of *Science—The Endless Frontier.*" *Isis* 68, no. 241 (1977): 4–26.

Kirp, David L. *Shakespeare, Einstein, and the Bottom Line: The Marketing of Higher Education.* Cambridge, MA: Harvard University Press, 2003.

Kitcher, Philip. *Science, Truth, and Democracy.* Oxford: Oxford University Press, 2001.

Klein, Julie Thompson. *Interdisciplinarity: History, Theory, and Practice.* Detroit, MI: Wayne State University Press, 1990.

———. "A Taxonomy of Interdisciplinarity." In *The Oxford Handbook of Interdisciplinarity.* Edited by Robert Frodeman, Julie Thompson Klein, and Carl Mitcham, 15–30. Oxford: Oxford University Press, 2010.

Klenow, Peter J., and Andrès Rodríguez-Clare. "The Neoclassical Revival in Growth Economics: Has It Gone Too Far?" *NBER Macroeconomics Annual* 12 (1997): 73–103.

Kotkin, Joel, and Ross DeVol. *Knowledge-Value Cities in the Digital Age.* Santa Monica: Milken Institute, 2001.

Kristof, Nicholas. "Smart Minds. Slim Impact." *New York Times* (February 16, 2014).

Kuhn, Thomas S. *The Structure of Scientific Revolutions*, 3rd ed. Chicago: University of Chicago Press, 1996. First published 1962.

Lemann, Nicholas. "The Soul of the Research University." *Chronicle of Higher Education* (April 28, 2014).

Leslie, Stuart W. *The Cold War and American Science: The Military-Industrial-Academic Complex at MIT and Stanford.* New York: Columbia University Press, 1993.

Levine, Lawrence W. *The Opening of the American Mind: Canons, Culture, and History.* Boston: Beacon Press, 1996.

Liedman, Sven-Eric. "General Education in Germany and Sweden." In *The European and American University since 1800: Historical and Sociological Essays.* Edited by Sheldon Rothblatt and Björn Wittrock. Cambridge: Cambridge University Press, 1993.

Lightman, Alan, Daniel Sarewitz, and Christina Desser, eds. *Living with the Genie: Essays on Technology and the Quest for Human Mastery.* Washington DC: Island Press, 2003.

Lingenfelter, Paul E. "The Financing of Public Colleges and Universities in the United States." In *Handbook of Research in Education Finance and Policy.* Edited by Helen F. Ladd and Edward B. Fiske. New York: Routledge, 2008.

Link, Arthur. "Woodrow Wilson." In *A Princeton Companion.* Compiled by Alexander Leitch. Princeton, NJ: Princeton University Press, 1978.

Lombardi, John V. *How Universities Work.* Baltimore: Johns Hopkins University Press, 2013.

Lowen, Rebecca S. *Creating the Cold War University: The Transformation of Stanford.* Berkeley: University of California Press, 1997.

Lundvall, Bengt-Åke. "Innovation as an Interactive Process: From User-Producer Interaction to National Systems of Innovation." In *Technical Change and Economic Theory.* Edited by Giovanni Dosi et al. London: Pinter, 1988.

Machlup, Fritz. *Knowledge: Its Creation, Distribution, and Economic Significance*. Volume II: *The Branches of Learning*. Princeton, NJ: Princeton University Press, 1982.

Macilwain, Colin. "The Arizona Experiment." *Nature* 446, no. 7139 (April 26, 2007).

Madsen, David. *The National University: Enduring Dream of the United States*. Detroit: Michigan State University Press, 1966.

Mansfield, Edwin. "Academic Research and Industrial Innovation." *Research Policy* 20 (1991): 1–12.

March, James G., and Herbert A. Simon. *Organizations*, 2nd ed. Cambridge, MA: Blackwell, 1993.

Marcus, Steven. "Humanities from Classics to Cultural Studies: Notes toward the History of an Idea." *Daedalus* 135, no. 2 (Spring 2006): 15–21.

Marsden, George M. *The Soul of the American University: From Protestant Establishment to Established Nonbelief*. New York: Oxford University Press, 1994.

Mau, Bruce, and Jennifer Leonard. *Massive Change*. London: Phaidon Press, 2004.

Mayer, Jane. "State for Sale," *New Yorker* (October 10, 2011).

McClelland, Charles E. *State, Society, and University in Germany, 1700–1914*. Cambridge: Cambridge University Press, 1980.

McNamee, Stephen J., and Robert K. Miller. *The Meritocracy Myth*, 2nd ed. Lanham: Rowman and Littlefield, 2009.

McPherson, Michael S., and Morton Owen Schapiro. "Economic Challenges for Liberal Arts Colleges." In *Distinctively American: The Residential Liberal Arts College*. Edited by Steven Koblik and Stephen R. Graubard, 47–76. New Brunswick, NJ: Transaction, 2000.

Meacham, Jon. *Thomas Jefferson: The Art of Power*. New York: Random House, 2012.

Meadows, Donella H., Dennis L. Meadows, Jørgen Randers, and William W. Behrens. *The Limits to Growth: A Report for the Club of Rome's Project on the Predicament of Mankind*. New York: Universe, 1972.

Menand, Louis. "College: The End of the Golden Age." *New York Review of Books* (October 18, 2001)

———. *The Marketplace of Ideas: Reform and Resistance in the American University*. New York: W. W. Norton and Company, 2010.

———. *The Metaphysical Club: A Story of Ideas in America*. New York: Farrar, Straus and Giroux, 2001.

Merton, Robert K. *On the Shoulders of Giants: A Shandean Postscript*. Chicago: University of Chicago Press, 1993.

———. *The Sociology of Science: Theoretical and Empirical Investigations*. Chicago: University of Chicago Press, 1973.

Merton, Robert K., and Elinor Barber. *The Travels and Adventures of Serendipity: A Study in Sociological Semantics and the Sociology of Science*. Princeton, NJ: Princeton University Press, 2004.

Mettler, Suzanne. *Degrees of Inequality: How the Politics of Higher Education Sabotaged the American Dream*. New York: Basic Books, 2014.

Metzger, Walter P. "The Academic Profession in the United States." In *The Academic Profession: National, Disciplinary, and Institutional Settings*. Edited by Burton R. Clark, 123–208. Berkeley: University of California Press, 1987.

Miller, Hugh T., and Charles J. Fox. "The Epistemic Community." *Administration and Society* 32, no. 6 (2001): 668–685.

Mokyr, Joel. *The Gifts of Athena: Historical Origins of the Knowledge Economy.* Princeton. NJ: Princeton University Press, 2002.

——. *The Lever of Riches: Technological Creativity and Economic Progress.* Oxford: Oxford University Press, 1990.

Moretti, Enrico. "Estimating the Social Return to Higher Education: Evidence from Longitudinal and Repeated Cross-sectional Data." *Journal of Econometrics* 121 (2004): 175–212.

Mortenson, Thomas. "Bachelor's Degree Attainment by Age 24 by Family Income Quartiles, 1970–2010." Oskaloosa, IA: Pell Institute for the Study of Opportunity in Higher Education, 2010.

Mortenson, Thomas et al. "Why College? Private Correlates of Educational Attainment." *Postsecondary Education Opportunity: The Mortenson Research Seminar on Public Policy Analysis of Opportunity for Postsecondary Education* 81 (March 1999).

Mowery, David C., Richard R. Nelson, Bhaven N. Sampat, and Arvids A. Ziedonis. "The Growth of Patenting and Licensing by U.S. Universities: An Assessment of the Effects of the Bayh-Dole Act of 1980." *Research Policy* 30 (2000): 99–119.

——. *Ivory Tower and Industrial Innovation: University-Industry Technology Transfer Before and After the Bayh-Dole Act.* Stanford: Stanford University Press, 2004.

Mowery, David C., and Nathan Rosenberg. *Paths of Innovation: Technological Change in Twentieth-Century America.* Cambridge: Cambridge University Press, 1998.

Mumper, Michael, Lawrence E. Gladieux, Jacqueline E. King, and Melanie E. Corrigan. "The Federal Government and Higher Education." In *American Higher Education in the Twenty-First Century: Social, Political, and Economic Challenges*, 3rd ed. Edited by Philip G. Altbach, Patricia J. Gumport, and Robert O. Berdahl, 113–138. Baltimore: Johns Hopkins University Press, 2011.

Murray, Charles. "Narrowing the Class Divide." *New York Times* (March 7, 2012).

Narin, Francis, Kimberly Hamilton, and Dominic Olivastro. "The Increasing Linkage between U.S. Technology and Public Science." *Research Policy* 26 (1997): 317–330.

National Academies. Committee on Facilitating Interdisciplinary Research and Committee on Science, Engineering, and Public Policy. *Facilitating Interdisciplinary Research.* Washington, DC: National Academies Press, 2005.

National Academies. Committee on Prospering in the Global Economy of the Twenty-First Century. *Capitalizing on Investments in Science and Technology.* Washington, DC: National Academies Press, 1999.

National Academies. *Rising above the Gathering Storm: Energizing and Employing American for a Brighter Economic Future.* Washington, DC: National Academies Press, 2007.

——. *Rising above the Gathering Storm Revisited: Rapidly Approaching Category 5.* Washington, DC: National Academies Press, 2010.

National Research Council. *Convergence: Facilitating Transdisciplinary Integration of Life Sciences, Physical Sciences, Engineering, and Beyond.* Washington, DC: National Academies Press, 2014.

National Research Council. Committee on Management of University Intellectual Property. *Managing University Intellectual Property in the Public Interest.* Washington, DC: National Academies Press, 2011.

National Research Council. Committee on Research Universities. *Research Universities and the Future of America: Ten Breakthrough Actions Vital to Our Nation's Prosperity and Security*. Washington, DC: National Academies Press, 2013.

Nelson, Richard R. "The Simple Economics of Basic Scientific Research." *Journal of Political Economy* 67, no. 3 (June 1959): 297–306.

Nelson, Richard R., Kristin Buterbaugh, Marcel Perl, and Annetine Gelijns. "How Medical Know-How Progresses." *Research Policy* 40 (2011): 1339–1344.

Nelson, Richard R., and Sidney G. Winter. *An Evolutionary Theory of Economic Change*. Cambridge, MA: Harvard University Press, 1982.

Nevins, Allen. *The State Universities and Democracy*. Urbana: University of Illinois Press, 1962.

Newfield, Christopher. "The End of the American Funding Model: What Comes Next?" *American Literature* 82, no. 3 (September 2010): 611–635.

Newman, John Henry. *The Idea of a University*. Notre Dame: University of Notre Dame Press, 1982. Reprint of the edition published by Longmans, Green, and Company, 1873.

Niosi, Jorge, Paolo Saviotti, Bertrand Bellon, and Michael M. Crow. "National Systems of Innovation: In Search of a Workable Concept." *Technology in Society* 15 (1993): 207–227.

Noer, Michael. "America's Top Colleges." *Forbes* (August 20, 2012).

Nussbaum, Martha. *Not for Profit: Why Democracy Needs the Humanities*. Princeton, NJ: Princeton University Press, 2010.

Oleson, Alexandra, and John Voss, eds. *The Organization of Knowledge in Modern America, 1860–1920*. Baltimore: Johns Hopkins University Press, 1979.

Ortega y Gasset, José. *The Mission of the University*. Edited and translated by Howard Lee Nostrand, with a new introduction by Clark Kerr. New Brunswick, NJ: Transaction Publishers, 1992. First published 1944.

Ostrom, Elinor. *Governing the Commons: The Evolution of Institutions for Collective Action*. Cambridge: Cambridge University Press, 1990.

Paradeise, Catherine, Emanuela Reale, Ivar Bleiklie, and Ewan Ferlie. *University Governance: Western European Comparative Perspectives*. Dordrecht: Springer, 2009.

Peck, Jeffrey M. "Berlin and Constance: Two Models of Reform and Their Hermeneutic and Pedagogical Relevance." *German Quarterly* 60, no. 3 (Summer 1987): 388–406.

Pew Center for the States. "Pursuing the American Dream: Economic Mobility across Generations." Washington DC: Economic Mobility Project, Pew Charitable Trusts, 2012.

Phillips, Elizabeth D. "Improving Advising Using Technology and Data Analytics." *Change: The Magazine of Higher Learning* (January–February 2013).

Piketty, Thomas. *Capital in the Twenty-First Century*. Translated by Arthur Goldhammer. Cambridge, MA: Belknap Press of Harvard University Press, 2014.

Piketty, Thomas, and Emmanuel Saez. "Income Inequality in the United States, 1913–1998." *Quarterly Journal of Economics* 118, no. 1 (February 2003): 1–39.

Pisano, Gary P., and W. C. Shih. "Restoring American Competitiveness." *Harvard Business Review* 87, no. 7–8 (July–August 2009): 114–125.

Polanyi, Michael. *The Tacit Dimension*. Garden City, NY: Doubleday, 1966.

Porter, Eduardo. "A Simple Equation: More Education=More Income." *New York Times* (September 10, 2014).

Porter, Michael E. "Clusters and the New Economics of Competition." *Harvard Business Review* 76, no. 6 (November/December 1998): 77–90.

Porter, Theodore M. *The Rise of Statistical Thinking, 1820–1900*. Princeton, NJ: Princeton University Press, 1986.

Powell, Walter W., and Kaisa Snellman. "The Knowledge Economy." *Annual Review of Sociology* 30 (2004): 199–220.

Price, Derek J. de Solla. "Is Technology Historically Independent of Science? A Study in Statistical Historiography." *Technology and Culture* 6, no. 4 (Autumn 1965): 553–568.

———. *Little Science, Big Science, and Beyond*. New York: Columbia University Press, 1986. First published 1963.

———. "Networks of Scientific Papers." *Science* 149 (1965): 510–515.

Readings, Bill. *The University in Ruins*. Cambridge, MA: Harvard University Press, 1996.

Reardon, Sean F. "The Widening Academic Achievement Gap between the Rich and the Poor: New Evidence and Possible Explanations." In *Whither Opportunity? Rising Inequality, Schools, and Children's Life Chances*. Edited by Greg J. Duncan and Richard J. Murname. New York: Russell Sage Foundation, 2011.

Rhoades, Gary. "Calling on the Past: The Quest for the Collegiate Ideal." *Journal of Higher Education* 61, no. 5 (September/October 1990): 512–534.

Rhoads, Robert A., Xiaoyang Wang, Xiaoguang Shi, and Yongcai Chang. *China's Rising Research Universities: A New Era of Global Ambition*. Baltimore: Johns Hopkins University Press, 2014.

Rhodes, Frank H. T. *The Creation of the Future: The Role of the American University*. Ithaca, NY: Cornell University Press, 2001.

———. "Sustainability: The Ultimate Liberal Art." *Chronicle of Higher Education* (October 20, 2006).

Romanelli, Elaine, and Michael L. Tushman. "Organizational Transformation as Punctuated Equilibrium." *Academy of Management Journal* 37, no. 5 (1994): 1141–1166.

Romer, Paul M. "Endogenous Technological Change." *Journal of Political Economy* 98, no. 5, pt. 2 (1990): S71–102.

Rorty, Richard, *Consequences of Pragmatism*. Minneapolis: University of Minnesota Press, 1982.

———. *Philosophy as Cultural Politics: Philosophical Papers, Volume 4*. Cambridge: Cambridge University Press, 2007.

———. "Postmodernist Bourgeois Liberalism." In *Pragmatism: A Reader*. Edited by Louis Menand, 329–336. New York: Random House, 1997.

Rosenberg, Nathan. "America's Entrepreneurial Universities." In *The Emergence of Entrepreneurship Policy: Governance, Start-ups, and Growth in the U.S. Knowledge Economy*. Edited by David M. Hart. Cambridge: Cambridge University Press, 2003.

———. *Inside the Black Box: Technology and Economics*. Cambridge: Cambridge University Press, 1982.

———. "Why Do Firms Do Basic Research (with Their Own Money)?" *Research Policy* 19 (1990): 165–174.

Rosenberg, Nathan, and L. E. Birdzell. *How the West Grew Rich: The Economic Transformation of the Industrial World*. New York: Basic Books, 1986.

Rosenberg, Nathan, and Richard R. Nelson. "American Universities and Technical Advance in Industry." *Research Policy* 23, no. 3 (1994): 323–348.

Rothblatt, Sheldon. "Historical and Comparative Remarks on the Federal Principle in Higher Education." *History of Education* 16, no. 3 (1987): 151–180.

Sarewitz, Daniel. *Frontiers of Illusion: Science, Technology, and the Politics of Progress.* Philadelphia: Temple University Press, 1996.

Saxenian, Anna Lee. *Regional Advantage: Culture and Competition in Silicon Valley and Route 128.* Cambridge, MA: Harvard University Press, 1994.

Schultz, Theodore W. "Investment in Human Capital." *American Economic Review* 51, no. 1 (March 1961): 1–17.

Schumpeter, Joseph A. *The Theory of Economic Development.* Cambridge, MA: Harvard University Press, 1934.

Shaffer, Elinor S. "Romantic Philosophy and the Organization of the Disciplines: The Founding of the Humboldt University of Berlin." In *Romanticism and the Sciences.* Edited by Andrew Cunningham and Nicholas Jardine, 38–54. Cambridge: Cambridge University Press, 1990.

Shils, Edward. "The Order of Learning in the United States: The Ascendency of the University." In *The Organization of Knowledge in Modern America, 1860–1920.* Edited by Alexandra Oleson and John Voss. Baltimore: Johns Hopkins University Press, 1979.

Shirky, Clay. *Cognitive Surplus: Creativity and Generosity in a Connected Age.* New York: Penguin, 2010.

Sieloff, Charles G. "If Only HP Knew What HP Knows: The Roots of Knowledge Management at Hewlett-Packard." *Journal of Knowledge Management* 3, no. 1 (1999): 47–53.

Simon, Herbert A. *Reason in Human Affairs.* Stanford: Stanford University Press, 1983.

———. *The Sciences of the Artificial,* 3rd ed. Cambridge, MA: MIT Press, 1996. First published 1966.

Slaughter, Sheila, and Larry L. Leslie. *Academic Capitalism: Politics, Policies, and the Entrepreneurial University.* Baltimore: Johns Hopkins University Press, 1997.

Slaughter, Sheila, and Gary Rhoades. *Academic Capitalism and the New Economy: Markets, State, and Higher Education.* Baltimore: Johns Hopkins University Press, 2004.

Snow, C. P. *The Two Cultures and the Scientific Revolution.* Cambridge: Cambridge University Press, 1960.

Solow, Robert M. "Technical Change and the Aggregate Production Function." *Review of Economics and Statistics* 39 (1957): 312–320.

Stahler, Gerald J., and William R. Tash. "Centers and Institutes in the Research University: Issues, Problems, and Prospects." *Journal of Higher Education* 65, no. 5 (September/October 1994): 540–554.

Stark, Jack. *The Wisconsin Idea: The University's Service to the State.* Madison, WI: Legislative Reference Bureau, 1996.

Steck, Henry. "Corporatization of the University: Seeking Conceptual Clarity." *Annals of the American Academy of Political and Social Science* 585 (January 2003): 66–83.

Stiglitz, Joseph E. "Knowledge as a Global Public Good." In *Global Public Goods: International Cooperation in the Twenty-First Century.* Edited by Inge Kaul, Isabelle Grunberg, and Marc Stern. Oxford: Oxford University Press, 1999.

———. *The Price of Inequality: How Today's Divided Society Endangers Our Future.* New York: W. W. Norton and Company, 2012.

Stokes, Donald E. *Pasteur's Quadrant: Basic Science and Technological Innovation.* Washington, DC: Brookings Institution Press, 1997.

Stuhr, John J. *Pragmatism, Postmodernism, and the Future of Philosophy.* New York: Routledge, 2003.

Swanson, Christopher B. "Closing the Graduation Gap: Educational and Economic Conditions in America's Largest Cities." Bethesda, MD: Editorial Projects in Education, 2009.

Swoboda, Wolfram W. "Disciplines and Interdisciplinarity: A Historical Perspective." In *Interdisciplinarity and Higher Education.* Edited by Joseph J. Kockelmans. University Park: Pennsylvania State University Press, 1979.

Taylor, Mark C. *Crisis on Campus: A Bold Plan for Reforming Our Colleges and Universities.* New York: Alfred A. Knopf, 2010.

Theil, Stefan. "The Campus of the Future: To Better Compete, A Few Bold Leaders Are Rethinking Their Schools from the Ground Up." *Newsweek* (August 9, 2008).

Thelin, John R. *A History of American Higher Education.* Baltimore: Johns Hopkins University Press, 2004.

Thiel, Peter. "College Doesn't Create Success." *New York Times* (August 25, 2011)

Tobin, Eugene M. "The Modern Evolution of America's Flagship Universities." In *Crossing the Finish Line: Completing College at America's Public Universities.* Edited by William G. Bowen, Matthew M. Chingos, and Michael S. McPherson, 239–264. Princeton, NJ: Princeton University Press, 2009.

Toma, J. Douglas. "Institutional Strategy: Positioning for Prestige." In *The Organization of Higher Education: Managing Colleges for a New Era.* Edited by Michael N. Bastedo, 118–159. Baltimore: Johns Hopkins University Press, 2012.

"Too Many Kids Go to College." *Intelligence Squared (IQ²)* debate series, Chicago, October 12, 2011, http://intelligencesquaredus.org/debates/past-debates/item/550-too-many-kids-go-to-college-our-first-debate-in-chicago.

Turner, Sarah E. "Going to College and Finishing College: Explaining Different Educational Outcomes." In *College Choices: The Economics of Where to Go, When to Go, and How to Pay for It.* Edited by Caroline M. Hoxby, 13–61. Chicago: University of Chicago Press, 2004.

"The University of the Future." *Nature* 446, no. 7139 (April 26, 2007).

Urahn, Susan K. et al. *Pursuing the American Dream: Economic Mobility across Generations.* Washington, DC: Pew Charitable Trusts, 2012.

Uzzi, Brian, Satyam Mukherjee, Michael Stringer, and Ben Jones. "Atypical Combinations and Scientific Impact." *Science* 342 (October 25, 2013): 468–472.

Vandenbussche, Jérôme, Philippe Aghion, and Costas Meghir. "Growth Distance to Frontier and Composition of Human Capital." *Journal of Economic Growth* 11, no. 2 (2006): 97–127.

Veysey, Laurence R. *The Emergence of the American University.* Chicago: University of Chicago Press, 1965.

Victor, David G. "Recovering Sustainable Development." *Foreign Affairs* 85, no. 1 (January/February 2006): 91–103.

Von Hippel, Eric. "Sticky Information and the Locus of Problem Solving: Implications for Innovation." *Management Science* 40: 429–439.

Voosen, Paul. "Microbiology Leaves the Solo Author Behind." *Chronicle of Higher Education* (November 11, 2013).

Wallerstein, Immanuel. "Anthropology, Sociology, and Other Dubious Disciplines." *Current Anthropology* 44, no. 4 (August–October 2003): 453–465.

Walsh, Taylor. *Unlocking the Gates: How and Why Leading Universities Are Opening Up Access to Their Courses.* Princeton, NJ: Princeton University Press, 2011.

Weber, Max. *On Charisma and Institution Building: Selected Papers.* Edited by S. N. Eisenstadt. Chicago: University of Chicago Press, 1968.

———. *The Protestant Ethic and the Spirit of Capitalism.* Translated by Talcott Parsons. New York: Charles Scribner's Sons, 1952. First published 1905.

———. "The Sociology of Charismatic Authority." In *Essays in Sociology.* Edited and translated by H. H. Gerth and C. Wright Mills. Oxford: Oxford University Press, 1946.

Weick, Karl E., and Robert E. Quinn. "Organizational Change and Development." *Annual Review of Psychology* 50 (1999): 361–386.

Weingart, Peter. "A Short History of Knowledge Formations." In *The Oxford Handbook of Interdisciplinarity.* Edited by Robert Frodeman, Julie Thompson Klein, and Carl Mitcham, 3–14. Oxford: Oxford University Press, 2010.

———. "Interdisciplinarity and the New Governance of Universities." *University Experiments in Interdisciplinarity: Obstacles and Opportunities.* Edited by Peter Weingart and Britta Padberg. Bielefeld: Transcript, 2014.

Wenger, Etienne. *Communities of Practice: Learning, Meaning, and Identity.* Cambridge: Cambridge University Press, 1998.

Westwick, Peter J. *The National Labs: Science in an American System, 1947–1974.* Cambridge, MA: Harvard University Press, 2003.

Wilson, Alan. *Knowledge Power: Interdisciplinary Education for a Complex World.* London: Routledge, 2010.

Winterer, Caroline. *The Culture of Classicism: Ancient Greece and Rome in American Intellectual Life, 1780–1910.* Baltimore: Johns Hopkins University Press, 2002.

Wittrock, Björn. "Institutes for Advanced Study: Ideas, Histories, Rationales." Keynote Address on the Occasion of the Inauguration of the Helsinki Collegium for Advanced Studies, University of Helsinki (December 2, 2002).

Wood, Peter, and Michael Toscano. "What Does Bowdoin Teach? How a Contemporary Liberal Arts College Shapes Students." Washington, DC: National Association of Scholars, 2013.

Yusuf, Shahid. "University-Industry Links: Policy Dimensions." In *How Universities Can Promote Economic Growth.* Edited by Shahid Yusuf and Kaoru Nabeshima, 1–25. Washington, DC: International Bank for Reconstruction and Development, 2007.

Zachary, G. Pascal. *Endless Frontier: Vannevar Bush, Engineer of the American Century.* Cambridge, MA: MIT Press, 1999.

Zemsky, Robert. *Making Reform Work: The Case for Transforming American Higher Education.* New Brunswick, NJ: Rutgers University Press, 2009.

Ziman, John, ed. *Technological Innovation as an Evolutionary Process.* Cambridge: Cambridge University Press, 2000.

# INDEX

AAU. *See* Association of American Universities; gold standard in American higher education; research universities, American; *names of member institutions*

Abbott, Andrew, 179, 185–86, 198

Abrams, M. H., 143–44

academia. *See* academic community (communities); higher education, American; research universities, American

academic charisma. *See* charismatic authority (academic charisma); William Clark

academic community (communities): Arizona State University, ix–xi, xiii, 60–61, 242, 257, 259; ASU charter statement, 62, 255; differentiation, 64, 304–5; dissensus within, 3; Robert Maynard Hutchins, 129–30; inquiry, correlation with, 178, 205–6; lineage, 308; multiversity, 18; New American University conception of, 8, 64, 218–19, 248, 255, 308. *See also* communities of practice; epistemic communities; invisible colleges

academic departments: disciplinary correlation, 126, 179, 185–86, 187–88; German academic model, 77, 80, 83; interdisciplinary reconfiguration, 187–88, 199–201, 212–13n79; Johns Hopkins University, 76–77, 83; Clark Kerr on, 130. *See also* Arizona State University; interdisciplinarity

academic disciplines. *See* disciplinarity; interdisciplinarity; transdisciplinarity

academic enterprise: Arizona State University, 253, 268–72, 275; as characteristic in emergence of American research universities, 102–3, 104 (figure 13), 159; as characteristic of land-grant institutions, 159–60; as characteristic of research universities, 102–3, 120, 160, 268–69; in contradistinction to bureaucratic agencies, 103, 245, 307; as correlate of academic charisma, 120; as correlate of creativity, discovery, and innovation, 159; design aspiration, 62, 242, 244, 268–70. *See also* knowledge enterprises

academic freedom, 128–30, 178, 219, 243, 248, 307; German academic culture, correlation with, 79–81, 82–83. *See also* German academic model; Wilhelm von Humboldt; University of Berlin

academic models. *See* Cambridge University; German academic model; land-grant colleges and universities; New American University; Oxbridge model; Oxford University; research universities, American; University of Berlin

academic organization. *See* design, institutional

Academic Ranking of World Universities (ARWU), 21, 65n9, 265, 301n41

academic rankings. *See* rankings of colleges and universities

academic tradition. *See* filiopietism; tradition, academic

accessibility: Arizona State University as representative of research-grade institution, vii, 59–62, 241–42, 251–52, 255, 293–96; colleges and universities generally, 5, 9, 30, 245, 252; comparative, 251–52, 260 (figure 14); federal programs, 94; historical, 32–33, 240, 245; national imperative, 304–6; online learning, 138, 273–75; quality, extraneous to evaluation of, 264–65; research universities, vii, 7, 18, 23, 32, 38, 49, 99, 103, 260 (figure 14), 304–6; socioeconomically disadvantaged, 30–31, 36–38, 42–47, 48–49, 53–60, 293–96; socioeconomic mobility, 9, 24, 30–31, 36–38, 42–47, 48–49, 53–60. *See also* admissions

Adams, John, 27–28, 98

adaptation (adaptivity), institutional, 20, 26, 139, 223, 306; academic enterprise, correlate of, 182, 269; Complex Adaptive Systems Initiative (CASI), 279, 281; design process, factor in, 248; evolutionary model, 63, 102–3, 180–82; knowledge enterprises, characteristic of, 8, 63, 103, 182, 204, 218, 240; New American University model, adaptation (adaptivity), institutional (*cont.*) characteristic of, viii–ix, 8, 19, 181, 240, 289; pedagogical models, 80, 142, 274; pragmatic conception of knowledge, 159, 218, 224. *See also* knowledge enterprises

admissions: correlation with family income, 42–45, 44 (figures 5, 6), 46 (figures 7a, 7b), 47–49, 54–55, 56 (figure 10), 59–60, 71n82; egalitarian vs. elitist, 5, 8–9, 27–28, 34, 36–38, 70n59, 88–89, 92; selective colleges and universities, 5, 9, 23, 30, 34, 61, 241, 251, 305–6. *See also* exclusivity (exclusion) in admissions practices; selectivity of colleges and universities

affordability (higher education), 1–2, 4–5, 53, 134, 138–40, 210n44, 260 (figure 14); Arizona State University, 253–54, 258–59, 274–75, 288–92, 291 (figure 17); cost disease, 135–38; University Innovation Alliance, 297

Allen, Douglas W. ("institutional revolution"), 89–90

American Century, 9, 38–39

American Dream, 8, 27, 38, 45, 48

American research universities. *See* research universities, American; research universities, private; research universities, public; *names of individual universities*

American Revolution, vii, 17, 27, 38, 92, 100

Arizona, 241, 253, 267, 271, 277; demographic trends, 249–51, 296; funding of higher education, 29–30, 288–90, 289 (figure 16), 291. *See also* Arizona State University

Arizona State University: academic community, ix–xi, xiii, 60–61, 242, 257, 259; accessibility, 59–62, 241–42, 251–53, 255, 293–96; accessibility, comparative, 252–52, 260 (figure 14); accessibility as extraneous to evaluation of quality, 264–65; accessibility to research-grade academic platform likened to conflation of University of California and Cal State systems, 252; accessibility to socioeconomically disadvantaged, 293–96; affordability, 253–54, 258–59, 274–75, 288–92, 291 (figure 17); charter statement, 62, 255; enrollment, 60–62; financial aid, 258–59, 260 (figure 14), 291, 293–96, 295 (figure 18); foundational prototype for New American University, viii, 12, 60–62, 240–42, 255, 296; graduate programs, ASU, vii, 256, 257–58, 265–66, 269–70, 275, 288–89, 292, 301n43; graduation

rates, 241, 253, 256–57, 290; institutional peers, 246, 262–63, 289–90, 292; online learning (ASU Online), 273–75; socioeconomic diversity, vii, 7–8, 12, 60–61, 240–42, 251, 253, 297; students, 257–58, 264–65, 266–67; tuition, 258, 275, 289–90, 291 (figure 17); vision statement, 60, 242. *See also* Arizona State University: design aspirations; design limitations; design process; faculty; research enterprise; research initiatives, centers, and institutes; schools

Arizona State University: design aspirations, 62–62, 218, 242–44, 267–77; academic enterprise, Arizona State University, 253, 268–72, 275. *See also* academic enterprise; use-inspired research

Arizona State University: design limitations, 18, 19, 229–30, 235; design process, viii–xi, 12, 60–64, 179–80, 240–49, 278, 298n4; interdisciplinary reconfiguration, 62–63, 64, 245–47, 270, 277–78; school-centrism, 62–63, 245–47

Arizona State University: faculty, 241, 243, 245, 254, 259, 261–62; diversity, 261; growth, 256, 261, 262, 301n35; honors, 256, 259, 261; productivity, 266–67

Arizona State University: research enterprise, ix, 62, 204, 241, 254, 261, 277–88; Arizona Technology Enterprises (AzTE), 263–64; research expenditures, 255–56, 261–64, 264 (figure 15), 267; technology transfer, 271–72

Arizona State University: research initiatives, centers, and institutes, 277–88; Biodesign Institute, 270, 279, 280; Center for the Study of Religion and Conflict, 279, 282–83; Complex Adaptive Systems Initiative (CASI), 279; Consortium for Science, Policy, and Outcomes (CSPO), 279, 283–88; Flexible Display Center, 279; Global Institute of Sustainability (GIOS), 270, 278–79, 281–82; Herberger Institute for Design and the Arts, 279; Institute for Humanities Research, 279; Institute for Social Science Research, 279; LightWorks, 279; Security and Defense Systems Initiative (SDSI), 279

Arizona State University: schools: Ira A. Fulton Schools of Engineering, 269, 273, 276, 280, 282; School of Earth and Space Exploration (SESE), 270, 280–81; School of

Historical, Philosophical, and Religious
Studies, 278; School of Human Evolution
and Social Change (SHESC), 278, 281;
School of Life Sciences (SOLS), 278;
School of Sustainability (SOS), 279,
281–82
Arizona Technology Enterprises (AzTE). *See
under* Arizona State University: research
enterprise
Arum, Richard, and Josipa Roksa, *Academically Adrift*, 2, 14n5
Association of American Universities (AAU),
31–32, 34, 84, 108n46, 290; aggregate
enrollment in member institutions,
31–32, 68–69n45, 101–2; land-grant member
institutions, 84–85. *See also* gold standard
in American higher education
authority. *See* charismatic authority (academic
charisma)
Autor, David H., 41–42, 54

baccalaureate attainment. *See* Arizona State
University: graduation rates; educational
attainment
basic research. *See* Bohr's quadrant;
discovery; science (scientific research)
Baumol, William J. (cost disease), 135–38
Bayh-Dole Act of 1980, 162–63, 174n45
Berkeley. *See* University of California,
Berkeley
Berkeley envy, 118, 121, 122. *See also*
Harvardization; isomorphism; prestige;
University of Michigan
*Bildung*, 79, 272. *See also* German academic
model; University of Berlin; Wilhelm von
Humboldt
Biodesign Institute. *See under* Arizona State
University: research initiatives, centers,
and institutes
Bloom, Allan, *Closing of the American
Mind*, 3
Bloom, Harold, 120
Bohr's quadrant, 202. *See also* Donald E.
Stokes; Pasteur's quadrant
Bok, Derek, 3. *See also* Harvard University
Bowdoin College, 4, 14n11, 99, 121. *See also*
liberal arts colleges; liberal bias in
academia; scale of American higher
education
Bowen, William G., 35–36, 42, 47, 50, 53; cost
disease (William J. Baumol), 135–38

Bozeman, Barry: on John Dewey, 222–23;
pragmatic idealism, 222; pragmatist stance,
221–23; public interest, 222–23; public
values, 222–23, 285; social consensus,
222. *See also* pragmatism
British academic model. *See* Cambridge
University; gold standard in American
higher education; Ivy League; Oxbridge
model; Oxford University
Brooks, David, 47, 54, 59
Brooks, Frederick P., 179–80, 181. *See also*
design (concept); design, institutional
Brown, John Seely, 117–18, 177, 189, 201,
207–8n3, 210n39; pragmatism, 221, 238n29
bureaucracy (bureaucratization): academic
enterprise, in contradistinction to, 245,
269; Anthony Downs, 124–25; German
academic culture, 80–81; "institutional
revolution" (Douglas Allen), 89–90;
isomorphism, 124–25; research universities, 10–11, 26, 85, 96–97, 103, 117, 135, 181–82,
307; Max Weber, 119–20, 124–25. *See also*
academic enterprise; isomorphism; Max
Weber
Bush, Vannevar, 10, 94–95, 111n89. See also
*Science: The Endless Frontier*
business and industry. *See* triple helix
(university-industry-government)

California Institute of Technology (Caltech),
99, 260 (figure 14), 262, 263
California Master Plan for Higher Education,
33, 69n50, 133–34, 252–53, 299–300n22;
Arizona State University accessibility to
research-grade academic platform likened
to conflation of University of California
and Cal State systems, 252. *See also* Clark
Kerr; University of California; University
of California, Berkeley
Cambridge University, 9–10, 17–18, 75–78, 80,
126, 166; C. P. Snow lecture, 183, 205;
elitism, 88–89, 110n74. *See also* Oxbridge
model; Oxford University
Carnegie Corporation for Higher Education,
151
Carnegie Foundation for the Advancement of
Teaching, 14, 20–21, 65n8, 262–63
Carnevale, Anthony, 32–33, 45–47, 54, 59,
74n128, 123
Centre National de la Recherche Scientifique
(CNRS), 93

charismatic authority (academic charisma),
119–21, 146n16, 146n19. *See also* filiopietism;
Max Weber; tradition, academic; William
Clark
Chinese universities, 19, 142, 276–77
Christensen, Clayton, 4–5, 15nn14–15, 126. *See
also* disruptive innovation; Henry Eyring
Clark, Gregory, 154–55, 226–27
Clark, William, 77, 119–20, 121, 146n16,
146n19. *See also* charismatic authority
(academic charisma)
Cold War university ("military-industrial-
academic complex"), 10, 96–97, 218–19
Cole, Jonathan R., xi, 78, 83; Chinese universities, 19; German research university model,
77; interdisciplinarity, 95, 185; Clark Kerr,
133–34; knowledge production, 152–54,
170nn3–4; national innovation system,
168–69; Cardinal Newman, 78; research
universities, 21, 83, 127, 131, 152–54, 167
collaboration, 62, 139–40, 162, 168–69, 182,
188–89, 226, 234, 255, 267–68, 275–77;
historic institutional prototypes, 197–201;
interdisciplinary, 187–89, 190–97, 206,
208n4, 306–7; solitary investigator, 197–201.
*See also* Arizona State University: research
initiatives, centers, and institutes; interdisciplinarity; transdisciplinarity; triple helix
(university-industry-government)
Columbia University: Center for Science,
Policy, and Outcomes (CSPO), 284–85;
graduate education, 131; interdisciplinary
programs, 199; as member institution of
Ivy League, 100; as representative of gold
standard in American higher education,
vii, 17–18; research enterprise, 263; role
in emergence of American research
universities, 83, 88
commercialization. *See* technology transfer
communities of practice, 190, 192–94, 197
community. *See* pragmatism
community colleges, 121, 253–54; California
Master Plan for Higher Education, 133–34,
252; enrollments, 29–30, 34, 49, 53, 100–101;
graduation rates, 53
competition (among universities), 17–18,
26–27, 81, 83–85, 91–93, 261, 307; ASU,
60–61, 253; decentralization, 10, 85;
historical trajectory, 102–5, 104 (figure 13);
isomorphism, 122–24, 139; selectivity, 47,
73n114

complex adaptive knowledge enterprises. *See*
Arizona State University; complexity;
knowledge enterprises
Complex Adaptive Systems Initiative (CASI).
*See under* Arizona State University:
research initiatives, centers, and institutes
complexity: complex adaptive knowledge
enterprises, viii, 8, 13, 19, 63, 218, 240–41,
298n1; social condition, 13, 26–27, 62–63,
181–83, 202, 204, 307–9. *See also* knowledge
enterprises
comprehensive knowledge enterprise. *See*
knowledge enterprises
Consortium for Science, Policy, and
Outcomes (CSPO), 279, 283–88. *See also*
Daniel Sarewitz
Constitution of the United States, 27, 91–92,
93, 235, 306
Cornell University: Ezra Cornell, 87;
land-grant status, 84; as representative
of gold standard in American higher
education, 18; as representative of
utilitarian values of Morrill Act, 86–88;
research enterprise, 263; role in emergence
of American research universities, 87–88;
Weill Cornell Medical College in Qatar, 276
Cornford, F. M., *Microcosmographia
Academica*, 126–27
cost disease (William J. Baumol and William G.
Bowen), 135–38
creative destruction, 22, 66n16, 103, 120, 160.
crisis in higher education. *See* higher
education, American: perception of crisis in
Critchley, Simon, 118, 145n13
Crow, Michael M., 18, 74n131, 284, 291–92,
298n1
Curtius, Ernst Robert, 114n129, 140, 149n84,
308

Dartmouth University, 7, 76, 87, 100, 115, 130
decentralization of American higher
education, 10, 19–20, 85, 91–93, 210n36, 246,
305–6
Delbanco, Andrew, 115
democracy: higher education, significance
for, 3, 22, 27–28, 29, 35, 38, 111n89, 143, 154,
158, 309; pragmatism, 218, 220, 223, 235,
237n17
design (concept), 11–12, 117–18, 177–80,
247–48; Frederick Brooks, 179–80, 181;
bureaucracy, correlation with, 124–26;

coevolution (between problem and solution), 181; human limitation, 229–30; interdisciplinarity, correlation with, 184–86, 187–90, 190–97; Bruce Mau, 182–83; models, 190–97; Herbert A. Simon, 180, 208–9n13; Vitruvius, *De Architectura*, 180. *See also* Arizona State University: design process; design, institutional; interdisciplinarity

design, institutional, 11, 117–18, 177–83, 189–90, 190–97, 208n4, 208–9n13, 227. *See also* Arizona State University: design limitations; design process; knowledge production; New American University; research universities, American

design aspirations. *See* Arizona State University: design aspirations

design limitations. *See* design, institutional

design process, viii–xi, 12, 60–64, 179–80, 240–49, 278, 298n4. *See also* Arizona State University: design process; design (concept); design, institutional

DiMaggio, Paul J., 122, 123, 124, 155. *See also* Walter W. Powell

disciplinarity, viii, 3, 82, 117, 191, 201, 206–7, 231–32, 234; Andrew Abbott, 179, 185–86, 198; departmental correlation, disciplinary departments, 77, 80, 83, 126, 179, 185–86, 199–201, 212–13n79; disciplinary hierarchies, 206; Immanuel Wallerstein, 117, 186, 197. *See also* interdisciplinarity; specialization; transdisciplinarity

disciplines. *See* disciplinarity; interdisciplinarity; specialization; transdisciplinarity

discovery (discoveries, creativity, and innovation), 10–11, 25–26, 161–64, 232–33; basic (fundamental) versus applied research, 25–26, 142, 152, 158–69, 171n15, 202–3; economic growth, correlate of, 5, 10–11, 20–21, 22–23, 25–26, 29, 39, 59, 61–62, 66n16, 89, 154–58, 158–69; federal investment, 10, 92–97, 98, 151, 161–64, 173n41; humanities, 152–54; interdisciplinary, 189–90, 198, 212–13n79, 277–78; social sciences, 152–54; specialization, viii, 3, 17–18, 25–26, 76, 81–82, 92, 191, 206–7, 231–32, 234; technological innovation, correlate of, 10–11, 11–12, 22–23, 25–26, 39, 65n7, 84, 96, 121, 137, 141, 152–54, 158–69. *See also* innovation, technological; knowledge production; research and development

(R&D); research universities, American; science (scientific research)

disruptive innovation, 4–5, 15nn14–15, 126. *See also* Clayton Christensen

diversity. *See* socioeconomic diversity

Douglass, John Aubrey, 29, 33, 69n50, 133, 299n22, 306

Downs, Anthony, 15n29, 124–25. *See also* bureaucracy (bureaucratization); isomorphism

Duderstadt, James J., viii, xi, 5–6, 142, 186. *See also* University of Michigan

earnings: of baccalaureate degree recipients. *See* educational attainment; employment (correlation with educational attainment)

economic growth: innovation and, 5, 10–11, 20–21, 22–23, 25–26, 29, 39, 59, 61–62, 66n16, 89, 154–58, 158–69

economic mobility. *See* socioeconomic mobility

educational attainment: across generational cohorts, 50, 52 (figure 9), 72–73n104; correlation with employment, 4, 41–42, 54–55, 56 (figure 10), 59–60, 161, 163–64; correlation with family income, 42–45, 44 (figures 5, 6), 46 (figures 7a, 7b), 47–49, 54–55, 56 (figure 10), 59–60, 71n82; correlation with inequality, 9, 33–34, 35–38, 40–42, 48, 153–54, 250, 295; correlation with middle class, 54, 56 (figure 10), 59–60; international comparisons of, 49–50, 51 (figure 8); wage differentials, 54–55, 59–60. *See also* employment; graduation rates

egalitarian conception of American higher education, 5, 8–9, 27–28, 34, 36–38, 70n59, 88–89, 92; land-grant colleges and universities, 84–85, 251; New American University, 60–61, 242, 251. *See also* meritocracy

Eisenhower, Dwight D., 93–94, 115

electives, system of, 127–28, 129. *See also* Thomas Jefferson; University of Virginia

elitism in American higher education, vii, 1, 5, 9, 13, 19, 23, 30, 34–38, 60–61, 75–77, 101–2, 110n74, 241, 251, 305–6. *See also* egalitarian conception of American higher education; exclusivity (exclusion) in admissions practices; gold standard in American higher education; liberal arts colleges; selectivity of colleges and universities employment (correlation with educational attainment), 4, 41–42, 54–55, 56 (figure 10), 59–60, 161, 163–64. *See also* educational attainment

engineering, 22; industry, relation to, 167; interdisciplinarity, 188, 205; liberal arts, constituent discipline of (Duderstadt), 142; José Ortega y Gasset on, 245; research universities, role in, 84–85, 87, 88, 96; specialization, 142, 245; STEM, constituent discipline of, 28–29, 49, 141, 270; techno-logical innovation, 22, 155, 156–57, 160, 171n15; "two cultures" (C. P. Snow), constituent discipline of, 183–84. *See also* Arizona State University: schools

English academic model. *See* Cambridge University; gold standard in American higher education; Ivy League; Oxbridge model; Oxford University

enrollments, 34–38, 53–54, 59–60, 97–102, 103–5, 104 (figure 13), 256; Ivy League, 31, 34–35, 68n44, 99–100, 113n114, 300n27. *See also* Arizona State University; scale of American higher education; *names of individual universities*

enterprise: *See* academic enterprise

epistemic communities, 138, 190, 194–95, 197, 208n4, 219

Etzkowitz, Henry (triple helix), 88, 102–3, 155–56, 159–61, 187–88, 195–96

exclusivity (exclusion) in admissions practices, 5, 9, 23, 30, 34, 61, 241, 251, 305–6; Chinese universities, 19; Great Britain, 89, 105–6n9, 110n74; Stanford University, 33; University of California, 33, 69n50, 251–52. *See also* Arizona State University: accessibility; *names of individual universities*

Eyring, Henry J., 4. *See also* Clayton Christensen; disruptive innovation

faculty (professors, professoriate), ix, 3, 14n8, 32, 36–37, 50, 127, 128, 139; correlation with research, 3, 10, 18, 20, 25, 37, 60, 76, 78–82, 182, 261, 306–7; disciplinary affiliation, 126, 186–87; "disengagement compact," 2; governance, 126, 128, 129; interdisciplinar-ity, 169, 184–85, 196–97, 198, 199, 206–7, 212–13n79, 246–47; Clark Kerr on, 130; José Ortega y Gasset on, 245. *See also* Arizona State University: faculty; teaching

family income: educational attainment, correlation with, 42–45, 44 (figures 5, 6), 46 (figures 7a, 7b), 47–49, 54–55, 56 (figure 10), 59–60, 71n82; educational attainment across generational cohorts, 50, 52 (figure 9), 72–73n104; inequality, 9, 33–34, 35–38, 40–42, 48, 153–54, 250, 295; low-income high achievers (Caroline Hoxby and Christopher Avery), 53–54, 73n114, 293–96; middle class, correlation with, 54, 56 (figure 10), 59–60. *See also* educational attainment; socioeconomic disadvantage

federal government: Arizona State University, 261–64, 264 (figure 15); national laborato-ries (U.S. Department of Energy), 94–95, 111n90, 168–69, 173n41, 176n68, 187–88; research funding, 10, 92–97, 98, 151, 161–64, 173n41. *See also* Pell Grants; state governments

filiopietism, 10–11, 116–19, 121–22, 134, 240; isomorphism, correlation with, 118–19, 122–26; prestige, correlation with, 123–24; tradition, correlation with, 122, 182. *See also* isomorphism; prestige; tradition, academic

financial aid. *See* Arizona State University: financial aid

flagship universities. *See* research universi-ties, American; research universities, public

Fogel, Daniel Mark, 28–29, 143–44

for-profit colleges and universities, 30, 101

Franklin, Benjamin, 214n110

Frodeman, Robert, 24–25, 66n22, 234; interdisciplinarity, 184–85, 197, 204–5

fundamental research. *See* Bohr's quadrant; discovery; science (scientific research)

Gee, Gordon, 6

Geiger, Roger L., 16n35, 17–18, 76, 84, 93, 101, 113n118

generational cohorts: educational attain-ment across, 50, 52 (figure 9), 72–73n104. *See also* educational attainment; family income

Generic Public University, 10–11, 121, 123, 125, 182, 245. *See also* Berkeley envy; Harvard-ization; isomorphism; prestige

Georgetown University Center on Education and the Workforce, 32–33, 45–47, 54, 59, 74n128, 123. *See also* Anthony P. Carnevale

German academic model, 9–10, 17–18, 75–83, 89, 104 (figure 13), 106n25, 107n30, 244, 272, 307. *See also* University of Berlin; Wilhelm von Humboldt

GI Bill of Rights (Serviceman's Readjustment Act of 1944), 94

Global Institute of Sustainability (GIOS). *See under* Arizona State University: research initiatives, centers, and institutes

global knowledge economy. *See* knowledge economy

Golden Age in American higher education, 29, 100–101

Goldin, Claudia, and Lawrence F. Katz, 39–40, 49–50

gold standard in American higher education, vii, 7, 10, 18, 60, 90–91, 97, 103–5, 104 (figure 13), 115, 178, 221, 250–51. *See also* Berkeley envy; elitism in American higher education; Harvardization; Ivy League; *names of individual universities*

Google X, ix–x. *See also* Astro Teller; moonshot project

Gordon, Robert J., 29–30, 35, 53

government. *See* Henry Etzkowitz; federal government; state governments; triple helix (university-industry-government)

graduate education, 3, 9–10, 14n8, 17–18, 22, 28–29, 34, 92–93, 131, 142; AAU member institutions, 68–69n45; ASU, vii, 256, 257–58, 265–66, 269–70, 275, 288–89, 292, 301n43; Caltech, 99; enrollments, percentage increase in, 29, 67n36, 100–101; German academic model, 75–76, 80, 83; Harvard University, 98, 112n107; Johns Hopkins University, 76–77, 83, 199; MIT, 99; Princeton University, 130–31; research and development (R&D), correlate of, 158–59, 261, 307; Syracuse University, 198–99; University of Michigan, 112n107; University of Toronto, 34, 290–91; Woodrow Wilson, 130–31. *See also names of individual universities*

graduation rates: baccalaureate attainment across generational cohorts, 50, 52 (figure 9); baccalaureate attainment among OECD member nations, 49, 51 (figure 8); baccalaureate attainment in STEM fields, 49; baccalaureate correlation with family income, 43–45, 44 (figures 5, 6), 46 (figures 7a, 7b); baccalaureate correlation with

selectivity, 36–37; community colleges, 53; correlation with initial college type, 53; high schools, 49; undermatching, 53–54. *See also* Arizona State University: graduation rates; educational attainment

Gregorian, Vartan, xi, 128

Habermas, Jürgen, 216, 219–20. *See also* pragmatism

Hacker, Andrew, and Claudia Dreifus, 2

Harvardization (Harvard envy), 11, 118, 121–22. *See also* Berkeley envy; isomorphism; prestige

Harvard University, 3, 4, 10, 220; American research universities, role in emergence of, 83, 87–88; budget, 98; correlation between admission and family income, 47; curriculum, 127, 129, 149–50n91, 198; Charles W. Eliot and, 127; endowment, 97; enrollment, 98–99, 100–101, 256, 300n28; graduate schools, 83, 98, 131; humanities majors, 149–50n91; interdisciplinarity, 198, 199, 212–13n79; libraries and museums, 97–98; Oxbridge model, 75–76; pragmatism, role in, 215; prestige as factor in isomorphism, 97, 122–23; regional innovation cluster, 166–67; relationship with MIT and Route, 128, 11, 166–67; as representative of colonial colleges that comprise Ivy League, 13, 27, 75; as representative of gold standard in American higher education, 13, 17–18, 28, 75–76; research enterprise, 87, 98; research expenditures, 98, 263; resources, 97–98, 122. *See also* Ivy League; Oxbridge model

Hewlett-Packard, 189

higher education, American: critique of, 1–8; decentralization of ("academic marketplace"), 10, 19–20, 85, 91–93, 210n36, 246, 305–6; egalitarian conception of, 5, 8–9, 27–28, 34, 36–38, 70n59, 88–89, 92; perception of crisis in, 1–8; as socially divisive, 9, 45, 46 (figures 7), 47–49 (*see also* social stratification)

Hoxby, Caroline M., and Christopher Avery, 53–54, 73n114, 293–96. *See also* socioeconomic disadvantage; undermatching

human capital, 2, 24, 50, 153, 66n19; economic growth, correlation with, 157, 167–68; research universities, role in formation of, 157, 164 humanities, 22; China, perception of value in, 142; Cornell University, 87; curricula, 154; developing economies, perception of value in, 142; discovery, perception of as, 152–53; federal investment in, 95; interdisciplinarity in, 198, 199–200, 254, 282–83; legitimation, modes of, 120; liberal arts, integral to, 140; Cardinal Newman, 78; C. P. Snow category ("literary intellectuals"), 183–84; societal impact, 154; undergraduate majors, 149–50n91; value, perception of, 142–44, 152–53, 244–45. *See also* Arizona State University; liberal arts

Humboldt, Wilhelm von, 77–83, 89, 106n25, 272, 307. *See also* German academic model; University of Berlin

Hutchins, Robert Maynard, 116–17, 129–30, 199. *See also* University of Chicago

income. *See* educational attainment; family income; inequality

Industrial Revolution, 89–90, 136, 154–55, 156, 224–26. *See also* innovation, technological

industry. *See* research and development (R&D); transdisciplinarity

inequality: and educational attainment, 9, 33–34, 35–38, 40–42, 48, 153–54, 250, 295; Claudia Goldin and Lawrence F. Katz, 39–40, 49–50. *See also* Thomas Piketty

innovation, institutional, 11–12, 26–27, 63, 76–77, 80–81, 102–3, 139, 179–83, 183–90, 190–97; historical, 197–201

innovation, technological, viii–x, 5, 8, 19, 20–21, 29, 59, 66n16, 89, 135–37, 152–54, 154–58

innovation: basic research. *See* discovery

innovation: economic growth, correlate of, 5, 20–21, 22–23, 25–26, 29, 39, 59, 61–62, 66n16, 89, 154–58, 158–69

innovation: national system of innovation (national innovation system), 11, 25, 160, 168–69, 175n66, 195

innovation: research universities, American, 8, 10–11, 13, 20–21, 22–23, 25–26, 26–27, 61–62, 84, 93, 96, 102–3, 124–25, 135, 137, 152–54, 158–69

innovation: scientific discovery as correlate of technological innovation, 10–11, 11–12, 22–23, 25–26, 39, 65n7, 84, 96, 121, 137, 141, 152–54, 158–69. *See also* Arizona State University: research initiatives, centers, and institutes; discovery

innovation clusters, 11, 164–67, 172n25, 174n50

Institute of Higher Education, Shanghai Jiao Tong University, Academic Ranking of World Universities. *See* Academic Ranking of World Universities (ARWU)

institutional design. *See* design, institutional

institutional organization. *See* design, institutional

interdisciplinarity, 12, 24, 184–86, 187–90, 198–99, 212–13n79; categories, 184–85; design, institutional, correlate of, 178; disciplinary entrenchment, disciplinary departments, 77, 80, 83, 126, 179, 185–86, 199–201, 212–13n79; historical models, 197–201; historical trajectory, 95, 197–201; implementation, 184–85, 189–90; invisible colleges, 138, 190–92, 197, 200–201, 239n44; knowledge networks, 189; matrix model, 187–88; models, 183, 190–97; National Academies, *Facilitating Interdisciplinary Research*, 187–88, 210n36; serendipity, 189–90; teaching, 169, 184–85, 196–97, 198, 199, 206–7, 212–13n79, 246–47; transdisciplinarity, 62, 184, 198, 204–5, 242, 244, 246. *See also* Arizona State University: design aspirations; collaboration; design, institutional; disciplinarity; knowledge production; C. P. Snow, *The Two Cultures and the Scientific Revolution*

invisible colleges, 138, 190–92, 197, 200–201, 239n44

isomorphic replication. *See* Berkeley envy; Harvardization; isomorphism; prestige

isomorphism, 10–11, 240; bureaucracies, correlation with, 124–25; caveat against, 63–64, 296; filiopietism, correlation with, 118–19, 122–26; prestige, correlation with, 123–24; tradition, correlation with, 182. *See also* Berkeley envy; Harvardization; prestige

Ivy League, vii, 19, 33, 35, 87; American research universities, role in emergence of, 60, 75–78, 250–51; enrollments, 31, 68n44, 99–100, 113n114, 300n27. *See also* research universities, American; research universities, private; selectivity of colleges and universities; *names of individual universities*

Jefferson, Thomas, 28, 127–28, 308–9. *See also* electives, system of; University of Virginia

Johns Hopkins University: Daniel Coit Gilman, 76; graduate education, 76, 83; Humanities Center, 199–200; interdisciplinarity, 199–200; Clark Kerr on, 76–77, 77–78; land-grant institutions, contemporaneous emergence with, 83–84; model (conflation of British and German), 75–78; pragmatism, contemporaneity of establishment with emergence of, 215–16; prototype for American research university, 9, 17, 75–76; as representative of gold standard in American higher education, 17–18, 75–76; research expenditures, 98, 263

John William Pope Center for Higher Education Policy, 3–4

Julie Ann Wrigley Global Institute of Sustainability (GIOS). *See under* Arizona State University: research initiatives, centers, and institutes

Kerr, Clark, 307, 309n6; California Master Plan for Higher Education, 133–34; on faculty grievances, 130; on German academic model and research universities, 80; on Robert Maynard Hutchins, 117, 130; on Johns Hopkins University as prototype for American research university, 76–77; "multiversity," 18; on traditional pedagogy, 117; University of California, 130, 133–34. *See also* California Master Plan for Higher Education

King's College, vii. *See also* Columbia University

King's College London. *See* University of London

knowledge: *episteme* versus *techne*, 202–3, 238n29; as know-how, 48, 165, 171n15, 202–3; proliferation of, 202, 203–4; propositional ("knowledge what") versus prescriptive ("knowledge how"), 202–3, 238n29; as a public good, 22, 61, 96, 103, 171n17, 235, 242, 268; reflexive relationship with institutional matrix, 11, 117, 177, 179, 181–82, 185, 208n4. *See also* discovery; educational attainment; tacit knowledge

knowledge economy: global dimension of, 19, 21, 26, 30, 59, 80, 158, 268; historical origins (Joel Mokyr), 22, 154–56, 170n9, 171n15, 190–91, 202–3, 210n44, 238n29; research universities and, 6, 11, 21, 24–25, 272, 282, 284, 305. *See also* knowledge production: research universities; technological innovation

knowledge enterprises (complex adaptive knowledge enterprises), viii, 8, 13, 19, 63, 218, 240–41, 298n1. *See also* Arizona State University; complexity

knowledge production: accessibility to, 32, 37–38, 49, 59–60, 99–100, 138, 240–49; Arizona State University, 12, 60–61, 62, 240–49, 285, 292; design, institutional, 11, 117–18, 177–78, 178–83, 189–90, 190–97, 208–9n13; economic growth, 151–54, 154–69; federal investment, 10, 92–97, 98, 151, 161–64, 173n41; filiopietism and, 117–18; innovation, institutional, 155–56, 227, 230; New American University, vii–viii, 7, 11, 36, 60–61, 62, 240–43, 255; research universities, 11, 18, 23, 24–25, 27, 121, 137–38, 234, 305–8; technological innovation, 155–56, 156–58; transinstitutional (university-industry-government), 102, 169, 195–96, 204–5, 268, 276. *See also* discovery; interdisciplinarity; New American University; research universities, American; transdisciplinarity; triple helix (university-industry-government)

Kristof, Nicholas, 3

Kuhn, Thomas, 118, 120, 194, 208n4

Kuznets, Simon, 156, 171n15

laboratories: industrial; 25, 167–68, 168–69, 176n68, 187–88. *See also* innovation, technological; national laboratories

land-grant colleges and universities, 83–84, 107–8n42; academic enterprise (entrepreneurial universities), 85, 159–60; agriculture and "mechanical arts," 84–85; American research university, role in emergence of, 9–10, 83–85, 86–87, 88; as egalitarian, 84–85, 251; federal lands, provisions for sale of, 84; federal support for higher education, 93; scientific discovery and technological innovation (applied science), correlation with, 88; university-industry relations, 87; utilitarian predication, 86–87. *See also* Morrill Act

Leiden Rankings, Center for Science and Technology Studies, Universiteit Leiden, 265–66, 301n42

liberal arts, 11; academic enterprise,
    integration with at Stanford University,
    88; antiquity (trivium and quadrivium),
    140–41; *Bildung* (character formation), role
    in, 78; curricula, 140; defense; engineering,
    relevance to, 142; general education, 81,
    142; humanities, correlation with, 78;
    innovation, basis for, 142–43; relevance,
    140–42; tradition, representative of, 118;
    trivium and quadrivium (seven traditional
    liberal arts), 140, 142, 308; value, perception
    of, 142–44. *See also* liberal arts, arguments
    on behalf of
liberal arts, arguments on behalf of: M. H.
    Abrams, 142–44; Daniel Mark Fogel, 143;
    Martha Nussbaum, 143; Frank Rhodes,
    234–35; Herbert A. Simon, 144
liberal arts colleges, 13, 14n11, 138; curricula,
    140–42; enrollments, 31, 73n114, 99, 101, 115,
    300n27; gold standard in American higher
    education, 60; isomorphism, 118–19, 122–26;
    Oxbridge model, 75–76, 77, 89, 119; prestige,
    correlation with, 123–24; scale of, 31, 99,
    101, 300n27; selectivity, 73n114, 99, 115;
    tradition, association with, 115. *See also*
    *names of individual colleges*
liberal bias in academia, 3–4, 14n11
Lincoln, Abraham, 9, 83. *See also* land-grant
    colleges and universities; Morrill Act
Lombardi, John, 6–7, 126, 137, 249. 261, 268

Madison, James, 28, 29, 91, 110n78
Manhattan Project, 95, 198. *See also*
    interdisciplinarity; transdisciplinarity
Massachusetts Institute of Technology
    (MIT), 7, 88; enrollment, 99; industry,
    relations with, 88; land-grant status, 84,
    86; Morrill Act, 84, 86; regional innovation
    cluster, 166–67; relationship with Harvard
    and Route, 128, 11, 166–67; as representative
    of gold standard in American higher
    education, 17–18; research expenditures,
    263, 300n26; utilitarian ideals, correlation
    with, 86
massive change (Bruce Mau), 182–83, 297
Max Planck Society, 93
Menand, Louis, 128, 130; German academic
    culture, 82–83; Golden Age of American
    higher education, 29, 100–101; knowledge,
    23–24, 63, 79; pragmatism, 215, 216, 217, 218,
    220, 223–24, 236n1, 236n3

meritocracy, 8–9; American higher
    education, presumption of in, 8–9, 30–31,
    34, 46, 89, 306; American society, 8, 37–38,
    38–39; egalitarian presumptions, 5, 8–9,
    27–28, 34, 36–38, 70n59, 88–89, 92; elitism,
    correlation with, 34; exclusion, correlation
    with, 34; merit, assessment (measurement)
    of, 88–90; myth (Stephen J. McNamee and
    Robert K. Miller), 38–39; New American
    University, 37–38
Merton, Robert K., 153, 190, 208n4
middle classes, 5, 33, 35, 41–42, 45, 46 (figure 7),
    48, 54–60, 82n71, 304–5; land-grant colleges
    and universities (Morrill Act), 83–87
military-industrial-academic complex, 10,
    96–97, 218–19
MIT. *See* Massachusetts Institute of
    Technology
models (of academic institutions). *See*
    Cambridge University; German academic
    model; land-grant colleges and universi-
    ties; liberal arts colleges; New American
    University; Oxbridge model; Oxford
    University; research universities, American;
    University of Berlin
Mokyr, Joel, 22, 154–56, 170n9, 171n15, 190–91,
    202–3, 210n44, 238n29. *See also* knowledge:
    propositional versus prescriptive
moonshot project, ix–x. *See also* Astro Teller;
    Google X
Morrill Act: Abraham Lincoln, 9, 83;
    academic enterprise (entrepreneurial
    universities), 85, 159–60; agriculture and
    "mechanical arts," 84–85; American
    research university, role in emergence of,
    9–10, 83–85, 86–87, 88; as egalitarian, 5,
    8–9, 27–28, 34, 36–38, 70n59, 88–89, 92;
    federal lands, provisions for sale of, 84;
    federal support for higher education, 93;
    land-grant institutions, 83–84, 107–8n42;
    scientific discovery and technological
    innovation (applied science), correlation
    with, 88; university-industry relations,
    87; utilitarian predication, 86–87.
    *See also* land-grant colleges and
    universities
multiculturalism. *See* socioeconomic
    diversity
multidisciplinarity. *See* interdisciplinarity;
    transdisciplinarity
Murray, Charles, 4, 5

National Academies, 287, 302–3n56; Arizona State University faculty, 256, 259; reports: *Facilitating Interdisciplinary Research*, 187–88, 202, 204; *Rising Above the Gathering Storm*, 22, 39, 59, 157, 159
National Association of Scholars, 4, 14n11
national laboratories (U.S. Department of Energy), 94–95, 111n90, 168–69, 173n41, 176n68, 187–88. *See also* discovery; innovation, technological
National Research Council, 161, 205, 225; "Data-Based Assessment for Research-Doctorate Programs in the United States" (2010), 265–66, 301n43
National Science Foundation, 94, 95, 259, 262, 286
national system of innovation (national innovation system). *See under* innovation
national university, 29, 91, 110n78, 305–6. *See also* James Madison
Nelson, Richard R., 86–87, 88, 95–96, 202–3
New American University, vii–x, 7–8; academic community, conception of, 8, 64, 218–19, 248, 255, 308; Arizona State University as prototype, viii, 12, 60–62, 240–42, 255, 296; *Bildung*, commitment to, 272; complement to set of American research universities, 7–8, 18, 27, 37–38, 63–64, 103, 240–41; concept as broadly applicable, 7–8, 296–97; conceptualization, 18–19; as egalitarian meritocracy, 5, 8–9, 27–28, 34, 36–38, 70n59, 88–89, 92; fifth wave in American higher education, 13; historical context, 9, 17–18, 75–105; inclusiveness to a broad demographic, 7–8, 35–37, 60–62; isomorphism, caveat regarding, 63–64, 296; as knowledge enterprise, viii–ix, 8, 19, 63, 102–3, 218, 240, 254; José Ortega y Gasset on, 244–45; pragmatism, correlation with, 12, 248; Frank Rhodes on, 243–44; societal transformation, 308; socioeconomic diversity, 7–8, 18–19, 60–61, 240–42. *See also* accessibility; Arizona State University: design aspirations; research universities, American
Newfield, Christopher, 34, 36–37, 70n59
Newman, John Henry (Cardinal Newman), 77–78, 89
Newton, Isaac, 116, 145n5

Obama, Barack, 23, 32, 53, 98, 151, 304; Arizona State University, President Barack Obama Scholars Program, 258, 295
OECD. *See* Organisation for Economic Co-operation and Development
Ohio State University, 6, 7, 263, 292, 297
Organisation for Economic Co-operation and Development (OECD), 23, 39, 49–50, 51 (figure 8), 52 (figure 9), 72–73n104, 173n29, 197–98
Ortega y Gasset, José, 244–45
Oxbridge model, 9–10, 17–18, 75–76, 77–78, 88–89, 110n74, 119, 183, 200
Oxford University, 183, 200; elitism, 88–89, 110n74; historical preeminence, 77, 80, 88–89; as model for American research university, 9–10, 17–18, 75–78, 80. *See also* Cambridge University; gold standard in American higher education; Ivy League; Oxbridge model

parental educational attainment. *See* socioeconomic mobility
Pasteur's quadrant (use-inspired research), 26, 183, 201–5, 216, 218, 244, 273; design aspirations, 62, 242–43. *See also* Arizona State University: design aspirations; Bohr's quadrant; Donald E. Stokes
Pell Grants, 94, 258–59, 260 (figure 14), 291
Piketty, Thomas, 40–41, 48. *See also* inequality
Polanyi, Michael, 174–75n52, 196, 203. *See also* tacit knowledge
Pope Center for Higher Education Policy. *See* John William Pope Center for Higher Education Policy
Powell, Walter W., 122, 123, 124, 155. *See also* Paul J. DiMaggio
pragmatism: American research university, impact on, 12, 215, 248; John Dewey, 216–17, 218, 221–22, 223, 236n10, 237n13, 237n17; Jürgen Habermas, 216, 219–20; William James, 215–16; knowledge interrelated with action, 12, 215–18, 220–24; Louis Menand on, 215–16, 217, 218, 223–24, 236n1, 236n3; Metaphysical Club, 215–16; neopragmatism, 216, 219; New American University, impact on, 12, 215, 219; C. S. Peirce (principle of Peirce), 215–16; Richard Rorty, 216, 219, 220–21;

pragmatism (*cont.*)
    social consensus, 12, 217–20, 221–23;
    truth claims, 217, 219–20, 237n11. *See also*
    Barry Bozeman
prescriptive knowledge. *See under*
    knowledge
prestige, 10–11, 25, 99, 134; discovery,
    correlation with, 201, 206; exclusion,
    correlation with, 30–31, 33–34, 99; Harvard
    University, attribute of, 97; isomorphism,
    correlation with, 97, 118–19, 122–24;
    rankings, 264–65. *See also* Berkeley envy;
    filiopietism; gold standard in American
    higher education; Harvardization;
    isomorphism; tradition, academic
Princeton University: curriculum, 199;
    endowment, 97; enrollment, 100; graduate
    schools, 130–31; interdisciplinarity, 199;
    James Madison, 28; James McCosh,
    128–29; Oxbridge model and, 75–76; as
    representative of colonial colleges that
    comprise Ivy League, 17–18, 76; as
    representative of gold standard in
    American higher education, 17–18, 76;
    Woodrow Wilson, 130–31. *See also* Ivy
    League; Oxbridge model
professors (professoriate). *See* faculty; teaching
propositional knowledge. *See under*
    knowledge
public research universities. *See* research
    universities, American; research
    universities, public; *names of individual
    universities*

rankings of colleges and universities:
    Academic Ranking of World Universities
    (ARWU), 21, 65n9, 265, 301n41; Leiden
    Rankings, Center for Science and
    Technology Studies, Universiteit Leiden,
    265–66, 301n42; National Research
    Council, "Data-Based Assessment for
    Research-Doctorate Programs in the
    United States" (2010), 265–66, 301n43;
    *Times Higher Education* World University
    Rankings, 21, 34, 265–66, 290–91; *U.S.
    News and World Report*, 1, 68n44, 113n114,
    121–22, 146n27, 266, 300n27, 302n44; *Wall
    Street Journal*, 266, 296. *See also names of
    individual rankings*
Readings, Bill, 3, 14n8, 77–78
reconceptualization. *See* design process

replication. *See* Berkeley envy; Generic Public
    University; Harvardization; isomorphism;
    prestige
research, basic (fundamental). *See*
    discovery; innovation, technological;
    research and development (R&D);
    research universities, American; science
    (scientific research)
research and development (R&D), 10–11, 22,
    28, 61, 94–95, 154–55, 158–69, 173n41, 174n45,
    195, 262–64, 268, 277
research universities, American, vii–xi, 4, 7,
    13; Carnegie Foundation for the Advance-
    ment of Teaching institutional classifica-
    tions, 14, 20–21, 65n8, 262–63; endowments,
    97, 101n112; faculty, ix, 3, 10, 14n8, 18, 20, 25,
    27, 32, 36–37, 50, 60, 76, 78–82, 127, 128, 139,
    182, 261, 306–7; federal investment, 10,
    92–97, 98, 151, 161–64, 173n41; historical
    context, 17–18, 75–105; innovation, 8, 10–11,
    13, 20–21, 22–23, 25–26, 26–27, 61–62, 84, 93,
    96, 102–3, 124–25, 135, 137, 152–54, 158–69;
    international status, 19–21; knowledge
    production, 11, 18, 23, 24–25, 27, 121, 137–38,
    234, 305–8; research integrated with
    teaching, 10, 18, 20, 25, 60, 76, 78–82, 182,
    261, 306–7; scale of, 31, 34–38, 53–54, 59–60,
    68n44, 97–102, 103–5, 104 (figure 13),
    113n114, 113nn118–119, 256, 300n27; societal
    impact, 9, 24, 30, 36–38, 42–47, 48–49,
    53–60, 71n82, 251. *See also* Association of
    American Universities (AAU); innovation,
    technological; innovation: scientific
    discovery; knowledge production;
    land-grant colleges and universities; New
    American University; research universities,
    private; research universities, public; scale
    of American higher education; socioeco-
    nomic mobility; *names of individual
    universities*
research universities, private. *See* Associa-
    tion of American Universities (AAU);
    Harvardization; research universities,
    American; research universities, public;
    *names of individual universities*
research universities, public: egalitarian
    conception, 5, 8–9, 27–28, 34, 36–38, 70n59,
    88–89, 92; as de facto national university,
    29, 306. *See also* research universities,
    American; research universities, private;
    *names of individual universities*

Rhodes, Frank H. T., vii, xi, 6, 17, 18; assessment of Arizona State University, 13; assessment of Cardinal Newman, 78; on electives, 127–28, 129; as inspiration for design aspirations, 243–44; on liberal arts, 235; on role of knowledge, 21–22; on sustainability, 235. *See also* Cornell University

Rosenberg, Nathan, 16, 85, 86, 87, 88, 96, 157, 203

Rothblatt, Sheldon, 105–6n9, 110n74, 299n10

Saez, Emmanuel, 40–41. *See also* Thomas Piketty

Sarewitz, Daniel, 283–84, 286. *See also* Arizona State University: research initiatives, centers, and institutes: Consortium for Science, Policy, and Outcomes (CSPO)

scale of American higher education, 31, 34–38, 53–54, 59–60, 68n44, 97–102, 103–5, 104 (figure 13), 113n114, 113nn118–119, 256, 300n27. *See also* enrollments; research universities, American

Schelling, F. W. J., 79, 80, 81, 107n30. *See also* German academic model; University of Berlin; Wilhelm von Humboldt

science (scientific research): disciplinary hierarchies, 206; interrelationship between science and technology and the political, 283–88; perception of chasm between humanities and, 183–85; research and development (R&D), 10–11, 22, 28, 61, 94–95, 154–55, 158–69, 173n41, 174n45, 195, 262–64, 268, 277; *Science: The Endless Frontier*, 10, 94–96, 111n89; scientific discovery as correlate of technological innovation, 10–11, 11–12, 22–23, 25–26, 39, 65n7, 84, 96, 121, 137, 141, 152–54, 158–69. *See also* discovery; innovation, technological; innovation: scientific discovery; sustainability

*Science: The Endless Frontier*, 10, 94–96, 111n89. *See also* Vannevar Bush

selectivity of colleges and universities, vii, 1, 5, 9, 23, 30, 34–38, 61, 241, 251, 305–6; Barron's *Profiles of American Colleges*, 73n114, 293; family income, correlation with, 47–48; Ivy League, 31, 68n44, 99–100, 113n114, 300n27; liberal arts colleges, 31, 73n114, 99, 101, 115, 300n27; Christopher

Newfield on, 34, 36–37, 70n59; scale, correlation with, 31, 73n114, 99, 101, 115; Stanford University, 33; University of California, 33, 69n50; undermatching, correlation with, 50, 53, 53–54, 73n114, 293–96. *See also* accessibility; elitism in American higher education; exclusivity (exclusion) in admissions practices

serendipity, 189–90. *See also* Robert K. Merton

Shanghai Jiao Tong University, Academic Ranking of World Universities. *See* Academic Ranking of World Universities (ARWU)

Shanghai Rankings Consultancy. *See* Academic Ranking of World Universities (ARWU)

Simon, Herbert A., 144, 180, 208–9n13, 253. *See also* design (concept); design, institutional

Snow, C. P., *The Two Cultures and the Scientific Revolution*, 183–85, 205, 209n22. *See also* interdisciplinarity; transdisciplinarity

social stratification ("reproduction of privilege"), 9, 45, 46 (figure 7), 47–49. *See also* socioeconomic mobility

socioeconomic disadvantage, 30, 35–37, 42, 47–48, 50, 53, 60–62, 100, 140–41, 153, 293–94, 304–6; Arizona State University, 240–41, 249–51, 253–55, 258–59, 260 (figure 14)

socioeconomic diversity, 29. 30, 35–36; ASU as representative of, vii–viii, 7–8, 12, 60–61, 240–42, 251, 253, 297; ASU charter statement, 62, 255–56; ASU design aspiration, 242; ASU faculty, 259, 261; ASU students, 257–58, 264–65, 266–67; New American University as representative of, 7–8, 18–19, 60–61, 240–42; public research universities, 60, 304–6

socioeconomic mobility: educational attainment, 9, 24, 30, 36–38, 42–47, 48–49, 53–60, 71n82, 251

Solow, Robert M., and Moses Abramowitz, 157, 171n18

specialization: disciplinarity, viii, 3, 82, 191, 201, 206–7, 231–32, 234; electives, 129; German academic model, 9, 76, 82, 107n30 (F. W. J. Schelling on unity of knowledge); graduate education, 9, 17–18, 76, 81; interdisciplinarity, 189–90, 198, 212–13n79,

specialization (*cont.*)
277–78; knowledge networks, 195; José Ortega y Gasset on, 245; research universities, 17–18, 25–26, 76, 81, 92. *See also* disciplinarity; interdisciplinarity; transdisciplinarity

Stanford University, 1, 11, 90–91, 146n27; academic enterprise, integration with, 88; admissions standards, 33; correlation between admission and family income, 47; endowment, 97; humanities majors, 149–50n91; industry, relations with, 88, 166–67; interdisciplinarity, 199–200; Program in Modern Thought and Literature, 199–200; regional innovation cluster, 166–67; as representative of gold standard in American higher education, 17–18; research expenditures, 263; role in emergence of American research universities, 76, 88; Silicon Valley, relation with, 166–67

state governments: citizens, 55; decentralization in higher education, 91–92, 305–6; higher education policies, 53, 161, 162–63, 249, 261; public disinvestment, 5, 29–30, 68n38, 141, 250, 288–90, 289 (figure 16), 291 (figure 17); states' rights, 91–92; Tenth Amendment, 92

state universities, 13: egalitarian conception, 5, 8–9, 27–28, 34, 36–38, 70n59, 88–89, 92; "flagship" public universities, 17–18, 33; gold standard in American higher education, 17–18; Morrill Act, 83–87, 108n47. *See also* research universities, American; research universities, public; state governments; *names of individual universities*

Stiglitz, Joseph, 22, 40, 42, 171n17

Stokes, Donald E., 202. *See also* Bohr's quadrant; Pasteur's quadrant; use-inspired research

sustainability, 4, 12, 224–29, 229–35, 238n37; sustainability science, 225–26; sustainable development, 12, 225–27. *See also* Global Institute of Sustainability (GIOS)

tacit knowledge, 165, 174–75n52, 195–96, 203. *See also* Michael Polanyi

Taylor, Mark C., 2

teaching, viii–ix, 3, 4, 13, 85, 88, 98, 102, 136–37, 195, 275; German academic model,

78–82; integration with research, 10, 18, 20, 25, 60, 76, 78–82, 182, 261, 306–7; interdisciplinarity, 169, 184–85, 196–97, 198, 199, 206–7, 212–13n79, 246–47; Oxbridge model, 9, 75–76, 77–78, 89, 119. *See also* Arizona State University: faculty; Arizona State University: research initiatives, centers, and institutes

technological innovation. *See* innovation, technological; innovation: scientific discovery

technology. *See* innovation, technological; innovation: scientific discovery; knowledge

technology transfer, 160, 161, 162, 172n25, 174n45. *See also* innovation, technological. *See also under* Arizona State University: research enterprise: Arizona Technology Enterprises (AzTE)

Teller, Astro, ix. *See also* Google X; moonshot project

tenure, 3, 14n8, 187; Arizona State University, 259, 261, 301n35

Thiel, Peter (Thiel Fellowships), 2

*Times Higher Education* World University Rankings, 21, 34, 265–66, 290–91

Tocqueville, Alexis de, 38, 87–88

Toma, J. Douglas, 97, 123, 124

tradition, academic, 6–7, 10–11, 17, 31; as bureaucratic, 124–25; as constructive force, 17, 116; as entrenchment in dated institutional arrangements, 63, 90, 102–3, 115, 121; as filiopietistic, 116–119, 182 (*see also* filiopietism); historical function, 115–16; as manifestation of societal values, 48, 126; as manifest in academic practices, 119–21; as manifest in curricula, 87; national traditions, 77–80; Cardinal Newman, 77–78; as "normal science" (Kuhn), 120; resistance to reform, 126–34. *See also* filiopietism; isomorphism; liberal arts

tragedy of the commons, 153, 239n43

transdisciplinarity, 62, 184, 198, 204–5, 242, 244, 246. *See also* interdisciplinarity; knowledge production: transinstitutional; triple helix (university-industry-government)

triple helix (university-industry-government), 103, 160, 169, 187–88, 195–96, 204–5; academic enterprise, 268, 275–77. *See also* academic enterprise; collaboration; discovery; Henry

Etzkowitz; innovation, technological; knowledge production: transinstitutional; transdisciplinarity
tuition and fees, 30, 35, 135, 164; Arizona State University, 258, 275, 289–90, 291 (figure 17). *See also* affordability (higher education); Arizona State University

undermatching: William Bowen and colleagues, 50, 53; Caroline Hoxby and Christopher Avery, 53–54, 73n114, 293–96
Universität Bielefeld (Zentrum für interdisziplinäre Forschung), 200–201
University College London. *See* University of London
University Innovation Alliance, 297
University of Berlin (Humboldt-Universität), 9–10, 75–76, 77–80, 81–83, 89, 106n25, 107n30, 272, 307. *See also* German academic model
University of California: accessibility to, historical, 33, 69n50, 251–53, 299–300n22; admissions policies, 33, 69n50, 251–53, 299–300n22; American research university, role in emergence of, 17–18; Association of American Universities (AAU) member institutions, 84; enrollment, 292; *Fiat Lux*, 220; interdisciplinarity, 199–200; land-grant status, 84; multiple campuses, 132–33; research expenditures, 262, 300n26; University of California, San Diego, 132, 133, 167, 263; University of California, Santa Barbara, 133, 262; University of California, Santa Cruz, 133, 199, 200. *See also* California Master Plan for Higher Education; Clark Kerr; University of California, Berkeley; University of California, Los Angeles (UCLA)
University of California, Berkeley, 99, 130; accessibility, 33, 69n50, 252, 299–300n22; admissions policies, 33, 69n50, 251–53, 299–300n22; American research university, role in emergence of, 17–18; Association of American Universities (AAU) member institution, 84; "Berkeley envy," 121; enrollment, 99; David P. Gardner, 128; Daniel Coit Gilman, 76; William James, 216; land-grant status, 84; prestige, 121; research expenditures, 300n26; Benjamin

Ide Wheeler, 109n61. *See also* Clark Kerr, University of California
University of California, Los Angeles (UCLA), 132–33, 292; admissions standards, 251–52; research expenditures, 263. *See also* University of California
University of Chicago: American research university, role in emergence of, 17–18, 76, 83; gold standard in American higher education, 1, 18; graduate education, 83; Robert Maynard Hutchins, 129–30; interdisciplinarity (Committee on Social Thought), 199; sociology, 126
University of London, 77, 89, 105–6n9, 110n74, 246, 299n10, 302–3n56
University of Michigan: American research university, role in emergence of, 83; family incomes of students, 47; gold standard in American higher education, 17–18, 121; Michigan Stadium, 31; research expenditures, 263
University of Oxford. *See* Oxbridge model; Oxford University
University of Pennsylvania, as representative of colonial colleges that comprise Ivy League, 17–18, 100; as representative of gold standard in American higher education, 17–18; research expenditures, 263
University of Toronto, 34, 290–91
University of Virginia, 28, 127, 308. *See also* electives, system of; Thomas Jefferson
University of Wisconsin: American research university, role in emergence of, 84; gold standard in American higher education, 17–18, 121; Wisconsin Idea, 131–32; research expenditures, 263
useful knowledge, 22, 63, 206, 214n110; access, function of, 156, 191; design, institutional, correlation with, 179; economic growth, correlate of, 156–57; Benjamin Franklin, 214n110; Simon Kuznets, 156–57; James Madison, 91; knowledge enterprises, 63; Morrill Act, 84–85; societal outcomes, 25–26, 181. *See also* Morrill Act
use-inspired research, 26, 183, 201–5, 216, 218, 244, 273; design aspirations, 62, 242–43. *See also* Arizona State University: design aspirations; Pasteur's quadrant; Donald E. Stokes

*U.S. News and World Report,* 1, 68n44,
  113n114, 121–22, 146n27, 266, 300n27,
  302n44

Wallerstein, Immanuel, 117, 186, 197. *See also*
  disciplinarity; interdisciplinarity
Weber, Max: bureaucratization, 124;
  charismatic authority, 119, 120, 146n19

Weingart, Peter, 82, 190, 204–5, 206
Wrigley Global Institute of Sustainability
  (GIOS). *See under* Arizona State University: research initiatives, centers, and
  institutes

zip code. *See* family income: educational
  attainment, correlation with